D0939018

The Metaphysics of Knowledge

The Metaphysics
of Knowledge

Keith Hossack

OXFORD
UNIVERSITY PRESS

OXFORD
UNIVERSITY PRESS

Great Clarendon Street, Oxford OX2 6DP

Oxford University Press is a department of the University of Oxford.
It furthers the University's objective of excellence in research, scholarship,
and education by publishing worldwide in

Oxford New York

Auckland Cape Town Dar es Salaam Hong Kong Karachi
Kuala Lumpur Madrid Melbourne Mexico City Nairobi
New Delhi Shanghai Taipei Toronto

With offices in

Argentina Austria Brazil Chile Czech Republic France Greece
Guatemala Hungary Italy Japan Poland Portugal Singapore
South Korea Switzerland Thailand Turkey Ukraine Vietnam

Oxford is a registered trade mark of Oxford University Press
in the UK and in certain other countries

Published in the United States
by Oxford University Press Inc., New York

© Keith Hossack 2007

The moral rights of the author have been asserted
Database right Oxford University Press (maker)

First published 2007

British Library Cataloguing in Publication Data
Data available

Library of Congress Cataloging in Publication Data
Hossack, Keith.
The metaphysics of knowledge / Keith Hossack.
p. cm.
Includes bibliographical references (p.   ) and index.
ISBN 978-0-19-920672-8
1. Knowledge, Theory of.   2. Metaphysics.   I. Title.
BD161.H625 2007
121—dc22
2007024939

Typeset by Laserwords Private Limited, Chennai, India
Printed in Great Britain
on acid-free paper by
Biddles Ltd., King's Lynn, Norfolk

ISBN 978–0–19–920672–8

10 9 8 7 6 5 4 3 2 1

In memory of my father,
George B. Hossack.

Contents

Preface

If a meaningful term is indefinable, it is said to be primitive. An example is the word 'not,' which everyone understands, but no one knows how to define. It is clear that if there is to be such a thing as a correct chain of definitions, then there must be primitive terms to terminate the chain. Therefore if any chain of definitions is correct, there exists a primitive term; if not, then every term is primitive. Thus there certainly exist primitive terms.

The thesis of this book is that 'knowledge' is a primitive term. The reason it is primitive is because the relation it names between a mind and a fact is a simple relation. Because knowledge is simple, it is unanalysable; there is nothing simpler than knowledge, in terms of which knowledge might be analysed, explained or defined. But knowledge is simpler than other things, which can be analysed in terms of it. The book's targets for such metaphysical analysis include the following: concepts, truth, necessity, consciousness, persons and language.

Perhaps not every simple relation deserves to be called fundamental. However, if a relation is simple, it seems plausible that it is at least a candidate for being metaphysically fundamental. For example, spatial betweenness is a simple relation. It is also metaphysically fundamental, for it picks out for us an important natural kind of particulars, namely the material beings. A particular is material, or a body, only if it is between some things; even if there were only one material particle in the whole universe, still it would be between itself and itself. Thus betweenness might be said to be the very essence of matter.

Is knowledge a metaphysically fundamental relation like betweenness? We can use the relation of knowledge to pick out an important natural kind of particulars, namely the mental beings. For an individual is mental or a mind only if it knows something: that which never knows anything is not a mind. Just as betweenness is the essence of matter, so knowledge is the essence of mind. This hypothesis echoes the claim of Descartes that extension is the essence of body and thought the essence of mind. But it is not the same as Descartes' claim. In the first place, betweenness and knowledge are binary relations, whereas Descartes conceived of extension and thought as unary qualities. In the second place, Descartes had a doctrine that distinctness of essence entailed disjointness of kind; hence if the essence of Descartes' body is extension, and the essence of Descartes' mind is thought, then his body and his mind belong to disjoint kinds and hence are different things. Thus Descartes' claim about essence entailed his familiar substance dualism.

In contrast, the present hypothesis, that betweenness is the essence of the material and knowledge the essence of the mental, does not entail substance dualism. For it does not exclude the possibility of the same thing being at once material and mental. So it leaves it an open question whether matter can think, i.e., whether every material being and every mental being are distinct. The hypothesis that knowledge is the essence of mind is therefore consistent both with substance monism and with substance dualism about the material and the mental.

However, the hypothesis that knowledge is a simple relation is certainly a form of property dualism, or rather, of relation dualism. If knowledge is a simple relation, it is not constituted by any other properties or relations, so in particular it is not constituted by physical properties and relations. That might seem to threaten philosophical naturalism. It would certainly undermine the case for the following claim:

> *Metaphysical Supervenience*: It is metaphysically necessary that two worlds that do not differ in any physical respect do not differ in any epistemic respect.

But we must distinguish materialism from philosophical naturalism. Materialism is the doctrine that every possible being is a material being, which does seem to require the truth of Metaphysical Supervenience. Philosophical naturalism, in contrast, is motivated only by the demand that everything that actually happens should have a complete natural explanation. Naturalism can therefore be content to require only the following weaker thesis:

> *Nomological Supervenience*: It is nomologically necessary that two worlds that do not differ in any physical respect do not differ in any epistemic respect.

This weaker thesis, I shall argue, is perfectly consistent with the claim that knowledge is a simple non-physical relation. Thus I do not think that anything in the present book is plainly inconsistent with philosophical naturalism. On the other hand, so far as I can see, nothing in the book is inconsistent with substance dualism either.

The plan of the book is as follows. Chapter 1 expounds the central thesis that knowledge is a relation of a mind to a fact. Epistemology is the theory of knowledge, so if knowledge is a simple relation, the task of epistemology cannot be the analysis of knowledge in terms of truth and warrant. Rather the task must be the study of warrant, taking the concept of knowledge for granted; as Williamson (2000) puts it, knowledge should be the 'unexplained explainer' in epistemology. Chapter 1 accordingly offers accounts of epistemic reliability, justification, warrant and defeasibility in terms of knowledge and its causation by mental acts.

The *relata* of the knowledge relation are minds and facts. Chapter 2 provides a theory of facts, according to which facts are combinations of particulars and universals. The relation of *combination*, which relates a fact and its constituents, is taken to be another simple and metaphysically fundamental relation. It is metaphysically fundamental, because it divides all beings into particulars and universals, and moreover it divides all particulars into individuals and facts. The chapter gives a theory of the combination relation, in terms of which we can speak of the structure of a fact. A theory of truth as correspondence to fact is presented; however, it turns out that if we are to avoid the Liar paradox, we cannot take the predicate 'true' to express a genuine property.

This result would be alarming if we wished to use *truth* as the centrally important theoretical primitive of the theory of content. But it is not alarming in the present context, for we can use knowledge instead of truth to found the theory of content. In Chapter 3 a knowledge-based account is developed, according to which a content is a mode of presentation of a fact (which fact, of course, need not exist). The account takes a content to be not an abstract object, but a property of a mental act. It is the property that determines the mental act's cognitive value, which Frege calls its 'value-for-the-getting-of-knowledge' (*Erkenntniswirt*). The chapter argues that a concept is not a part of a content; rather, it is the property of the mental subject that grounds the subject's capacity to have the thoughts which activate that concept. Given concepts, we can define reference, and hence truth, in terms of knowledge; the referent of a concept is that object knowledge of which is made possible by possession of the concept. A version of the picture theory of thought is now possible: a thought is a picture of a fact, in the sense that the thought is true if there is a fact that combines the referents of the concepts activated by the thought.

With the theory of modes of presentation in hand, Chapter 4 goes on to offer an epistemic account of necessity: a fact is necessary if it has an *a priori* mode of presentation, contingent otherwise. The chapter develops this account, which is just the doctrine of traditional rationalism. It then discusses what is currently taken to be the main obstacle to the rationalist doctrine, namely the existence of many supposed counterexamples to the coincidence of the necessary and the *a priori*. It examines these counterexamples, and argues that none of them is convincing. Finally it offers an account of the philosophical discourse of 'possible worlds' within an ontology that presupposes only knowledge and the one real world.

Chapter 5 applies the metaphysics of knowledge to the mind, the other *relatum* of the knowledge relation. The chapter discusses the problem of consciousness, and seeks to define consciousness in terms of knowledge. It says that a state is conscious if it instantiates a certain type of universal, namely a *quale*. *Qualia* are defined in terms of knowledge: one's knowing concerning one's experience that it has a certain *quale* is nothing over and above the experience itself; the experience, and one's knowledge of its instantiating the *quale* it does, are one and the same identical event. This Identity Thesis, which is adumbrated in Aristotle, was first explicitly stated by Thomas Reid. Brentano later gave a somewhat similar theory, but based his account on the concept of *appearance* rather than knowledge. The chapter argues that Brentano's account is inferior to Reid's, because only knowledge will do to define consciousness.

Chapter 6 continues the discussion of consciousness, and applies it to persons. Following Locke, the chapter argues that a person is a mind that can think of itself under the concept 'I'. Therefore a *person* can be defined in terms of knowledge, as a being that knows itself under that concept which is the intersection of a subjective and an objective mode of presentation of oneself. The subjective mode presents oneself as the subject of one's conscious states; the objective mode presents oneself as a psychological agent in the sense of functionalism, and as part of the objective order.

Persons desire to communicate, and Chapter 7 uses knowledge to give a metaphysics of language. The chapter begins by indicating how, using the apparatus of contents and concepts introduced in Chapter 3, we can go on to give a semantic theory for a language. It then proposes that understanding a language consists in one's capacity, on hearing a sentence of the language, to be the subject of a characteristic mental act whose content is the same as that of the heard sentence. In the right context, one's being the subject of this mental act causes one to know the fact of which the sentence's content is a mode of presentation. This is the mechanism of knowledge transmission by testimony: a sentence is an artefact for the production of the characteristic mental acts whereby testimony is transmitted, and a community's language is their collection of such artefacts.

Finally, Chapter 8 returns to the question of whether knowledge really is a simple and fundamental relation. An alternative hypothesis is the following Constitutive Thesis:

> To know that A is nothing over and above believing that A in the right circumstances.

The chapter examines arguments for and against the Constitutive Thesis. The arguments in its favour are mostly causal: beliefs and other psychological states, or the physical states that realise them, are the complete causes of our actions, so if knowledge is not to be epiphenomenal, it must be identical with belief. It is suggested that these arguments fail: the causal efficacy of knowledge is fully compatible with the completeness of physics, even if knowledge is not identical to any physical state. The chapter goes on to suggest that the Constitutive Thesis has troubles of its own in dealing with consciousness and the unity of the self.

To the extent that the arguments given in the book succeed, they suggest that the concept of knowledge is a theoretically fruitful one, in terms of which many other concepts can be analysed. Therefore we should not take knowledge to be an unscientific concept, useful only in practical life but of no theoretical value. Nor should we take knowledge to be definable in other terms, for example, as some kind of justified true belief. We should take the concept of knowledge to be primitive; and the thing itself to be metaphysically fundamental.

I have to thank many people for invaluable help while I was writing this book. The members of my graduate seminar over several years gave me much useful instruction, corrected many of my errors, and forced me to think more clearly about many issues. I was also greatly helped by comments from the group of London philosophers to which I belong, who meet weekly at King's to discuss each other's work. I am grateful too for comments from King's colleagues in our departmental research seminar, and from comments from many other philosophers at talks and conferences.

So many people have helped me that I cannot possibly mention them all by name. However, there are some that I must thank individually. My greatest debt, both intellectually and personally, is to my friend Mark Sainsbury, who spurred me on, sometimes with help and encouragement, sometimes with challenging criticisms. I have also to thank Andrew Jack, my former colleague, and Fraser MacBride, my former student and now a London colleague at Birkbeck. These two friends have had an immense influence on me: I learned from Andrew the importance of the problem of psychophysical causation, and from Fraser the importance of the topic of universals. I thank too my friends David Galloway and Mark Textor for detailed criticism and discussion of several drafts of this material; I am much indebted to these two good colleagues and good comrades.

My academic career has been spent entirely here in the philosophy department at King's College London, where I have been very happy. The department has a fine reputation for the way it succeeds in combining an atmosphere of amity with intellectual rigour in discussion. I am very grateful to all my King's colleagues for all their help. I should like to thank in particular Jim Hopkins, Chris Hughes, MM McCabe, David Papineau and especially Gabe Segal, who was a tolerant and supportive Chair while I was writing the book.

Finally I should like to thank my sister Ruth Metcalfe for her love and support. And a special thanks to Laura and Anna, best of nieces, who so often chased the clouds away.

K. G. H.

Acknowledgements

I am grateful to the editors and publishers concerned for kind permission to draw on material published previously elsewhere, as follows.

Chapter 3 contains material an earlier version of which appeared in 'Content and Concept' in Martin Stone (ed.) *Reason, Faith and History: Essays in Honour of Paul Helm*, Aldershot: Ashgate (2007).

Chapter 5 contains material an earlier version of which appeared in 'Self-Knowledge and Consciousness' *Proceedings of the Aristotelian Society*, 102 (2002): 163–81. An earlier version of other material from this chapter appeared in 'Consciousness in act and action', *Phenomenology and the Cognitive Sciences* 2 (2003): 187–203. (Copyright Kluwer Academic Publishers; with kind permission of Springer Science and Business Media.)

Chapter 6 is largely reprinted from 'Vagueness and Personal Identity' in F. MacBride (ed.) *Identity & Modality: New Essays in Metaphysics*, Oxford: Oxford University Press (2006), 221–41.

I also gratefully acknowledge two terms of sabbatical research leave granted by King's College London to enable me to work on this book.

1
'S knows that A'

What is the relation between knowledge and belief? It seems evident that we often know by believing, but the word 'by' is ambiguous between a constitutive sense and a causal sense. Someone may marry by saying 'I do,' which is the constitutive sense of 'by'. A stone may break a window by striking it, which is the causal sense of 'by'. Now, when we know by believing, is that the constitutive sense of 'by', or is it the causal sense?

There is a long philosophical tradition of trying to analyse knowledge in terms of belief. For example, according to the 'tripartite analysis', knowledge is justified true belief. If that were correct, knowledge would be a kind of belief, and the relation between knowledge and belief would be constitutive. When the tripartite analysis was decisively refuted by Gettier's (1963) counterexamples, many people sought to repair the analysis by complicating it. But an alternative conclusion to draw from Gettier is that knowledge is not a kind of belief at all. On this view, the relation between knowledge and belief is not constitutive but causal; an intrinsic state that realises a belief can cause knowledge, but the belief and the knowledge are two distinct things. It is this causal point of view that is recommended in this book. I make no attempt here to analyse knowledge as a kind of belief, or as anything else; instead I take the concept of knowledge to be primitive, and the relation of knowledge to be metaphysically fundamental.

Belief and experience are traditionally thought of as propositional attitudes, i.e., as psychological relations to a content. If knowledge were a kind of belief, then knowledge would be a propositional attitude too. But if belief causes knowledge rather than constituting it, the way is open for a conception of knowledge that does not regard it as a propositional attitude. We can instead take knowledge to be a relation to a fact rather than a content.

On this alternative conception, our human epistemic faculties are powers of the mind to cause itself to know. When we become aware of a fact, typically it is because the fact caused a faculty to cause a mental act with a certain content; if the faculty is working correctly, and the context is favourable, the mental act causes the mind to know the fact. On this conception, an English knowledge attribution with a 'that' clause is not a propositional attitude report; rather, it gives the content of the mental act that caused the knowledge.

If we adopt the hypothesis that there is nothing more fundamental than knowledge, then instead of trying to analyse knowledge in terms of other things, we do better to analyse other things in terms of knowledge. In the present chapter I discuss epistemology, a subject whose project some have seen as the definition of knowledge in terms of such notions as justification, warrant and reliability. Here I reverse that order of explanation, and instead seek definitions of justification, warrant and reliability in terms of knowledge.

Justification, in the sense of epistemic faultlessness, can be defined as follows: one is justified if one has reasoned correctly, i.e., if one has been the subject of a sequence of mental acts which in a favourable context would cause knowledge. In this sense even the brain in a vat is justified in its opinions, for in a more favourable context the brain's ruminations would indeed give it knowledge of the external world—it is guilty of no irrationality. But the opinions of the brain are not warranted, for however conscientiously it reasons, it never gets any closer to the truth. Even if all its beliefs did chance to be true, still they are not reliably true, and so they are not warranted. Reliability can be defined in terms of knowledge; S is reliable about A on condition that if S were to have the true belief that A, then S would know that A. Warrant can then be defined as the property that underlies epistemic reliability, i.e., as the disposition to know if one believes.

The plan of this chapter is as follows. Section 1 argues that knowledge is not a propositional attitude. Section 2 classifies knowledge as a relation between a mind and a fact. Section 3 discusses whether the connection between knowledge and mental acts is causal or constitutive. Section 4 discusses epistemic faculties, and section 5 defeaters. Section 6 discusses some unsuccessful attempts to define reliability. Section 7 defines reliability as knowing if one believes, and warrant as being disposed to know if one believes; section 8 concludes that explaining other things in terms of knowledge can be a fruitful strategy.

1.1 Is Knowledge a Propositional Attitude?

A knowledge attribution in English is a sentence that attributes knowledge to someone. Typically it will have the grammatical form 'S knows that A'. That is grammatically similar to the belief attribution 'S believes that A' and to the desire attribution 'S desires that A'. The grammatical similarity makes it natural to assume that knowledge attributions share a common logical form with belief attributions and desire attributions. Since belief and desire are propositional attitudes, it would follow that knowledge is a propositional attitude too. But I shall suggest that this natural assumption is mistaken, and that the grammatical similarity is more apparent than real.

A propositional attitude has relational logical form. For example, if Pharaoh believes that Hesperus is shining, then the logical form is *Rab*, where *R* is the *belief* relation, *a* is Pharaoh, and *b* is the entity named by the phrase 'that Hesperus is shining'. But what is the entity named by this phrase? Certainly it cannot be the fact that Hesperus is shining. For Pharaoh may believe that Hesperus is shining and be mistaken, since he is fallible on such matters. But then he does not have the belief in virtue of standing in the belief relation to the fact that Hesperus is shining, since that fact does not exist.

Thus if belief is a relation to anything, it is not a relation to a fact. What then can it be a relation to? One suggestion is that it is a relation to a *proposition*. A proposition is a hypothetical entity characterised by its postulated capacity to be true or false; it is true upon a certain condition, and false otherwise. For example, the proposition *that Hesperus is shining* is true on condition that Hesperus is shining. We may therefore define the constituents of a proposition as the sequence of entities that enter its truth condition. For example, the proposition *that Hesperus is shining* will have as its constituents the planet Venus and the property of *shining*. We may define identity of propositions by identity of constituents: if x and y are propositions, then $x = y$ only if the constituents of x are $x_1, \ldots, x_n$, the constituents of y are $y_1, \ldots, y_n$, and $x_1 = y_1, x_2 = y_2, \ldots$ and $x_n = y_n$.

It is evident that propositions so defined cannot be the *relata* of the belief relation. For the proposition that Hesperus is shining and the proposition that Phosphorus is shining are the same proposition by our criterion, since each has as its two constituents the property of *shining* and the planet Venus. Yet Pharaoh, who lived before it was known that Hesperus is Phosphorus, may believe that Hesperus is shining but not believe that Phosphorus is shining. Since the propositions are the same and the beliefs different, it follows that belief is not a relation to a proposition.

Since the main purpose of propositions is to serve as the objects of belief, and since unassisted they are inadequate for that purpose, we might be inclined to reject the hypothesis that there are such things as propositions. But we need not yet reject the theory that belief is an attitude, i.e., a diadic relation between a mind and a content. The content must however be some entity that is finer-grained than a proposition, so as to differentiate believing that Hesperus is shining from believing that Phosphorus is shining.

What then is a content? It might be suggested that we could identify the content of the sentence 'Hesperus is shining' with the inferential role of the belief it expresses. But the notion of an inferential role is ambiguous. On one disambiguation, the inferential role is a functional role, specified descriptively by the way human beings do in fact reason. On a different disambiguation, it is specified normatively, by the way human beings ought to reason, if they wish to conform their beliefs to the facts. It is the normative disambiguation that is required here, for beliefs are often the premises of inferences, and for logical purposes what we are concerned with is the rational correctness of the inference, not the psychological normality of the human being making the inference.

On the normative conception of content, we can say to a first approximation that the content of A is equal to the content of B if it is impossible coherently to believe A and disbelieve B. This is Evans' 'Intuitive Criterion of Difference' (1982: 18–19). By 'coherently', Evans means rationally: but what is rationality? It must be more than mere conformity of one's beliefs to the facts, for beliefs can be true by chance, whereas rationality is a matter of reliable conformity to the facts. The reliability in question is clearly epistemic, so we may conclude that a way of forming beliefs is rational only if it is a way of possibly getting knowledge. Thus Evans' criterion by its mention of irrationality implicitly relies on the concept of knowledge.

Rational correctness cannot be defined in terms of any non-epistemic notion. For example, rational correctness is not the modal validity of one's reasoning, as the following inference shows:

Hesperus shines.
Therefore, Phosphorus shines.

This inference is valid in the modal sense, for it is impossible for its premiss to be true and its conclusion false. But it is not rationally correct: someone who did not know that Hesperus is Phosphorus would not be justified in inferring its conclusion from its premiss. It may be suggested that what is wrong with the inference is that it is not logically valid, where 'logical validity' is the property an argument has if its conclusion is true on every interpretation on which its premisses are true. But rational correctness is not logical validity either, as the following inference shows:

Your nag kicked my steed.
Therefore, your horse kicked my horse.

This is not logically valid, since the conclusion is not true upon every interpretation on which its premisses are true. But it is rationally correct, for the terms 'nag', 'steed' and 'horse' differ only in Fregean tone.

It therefore appears that rational correctness must be defined in terms of knowledge: an inference is rationally correct only if it is possible by its means to pass from knowledge of the premisses to knowledge of the conclusion. The 'irrationality' of which Evans speaks can then be defined in terms of obvious rational correctness: one cannot without irrationality believe A, and disbelieve B, if there is an obvious rationally correct inference from A to B. So interpreted, Evans' criterion tells us that 'Hesperus shines' and 'Phosphorus shines' have different contents, since there is no obvious rationally correct inference from the one to the other. But 'Your nag kicked my steed' and 'Your horse kicked my horse' differ only in tone: they have the same content, for there is a trivially rationally correct inference from the one to the other. Thus contents are individuated in terms of knowledge. If belief must be explained as a relation to a content, and if the individuation of contents must be explained in terms of knowledge, then it looks as if belief must be explained in terms of knowledge, and not the other way round.

If belief is a diadic relation between a believer and a content, then it relates the believer to a proposition only indirectly: the believer believes a content, and the content is a 'mode of presentation' of the fact represented by the proposition. So we can analyse 'Pharaoh believes that Hesperus is shining' as of the logical form R_1ab, where R_1 is the *belief* relation, a is Pharaoh, and b is the content *that Hesperus is shining*. Desire receives an analogous analysis: if Pharaoh desires that Hesperus is shining, that will be of the form R_2ab, where R_2 is the *desire* relation, and a and b are as before. Other propositional attitudes such as hoping, expecting, fearing, etc., will in the same way be treated as further relations R_3, R_4, R_5, etc., between a believer and content. And now it might seem natural to take 'Pharaoh knows that Hesperus is shining' as also of the logical form R_kab, where R_k is the *knowledge* relation, a is Pharaoh, and b is the content *that Hesperus is shining*.

But is it right to treat knowledge as a relation between a knower and a content? We may note straight away that there is not the same reason to take knowledge as a relation to a content as there is in the case of the paradigm propositional attitudes. For unlike belief or desire, knowledge is factive: if S knows that A, then it follows that A states a fact. Since knowledge is never in error, there is no need to make room for mistaken knowledge by invoking contents, and so there is no need to take contents to be the objects of knowledge; we can simply take the facts themselves as the objects of knowledge.

But although contents are not needed as the objects of knowledge, they may still be needed in reports of knowledge, for often a report will indicate not only the fact known, but also the provenance of the knowledge. If the knowledge arises from some mental act of the subject, then the content of the mental act is relevant to provenance. My suggestion is that an English knowledge attribution mentions a content not to report the object of knowledge, but to report the content of the mental act in virtue of which the subject has knowledge. The knowledge itself is not a relation to this content: rather, it is that relation **K**ab that holds between a mind a and a fact b if the mind is aware of the fact. The English knowledge attribution 'S knows that A' therefore does more than merely state that this relation obtains; it also gives an indication why it obtains, by giving the content of the mental act in virtue of which S has the knowledge. So my proposal is that its logical form is as follows:

'S knows that A' $=_{df}$

$(\exists x)(\exists p)(x$ is a mental act $\wedge$ p is a fact $\wedge$ content$(x) = $ *that-A* $\wedge$ *that-A* is a mode of presentation of $p \wedge S$ knows of p in virtue of $x)$

Thus the knowledge attribution 'S knows that A' reports that S knows of a fact p in virtue of some unspecified mental act with the content *that-A*. If we wish, English allows us to be more specific about the kind of mental act: 'S sees that A', 'S recollects that A', 'S proves that A', etc., each indicate the kind of mental act whereby S became aware of the fact presented by *that-A*.

1.2 Knowledge is a Relation Between a Mind and a Fact

To develop this account of knowledge, a background metaphysics is needed. I shall be assuming that the world, i.e., the totality of all the things there are, includes not only individuals, but also universals and facts. All these things can stand in various relations to each other, and among the relations in which they may stand is knowledge. A thing that stands in the knowledge relation to something is a mental individual—in other words, it is a *mind*. I take it to be constitutive of an individual's status as a mental being that it is an individual that at some time knows something.

For any given mind, there will be some things in the world that have come to its notice, while other things remain unnoticed by it. If something x has come to the notice of a person S, we say that S is aware of x, that S is conscious of x, that S is cognisant of x; in short, that S knows of x. This 'knows-of' construction is not the same as the English knowledge attribution 'knows-that'. The two constructions signify different things, which Russell (1959: 44) distinguished sharply, calling the former 'thing-knowledge' and the latter 'knowledge-of-truths'. Russell does not suggest that 'knowledge-of-truths' is a simple relation, and I think we can safely take it to be just the complex state of affairs which I have been suggesting is reported in English knowledge attributions.

Knowledge-of-truths is always reported in English with a 'that' clause, but thing-knowledge, which Russell also calls *acquaintance*, always has a single thing as its object. According to Russell, thing-knowledge is a relation in which, in principle, a mind can stand to any thing whatever, of which it is aware. Now on the metaphysics presupposed in the present book, the things there are include not only individuals but also facts. Thus for example there exists the individual Socrates, and also the fact *that Socrates was wise*. Both of these really exist: according to Russell, both are things of which one can have thing-knowledge; thus a person might know of Socrates, or of the wisdom of Socrates. But Russell's undifferentiated notion of thing-knowledge, which treats knowledge of an individual and knowledge of a fact as the same relation, seems to me to be a mistake. Certainly one may speak with equal propriety in English of knowing individuals and knowing facts, but the word 'know' is used in different senses in the two uses. To know an individual is to recognise or identify it, or at least to have the capacity to do so; or to know it in the sense of being familiar or acquainted with it, or of having personal experience of it. Knowledge of a fact lacks these connotations: knowing a fact is not identifying it, and does not imply familiarity with it, or personal experience of it. Therefore I think we need to subdivide Russellian 'thing-knowledge' into two sub-kinds, according to the metaphysical category of the thing known, i.e., according as what is 'known' is an individual or a fact. Knowledge of an individual is the sense of 'to know' that corresponds to German *kennen* and French *connaître*. Object-knowledge seems not to be a simple relation, for as noted it is a complex and context-dependent matter; therefore I do not believe that it is a fundamental relation. Knowledge of fact is the sense of English 'to know of' that corresponds to German *wissen* and French *savoir*. Fact-knowledge is the relation that I take to be conceptually primitive and metaphysically fundamental, and on which I shall be focusing in this book.

If fact-knowledge is a simple relation between a mind and a fact, then it should be possible to report fact-knowledge in a way that is referentially transparent. Thus if Pharaoh is aware of the fact that Hesperus is shining, he must also be aware of the fact that Phosphorus is shining, since these are one and the same fact. Transparent reports of fact-knowledge do indeed occur in English; two such occurred in the preceding sentence.

Another way to report fact-knowledge transparently is to refer to the fact known by utilising a construction such as sentence nominalisation. For example, if A is the sentence 'Phosphorus shone at dawn yesterday' then its nominalisation A^* is 'the shining of Phosphorus at dawn yesterday'. In general, if A is the sentence 'a is F at t,' then its nominalisation A^* will be 'the F-ness of a at t', or 'a's being F at t'. Here the positions occupied by F, a and t are all referentially transparent, because the sentence nominal denotes a fact by listing the fact's constituents, which are the same regardless of which terms we use to designate them. Thus for example, if dawn yesterday was at 6 a.m., then the shining of Phosphorus at dawn yesterday is identical with the shining of Hesperus at 6 a.m. yesterday. Because sentence nominalisations are referentially transparent, knowledge-reports that use them are referentially transparent also. If Pharaoh was aware that Phosphorus was shining at dawn, then what Pharaoh was aware of was the shining of Phosphorus at dawn; which was the shining of Hesperus, so Pharaoh was aware of the shining of Hesperus at 6 a.m. yesterday. Of course if we report Pharaoh's awareness by saying he was aware of the shining of Hesperus, we usually imply that Pharaoh was aware that Hesperus was shining. However, this is only an implicature, and not part of the semantic content. For the implicature is cancellable; thus one might say without absurdity 'Pharaoh was aware of the shining of Hesperus, though I do not imply he was aware that it was Hesperus that was shining'.

If the account is correct that I gave in section 1 of the logical form of knowledge attributions, then whenever we have 'S knows that A', we shall also have 'S knows of A*', where A* is the nominalisation of A. This pair of constructions with 'of' and 'that' occurs with several other verbs of cognition; the 'that' construct always entails the 'of' construct, but the converse entailment does not hold, as Pharaoh's case shows. Thus 'S is aware that A' entails 'S is aware of A*', 'S is conscious that A' entails 'S is conscious of A*', 'S is apprised that A' entails 'S is apprised of A*', but none of the converse entailments hold. This shows that the grammatical similarity between 'believes' and 'knows' is quite superficial, since there is no such thing as the 'of' construction with genuine propositional attitudes; one cannot 'believe of', 'hope of' or 'fear of' the shining of Hesperus. One can of course believe of x that it is thus and so, for example, one can believe of the shining of Hesperus that Pharaoh was aware of it. But 'believe of' does not take a sentence nominal to make a sentence: one cannot simply believe of the shining of Hesperus.

What now of Frege's puzzle? Pharaoh does not know that Hesperus is Phosphorus, but does he know of Hesperus's being Phosphorus, i.e., of the identity of Hesperus and Phosphorus? Since the fact of the identity of Hesperus and Phosphorus is the same fact as the fact of the identity of

Hesperus and Hesperus, it seems this is a fact of which Pharaoh is indeed aware. But Pharaoh lacks knowledge-of-truths: he does not know that Hesperus is Phosphorus. For Pharaoh is not in a position to judge that Hesperus is Phosphorus. It is not a judgement he is prepared to make; even if he were prepared to make it, it would not be justified, and so he is unable to derive any knowledge by means of this judgement. Now the knowledge attribution 'S knows that A' requires that S arrives at knowledge of the fact named by the nominalisation of A by a judgement or other mental act with the content that A; that is why, although Pharaoh knows of Hesperus's being Phosphorus, we do not say that he knows that Hesperus is Phosphorus. We could only use the 'knows that' locution if Pharaoh knew of the identity of Hesperus and Phosphorus specifically by a judgement or other mental act with the content *that Hesperus is Phosphorus.*

It may be objected that this does not do justice to the importance of the Babylonian discovery that Hesperus is Phosphorus. For on our account, the fact stated by 'Hesperus is Phosphorus' was not a new discovery by the Babylonians, since it is identical with the fact stated by 'Hesperus is Hesperus,' which they already knew. To this I reply that the great achievement of the Babylonians was not their apprehending a new fact about identity, but their attaining justification for a new belief. They were not the first to apprehend the self-identity of Hesperus, but they were the first to attain justification for the belief that Hesperus is Phosphorus. By adding this belief to their existing knowledge of astronomy, they were able to deduce knowledge of many new facts—for example, the fact that there is only one planet between Earth and Mercury. The new belief was thus a first-rate discovery, in the sense that it led to a flood of new knowledge; but the flood did not include new knowledge of the self-identity of Hesperus, for that was a fact they already knew.

1.3 Knowledge and Mental States

When a mind knows of some fact, usually there will be some mental events in virtue of which the mind has the knowledge. For example, if the knowledge is perceptual, the knowledge will be caused by the senses. The activity of a sense causes a mental act in the perceiver, and it is in virtue of this mental act that the perceiver knows of the fact. The locution 'in virtue of' is ambiguous as between a causal sense and a constitutive sense. We say the spark caused the fire in virtue of the presence of oxygen; the presence of oxygen was a contributory cause of the fire. We also say an apple is red in virtue of its skin being red, but the red skin constitutes rather than causes the redness of the apple.

The 'tripartite analysis' and its descendants say that knowledge is a species of justified true belief—having the knowledge is nothing over and above having the belief in the right circumstances. On such an account, one has the knowledge in virtue of the belief, in the constitutive sense of 'in virtue of'. This is a 'doxastic priority' theory, in that it takes belief to come before knowledge in the order of philosophical explanation, since it takes knowledge to be a kind of belief. But there is also the possibility of an entirely different sort of account, in which knowledge comes before belief in the order of explanation. An 'epistemic priority' theory will not explain knowledge as a kind of belief; rather, it will explain belief as a kind of knowledge-causing state. An epistemic priority theory can recognise other kinds of mental state, besides belief, as knowledge-causing; for example, it can recognise perceptual experience as directly knowledge-causing also.

The contrast between a doxastic priority theory and an epistemic theory is seen in the following two theses about the relation between knowledge and other psychological states. If S is aware of the fact p in virtue of S being in psychological state M in a context C, we can ask whether the knowledge is anything over and above S being in state M in context C. According to the Constitutive Thesis, it is not:

> *Constitutive Thesis*: Knowledge is constituted by being in the right psychological state in a favourable context.

The Constitutive Thesis is a thesis of psychological priority: it takes psychological states to come before knowledge in the order of explanation. But if we think that knowledge is a simple and unanalysable relation, we will deny that knowledge is constituted by other states. We shall prefer to understand the 'in virtue of' relation causally, and to endorse instead the following thesis:

> *Causal Thesis*: Knowledge is caused by being in the right psychological state in a favourable context.

The difference between the Constitutive Thesis and the Causal Thesis is a deep one, which raises fundamental issues in the philosophy of mind. For example, functionalism is a philosophy of mind that goes well with the Constitutive Thesis. Functionalism identifies mental states with inner states that interact with each other to cause behaviour, in response to sensory input. Functionalists suppose that, in principle at least, there is a definition of belief and other psychological states that does not presuppose the concept of knowledge; they take knowledge itself to be only a belief of a certain sort. But the Causal Thesis prefers to define belief in terms of knowledge. According to the Causal Thesis, a system of functional states can be a system of beliefs only if some at least of them cause knowledge. On this view, a being that was a functional duplicate of a human person would not necessarily have psychological states; only if its functional states caused knowledge would it be correct to classify it as having genuinely psychological states such as beliefs and experiences.

A small point in favour of the Causal Thesis is the great variety of mental acts and mental states in virtue of which we have knowledge. Examples of knowledge in virtue of a mental act include 'seeing' by a sudden insight that a mathematical theorem is true; perceiving a thing, an event or a fact; making an inference; judging that something is the case. Examples of knowledge in virtue of a standing mental state include: believing that the Battle of Hastings was in 1066; remembering that it was in 1066. Thus there are several quite different types of mental acts and states, in virtue of which one may have knowledge. This presents the difficulty for the Constitutive Thesis that if knowledge can be constituted by any of such a miscellany of states, it would appear that knowledge is not one thing, but a disunified and miscellaneous relation.

We could recover unity under the Constitutive Thesis by insisting that all the miscellaneous states give rise to belief, and that it is the belief that constitutes the knowledge. But there can be knowledge without belief. For example, when we judge we often form the corresponding belief, but we need not always do so. It is certainly conceivable that someone might make a judgement on an occasion, and so arrive at knowledge, without forming any disposition to judge the same way again on a future occasion; in such a case the person would have knowledge without belief. Perception also yields examples of knowledge without belief. For example, a simple creature may not be capable of such a complex mental state as belief, but may still have knowledge; it may notice things in its environment perceptually, and so be aware of them, even if it is incapable of conceptual thought about the things it notices. Moreover, in the case of human perception, we note that perceptual states have a very rich content, which many claim to be a non-conceptual content. We can put this by saying that some perceptual contents are so complex that they are unsuited to be the contents of any belief. Yet these perceptual contents give rise to immediate and detailed knowledge of the environment, which knowledge therefore cannot be any kind of belief. Of course, one might judge, concerning a perceptually presented scene, that it looks like *that*; but a demonstrative, as I shall argue later, can refer only if one already has knowledge of the referent. Thus one does not have knowledge of how the scene looks by believing it looks like that; rather, one is in a position to believe that it looks like *that* because one already has knowledge of how it looks.

Thus I think that we may doubt that knowledge is justified true belief, or any other kind of belief, on the grounds that belief is not the only mental state in virtue of which we have knowledge. Other 'verdictive' mental acts, such as perception, also give rise to knowledge. And this gives some support to the view that the connection between the verdictive mental act and the knowledge is not constitutive but causal.

1.4 Epistemic Faculties

Traditionally, a faculty is a power of the mind of any sort. Here it will be convenient to restrict the term to *epistemic* faculties, by which I mean a power of the mind to cause itself to know. Thus the very idea of a faculty presupposes the rejection of scepticism: our actual faculties are defined in terms of our actual knowledge. It would be possible to seek to define a faculty as a belief-forming mechanism of some special kind. For example, we might follow Plantinga (1993) and appeal to teleology, defining a faculty as a well-designed belief-forming mechanism designed (by its creator or by natural selection) to form true beliefs. Plantinga hopes to define knowledge as a true belief formed by the normal operation of a well-designed faculty working in its design environment. But no such attempt to define knowledge is being made here: instead I take knowledge to be primitive, and define the faculties in terms of the knowledge to which they give rise.

Perception is the faculty that gives us knowledge of facts about our environment. Our knowledge is not static, for we are constantly acquiring new knowledge. Some new knowledge is not derived from what we already know, so we must suppose that there are causal mechanisms that cause the world to cause us to acquire new knowledge in response to the changing environment. But often we acquire new knowledge from knowledge we already have, without further perceptual interaction with the world. Therefore we must also recognise the faculty of inference, a causal mechanism that causes what we already know to cause us to acquire new knowledge. And of course we have a faculty of memory, a power of continuing to know what we have once discovered.

Thus new knowledge is caused by the world, or by old knowledge, or by both. These cause the faculty to cause in us a new mental state, for example a new belief. The question then arises whether the new belief gives rise to knowledge. Clearly it will not do so if the mechanism that forms the belief is not alethically reliable. But mere reliability with respect to truth is not enough, for there could be a mechanism that was alethically reliable but which did not confer warrant. For example, someone might acquire clairvoyant powers that caused them to form new beliefs that were in fact reliably true. But if they had no idea whether the mechanism was reliable, then even though the beliefs it forces upon them are true, they are not warranted and do not (yet) give knowledge. This is not to deny that someone could eventually come to have immediate and non–inferential knowledge from the deliverances of a power of clairvoyance. They would have knowledge if they had come to know, by the use of some of their natural faculties, that the clairvoyant beliefs are reliable. But here the ultimate warrant is not the clairvoyance, but the faculty by means of which they discovered that the beliefs formed by the clairvoyance are a reliable sign of the truth.

The epistemic dependence of new belief-forming mechanisms on old faculties is shown also by the fact that beliefs formed by a mechanism that is in fact reliable will be open to defeat. Suppose someone has newly acquired a power of clairvoyance, and is consulting an expert to find out whether the clairvoyant beliefs are reliable. Suppose the expert mistakenly says that the clairvoyance mechanism is somehow faulty. Then the person may lose the warrant they previously had for trusting the deliverances of their new power; the old faculty, in this case the power of understanding testimony, has trumped the new power, however reliable the new power may actually be. I conclude that if one acquires a new belief-forming mechanism, then however reliable the mechanism may be, the beliefs it causes to arise in one have no epistemic warrant unless the alethic reliability of the new belief-forming mechanism is first established by some natural faculty.

But what of the natural faculties themselves? There are plenty of sceptics who have cast doubt on the reliability of our faculties. Do the faculties themselves need to be validated and proved reliable before they can give us knowledge? It is clear that our faculties, even if they are actually working perfectly, are not guaranteed to give us knowledge. Let us say that S and S^* are epistemic counterparts at time t, if they are exact duplicates, and if their seeming experiences and seeming memories are exactly the same. Then every knower has an unlucky epistemic counterpart. For example, I rely on my senses to tell me what is going on in my environment. But I have an unlucky counterpart who is the victim of a Cartesian deceiver. I see what is going on around me, but my unlucky counterpart does not see what is going on around him. There is nothing wrong with the counterpart's senses, but they are being controlled by the deceiver rather than by facts about the environment. The state of the counterpart is phenomenologically the same as mine, and he is in a situation I could not discriminate from my actual situation: for if I were in his situation, I would not know I was not in my actual situation. With what right, then, do I claim to know that I am not in his situation? My knowledge, if I have it, relies on my senses, which in the actual world are a reliable belief-forming mechanism. But if I am to be warranted in trusting my senses, must I not validate their operation in some way, by proving that they are a reliable belief-forming mechanism?

Perception is not the only faculty whose capacity to deliver knowledge depends upon one's context. It is the same with memory. I remember some of the past—a day ago, a month ago, a year ago. But I have an unlucky counterpart who was created five minutes ago with a lot of false memories about the past. There is nothing wrong with the counterpart's faculty of memory; on the contrary, the faculty is in perfect working order, and it is only the causation of its initial state that is unsatisfactory. Thus I and this counterpart have the same faculties, and are in subjectively indiscriminable states. My unlucky counterpart is ignorant about the past. With what right do I claim not to be ignorant?

It is the same with knowledge of the future. I know that the sun will rise tomorrow, but I have an unlucky counterpart who does not know it, for at his world the future will not resemble the past. There is nothing wrong with his faculty of inference, which works identically to my own. Like me, he takes certain regularities which have held throughout the past to be laws, but in his context the regularities are not laws, for they will cease to hold tomorrow. His situation is subjectively indiscriminable from my situation. He does not know the sun will rise tomorrow, so with what right do I claim that I know that the sun will rise tomorrow?

One response to this is to agree with the sceptic that after all I do not know what I took myself to know. The argument is:

1. I have the same faculties as my counterpart.
2. The state of my counterpart is indiscriminable from my own state.
3. Counterparts who are in indiscriminable states have the same knowledge.
4. My counterpart does not know the fact p.
5. I do not know the fact p.

This argument is internalist. It assumes that counterparts have the same epistemic status, if they are in subjectively indiscriminable states. To avoid scepticism, we must reject this assumption: contrary to internalism, counterparts may vary in knowledge, according as their context does or does not enable them to know. We must therefore introduce the notion of a context favourable for knowledge, and refine our definition of a faculty as follows: a faculty is a power of the mind, such that if a fact p is in the range of the faculty, the faculty is working normally, and the context is favourable, then p can cause the faculty to cause the mind to know the fact p.

Whether a context is favourable or not depends on the kind of fact in question, and on the faculty that is to produce knowledge of the fact. For example, a context where the future will not resemble the past is unfavourable for inductive knowledge about the future, but it does not follow that it is unfavourable for every faculty. It may be favourable with respect to memory, if it is possible even in this context to have memory knowledge of facts about the past. It may be favourable with respect to perception, if it is possible even in this context to have knowledge of the environment by means of the senses. Thus favourableness of a context is relative to a faculty, and relative to the range of facts knowledge of which is in question.

For perception, the range of the faculty is certain facts about the environment. The environmental fact p causes an experience with a content which in the context represents the fact that p. If the context is a favourable one, the experience causes the subject to know the fact p. The experience is a causal intermediary between the mind and the fact, but it is not an epistemic intermediary, so one's awareness of an experientially presented fact is just as immediate as one's awareness of the experience itself. It has however sometimes been suggested that the phenomenology of the perceptual experience has a specially important epistemic role. For example, it has been suggested that in perception what we are immediately aware of is the phenomenal character of our current perceptual experience; and that from this we go on to infer the state of the environment which we take to be the cause of this experience. This is a most implausible suggestion. Certainly the experience has a characteristic phenomenology, but it seems wrong to suggest that we infer the fact it presents from the phenomenology. For any mental act has a phenomenology. For example, an occurrent memory has a phenomenology, since there is something it is like to have that memory. But it is absurd to suppose that we infer the fact the memory presents from what it is like to have the memory. It seems equally absurd to suppose that we infer the experientially presented fact from what it is like to have the experience. The experience is a causal intermediary between the mind and the fact, but it is not an epistemic intermediary.

If we had no sense-perception, we could not make up for its lack by our other faculties. Thus outright scepticism about the senses cannot be answered. But this does not mean that we cannot tell that our senses are functioning correctly. On the contrary, we can confirm their correct functioning by memory and inference. For in the light of current sensory experience we can predict future sensory experience by induction. When the predictions turn out to be correct this confirms the correct functioning of the senses. However, this has to be distinguished from validation of the reliability of the senses *ab initio* by the other faculties. That kind of validation is not feasible. It would involve treating our experience as only an indication of what is going on in the environment, with the reliability of the indicator having to be independently confirmed by the other faculties.

But that is impossible, for if we do not trust our senses we have no other epistemic access to what is going on in the environment.

Just as perception is the faculty that gives us knowledge of facts about the environment, so memory is the faculty that gives us knowledge of facts about the past. If we did not trust our memory, we would be able to know nothing of the past, for even the hypothesis that there was a past would have nothing to commend it. Thus someone who rejected the evidence of memory would be deprived of all knowledge of the past; the other faculties could not replace memory as a source of knowledge. Neither can the other faculties validate memory, since we cannot regard all our memories as mere indicators of past facts. However, the other faculties can serve to confirm that memory is functioning correctly. We can certainly notice if there is a good match between what follows from our seeming memories and what is currently observed to be the case, and this can be the basis of confirmation by the other faculties that memory is functioning correctly.

We rely on the faculty of inference for knowledge of facts about the future. Induction allows us to infer the future from what we already know about the present and the past. Of course induction cannot be validated by any other faculty, for no other faculty knows the future. Therefore total scepticism about induction cannot be refuted. However the performance of induction in the past can be checked by perception and memory, from which we may learn by induction how to learn better in future.

Thus the various faculties are each indispensable, for if we came to distrust any of our faculties none of the others could replace it. Moreover, a general scepticism about all our faculties is unanswerable. However each individual faculty can be checked to some extent by the others, so that if the correct operation of any one faculty is in doubt, it can receive support from the others.

1.5 Defeaters

The simplest version of the Constitutive Thesis is the tripartite analysis, which says that knowledge is the true, justified kind of belief. But we know from Gettier that context enters the question too, so a more refined version of the Constitutive Thesis will try to separate intrinsic and contextual factors. The obvious suggestion is that knowledge is the sort of true belief where the intrinsic state of the subject is knowledge-conducive, and the context is knowledge-conducive too.

But Williamson (2000:66–72) has shown that knowledge cannot be 'factorised' into an intrinsic state component and a context component. For we can find a state type that is conducive to knowledge, and a context type that is conducive to knowledge, such that there can be a token of the state type, and a token of the context type, whose conjunction is not a token of knowledge. For example, let σ_1 be a type of intrinsic state in which S can speak English but not French, and let σ_2 be a type of intrinsic state in which S can speak French but not English. Let C_1 be a type of context in which S meets two strangers, and asks them where the Post Office is: the English-speaking stranger is reliable and sincere, and says in English that the Post Office is straight ahead; the French-speaking stranger is a liar, and says in French that it is to the left. Let C_2 be just like C_1, except that in C_2 it is the French-speaking stranger who is reliable and sincere, and the English speaker who is a liar.

In context C_1, if S is in state σ_1, then S hears and understands only the truthful English-speaker, and learns that the Post Office is straight ahead. Thus σ_1 and C_1 are a state-context pair in which S gains knowledge, so σ_1 and C_1 are both knowledge-conducive. In context C_2, if S is in state σ_2, then S hears and understands only the truthful French-speaker, so σ_2 and C_2 are also both knowledge-conducive. But we cannot mix and match state and context. For example, in the state-context pair σ_1 and C_2, S understands only English; S is justified in believing what the English-speaking liar says, but gains no knowledge. So not just any combination of a knowledge-conducive belief-state with a knowledge-conducive context will do. Therefore it is impossible to analyse knowledge by a conjunctive definition, whose first conjunct lays down an appropriate condition on the knower's intrinsic state, and whose second conjunct lays down an appropriate condition on the knower's context. What fact one learns in a context, and indeed whether one learns any fact at all, depends on intrinsic state and context not separately, but in combination. How is it that knowledge can be the upshot of an intrinsic state in a context? According to the Causal Thesis, the explanation is causal: the state and the context jointly cause the knowledge. Since joint causation has no simple logical analysis, we should not expect a simple analysis of how knowledge depends on intrinsic state plus context.

According to the Constitutive Thesis, however, a logical analysis must exist, at least in principle; so it is incumbent on the Constitutive Thesis to give some account of how context affects the possibility of knowledge. Here appeal might be made to the notion of a *defeater*. For any given item of knowledge that A, there will be a great many facts I might learn that would cause me to lose my justification for believing that A. For example, perhaps I know that there is a blue carpet in the room I am in. But if I learned that there is something wrong with my colour vision, I might cease to be justified in believing that there was a blue carpet in the room. Or if I learned that there was a blue filter on the light in the room, again I might lose my justification. These potential discoveries are *defeaters*:

> *Defeater*: A fact d is a defeater of S's knowledge that A if, if S were to learn of d, S would no longer be rationally justified in believing that A.

For any given A, there are many possible defeaters $d_1, d_2, \ldots, d_n, \ldots$ any one of which would defeat my knowledge that A. Let D be the disjunction of all these possible defeaters. Then my subjective credence for $\neg D$ is a measure of my certainty that A, since it will reflect my subjective probability of learning some fact that will make me lose justification for my belief that A. (Note that on this account one's *certainty* that A, i.e., one's credence for $\neg D$, is to be distinguished from one's *confidence* that A, which is one's credence for A itself.)

If I am completely certain that A, I believe there is nothing I might learn that would cause me to lose justification for my belief that A. If I am right about this, my belief is *indefeasible*: it is not possible that I will learn something such that, if I learned it, I would not be rationally justified in continuing to believe that A. Conversely a belief is defeasible and therefore less than objectively certain if a defeater is possible, i.e., if it is possible that I will learn something that will remove my justification for believing that A. If we require that knowledge be certain or indefeasible, scepticism about the external world follows directly. As every reader of Unger (1975) knows, one cannot be entirely confident that life is not a dream, and hence one must give non-zero credence to this hypothesis; but if we learned the hypothesis is true, our former beliefs about the external world would no longer be justified. Therefore if knowledge of the external world requires certainty that life is not a dream, we do not know there is an external world. Rather than drawing a sceptical conclusion from this, we should of course reverse the argument, and deduce that knowledge does not require certainty; similarly, it does not require indefeasibility.

The concept of a defeater may seem to help the Constitutive Thesis to say when a belief in a context constitutes knowledge: the context must be one in which the believer is justified, the belief is true, and where there exist no defeaters. But then the challenge for the Constitutive Theory is to explain why a defeater precludes knowledge. The defeater d is a fact such that if one knew of it one would not continue to be justified in believing that A: however one does not actually know of d; so how does the mere existence of d preclude one from knowing that A?

For example, if a candle is a metre in front of me, and it looks to me as if a candle is a metre in front of me, I have a justified true belief that I face a candle. But if there is a mirror placed between the candle and me, and it is the reflection of a different candle that I see in the mirror, then I do not know that I face a candle. Now if I knew I faced a mirror, I would not be justified in continuing to believe that I faced a candle; but I do not know I face the mirror, so how does it block my knowledge?

It may be held to be obvious that I cannot know that A, if there is a fact such that, if I knew of it, I could not rationally continue to believe that A. For example, suppose that two subjects are looking at the reflection of the candle in the mirror. One subject does not know of the mirror, the other does. The better-informed subject who does know of the mirror is not justified in believing in the presence of the candle; so how can the subject who is ignorant of the mirror know of the candle? Thus we might propose it as an axiom, that if S does not know that A, because S knows something relevant that S^* does not know, then S^* does not know that A either. This proposed axiom, however, is incorrect, for it overlooks the possibility of misleading defeaters: if S learns of a defeater which is in fact misleading, learning of it may destroy S's knowledge, while S^*, who remains ignorant of the defeater, continues to know. For example, you and I may both know that Billy the Kid was the robber, for we recognised him when his mask slipped. But if next day someone you trust tells you falsely that Billy has an indiscriminable twin Benny, you may give up your belief that it was Billy. I did not hear the false testimony about the non-existent twin, so I continue to know it was Billy. You know something relevant that I do not know, yet I know it was Billy, and you do not. Thus the mere existence of the defeater—the fact of the giving of the false testimony—does not destroy my knowledge; it is only if I knew of the defeater that it would destroy my knowledge, by causing me to give up my belief.

A response to this is to suggest that we should talk of defeater-defeaters, defeaters of defeater-defeaters, and so on. It might then be proposed that a justified true belief constitutes knowledge if all its defeaters are themselves defeated—it is an 'ultimately undefeated' belief. Thus in the present example, although the fact of the false testimony defeats my evidence that Billy did it, the fact that the testimony is false defeats the fact of the testimony. Then the defeater is defeated, and my evidence for believing Billy did it is 'ultimately undefeated', and therefore it is knowledge. But this manoeuvre will not save the Constitutive Thesis. The trouble is that a defeater of knowledge of p may itself be defeated by the fact p. In the example of the candle, the fact of the presence of the mirror defeats one's belief that one faces a candle, but the fact that the mirror obscures a candle defeats this defeater. So my initial belief that I faced a candle is an ultimately undefeated true justified belief; nevertheless I did not initially know that I faced a candle.

1.6 Reliability

The defeater d is a fact such that if one knew of it one would not continue to be justified in believing that A: however one does not know of d; so how can the mere existence of d preclude one's knowing that A? I suggest that the answer must be causal: the existence of d causes one to be unreliable about A. For example, the right thing to say about the case of the mirror and the candle is that the mirror blocks one's knowledge simply because it blocks one's view. The mirror disrupts the information link between the subject and the candle, and therefore causes the subject to be unreliable about the candle. If this is right, we must expect to find many other types of case where a fact which is not a defeater nevertheless prevents knowledge by causing unreliability.

An example is what Williamson (1992) has called 'inexact knowledge'. Suppose S is skilled at estimating visually the number of apples in a box. S can put a lower bound on the number of apples just by looking, provided there is allowed a sufficient margin of error. Thus if there are more than 52 apples, S knows there are more than 50, but if there are 52 or fewer, S is alethically unreliable about whether there are more than 50. Consider an occasion when there are exactly 51 apples, and S confidently judges there are over 50 apples. S's belief is true, and is justified by S's known skill in estimation. However, S does not know there are over 50 apples. The fact that there are 51 prevents S from knowing that there are over 50, for there is insufficient margin of error. Yet the fact that there are 51 is not a defeater; on the contrary, if S learned that fact, S would be conclusively justified in thinking there are over 50. The circumstance that there are 51 precludes S from knowing not by acting as a defeater, but by being a cause of unreliability.

The notion of a defeater as we have defined it is not an internalist notion, but it might be thought to be internalist in spirit. For a defeater is something that would destroy one's justification if one knew of it, so we are thinking of it as something that can potentially come within one's epistemic purview. Perhaps the Constitutive Thesis needs to adopt a more radically externalist strategy. Perhaps it should adopt reliabilism, and explain knowledge as the reliable sort of true belief. Certainly there is some connection between knowledge and reliability: let us define *epistemic reliability* about A as the kind of reliability one has if and only if one knows that A. Then reliabilism would shed light on the nature of knowledge, if we could define reliability without appeal to knowledge.

Can we define reliability in terms of probability? It is evident that there is a conceptual connection between reliability and probability. For we are willing to test a claim to knowledge by asking whether there is a high probability that the belief is true, given that the belief is held. Thus we seem to have:

$$S \text{ knows that } A \rightarrow P(A|S \text{ believes that } A) \text{ is high}$$

If A is not itself very probable, but there is a high probability of A conditional upon S believing that A, then normally there is an information link of some kind between S and the fact that A. It is the information link that makes S reliable. The existence of an information link does not require knowledge of the existence of an information link, so reliabilism can be a radically externalist epistemology.

But it turns out that a definition of epistemic reliability in terms of probability is none too easy to give. We cannot say reliability requires that the probability of A, conditional upon S believing that A, is unity. For example, I have arranged to meet my friend Mark at noon tomorrow, so since he is a punctual person, I know he will be there at noon. I know, so I am epistemically reliable. Nevertheless there is a chance he will not be there at noon, since any number of chance events might delay him. Thus the conditional probability that Mark will be there at noon, given that I believe Mark will be there at noon, is less than unity. Knowledge is possible even in a chancy world like ours; therefore reliability does not require a conditional probability of unity.

It may be objected that one surely cannot know something, if there is a chance it will not happen. There is a chance that Mark will not be there at noon; therefore, I do not know that he will be there at noon. But the point at issue is not specifically an epistemic one. The objector might with the same right insist that it cannot be true today that Mark will be there at noon, since there is a chance today that he will not be there. Or it might be insisted that the fact that Mark will be there on 10 July cannot exist on 9 July, since on 9 July there is a chance he will not be there. But in each case the mistake is the same. Whether something is known, or true, or a fact depends only on the actual world; whereas whether something has a chance of not being known, or of not being true, or of not being a fact depends on nearby worlds. The present chance that Mark will be there at noon tomorrow is the percentage of nearby worlds with the same laws as the actual world, and the same past up to the present moment, at which he is there at noon tomorrow. Thus it can be the case both that he will be there, and that there is a chance he will not be there: he will be there, because at the actual world there exists the fact that he is there at noon on 10 July; there is a chance he will not be there, because this fact is absent at some nearby worlds which have the same laws as the actual world, and the same history up to 9 July. The fact that he will be there exists actually on 9 July, and is therefore available actually on 9 July to be a term of the knowledge relation, despite its absence at some nearby worlds. We must suppose that such facts about the future can be known beforehand, despite being chancy; the alternative is inductive scepticism in a chancy world.

I conclude that epistemic reliability does not require a conditional probability of unity. Nor can we correct the definition by requiring only that the conditional probability be 'close enough' to unity. Variants of the lottery paradox show that no matter how high $P(A|\mathbf{B}A)$ is, if it falls short of unity we may not have the kind of reliability necessary for knowledge.

For example, suppose N owns exactly £1, and that there is a 50% chance that N spends the £1 to buy a lottery ticket. Since the ticket is unlikely to win, the unconditional probability that N has no money at all after the draw is about 50%. Suppose that if S has in fact formed the belief that after the draw N has no money, that will be because S saw N buy the ticket, believes the ticket will not win, and has inferred that after the draw N has no money. Then the conditional probability that N has no money, given that S believes that N has no money, can be made as close to unity as we please; so it much exceeds the unconditional probability that N has no money. But N might be a millionaire after the draw! So S does not know that N has no money, and therefore S's belief that N has no money lacks epistemic reliability. It follows that epistemic reliability about A cannot be defined in terms of $P(A|\mathbf{B}A)$.

We might instead try to define reliability in terms of truth-tracking. Since we require S to show sensitivity to whether or not A is the case, we might suggest Nozick's (1981: 172–96) truth-tracking counterfactuals:

S is reliable about $A =_{\mathrm{df}}$

   (i) $A \,\Box\!\!\rightarrow\, \mathbf{B}A$, and
   (ii) $\neg A \,\Box\!\!\rightarrow\, \neg\mathbf{B}A$

But, as Nozick notes, there are counterexamples to this. There is the Lucky Glimpse: the bank robber's mask slips, and S recognises Billy the Kid, so S knows Billy did it. But there are plenty of close worlds where the mask did not slip, i.e., worlds where Billy did it, but S does not believe that Billy did it. Nevertheless, as things actually are, S is perfectly reliable about the fact that Billy did it, which violates the suggested condition that $A \,\Box\!\!\rightarrow\, \mathbf{B}A$. An example that violates the other suggested condition is the Hypochondriac, who would convince himself he was in pain even if he was not in pain. But in fact he is in pain, he knows he is, and his belief is epistemically reliable, which violates $\neg A \,\Box\!\!\rightarrow\, \neg\mathbf{B}A$.

Nozick himself suggests a shift to *methods*: S knows that A if S arrives at the true belief that A by a method M that 'tracks the truth'. Thus in the case of the Lucky Glimpse, the method is to look at the robber when his mask has slipped; the mask might easily not slip, but that would not make the method itself unreliable, just inapplicable. In the case of the Hypochondriac, the method is to rely on conscious introspection when one is in pain, not morbid imaginings when one is not in pain. But the appeal to methods is known not to succeed, for it depends too much on the description of the method. If the description is made too specific, then everyone with a true belief can be represented as relying on some reliable method; but if it is made too general, then every knower can be represented as relying on an unreliable method. Since we are given no guidance on which description of the method M is the appropriate one in a given case, this attempt to define reliability fails.

A related suggestion, discussed in Sainsbury (1997), is that we should explain reliability in terms of the modality 'it could easily happen that'. Then S is reliable about A, if it could not easily happen that S is mistaken about A. This blocks the counterexample of the Lucky Glimpse. S is not in fact mistaken that Billy did it; and had the mask not slipped, S would have had no opinion about whether Billy did it, and so would not easily have been mistaken. But it is straightforward to construct a modified counterexample. There is the Misleading Mask: Billy robs the bank wearing the trademark mask of Jesse James; the mask slips, so S knows Billy did it; but the mask might easily not have slipped, in which case S would have mistakenly believed that Jesse did it. Thus S could easily have been mistaken, despite being actually perfectly reliable. Here it may be replied that S does not use the same method throughout the possibilities under discussion, since sometimes S relies on recognising a face, and sometimes on recognising a mask; but as before this reply does not help, because we do not know sufficiently exactly how to define the relevant methods.

1.7 Epistemic Priority

Can we reverse the order of explanation, and throw light on the concepts of justification, defeat and reliability by means of the concept of knowledge? If we can, that would speak in favour of the thesis that knowledge comes first in the order of explanation.

Justification can be defined in terms of knowledge. If one believes that A, then whether one's belief is justified or not will depend on how one arrived at it. Suppose that one is in possession of background knowledge E, that one is the subject of a sequence Σ of one or more mental acts, and that it is in virtue of Σ that one has arrived at the belief that A. Then justification may be defined as follows: E and Σ justify one's belief that A if in a favourable context E and Σ would cause one to know that A. Given E, one has in virtue of Σ fully carried out one's epistemic duty, for one has done everything required of one to arrive at knowledge; the rest is up to the context. Note that this definition of justification is not internalist, since one can be justified, without being in a position to know that one is justified. For given Σ, one is justified if one has background knowledge E; but one can have E without being in a position to know that one has E.

Defeat can be defined in terms of justification, and hence in terms of knowledge. Suppose one is in possession of background knowledge E, that one is the subject of mental acts Σ, and that $E(d)$ is the background knowledge one would have, if one learned that d. Then d is a defeater of one's justification for A if E and Σ justify one's belief that A, but $E(d)$ and Σ do not justify one's belief that A.

I argued in the previous section that epistemic reliability cannot be analysed in non-epistemic terms. But we can certainly accept the doctrine that reliability is that property of the subject which when added to true belief gives knowledge. The reliabilist equation 'knowledge = reliably true belief' is perfectly acceptable, provided we treat it simply as an implicit definition of reliability. It remains to try to extract an explicit definition.

Clearly it would serve no useful purpose to define reliability as the logically weakest condition that must be added to true belief to give knowledge. That would yield only the trivial :

$$R \equiv ((A \wedge \mathbf{B}A) \rightarrow \mathbf{K}A)$$

That is unsatisfactory because intuitively we want reliability to be what distinguishes knowledge from belief that merely chances to be true. The material conditional will not serve our purpose: being such that (either one does not believe truly that A, or one knows that A) does not guarantee that, if one believed truly that A, one would know that A; any more than being either unwise or tall guarantees that, if one were wise, one would be tall.

Reliability is not that which must be added to true belief to materially imply knowledge. Rather, it must be a property of a subject S which guarantees that, if S believes that A, then S knows that A. Therefore the condition we need is the counterfactual conditional:

$$R \equiv ((A \wedge \mathbf{B}A) \; \Box\!\!\rightarrow \mathbf{K}A)$$

This is the right condition, because if S does believe truly that A, then the counterfactual tells us that S knows that A, so certainly S is reliable about A. And if A is false, or if S does not believe that A, we know that if S were to believe truly that A, then S would know that A, so that again S is reliable about A. So we can define reliability as follows: S is reliable about A if S would know that A if S had the true belief that A. Note that being reliable about A, as just defined, does not entail being reliable about $\neg A$: so we must distinguish reliability about A from reliability about whether A.

Many epistemologists discuss warrant, which they conceive of as a strongly externalist species of justification, which takes into account not only the subject's mental acts and background knowledge, but also certain favourable features of the context which confer entitlement. Warrant must be distinguished from reliability, for the truth of the reliability counterfactual '$(A \wedge \mathbf{B}A) \; \Box\!\!\rightarrow \; \mathbf{K}A$' does not suffice for warrant. For example, suppose Midas stands with his eyes closed facing a heap of gold. He has not seen the gold, so he has no warrant for the belief that he faces gold. But if he believed he faced gold, he would open his eyes, and so he would know that he faced gold. Midas satisfies the reliability counterfactual, but until he opens his eyes he is not warranted in believing he faces gold.

Reliability was characterised by a counterfactual conditional. It might be proposed that warrant is characterised by the corresponding strict conditional:

$$W \equiv \Box((A \wedge \mathbf{B}A) \rightarrow \mathbf{K}A)$$

But this is not satisfactory, because there will be many cases where one is warranted, but one has only a defeasible warrant, so that one does not satisfy the strict conditional. Then actually one is warranted, but the strict conditional is not true, for there is a possible world where one has the same justification E and Σ for one's true belief that A, but one does not know that A, because of the presence of a defeater.

However strict we make the conditional, being warranted is not being such that if one believes truly that A, then one knows that A. Let us therefore shift attention from the conditional property to the corresponding dispositional property. If warrant is not knowing if one believes, perhaps it is the disposition to know if one believes. And indeed it does seem reasonable to suppose that warrant is a disposition, because there is a close analogy between it and other properties that are uncontroversially dispositional.

The analogy can be spelled out as follows: a thing has its dispositional properties partly on account of its own intrinsic nature, and partly on account of contextual factors. For example, *fragility* is the disposition to break if struck, and fragility is the upshot of factors that are partly intrinsic and partly contextual. Relevant intrinsic factors include complex microstructural properties of the fragile object; contextual factors include features of the kind of objects in the environment which might possibly strike it. Analogously, warrant is the upshot of factors that are partly intrinsic, and partly contextual. For example, in the case of visual reliability, intrinsic factors will include the acuity of one's vision, and whether one's visual system is in good working order. Contextual factors will include factors that enable one's visual system to work properly, for example the strength of the lighting, the presence of suitable visual cues, etc., etc. We therefore seem justified in treating warrant as a disposition.

Whenever there is a disposition, there is the possibility of a preventer—something that can block the disposition from having its normal effect. A fragile vase will not break if dropped, if a guardian angel stands ready to catch it if it falls. The angel is a preventer of the vase breaking, despite its fragility and its fall. In the same way, a warranted person's disposition to know if they believe may be blocked. For example, if it looks to S as if S faces a candle, then S has warrant for the belief that S faces a candle, for S has good eyesight and knows what candles look like. Thus S is disposed to know S faces a candle if S believes S does. But in the context where the blocking mirror is present, S does not know S faces a candle; the presence of the mirror prevents S's true belief from yielding knowledge in this context. This suggests that what makes a context unsuitable for knowledge is not constitutive but causal: some factor prevents even a warranted subject from knowing, by blocking their disposition to know if they believe.

The suggestion that warrant is a disposition fits very well with the Causal Thesis. For if D is a disposition to E if C, then if indeed E when C, then probably D caused C to cause E. For example, the fragility of the fragile vase is its disposition to break when struck: if when struck it does break, then probably it was its fragility that caused the striking to cause the breaking. Similarly, one's warrant about A is one's disposition to know that A if one has the true belief that A: so if when one believes one does know, probably one's warrant caused one's believing to cause the knowing. Just as the fragility of the vase causes the striking to cause the breaking, so one's warrant causes one's belief to cause one to know. Thus belief causes knowledge, in accordance with the Causal Thesis.

It may be objected that from 'D is a disposition to E when C' we cannot always infer 'C causes E'. For it sometimes happens that a disposition suppresses an effect rather than causing it. For example, if a fragile vase is cushioned by being wrapped in protective packaging, the cushioning disposes the vase not to break when struck. When the vase is struck, it does not break; but it hardly follows that the cushioning caused the striking to cause the vase not to break. Here it is necessary to distinguish dispositions that enable from dispositions that prevent. Fragility is an enabling disposition to break if struck; being cushioned is a preventing disposition that suppresses breaking. The difference between enabling and suppressing is not formal, but lies in the pattern of causation. In the case of fragility, we have iterated causation: the fragility causes a striking to cause a breaking. In the case of the cushioning, we have prevented causation: the cushioning prevents a striking from causing a breaking. It is iterated causation that we have in the case of warrant, for warrant enables belief to cause knowledge, rather than preventing it. Therefore if warrant causes one to know when one believes, it seems reasonable to infer that one's warrant causes one's believing to cause one to know.

1.8 Conclusion

This chapter has treated the concept of knowledge as primitive, and knowledge itself as an unexplained fundamental relation. It has introduced the Causal Thesis, according to which belief is a means whereby we may apprehend a fact, but is not itself our awareness of the fact. Not even a true, justified, ultimately undefeated belief is knowledge—it is only a cause of knowledge. Similar remarks apply to other mental acts and states. For example, perception can cause awareness of the visible scene, but not even a veridical and appropriately caused visual experience is visual knowledge; it is only the cause of visual knowledge.

With knowledge as our starting-point, it proves possible to provide accounts of a number of other topics that are of interest in epistemology. In what follows I will suggest that the same approach can be fruitful in metaphysics generally, and that even if we cannot say what knowledge is, we can still use the concept of knowledge to shed light on several other topics in metaphysics. But first it is necessary to have available a background metaphysics. So in the next chapter I will temporarily set aside the topic of knowledge, in order to sketch a metaphysic of facts and universals. That background will provide a framework for the subsequent discussion of connections between knowledge and other topics.

2

Facts

The operation of our faculties gives rise in us to knowledge, by causing the thoughts in virtue of which we come to know facts. Thoughts have structure, reflecting the concepts they activate; sentences are the verbal expressions of thoughts, and they also have structure. So it would be convenient for theory if facts had structure too. Then the referent of a component of a thought could be read off as the corresponding component of the fact of which the thought gives us knowledge. Once a referent has been assigned to a concept, the word that expresses the concept will inherit the same referent. Thus we can use knowledge to found the theory of reference, without appeal to the concept of truth; provided that facts genuinely exist, and provided that they have a suitable structure.

Part of our inheritance from the 'linguistic turn' in philosophy is the doctrine that facts do not genuinely and separately exist as 'things in the word'. According to Strawson:

Facts are what statements (when true) state; they are not what statements are about. ... There is no nuance, except of style, between 'That's true' and 'That's a fact'. (Strawson 1950: 196)

Davidson writes:

Talk about facts reduces to predication of truth ... : this might be called the *redundancy theory* of facts. (Davidson 1967: 43)

On this view, there is no separate ontology of facts: facts are a kind of truth-bearer, namely the true kind; they are not a separate class of 'things in the world'. Strawson puts it vividly:

If you prise the statements off the world, you prise the facts off too. (You don't also prise off what the statements are about—for this you would need a different kind of lever.) (Strawson 1950: 197)

The view I advocate here is exactly the opposite of this. There certainly are facts, and *pace* Strawson (1950: 196), facts can indeed be 'witnessed or heard or seen', and thereby become known.

Why should we believe in facts? If facts were merely true truth-bearers, we should have only semantic reasons to believe in them. But if facts are a separate kind of entities in their own right then we will expect to find reasons to believe in them from general metaphysics. And metaphysics does give us a variety of good reasons to believe in facts. For example, facts are needed as the causal relata: as Mellor (1995: 130–9) has argued, it was the fact that Don did not fall that caused him not to die. Facts are needed in the theory of material beings, for we can found the theory in plural logic and the theory of facts (Hossack 2000). Facts are the metaphysical glue that 'tie' particular and universal together, thus allowing us to escape Bradley's Regress. In the theory of content and the theory of modality, facts can replace such dubious entities as propositions, states of affairs and possible worlds. Facts can ground logic: if there are facts, and if there are laws of coexistence of structurally related facts, then these 'laws of fact' can take the place of Frege's 'laws of truth' (1967: 13) as the objective correlate of the rules of inference of a correct logic. The usefulness of facts in so many branches of metaphysics gives us good reason to believe in them, and to make full use of them in the metaphysics of knowledge.

In this chapter I outline a theory of facts. Section 1 discusses the relation between the theory of facts and Realism, the traditional metaphysical doctrine of universals. Section 2 places at the centre of the theory of facts and universals the relation of *combination*, a multigrade relation taking a variable number of terms. Section 3 discusses the 'vector logic' of multigrade relations. Section 4 introduces 'the problem of the unity of the proposition', i.e., the problem of why it is impossible to judge 'nonsense'. This turns out to be the same as the problem of the distinction between particulars and universals. Section 5 rejects solutions that invoke extra entities such as propositions or states of affairs. Section 6 offers a solution *via* the theory of negative facts. Section 7 extends the theory of negative facts to other complex facts, namely conjunctive and general facts. Section 8 further extends the theory of complex facts to allow it to cope with multiple generality, without the need to resort either to 'logical forms' or to 'variables'. Section 9 suggests that an adequate semantic theory for the Predicate Calculus can be developed within the theory of facts. A proof of this is given in the Appendix to this chapter.

2.1 Resemblance

The theory of facts to be developed here presupposes Realism, the traditional metaphysical doctrine according to which there exist universals as well as particulars. Realism stands opposed to Nominalism, traditionally the alternative doctrine that there are no universals. The theory of facts needs Realism, for facts are individuated by the universals and particulars they combine. But conversely, I shall argue, Realism needs the theory of facts, for without facts universals cannot do the explanatory work for which they are needed; indeed, without facts the very distinction between particular and universal is difficult to draw.

Realism is a metaphysical doctrine. According to the traditional conception, metaphysics is a science. A science seeks by rational inquiry to discover natural kinds and the laws that govern them. A special science restricts its attention to some only of all the things there are; for example, biology studies only living things, and psychology studies only things with minds. In contrast, metaphysics studies everything. The natural kinds studied by metaphysics are called categories: the claim of metaphysics is that everything there is falls within one or other of its categories. This is not to say that metaphysics subsumes the other sciences; metaphysics seeks knowledge of all things, not all knowledge of things. There is plenty of knowledge that falls to some special science, outside the sphere of metaphysical knowledge. But there is no thing that falls outside the metaphysical categories, for the categories are the highest *genera* or natural kinds.

Different metaphysical theories have different hypotheses about which are the true metaphysical natural kinds. Realism takes the highest categories to be *particular* and *universal*: it claims that without exception, everything that exists falls into the one category or the other. This division of all things into particular and universal has traditionally had two fundamental motivations, one semantic, the other metaphysical. The semantic motivation is to give an account of the difference between subject and predicate. Realism says that only a universal can occur in thought as predicate, and that a particular can occur only as subject; so universals are needed as the semantic value of predicates. The metaphysical motivation for Realism is to explain resemblance. Out of all the numberless classes there are, only a few are similarity classes whose members all resemble each other. Realism says that things resemble because they literally have something in common, namely a universal. In this section, it is this metaphysical motivation that I will be discussing.

It is central to Realism that resemblance is an objective matter: it is not just that some things strike us humans as similar by human standards; some things really are similar, whether they strike us as similar or not. Realism concedes, indeed it insists, that some classes are arbitrary or miscellaneous collections, grouped together only because of some subjective interest of the classifier. But it says there are other classes that are not mere arbitrary groupings; the members of these classes have a real or natural resemblance to each other. Plato puts the point succinctly in the *Statesman* 262, d–e:

A man might think he was dividing number into its true classes if he cut off the number 10,000 from all the others and set it apart as one class. He might go on to invent a single name for the whole of the rest of number and then claim that because it possessed the invented common name it was in fact the other true class of number—'number other than 10,000'. Surely it would be better and closer to the real structure of the forms to make a central division of number into odd and even ... a true division into two groups each of which after separation is not only a portion of the class to be divided but also a real subdivision of it. (Plato 1963: 1026)

Here Plato distinguishes between a mere portion of a class and a 'real' subdivision. What makes the difference is that a 'real' subdivision is 'closer to the real structure of the forms'. The same idea is also to be found in the *Phaedrus*, where Plato tells us that a good definition, a good subdivision into classes, 'cuts the great beast of being at the joints'. In a good definition, according to *Phaedrus* 265d–266a:

...we bring a dispersed plurality under a single form, seeing it all together... [t]hereby we are enabled to divide into forms, following the objective articulation; we are not to attempt to hack off parts like a clumsy butcher ... (Plato 1963: 511)

Plato is saying that there is an objective articulation to be found in nature. A good system of classification follows the objective boundaries, which are marked by the forms; a bad system of classification merely 'hacks off parts', without respecting the natural divisions. Plato's claim is that scientific progress requires the discovery of principles of classification that divide things according to their real resemblances and real differences. The laws of a science connect the properties that are of classificatory importance;

thus the very idea of a law of nature is inseparably connected with real or objective resemblance.

Universals

According to Realism, the world must contain universals, in addition to individuals, if objective resemblance is to be so much as possible. Nominalists deny this, for they hold that the resembling individuals themselves are all that is needed. Nominalists say it is no use trying to build a metaphysical theory to *explain* resemblance, for nothing explains resemblance. Things either resemble or not, and that is all that can be said, for resemblance is primitive and fundamental. The world does not need to contain anything extra to make Socrates resemble Plato, or even to make it possible that Socrates resembles Plato; it needs simply to be a world where Socrates does resemble Plato, or could do so. No extra entities are needed or wanted.

Nominalism comes under pressure when we take into account *respects* of resemblance. A red sphere resembles a red cube and a blue sphere: it resembles the red cube in respect of its colour, and the blue sphere in respect of its shape. Perfect duplicates resemble each other in every respect, imperfect duplicates in only some respects. The notion of a duplicate is indispensable in theoretical metaphysics, but to define 'duplicate' we must quantify over respects of resemblance. Nominalism is therefore obliged to give some account of what a 'respect of resemblance' is.

Two principal strategies are available here to Nominalism. The first is Representation Nominalism, the psychologistic doctrine that a respect of resemblance is a human representation, such as a concept we actually possess, or a predicate of our actual language: then things resemble in a respect if they fall under the same concept of ours, or fall under the same predicate. For example, the whole account of what it is for a thing to be wise might be as follows:

(1) x is wise if and only if x falls under 'wise'.

According to this Nominalist strategy, (1) is all that needs to be said, or indeed that can be said, about resemblance in respect of being wise.

Two difficulties arise for this strategy. The first is to give some account of the relation of *falling under*. Socrates is wise, but there is more to his wisdom than merely one's own willingness to apply the concept *wise* to him, i.e., to judge concerning Socrates that he is wise. For it is required that one's judgement is actually correct. There is the same problem if we work with predicates instead of concepts. For Socrates to be wise, it is not enough that I am prepared to say of him that he is wise. It is not enough even if my whole speech-community agree that 'Socrates is wise' is a correct assertion, for it is at least conceivable that all of us are mistaken. It is required that one's predication is actually correct; now, what makes a predication objectively correct?

At this point a Representation Nominalist may appeal to the Tarskian notion of *satisfaction*, saying that to fall under a predicate is simply to satisfy it. Satisfaction in turn is explained by giving for each predicate of the language a condition upon which any object satisfies that predicate, e.g.:

(2) $(\forall x)(x$ satisfies 'wise' $\leftrightarrow x$ is wise)

But it is hard to see how this manoeuvre sheds any light on the matter. Such an axiom as (2) perhaps has its place in a recursive semantics for a formal language, but it is unhelpful at the level of metaphysical theory. What we wanted to understand was the *falls-under* relation. We wished to be told that single condition on any x and y which must obtain if x is to fall under y. What (2) gives us is for each y a different condition which must obtain if x is to satisfy that y. *Falls-under* is supposed to be a single relation, but *satisfaction* is not a relation at all, but only as it were a relation-schema, which gives a different relation for each predicate of the language. The motley collection of relations schematised by (2) does nothing to help us understand the unitary relation of resemblance. Thus Representation Nominalism fails to give a satisfactory account of the *falls-under* relation.

A second difficulty is that things can resemble in respects that are unknown to us. According to Representation Nominalism, a respect of resemblance is simply a concept of ours, or a predicate of our language; but an unknown respect of resemblance corresponds to no concept or predicate of ours. We know now of respects of resemblance that formerly were unknown: for example we have only recently come to know that quarks can resemble with respect to colour, strangeness and charm. Thus respects of resemblance and difference, and the laws that govern them, can exist whether or not human beings have words or concepts for them.

A non-psychologistic alternative to Representation Nominalism is Set Nominalism. This identifies respects of resemblance with the sets of resembling individuals themselves. Then x resembles y in a certain respect if x and y are both members of the same resemblance set. But Set Nominalism faces three serious difficulties. First, it might happen that a respect of resemblance had no instances, e.g., *wisdom* would have no instances if no one were wise. *Wisdom* would still exist as a respect of possible resemblance, even though the resemblance set of the wise was the empty set. To avoid this difficulty, the Set Nominalist can identify respects of resemblance not with actual extensions but with intensions. The intension of 'wise' is a set of ordered pairs: the first member of each pair is a possible world, and the second member is the set of things that are wise at that world. But if intensions are to play the role of respects of resemblance, it will be necessary to posit *possibilia*, i.e., things which exist but do not exist actually. For there could have been more things than there are actually, and some of these extra things could have been wise; hence these extra things must exist, if the intension of 'wise' is to exist actually. But things that exist without existing actually seem hard to take seriously; it is difficult enough to believe in the real existence of possible worlds, but even more difficult to believe in the real existence of their merely possible inhabitants.

The second difficulty for Set Nominalism is the case of the renates and the cordates. The animals with kidneys are actually all and only the animals with hearts, so the resemblance sets are the same, but *renate* and *cordate* are different respects of resemblance. To avoid this difficulty, appeal is again needed to intensions and their attendant *possibilia*.

A third difficulty is that Set Nominalism needs to say how the resemblance sets are defined. One suggestion is that a resemblance set is defined by some paradigms; e.g., paradigms for *red* might be a red post-box, a red brick, a red ball, etc. Then x is a member of the resemblance set for *red* if and only if x resembles each of the paradigms of *red* at least to the degree that the paradigms resemble each other. But what is the metaphysics of a degree of resemblance? A Realist can define degree of resemblance by a count of shared universals, but the only way for a Set Nominalist to get objective degrees of resemblance is by appeal to *possibilia* again (Lewis 1987; Cresswell 1990: 63–75).

Thus Set Nominalists need to admit into their ontology not only sets, but also objectively real *possibilia*. A set is an abstract particular that shares our world, but does not inhabit space and time; a *possibile* does not even inhabit our world. As serious metaphysics, sets seem dubious at best, and *possibilia* merit only an incredulous stare. Whatever initial reluctance one may feel about believing in the real existence of universals, at least they are less difficult to believe in than the Set Nominalist's alternative offering of sets plus *possibilia*. I conclude that if the world is to contain respects of objective resemblance, it must contain more things than just individuals; we need to posit also some things of an altogether different sort from the resembling individuals themselves; we must posit universals.

The proposal of Realism is that things that resemble in a given respect 'have in common', or 'share' the same universal, and that therein lies their resemblance in that respect. Thus Socrates and Plato resemble in respect of wisdom because they have the universal *wisdom* in common; both instantiate *wisdom*, so both are wise and resemble in respect of being wise. The theory of universals neatly explains the following features of the relation of resemblance: (1) the relation of perfect resemblance is transitive; (2) imperfect resemblance comes in degrees; and (3) imperfect resemblance is not transitive. The explanations are as follows: (1) perfect resemblance is transitive because perfect resemblers (duplicates) resemble in every respect, i.e., they share all the same universals; (2) degrees of resemblance can be explained as a (possibly weighted) count of shared universals; and (3) imperfect resemblance is not transitive because the universals which A shares with B need not be the universals which B shares with C. Thus the hypothesis of the real existence of universals neatly explains the phenomena of resemblance.

Relations

Resemblance can be plural as well as singular. This goes unrecognised by singularist logic, which admits only singular predications, and recognises only singular resemblances. But we should also acknowledge plural resemblances. For example, these stones are arranged in a circle, and those logs are arranged in a circle too. The stones resemble the logs in respect of their spatial arrangement, but an individual stone does not resemble an individual log. Thus the predicate 'arranged in a circle' should be taken to express a respect of plural resemblance. Number provides another example: the hills of Rome resemble the kings of Rome, because the hills were seven, and the kings were seven too; but an individual hill does not resemble an individual king. We can take *being arranged in a circle* and *being seven* to be plural universals.

But there are respects of plural resemblance that are not plural universals. The relation *love* is an example. Consider Romeo and Juliet, and Anthony and Cleopatra. Romeo loves Juliet, and Anthony loves Cleopatra; thus *love* is a respect in which Romeo and Juliet resemble Anthony and Cleopatra. The resemblance is plural. Suppose that Twin-Romeo is a perfect duplicate of Romeo, and that Twin-Juliet is a perfect duplicate of Juliet; it does not follow that Twin-Romeo and Twin-Juliet plurally are perfect duplicates of Romeo and Juliet. For if Twin-Romeo does not love Twin-Juliet, then *love* is a respect in which Romeo and Juliet plurally resemble Anthony and Cleopatra, yet fail to resemble Twin-Romeo and Twin-Juliet. Thus *love* is a respect not of singular but of plural resemblance.

Relations must be distinguished from plural universals. Every plural universal is *permutative*: for example, if 'x_1 and x_2 and ... and x_n are arranged in a circle' is true, then for any permutation π of the numbers from 1 to n, '$x_{\pi(1)}$ and $x_{\pi(2)}$ and ... and $x_{\pi(n)}$ are arranged in a circle' is also true. The hills of Rome are seven in whatever order you take them; and the kings of Rome are seven in whatever order you take them. But not every respect of plural resemblance is permutative. For example, *love* is not permutative. Romeo and Juliet are two, so it follows that Juliet and Romeo are two; but if Romeo loves Juliet, it does not follow that Juliet loves Romeo. Romeo and Juliet instantiate *two* plurally and regardless of order; but if Romeo and Juliet in that order instantiate *love*, it is a further question whether they also instantiate it in the opposite order. Thus not every respect of plural resemblance is permutative, and we must recognise relations, as well as plural universals. Relations are respects of objective resemblance, just as qualities are; thus just as there can be qualities of which we have no concept, there can be relations of which we have no concept.

Every non-permutative universal is a relation, but not every relation is non-permutative. For example, *is sibling to* is a relation, not a plural quality, yet it is permutative, since if x is sibling to y, it follows that y is sibling to x. Why then do we class *is sibling to* as a relation? The reason is that every respect of resemblance is also *eo ipso* a respect of difference: if things can resemble in a respect because both have a certain property, then they can differ in that same respect if one has the property and the other lacks it. Thus *is sibling to* is a respect in which only pairs resemble or differ, and for that reason we say that it is of arity 2. In contrast, a plural universal is a respect in which any number of things can resemble or differ from any number of things.

Bradley's Regress

As well as respects of resemblance, there are also the resemblances themselves to be considered. For example, Plato is wise. Socrates is also wise, so there is a resemblance in respect of wisdom between Socrates and Plato. This resemblance came into existence at the first moment when both Socrates and Plato were wise. So resemblances exist; but what sort of a thing is a resemblance? My suggestion is that it is not one thing, but two. A resemblance is a pair of *facts*: for example, the resemblance between Socrates and Plato is the pair of facts *that Socrates is wise* and *that Plato is wise*. I shall argue that Realism is an incomplete theory unless it incorporates a theory of facts.

To explain how it is possible for Socrates to be wise, i.e., to resemble other things in respect of being wise, we posited the existence of the universal *wisdom*. But the mere existence of the universal is not enough to make Socrates wise; what is needed is that Socrates should actually instantiate *wisdom*. But what is it to instantiate a universal? What is instantiation? The natural Realist suggestion is that the predicate 'instantiate' stands for a universal, namely the relation that obtains for example between Socrates and *wisdom* when and only when Socrates is wise.

However, this natural suggestion faces the well-known difficulty of Bradley's Regress. The difficulty is as follows. The programme of the theory of universals is to discover what things the world has to contain if, for example, Socrates is to be wise. We have been led by the theory to say successively that, in addition to Socrates himself, it needs to contain the universal *wisdom*, and also now the relation of *instantiation*. But even this is not enough. The world might contain Socrates, and *wisdom*, and *instantiation*, without Socrates being wise: the world does contain Socrates, and *foolishness*, and *instantiation*, yet Socrates is not foolish. So we have not succeeded yet in finding some things the existence of which is all that is required for it to be the case that Socrates is wise.

It is clear that nothing further in the way of positing universals will help solve Bradley's Regress. For example, suppose we posit, in addition to the universals wisdom and *instantiation*, a further universal, call it *meta-instantiation*, which relates Socrates, *wisdom* and *instantiation* if Socrates is wise. The problem recurs: even if we add *meta-instantiation* to the contents of the world, still it remains possible that Socrates is not wise.

Bradley's Regress brings us to a parting of the ways in the further development of Realism, and we must choose between alternative strategies. One strategy is to abandon the search for an entity which the world must contain if Socrates is to be wise. We can backtrack, and refuse to take *instantiation* as a relation. We can still say that for Socrates to be wise, Socrates must instantiate *wisdom*; but we decline to assign to the predicate 'instantiate' any entity as its semantic value. Instead we say with the Representation Nominalists that x instantiates y if x and y in that order satisfy 'instantiates'. That halts Bradley's Regress. In explaining what 'instantiate' means, we decline to go further than the following clause of a 'homophonic' truth-theory:

x and y satisfy 'instantiate' if x instantiates y.

This applies to the special case of *instantiation* the same strategy that Representation Nominalism applies to predicates generally. But because it applies the strategy only in the special case of the predicate 'instantiates', it escapes one of the objections we made against Representation Nominalism, namely, that there are unknown respects of resemblance for which we have no predicate. However, it does not escape the other objection: we still have no (metaphysical) understanding of what 'satisfy' means, that does not presuppose a prior understanding of what 'instantiate' means.

In any case we should reject this strategy, for in the context of metaphysical Realism, it is counter-systematic. A central motivation of the theory of universals is to explain predication by assigning universals as the referents of certain predicates. If a predicate is of scientific importance and marks a natural boundary, the doctrine of Realism is that either it introduces a universal, or it has a simple definition in terms of universals. So if Realism is to have any pretension to be by its own lights a correct theory of (metaphysical) science, it must take 'instantiates', its own centrally important theoretical predicate, either to refer to a universal, or to have a simple definition in terms of universals. Therefore to solve Bradley's Regress, the Realist needs some other strategy than a mere appeal to a satisfaction clause for 'instantiates'.

Realism does its best to regard Bradley's Regress not so much as a problem for the theory of universals, but as a proof that the theory requires to be supplemented by positing a further kind of entity. Adding more universals, even an *instantiation* universal, will not solve Bradley's Regress. What is required is a kind of entity which allows us to give a substantive metaphysical account of instantiation. For example, as well as Socrates and *wisdom*, we need an entity that exists if and only if Socrates resembles other wise things in respect of wisdom. The needed entity is the resemblance-maker for Socrates in respect of wisdom; and hence it is the truth-maker for the content *that Socrates is wise*.

What can the resemblance-making entities be? One suggestion is that they are *sets*. If we have sets in our ontology, we can say that x instantiates *wisdom* if and only if x is a member of the set of wise things. But this appears to be circular, for we must ask what makes a given set C deserve the title 'set of wise things'. Unless we posit some further substantive metaphysical relation between C and the universal *wisdom*, we seem reduced to saying that C deserves the title because all its members are wise. That gets us no further forward.

A second suggestion appeals to mereology. We might say that x instantiates y if x has y as a (non-spatio-temporal) part. Thus Socrates is wise because *wisdom* is part of Socrates, and Socrates resembles Plato in point of wisdom because they have *wisdom* in common, i.e., they have it as a common part. This suggestion fails because it cannot deal with the case of relations. Romeo and Juliet instantiate *love*, so on the mereological theory we should say that this is because *love* is part of Romeo and Juliet. But it is not enough to say that *love* is part of Romeo, and part of Juliet, for this could be true if they did not love each other, but each loved a third party. Nor can 'part of Romeo and Juliet' mean 'part of the mereological sum of Romeo and Juliet, but not part of Romeo, and not part of Juliet'; for since the sum of Romeo and Juliet is the sum of Juliet and Romeo, whenever *love* was part of Romeo and Juliet it would also be part of Juliet and Romeo, from which it would follow that love is a symmetrical relation, which it is not.

A third suggestion is the one I shall recommend. It is the hypothesis that instantiation consists in the existence of a suitable *instantiation*. If Socrates is to be wise, then what needs to exist, besides Socrates, and the universal wisdom, is a certain instantiation, viz., the instantiation by Socrates of *wisdom*. The suggestion is that there literally are such things as instantiations. We already have in English a conveniently short name for instantiations—we call them 'facts'. We reduce the metaphysics of instantiation to the theory of facts: Socrates instantiates wisdom if and only if the instantiation of wisdom by Socrates exists, i.e., if the fact *that Socrates is wise* exists.

The objection to the set theory of instantiation was that we were at a loss to specify without circularity the connection that must exist between a set C, and the universal *wisdom*, in virtue of which the set C is the set of wise things. The relation between the set of wise things and the universal wisdom is too indirect; the set has the things as its members, and the members instantiate the universal—this tells us precisely nothing about the metaphysics of instantiation. If fact theory is to be an improvement, we must say what it is that makes a given fact p deserve the title 'the fact *that Socrates is wise*'. Therefore we must suppose that there exists a simple relation between the fact p and *wisdom* and Socrates, in virtue of which p does indeed deserve to be called the fact *that Socrates is wise*. I shall call this relation between a fact and the universal and particulars it combines the *combination* relation. It is to be the main theoretical primitive of the theory of facts, and I shall represent it by the symbol '$\cdot$'. Thus if $p =$ the fact *that Socrates is wise*, I shall write:

$p \cdot (wisdom, \text{Socrates})$

We can define instantiation in terms of the combination relation:

y instantiates $x =_{\text{df}} (\exists p)(p \cdot (x, y))$

The hypothesis of the existence of facts allows Realism to complete its explanation of resemblance. If Socrates is to resemble Plato in point of wisdom, then what needs to exist, besides Socrates, Plato and wisdom, are the fact *that Socrates is wise*, and the fact *that Plato is wise*: the resemblance between Socrates and Plato in point of wisdom just is this pair of facts. By treating facts as resemblance-makers we complete the theory of resemblance: universals are the respects of resemblance, and facts are the resemblance-makers.

Resemblance-Making Principle If x_1 and x_2 are any two things, and if U is any universal, let p_1 denote the fact that combines U with x_1, and let p_2 denote the fact that combines U with x_2. Then p_1 and p_2 are the *resemblance-makers* for x_1 and x_2 in the respect U, i.e., x_1 and x_2 resemble in respect U if and only if p_1 exists and p_2 exists.

Universals and facts are thus best thought of as two components of a single theory; Realism is incomplete until facts are included in the theory too.

2.2 Combination

Realism, the theory of universals, needs to be completed by the addition of a theory of facts. Thus Realism will have at its centre a theory of the relation of *combination*, which holds between a fact, a universal and some other things if the fact is the instantiation of the universal by the other things. In this section I discuss the relation of combination.

Often in metaphysics, the theory of a type of entity is developed in terms of a certain relation that is treated as primitive by the theory. The relation is one which characteristically only entities of the type concerned enter into, and the theory of the entities is given by giving axioms that govern the relation. For example, the theory of sets is developed in terms of the relation of *membership*; axioms are given for the membership relation, and thereby the sets are characterised. Similarly the theory of mereological aggregates is developed in terms of the *part-of* relation; axioms are given for that relation, and thereby the aggregates are characterised. Here I propose to develop the theory of facts in terms of the relation of *combination*: axioms will be given for that relation, with the intention that thereby facts will be characterised.

The fact *that Socrates is wise* is the instantiation of *wisdom* by Socrates. We can say the fact 'combines' *wisdom* and Socrates—*wisdom* and Socrates are the two 'constituents' of the fact. This talk of 'combination' and 'constituents', which is due to Russell (1959: 127), has the disadvantage of making it sound as if some sort of mereological composition is intended; but as our discussion of asymmetrical relations showed, it cannot be the ordinary relation of part and whole that is in question here. The relation of *combination* that obtains between a fact and its constituents is *sui generis*; the terminology of 'combination' and 'constituents' should not be taken to have any mereological connotations.

We wish to say that the constituents of facts include not only particulars and qualities, but also relations. But the presence of relations of various arities as constituents of facts creates an immediate difficulty for the theory of the combination relation. For according to standard logic, a formula is syntactically well-formed only if it attaches the correct number of terms to its predicates. Every predicate has a fixed *adicity*, which is the number of terms that must be attached to the predicate to make a well-formed formula. Now consider p, the fact *that Socrates is wise*. We wrote:

(3) $p \cdot$ (*wisdom*, Socrates)

In the above sentence (3), the symbol '$\cdot$' is a predicate with a triadic occurrence—it combines with three terms to make a sentence. So the predicate '$\cdot$' appears to have three argument-places, one for the fact, a second for the universal and a third for the particular. But now let q be the fact *that Romeo loves Juliet*; the constituents of q are *love*, Romeo and Juliet, so we wish to write:

(4) $q \cdot$ (*love*, Romeo, Juliet)

But in (4) the predicate '$\cdot$' appears to be of adicity four, since it is combining with four other terms to make a sentence. But if '$\cdot$' is really triadic, as sentence (3) suggests, then sentence (4) is ill-formed according to standard logic, since it attempts to combine the triadic predicate '$\cdot$' with four terms. Thus standard logic seems to prevent us from so much as stating our theory of combination.

Three strategies now suggest themselves. The first is to treat combination in the same way that Quine once suggested we should treat belief (Quine 1956: 188–9). Instead of seeing combination as a single relation, we could posit the existence of a distinct combination relation for each possible arity n. Thus we would have combination$_1$, combination$_2$, combination$_3$, etc., and instead of (3) and (4) we would write:

$p \cdot_1$ (*wisdom*, Socrates)
$q \cdot_2$ (*love*, Romeo, Juliet)
$r \cdot_3$ (*between*, York, Edinburgh, London)
etc., etc.

However, the objection to this is that it fragments the theory of facts excessively, and does not display what is in common to all facts, however many constituents they may have. We should prefer to avoid a Quinean solution, if we can.

A second suggestion is to replace the relata of the combination relation, other than the combining fact, with some one thing that can stand as their surrogate. Thus in (4), if we can replace Romeo and Juliet with a single surrogate thing, then we can allow '•' to remain triadic. But the difficulty for this strategy is to find a suitable single surrogate thing. The mereological sum is unsuitable, for it is indifferent to order, whereas we need an intrinsically ordered thing, in order to preserve the distinction between Romeo loving Juliet and Juliet loving Romeo. It may be suggested that we should replace Romeo and Juliet with their set-theoretic ordered pair {Romeo, {Romeo, Juliet}}; in general we should need to replace *n* relata with their ordered *n*-tuple. But that would inextricably entangle the theory of facts with the theory of sets, to which we may not wish to commit ourselves at so early a stage of metaphysical inquiry. In any case, it would not solve our problem in full generality. For Romeo might have been a mathematician. Supposing there really are sets, Romeo might have loved not only Juliet, but also V, the proper class of all sets. But there is no set-theoretic ordered pair {Romeo, {Romeo, V}}, since V is too 'large' to be a member of any set. It would not help to invoke collections that can have proper classes as members. Call such a collection a *hyperclass*: Romeo might have loved the hyperclass of all proper classes, whereupon the difficulty would recur.

The third suggestion adopts an idea of Russell's (1994: 154–5) to dispense with the need for tuples. We can modify our logic, and relax the requirement that every predicate has exactly one adicity, by allowing *variably polyadic* predicates: if M is such a predicate, then '$Mt_1 \ldots t_n$' counts as well-formed for every *n*. In conventional logic every predicate has a fixed adicity, so the predicates can express only relations of fixed arity. But if we allow variably polyadic predicates, we can treat combination as a *multigrade* relation, i.e., a relation of multiple arity. In that case we shall count '$p • (t_1, \ldots, t_n)$' as well-formed for every *n*. It is this third strategy that I shall be recommending here.

2.3 Vector Logic

Since it is facts that combine things, a starting point for our inquiry can be this: what is the criterion of identity for facts? Can we give non-circular necessary and sufficient conditions for identity of facts in terms of the relation of combination?

We arrived at the concept of a fact in order to give a substantive account of the metaphysics of instantiation: facts *are* instantiations. Thus we identify the instantiation of a universal by a particular with the fact that combines that universal with that particular. For example, the fact that Socrates is wise is the instantiation of the universal *wisdom* by the particular Socrates. Here we are willing to use the definite article, 'the instantiation', because we suppose that there is at most one entity that is the instantiation of *wisdom* by Socrates. Hence if we switch to the terminology of 'combination', we must say there is only one fact that combines *wisdom* and Socrates. Since the same will apply to any other quality and any other particular, we are led to conclude that facts are the same if and only if they combine the same constituents in the same order. This gives the following Axiom of Extensionality:

(Ext$_2$) $p_1 \cdot (x_1, x_2) \wedge p_2 \cdot (y_1, y_2) \rightarrow (p_1 = p_2 \leftrightarrow (x_1 = y_1 \wedge x_2 = y_2))$

The axiom of extensionality for facts is analogous to the axiom of extensionality for sets and the axiom of extensionality for aggregates. Our concept of the hypothetical entity *set* is clarified by a postulate about the membership relation: sets are the same that have the same members. Similarly, our concept of *aggregate* is clarified by a postulate about *part-of*: aggregates are the same that have the same parts. The axiom (Ext$_2$) clarifies the concept of *fact*: facts are the same that have the same constituents in the same order. This guarantees that facts are independent of our ways of thinking of them.

Unfortunately axiom (Ext$_2$) deals only with facts that combine two things, i.e., facts of the form *Fa*. To deal with facts that combine three things, i.e., facts of the form *Rab*, we need a further axiom:

(Ext$_3$) $p_1 \cdot (x_1, x_2, x_3) \wedge p_2 \cdot (y_1, y_2, y_3) \rightarrow (p_1 = p_2 \leftrightarrow (x_1 = y_1 \wedge x_2 = y_2 \wedge x_3 = y_3))$

But facts can combine any number of things. So for each *n* we need yet another axiom:

(Ext$_n$) $p_1 \cdot (x_1, \ldots, x_n) \wedge p_2 \cdot (y_1, \ldots, y_n) \rightarrow (p_1 = p_2 \leftrightarrow (x_1 = y_1 \wedge \ldots \wedge x_n = y_n))$

Thus a complete axiomatisation of the theory of facts will need an infinite number of axioms. It is inconvenient to have to give so many axioms!

However, it is evident that there is a common pattern to all the axioms, so perhaps there is only a single thought that they are collectively expressing. Here I do not mean their infinite conjunction—an infinite conjunction is not a single thought that we are capable of thinking. But there does seem to be a single thought here that even a finite being can grasp; unfortunately standard logic does not allow us to give it finite expression.

For any given length n, standard logic allows us to have lists of variables '$x_1, \dots, x_n$' of length n, and to bind the variables in such a list by a list of quantifiers '$(\forall x_1) \dots (\forall x_n)$'. But it does not allow us to have variable length lists of variables. However, in the previous section we proposed to extend standard logic by allowing variably polyadic predicates. This in turn suggests that we need to introduce a new type of variable, the *vector variable*, which can occupy the argument place of a variably polyadic predicate, and serve in effect as a variable-length list of variables (Taylor and Hazen 1992).

One reason we need vector variables is to allow the truth theory for a language with variably polyadic predicates to be finitely stated. Suppose we give the truth theory by a clause saying when the variably polyadic predicate M is satisfied. If we let $\underline{M}$ be the translation of M into the metalanguage, we have to say:

(5) $x_1, \dots, x_n$ satisfy M if $\underline{M}(x_1 \dots x_n)$

If the metalanguage lacked vector variables we would therefore need an infinite set of axioms to explain the meaning of M. But in that case no human being could know the meaning of M, unless they knew all of the infinitely many axioms. However, with vector variables available, we can replace the infinitely many axioms of the above form (5) with the single axiom:

(6) θ satisfy M if and only if $\underline{M}(\theta)$

Thus if we assume that our language contains variably polyadic predicates, and if we further assume that we understand the meaning of these predicates, then we are driven to conclude that we must also have the capacity to understand vector variables. We must therefore propose a second extension of the standard predicate calculus, to allow not only variably polyadic predicates, but also vector variables. Thus if M is variably polyadic, then not only is '$M(t_1 \dots t_n)$' a well-formed formula for every n, but '$M(\theta)$' is also a well-formed formula.

What is the meaning of the vector variable? Roughly and informally, one may think of the vector variable θ as in effect a sequence, of variable length n, of the individual variables $x_1, \ldots, x_n$. More exactly, we can say that the vector variable is implicitly defined by the following Rules of Inference that govern deductions in which it occurs. Let M be a variably polyadic predicate, and let Σ be a premiss set. Then the Introduction Rule is:

Vector Variable Introduction: If from some premisses Σ you can infer for every n some formula $M(t_1 \ldots t_n)$, where none of the t_i occur in Σ, then you may infer $M(\theta)$ from the same premisses Σ.

The Elimination Rule is:

Vector Variable Elimination: If from some premisses Σ you can infer $M(\theta)$, then from the same premisses Σ you may for any n infer $M(t_1 \ldots t_n)$, where the t_i are any terms.

Using vector variables we can state our axiom of fact identity in a single sentence as follows:

Axiom 1 (Extensionality): $p_1 \cdot \theta_1 \wedge p_2 \cdot \theta_2 \rightarrow (p_1 = p_2 \leftrightarrow \theta_1 = \theta_2)$

Interpreting Vector Variables

But how exactly are we to understand the vector variables? The Introduction and Elimination Rules given above are infinitary, and this might be felt to be objectionable. There are other interpretations we could give the vector variable that avoid the need for infinitary Inference Rules. One is the *tuple interpretation*, according to which a vector variable is just an ordinary individual variable, restricted to range over those entities that are tuples. Another is the *metalinguistic interpretation*, which takes the vector variable to be an ordinary individual variable of the metalanguage.

The tuple interpretation says the vector variable θ is an ordinary first-order variable, restricted to range over tuples. But what is a tuple? We are familiar with the Kuratowski definition of the ordered pair $\langle a_1, a_2 \rangle$:

$$\langle a_1, a_2 \rangle = \{a_1, \{a_1, a_2\}\}$$

Ordered n-tuples can be defined similarly. However, no definition in terms of sets will suit our purpose here, for as we noted in the case of Romeo the possible mathematician, there are some vectors to which no Kuratowski tuple corresponds. For example, let V be the class of all sets. It is a fact that V is large, so:

$$(\exists p)(p \bullet (\text{largeness, } V))$$

However, we cannot take '$(\text{largeness, } V)$' to name a Kuratowski tuple, because V is a proper class and too large to be a member of any set.

We might try to build a theory of tuples from scratch, without any appeal to set theory. An initial objection to this is that tuples seem to do no other useful work in metaphysics; they provide something for vector variables to allegedly range over, but that is all. And tuples cannot even perform their allotted task of permitting our metaphysical theory to be finitely stated. For tuple theory requires a criterion of identity for tuples. For each n, we can give an axiom giving a criterion of identity for n-tuples:

(7) $\theta_1 = \langle x_1, \ldots, x_n \rangle \wedge \theta_2 = \langle y_1, \ldots, y_n \rangle \rightarrow (\theta_1 = \theta_2 \leftrightarrow (x_1 = y_1$
$\wedge \ldots \wedge x_n = y_n))$

But we cannot state a single axiom which gives, for any n, a criterion of identity for n-tuples. We can define tuple identity recursively:

(i) $(\theta_1 = x_1 \wedge \theta_2 = x_2) \rightarrow (\theta_1 = \theta_2 \leftrightarrow x_1 = x_2)$
(ii) $(\theta_1 = (\phi_1, x_1) \wedge \theta_2 = (\phi_2, x_2)) \rightarrow (\theta_1 = \theta_2 \leftrightarrow (\phi_1 = \phi_2 \wedge x_1 = x_2))$

But the recursive 'definition' is just equivalent to infinitely many axioms of the form (7). So the theory of tuples cannot be finitely axiomatised. But we only introduced tuples in the first place in order to make it possible to give a finite axiomatisation of the theory of facts! We must reject the metaphysics of tuples, and look for a different interpretation of the vector variables.

The metalinguistic interpretation treats the assertion '$(\forall \theta)M(\theta)$' as saying that each of its object language substitution instance '$(\forall x_1) \ldots (\forall x_n)M$ $(x_1 \ldots x_n)$' is true. In effect it treats the vector variable as an ordinary individual variable over expressions of the object language, by means of which we assert that all the object-language expressions of a described sort are true. That is to treat the vector variable as a device of 'semantic ascent'. (Quine 1986: 8–10). McGee has suggested the method of semantic ascent is one reason why the notion of truth is precious to us. He writes:

We can even apply this method where the sets of sentences involved are infinite, thus simulating a fragment of the infinitary language $L_{\infty \omega}$. This is a reason why the notion of truth is so precious to us; it is one of the means by which finite minds are able to apprehend the infinite. (McGee 1991: 124)

But I think this is an illusion: semantic ascent does not explain how a theory with infinitely many axioms can be of value to us. The metalinguistic schema asserts that all its infinitely many instances are true. That is not yet to *state* a theory, but only to *describe* it, and as it were to endorse it, without one's being able to state the theory one endorses. Knowledge that a theory is true need not be knowledge of any of the facts the theory states—one can know on good authority that a theory is true, even if one does not know what the theory says, for example because one does not understand the theory. Thus the metalinguistic interpretation of the vector variable does not explain how statements that employ it can be used to convey useful knowledge.

A second objection to the metalinguistic interpretation is that in the context of the present metaphysical project, the suggestion that vector quantification is equivalent to metalanguage quantification plus *truth* is unwelcome. Our project here is to define truth in terms of facts, so we do not want to build the concept of truth into the background logic. Knowledge and not truth is to be the central primitive concept in our theory of content, so we want vector logic to be independent of the concept of truth.

A third objection to the metalinguistic interpretation is that it is circular. For the method of semantic ascent presupposes some version or other of following schema:

(8) A is true if and only if $\underline{A}$

where A is the name of a sentence of the object-language, and $\underline{A}$ is a sentence of the metalanguage that translates A. We explain translation as follows. If σ is any simple symbol of the object language, and $\underline{\sigma}$ is a simple symbol of the metalanguage that expresses the same concept, then $\underline{\sigma}$ is the metalanguage translation of σ. Now let A be any sentence of the object language, and suppose A concatenates the symbols θ. If $\underline{\theta}$ is the vector obtained by replacing each symbol σ of θ by its metalanguage translation $\underline{\sigma}$, let $\underline{A}$ be the metalanguage sentence that concatenates $\underline{\theta}$. Then $\underline{A}$ is the translation of A. The circle is that the explanation of 'translation' itself employs vector variables in the metalanguage. The infinitary character of the vector variables is still with us. Clearly it is hopeless to attempt to explain metalanguage vector variables by semantic ascent to the meta-meta-language—that would lead to an infinite regress.

For these reasons I shall adopt a third interpretation, according to which the vector variable is a *sui generis* logical primitive, which has an infinitary character, and which cannot be reduced to the individual objectual variable. It is not a device of reference to individual ordered objects, such as tuples supposedly are, nor is it a metalinguistic device of reference to individual symbols for objects. In fact the vector variable is not an individual variable at all; rather, a sentence containing a vector variable is a *schema*—a device for asserting plurally all the facts for which the sentence is a schema. The vector variable enables us to affirm plurally a class of statements too numerous to be affirmed individually: the schema '$M(\theta)$' plurally asserts *all* of the following:

$$M(x_1), M(x_1, x_2), \ldots, M(x_1, \ldots, x_n), \ldots$$

At the level of language, the vector variable allows a single sentence to assert infinitely many facts. At the level of knowledge, to know that $M(\theta)$ is to possess plural knowledge of all these infinitely many facts; of course the knowledge is *only* plural or collective, for one knows them without knowing each of them.

The hypothesis of schematic expression of plural knowledge seems needed if we are to make theoretical room for the knowledge we actually possess. Despite the supposed finiteness of the human mind, we are able to know theories that cannot be finitely axiomatised, provided the infinity of axioms can be presented as schemata. Thus we know Peano arithmetic; we do not merely know that the theory is true; yet the theory cannot be finitely axiomatised. Semantic knowledge is another example; we know our language, but the truth theory for a natural language has infinitely many axioms. Thus reflection on our actual knowledge encourages us to conclude that there is indeed a sense in which a 'finite' mind can apprehend infinitely many facts; not individually of course, but plurally and schematically. According to the schematic interpretation, this is why vector variables are useful to us; not to allow us to quantify over tuples, or over object language expressions, but to allow us to state a body of schematic knowledge that cannot otherwise be finitely stated.

Vector Quantifiers

Can vector variables be bound with vector quantifiers? This raises delicate issues. On the schematic interpretation, to assert $M(\theta)$ with a free vector variable is to plurally assert, as it were for every n, all the instances $M(x_1, \dots, x_n)$. Similarly, to assert $\neg M(\theta)$ is to plurally assert all the instances $\neg M(x_1, \dots, x_n)$. Thus there is no difficulty in interpreting formulas with free vector variables. It might therefore at first seem that the schematic interpretation should also have no difficulty in making sense of vector quantification.

We can of course interpret an assertion of $(\forall\theta)M(\theta)$ as plural assertion of all the $(\forall x_1) \dots (\forall x_n)M(x_1, \dots, x_n)$; each of these is equivalent to the corresponding free variable formula $M(x_1, \dots, x_n)$; hence plural assertion of them all is equivalent to plural assertion, as it were for every n, of all the $M(x_1, \dots, x_n)$; which is equivalent to asserting $M(\theta)$. Thus we can make a sort of sense of the formula '$(\forall\theta)M(\theta)$'. But the sense we can make of it does not amount to treating the sign '$(\forall\theta)$' as a genuine universal quantifier. If it were, then '$\neg(\forall\theta)\neg$' would be well-defined, and so '$(\exists\theta)$' would be well-defined. But there is no interpretation in terms of plural assertion that can be given to the sign '$(\exists\theta)M(\theta)$'. Perhaps one might assert plurally all the $(\exists x_1) \dots (\exists x_n)M(x_1, \dots, x_n)$: certainly one might assert some specific one of them; but there is no such thing as asserting plurally some indefinite one of them. The schematic interpretation can therefore assign no meaning to the expression '$(\exists\theta)M(\theta)$'. Although we can make sense of vector variables, we cannot make sense of vector quantifiers.

Logics with free variables but no quantifiers are well known to logicians. For example, we can construct a formal language by allowing any predicate calculus formula with variables but no quantifiers. This free-variable language is intermediate in expressive power between a language with only individual constants, i.e., one which lacks variables and quantifiers altogether, and a language that has both variables and quantifiers. In fact the free-variable language is equivalent in expressive power to a predicate calculus language that does have quantifiers, but which allows only prenex universal quantification—i.e., the only quantifiers permitted are an initial block of universal quantifiers at the start of a formula.

On the schematic interpretation, a language with vector variables must be thought of as a free-variable language; equivalently, only prenex universal quantification with vector variables is allowed. Thus we can assert $(\forall\theta)M(\theta)$, but we cannot assert its negation, since it has none. For $\neg(\forall\theta)M(\theta)$ is not prenex, so it is not well-formed. This reflects the fact that '$M(\theta)$' asserts not one but many propositions: each proposition it schematises has a negation: a finite mind can plurally affirm all these negations, but cannot affirm the negation of them all. The schematic interpretation is therefore much more modest than the metalinguistic and tuple interpretations. On the tuple interpretation, '$(\exists\theta)M(\theta)$' can be read straightforwardly as asserting the existence of a tuple that falls under M. On the metalinguistic interpretation, it can be read as saying that one of the formulas that fits its schema is true. For an infinite mind, '$(\exists\theta)M(\theta)$' is the infinite disjunction '$(\exists x_1)Mx_1 \lor (\exists x_1)(\exists x_2)Mx_1x_2 \dots \lor (\exists x_1) \dots (\exists x_n)Mx_1 \dots x_n \lor \dots$' But on the schematic interpretation no meaning whatever can be assigned to '$(\exists\theta)M(\theta)$'. However, as will appear in connection with the semantic paradoxes, that is not altogether a bad thing.

2.4 The Problem of Sense and 'Nonsense'

Russell's 'multiple relations' theory of judgement centres on what he claims is the multigrade relation *Bel* of belief. According to Russell, if $Bel(x_1, x_2, \dots , x_n)$ then x_1 is a mind, and x_2 is a universal; the belief is true if the universal x_2 is a 'relating relation', i.e., if the remaining constituents $x_3, \dots , x_n$ do stand in the relation x_2 (1959: 129). Russell invokes what he calls a *complex* to explain truth: a belief is true if there exists a complex whose constituents are the constituents of the belief other than the subject. So the belief is true if a 'complex' combines $x_2, \dots , x_n$. It would appear that a Russellian 'complex' is what I have been calling a 'fact'; so a Russellian belief is true if and only if for some fact p, $p \cdot (x_2, \dots , x_n)$.

Russell took it to be an important advantage of his theory that it treats belief as a direct relation to the objects the belief is about; it is not a relation to any intermediary between one's thoughts and the objects of one's thoughts. Russell therefore took himself to be able to dispense with such entities as propositions and Fregean Thoughts. But against Russell's theory Wittgenstein brought the following important objection:

A proper theory of judgement must make it impossible to judge nonsense. (Wittgenstein 1961a: 97)

The objection is that Russell's theory does not explain why it is that there are certain sequences of objects $x_2, \dots , x_n$ which cannot occur as the constituents of a belief or judgement. For example, it is impossible to make a judgement whose constituents are (Plato, Socrates). It is not just that no one in fact makes such a judgement—it is impossible to make such a judgement. On the other hand, it is certainly possible to make the judgement that Socrates is wise, the constituents of which are (*wisdom*, Socrates). Why does the judgement that Socrates is wise make 'sense', while it is 'nonsense' to judge that Socrates Plato?

This is no problem for the believer in propositions (or Fregean Thoughts). If belief is a relation to a proposition, then it is only possible to stand in the belief relation to one of the propositions there actually are. There is no proposition *that Socrates Plato*, which is why it is not possible to believe that Socrates Plato. But Russell had dispensed with propositions and other intermediaries: how then was he to exclude the possibility of arbitrary combinations of objects occurring in the belief relation? The 'problem of the unity of the proposition' is another formulation of essentially the same problem. The string of words 'Plato Socrates' is a mere list of names, but the string 'Socrates is wise' is a sentence, for it expresses a complete thought. Thus the syntactic category *sentence* reflects an underlying unity at the level of thought. The challenge for Russell is to explain this 'unity of the proposition'; he must provide a solution to the problem of 'sense and nonsense'.

In the context of a theory of universals, there is an obvious solution to the problem. The solution is to say that a string of words is a sentence only if it is the sort of string that is capable of representing a fact: and this in turn is possible only if the names in the sentence name the sorts of things which taken in order could be the constituent of some fact. But every fact must contain a universal. Hence (Plato, Socrates) are 'nonsense' because they include no universal, and hence there is no possibility of their combination in a fact. But this solution can be no clearer than the distinction itself between particular and universal. Thus without propositions we cannot solve the problem of sense and nonsense until we can give a clear answer to the question of what a universal is. So Russell's theory of judgement can be defended only if it is possible to define the difference between particulars and universals. Note that this problem is distinct from the problem of whether there *are* any universals. Imagine someone who acknowledges the existence of Socrates, and of *wisdom* also, but who asks why Socrates and *wisdom* are to be assigned to different ontological categories. The problem is to explain the difference between the category of particulars and the category of universals. Why is it claimed that *wisdom* belongs to the category of universals, and not the category of particulars (MacBride 1999, 2004, 2005)?

Many well-known suggestions about how to draw the distinction between particular and universal are unsatisfactory in the context of fundamental metaphysics. For example, it is not possible to define universals by syntactic criteria. Suppose we say that a particular is that which can occur only as subject and never as predicate, whereas a universal can occur as either subject or predicate. Then we are obliged to provide a purely syntactic criterion for dividing subject and predicate, and as Ramsey's classic paper (1925) argues, this cannot be done. The universals and the natural kinds that they define are not shadows of syntax.

Nor can we define universals by saying that universals have multiple occurrences, whereas particulars occur only once. Suppose we say there are many instances of *wisdom*, but only one instance of Socrates. This is question-begging. If the wisdom of Socrates and the wisdom of Plato are multiple instances of *wisdom*, why are the wisdom of Socrates and the snub-nosedness of Socrates not multiple instances of Socrates? A related suggestion is that multiple occurrence means multiple spatial location: *wisdom* is located in many places at the same time, but Socrates can only be in one place at a time. This fails because there are multiply-located particulars: for example, the United Kingdom is a particular which is located in several places at the same time, namely in Britain, the north of Ireland and some islands off France. It may be replied that the United Kingdom has spatially scattered parts, whereas the universal *wisdom* has no parts, but is wholly located at each of its instances. But this makes the distinction between particular and universal dependent on controversial doctrines in the theory of spatial part and whole; which means that the correct theory of part and whole must treat particulars and universals differently; which in turn means that we must already know the difference between particular and universal, in order to determine whether any particular theory of spatial part and whole is correct.

But in any case we should in principle expect the metaphysics of universals to be prior to the metaphysics of space. It is counter-systematic to define universals in spatial terms. Space presupposes universals, since the points of space are themselves particulars, and the relation of spatial *between-ness* is itself a universal. We require universals in metaphysics to explain resemblance and predication, both of which are prior to the metaphysics of space; therefore we should not expect to distinguish universals from particulars by a spatial criterion.

A more promising suggestion is to define universals by reference to facts. Thus we could say that x is a universal if it occupies predicate position in some fact, i.e., if it is the first constituent of some fact:

$$\text{universal}(x) =_{df} (\exists\theta)(\exists p)(p \bullet (x, \theta))$$

The problem with this is that it uses an existentially quantified vector variable, something that we have rejected as meaningless on our schematic interpretation of vector variables. We can however define the natural kind *particular*:

$$\text{particular}(x) =_{df} (\forall\theta)(\forall p)(\neg p \bullet (x, \theta))$$

Particularity as just defined is the distinguishing characteristic of the meta-physical natural kind, or category, of particulars. The universals are a second natural kind that comprise everything that is not a particular.

$$\text{universal}(x) =_{df} \neg\text{particular}(x)$$

This definition gets round the schematic interpretation's prohibition on existential quantification with the vector variable. (Here it is important that the sign '$=_{df}$' does not signify that the *definiendum* is a mere verbal abbreviation of the *definiens*. I go more fully into the question of such definitions in section 3.6.)

Unfortunately the above definition fails to classify correctly a universal that has no instances. For example, at the present time, the universal *dodo* has no instances, but it is not true that at the present time the property of being a dodo is a particular. Similarly, *unicorn* has never had any instances; nevertheless, *being a unicorn* is a property, not a particular.

Might a modal formulation help? We might try the definition:

$$\text{particular}(x) =_{df} \Box(\forall\theta)(\forall p)(\neg p \bullet (x, \theta))$$

But even the modalised definition is inadequate, for it misclassifies any universal that could not possibly have any instances. For example, not only are there no unicorns, but according to Kripke (1980: 24, 156–7) there could not possibly be any. Yet the property *unicorn* is not a particular. Sim-ilarly, the proposed definition wrongly classifies $(\lambda x)(x \neq x)$, the property of self-difference, as a particular. The property has no instances, and could not have any, but it is not a particular.

A second difficulty with the modal formulation is that the notion of necessity itself remains to be explained. If we explain necessity in terms of possible worlds, or possibilities, we are faced with the difficulty of saying what these are. Lewis's (1986) answer was clear enough, but he complained that his concretism about possible worlds was too often met with an 'incredulous stare' rather than reasoned discussion. But if we give due weight to 'the vivid instinct as to what is real' that Russell (1918: 223) thought essential for logical studies, I believe we shall not find appealing any version of realism about possible worlds, concretist or otherwise. Therefore in Chapter 4 I shall be suggesting that we do better to define 'necessary' in terms of the *a priori*. A proposition is primitive *a priori* if one only needs to consider it to know it is true, but this test presupposes that the question we have under consideration is not 'nonsense': we cannot 'consider the question' whether Plato Socrates, because it does not make sense. Thus we are unable to determine whether it is *a priori* that Plato Socrates: so we are not in a position to define the *a priori*, and hence the necessary, unless we are already able to distinguish sense from nonsense. Thus if we set aside realism about possible worlds, a modal formulation cannot solve the problem of distinguishing particulars from universals.

2.5 Propositions and States of Affairs

Many philosophers reject talk of possible worlds as mere metaphor, yet find no difficulty in believing in propositions, which indeed they deem to be theoretically indispensable in semantics. They would advise us to reject Russell's theory of judgement, and to keep propositions in our ontology. Propositions will even allow us to distinguishing particulars and universals. Like a fact, a proposition is supposed to be a complex of particulars and universals. Let us use '*' to denote the relation of combination in a proposition. The main property of propositions is their supposed role as truth-bearers; it is their capacity to be true or false that defines them. In vector logic, however, we cannot give explicit definitions of 'true' and 'false' for propositions conceived of as single entities. The definition we should like to give is as follows:

$$\text{true}(Q) =_{\text{df}} (\exists\theta)(\exists p)(Q * \theta \land p \cdot \theta)$$

But this requires existential quantification over vectors, which is forbidden. However, we can give 'implicit' definitions as follows:

$$(\text{proposition}(Q) \wedge Q^* \theta) \rightarrow (\text{true}(Q) \leftrightarrow (\exists p)(p \cdot \theta))$$
$$(\text{proposition}(Q) \wedge Q^* \theta) \rightarrow (\text{false}(Q) \leftrightarrow \neg(\exists p)(p \cdot \theta))$$

Thus a proposition is true if some fact combines its constituents, and it is false otherwise. Given propositions, it is easy to distinguish sense from nonsense: some things in order are 'sense' just if they are the constituents of a proposition, and otherwise they are 'nonsense'.

$$\text{sense } (\theta) =_{\text{df}} (\exists Q)(\text{proposition}(Q) \wedge Q^* \theta)$$

Once we have the definition of sense and nonsense, we can define *particular*:

$$\text{particular}(x) =_{\text{df}} \text{nonsense}(x, \theta)$$

Equivalently,

$$\text{particular}(x) =_{\text{df}} (\forall Q)\neg(\text{proposition}(Q) \wedge Q^* (x, \theta))$$

This says that a particular is an entity that can never occupy 'predicate position' in a proposition. If an entity does ever occupy predicate position in a proposition, that entity is a universal. The definition correctly classifies uninstantiated and even uninstantiable universals. Such universals admittedly never occur in predicate position in a true (atomic) proposition, but they do occur in predicate position in some false propositions.

On this theory, the supply of propositions determines the supply of universals: if there were fewer propositions, fewer entities would be universals. The theory is silent on what determines the supply of propositions; why there should be exactly these propositions, and no more, is left mysterious. The nature of the propositions themselves is also mysterious. Russell writes:

To suppose that in the actual worlds of nature there is a whole set of false propositions going about is to my mind monstrous. (Russell 1918: 223)

Russell's reaction to the theory of propositions was an 'incredulous stare'. It seems to me that Russell was right: propositions do conflict with the 'instinct as to what is real', and we should avoid postulating them, if we can.

If we find it hard to believe in propositions, there might seem to be an alternative strategy for distinguishing particulars and universals, by appeal to another kind of entity, the *state of affairs*. Where the notion of a proposition is tailored for the concept of truth, the notion of a state of affairs is tailored for the concept of possibility: indeed, a state of affairs can be identified with a possibility, and a state of affairs that obtains can be identified with a possibility that is actual. Possible worlds can be identified with very comprehensive states of affairs, though the state of affairs theorist is not necessarily committed to the existence of such maximal possibilities.

Let us now reuse the sign '*' to represent the relation of combination in a state of affairs. The main property of states of affairs is their capacity to *obtain*; the obtaining of a state of affairs must be distinguished from its existence, since it can exist even if it fails to obtain. Using vector logic we can give an implicit definition of 'obtaining' as follows:

$$(\text{state-of-affairs}(Q) \wedge Q * \theta) \rightarrow (\text{obtains}(Q) \leftrightarrow (\exists p)(p \cdot \theta))$$
$$(\text{state-of-affairs}(Q) \wedge Q * \theta) \rightarrow (\text{non-actual}(Q) \leftrightarrow \neg(\exists p)(p \cdot \theta))$$

Thus a state of affairs obtains if some fact combines its constituents; it is non-actual, or fails to obtain, otherwise. Given states of affairs, we can again distinguish sense from nonsense:

$$\text{sense }(\theta) =_{df} (\exists Q)(\text{state-of-affairs}(Q) \wedge Q * \theta)$$

And we can define *particular*:

$$\text{particular}(x) =_{df} (\forall \theta)\neg(\text{sense}(x, \theta))$$

On this theory too, whether or not something is a universal depends on the actual supply of states of affairs; it is just a brute fact that there are exactly the states of affairs there actually are, neither more nor less.

But states of affairs are quite as repugnant to 'the sense of reality' as are propositions. It is equally 'monstrous' to suppose that there are a whole set of unactualised possibilities 'going about the world' as it is to suppose that there is a whole set of false propositions going about. The reason the degree of monstrousness is the same is that this is the same theory all over again. We turn the theory of propositions into the theory of states of affairs by merely verbal changes, as follows: substitute 'state of affairs' for 'proposition', 'actual' or 'obtaining' for 'true', and 'unactualised state of affairs' for 'false proposition'. We get nothing new by switching to states of affairs.

Instead of relying on propositions or states of affairs to distinguish particulars from universals, we might propose to rely instead on contents, i.e., Fregean Thoughts. A content does not indeed 'combine' particulars and universals, but its concepts do 'present' them. So we can regard the whole content as presenting in order what each of its associated concepts presents. We could define 'sense' and 'nonsense' in terms of contents, and go on as before to define the distinction between particular and universal in terms of sense and nonsense. Certainly we cannot complain this is the same theory again, for different contents can present the same things, and some contents present nothing, whereas different states of affairs have different constituents, and no state of affairs has no constituents. Moreover, contents seem not at all repugnant to the 'instinct' for reality, for we can identify contents with properties of our mental states. Nevertheless it seems undesirable to found the metaphysical distinction of particular and universal in the theory of content. The true order of explanation is surely exactly the reverse: the theory of content, and in particular the theory of the presentation relation, (i.e., the relation of reference) itself rests on the distinction between particular and universal, as I shall argue in Chapter 3. I conclude that there is no good way of drawing the distinction between particular and universal by adding to our ontology any new kind of item beyond those already presupposed by metaphysical Realism.

2.6 Negation

Ordinary positive facts are enough to allow us to class some things as universals. For example, we know that *wisdom* is a universal. Let $p =$ the fact that Socrates is wise. Then:

$p \cdot$ (*wisdom*, Socrates)

Because a fact combines them, we know that (*wisdom*, Socrates) are 'sense', and not 'nonsense', and hence we know that *wisdom* is a universal, since it occupies first position, or 'predicate position' among some things that are sense. But in the absence of the fact that Socrates is wise, we would lack this particular proof that *wisdom* is a universal. The presence or absence of facts is a highly contingent matter, and many things make sense, even if no fact combines them. For example, in a world at which the only individual is Socrates, there is no fact p and particular x such that:

$p \cdot$ (*foolishness*, x)

It might seem we would be unable to classify *foolishness* correctly as a universal at such a world. At least, we would be unable to do so if only positive facts exist. But are there perhaps *negative facts*, in addition to the positive facts?

It is a law of logic that for any sentence, if it is false, then its negation is true. So because 'Socrates is foolish' is false, its negation 'Socrates is not foolish' is true. What is the truth-maker for 'Socrates is not foolish?' One theory is that it is merely the *absence* of the positive fact that Socrates is foolish. A better theory is that it is the presence of the *negative fact* that Socrates is not foolish. Let q be this negative fact; if it really exists it will have *negation* as a constituent:

$q \cdot (\neg, foolishness, \text{Socrates})$

Suppose we adopt the point of view that there really is such an entity as *negation*. If there is, it must presumably be some kind of relation, since it occupies predicate position in the fact q; in that case a negative fact will simply be the fact that a universal and some other things stand in the *negation* relation. Then we can dispense with the ontology of propositions and states of affairs and possible worlds, and instead solve Russell's problem of sense and nonsense by means of negative facts. For we can say that things are 'sense' if either they are the constituents of a fact, or if together with *negation* they are the constituents of a negative fact:

Definition of 'sense': $\text{sense}(\theta) =_{\text{df}} (\exists p)(p \cdot \theta \lor p \cdot (\neg, \theta))$

According to this account, a negative fact combines *negation* and what would be the constituents of p, if the fact p existed. Our theory of sense and nonsense is that θ make 'sense' if either θ compose a fact, or *negation* and θ compose a fact.

What exactly is this mysterious entity, *negation*? Various proposals have been made. For example, negation has been said to be a truth-function: given a truth-value as argument, it returns the opposite truth-value. That makes *negation* a relation, namely the relation in which truth stands to falsity, falsity to truth, and in which nothing else stands to anything. But this proposal will not suit us here, for two reasons. First, the proposal seems obliged to posit propositions as single entities again, for neither sentences nor contents are necessarily guaranteed to have a truth-value, so they are not suited to be the arguments to truth-functions; only propositions will do for that, but we were professing incredulity about propositions. The second reason is that the notion of a truth-value requires that there be such a thing as truth, and such a thing as falsity, and this is something we should like to avoid if we can, because the primitive concept for the present theory is not truth but knowledge.

Pretend for a moment, however, that there really are propositions that are single entities. Now consider the property a proposition has, if no fact combines its constituents. This property of a proposition induces a relation in which its constituents stand to each other, if no fact combines them. My suggestion is that *negation* is this relation on the constituents of propositions. Since propositions have a variable number of constituents, *negation* must be a multigrade relation. So if propositions existed, we could define *negation* as that multigrade relation in which some things θ stand, if taken in order they compose a proposition, but do not compose a fact.

But now it seems nothing prevents us from dispensing with propositions, and giving a direct explanation of *negation* in terms of just the relation of combination. Of course we cannot really *define* negation, but we have two logical Principles that tell us all we need to know about it. The Principle of Double Negation tells us that $\neg\neg A \to A$. The Principle of Contradiction tells us that $\neg(A \land \neg A)$. Since these principles are correct *a priori*, we have the following laws of logic about the existence of facts:

Law of Double Negation: $\quad (\forall\theta)((\exists p)(p \cdot \theta) \leftrightarrow (\exists q)(q \cdot (\underline{\neg}, \underline{\neg}, \theta)))$

Law of Contradiction: $\quad (\forall\theta)(\neg(\exists p)(\exists q)(p \cdot \theta \land q \cdot (\underline{\neg}, \theta)))$

We can regard these as the axioms of the theory of *negation*. (Note that here the sign '$\underline{\neg}$' names the relation of *negation*—it is not the object language sign '$\neg$', which is a sentential connective.)

Can we extract an explicit definition of *negation* from these axioms? The first step would be to extract the 'Ramsey Sentence' of the Theory of Negation:

$$(\exists x)(\forall\theta)(((\exists p)(p \cdot \theta) \leftrightarrow (\exists q)(q \cdot (x, x, \theta)) \land \neg(\exists p)(\exists q)(p \cdot \theta \land q \cdot (x, \theta)))$$

We could then give an explicit definition of *negation* as follows:

$$\neg =_{df} [\text{the } x\text{: } (\forall\theta)(((\exists p)(p \cdot \theta)$$
$$\leftrightarrow (\exists q)(q \cdot (x, x, \theta)) \wedge \neg(\exists p)(\exists q)(p \cdot \theta \wedge q \cdot (x, \theta)))]$$

The objection to this is that the proposed 'Ramsey Sentence' contains a universal vector quantifier within the scope of an existential quantifier; it is not a prenex universal quantification, so it is not permitted under our schematic interpretation of the vector quantifier. While we hold to the restrictions of vector logic, we are unable to define *negation*. But that does not seem to constitute a difficulty for the theory of negative facts, for it seems quite plausible that *negation* is something absolutely simple and indefinable. The familiar laws of Double Negation and Contradiction are all we need to assure ourselves that we do know exactly what *negation* is.

Given *negation*, we can distinguish sense from nonsense, and hence particulars from universals. *Wisdom* is a universal, for there is a fact that combines *wisdom* with Socrates, since 'Socrates is wise' is true. *Foolishness* is a universal, for even though no fact combines *foolishness* and Socrates, still *foolishness* and Socrates stand in the *negation* relation, which is to say that a (negative) fact combines *negation, foolishness* and Socrates. That is why 'Socrates is foolish' makes sense, even though it does not state a fact. In contrast, Plato and Socrates do not stand in the *negation* relation, for no negative fact combines *negation* and them. But no positive fact combines them either, which is why 'Plato Socrates' is neither true nor false, but 'nonsense'.

We earlier rejected the suggestion that there are any such individual entities as propositions, for reasons of incredulity. But we need not leave the theoretical role of propositions unfilled, for we can use vectors to fill the role without any additional ontological commitment. A vector is just some things referred to in a given order, and we can say that any vector can play the role of a proposition, provided they are not 'nonsense'.

Russellian Proposition: θ are a *Russellian proposition* $=_{df}$ sense (θ)

Note that to say that θ are a *Russellian* proposition is by no means to say that θ *is* a proposition, i.e., a single entity: a Russellian proposition are not a 'one', but an ordered 'many': they are some entities fit to be the constituents of a (Russellian) judgement, not a single entity that is the propositional object of the judgement.

Given negative facts, we can give explicit definitions of *true* and *false* for Russellian propositions. We found it impossible earlier to define true and false explicitly for propositions as single entities, but because Russellian propositions are a 'many' and not a 'one', in their case vector logic presents no obstacle to an explicit definition:

Definition of 'true' for Russellian propositions: θ are *true* $=_{\mathrm{df}} (\exists p)(p \cdot \theta)$
Definition of 'false' for Russellian propositions: θ are *false* $=_{\mathrm{df}} (\exists p)$
$(p \cdot (\neg, \theta))$

The existence of negative facts increases the total supply of facts sufficiently to allow us to define the distinction between particular and universal, while allowing for uninstantiated and even necessarily uninstantiated universals. Our definition is that something x is a particular if, whatever θ may be, (x, θ) are 'nonsense'.

Definition of 'particular': x is a *particular* $=_{\mathrm{df}} (\forall \theta)(\mathrm{nonsense}(x, \theta))$

Thus a particular is anything that occupies 'predicate position' in no Russellian proposition; a universal is anything that is not a particular.

Arity

Negative facts not only distinguish universals from particulars, but also provide an account of the arity of universals. The arity of a property, or correspondingly the adicity of a predicate, is of great importance in logic, but is not very easy to define. We sometimes say loosely that a universal U has arity n if it has n 'slots' or 'argument-places'. But this can only be a metaphor, since it would sometimes require the same thing to 'occupy' more than one argument place. For example, the relation of *killing* appears to have two slots, so in the fact that Brutus killed Caesar, we might think that Brutus occupies the first slot, and Caesar the second. But a difficulty arises in the case of Cato, who killed himself. In the fact that Cato killed Cato, Cato occupies the first slot in the relation of *killing*, since he was the killer, but he also occupies the second slot, since he was also the killed. But how can a single particular be in two slots at the same time? Whatever an argument-place may be, a spatial metaphor of slots seems of little use in assisting our understanding.

Arity is a concept of logic, and it should be explained in terms of logical concepts, not quasi-spatial ideas like 'slot'. Given negative facts we can define arity by saying that U is a universal of arity n if the vector of U followed by any n other things are never nonsense:

Definition of arity: U has arity $n =_{df} (\forall x_1) \ldots (\forall x_n)(\text{sense}(U, x_1, \ldots, x_n))$

In logic it is customary to draw a distinction between simple predicates, such as 'wise', and complex predicates such as 'round or square'. We may suppose that the simple predicates refer to properties if they refer to anything. But what is the semantic value of a complex predicate? One hypothesis is the Naive Property Abstraction Principle, according to which for every complex predicate, there exists a property such that some things satisfy the complex predicate if and only if they instantiate the property. That hypothesis is ontologically inflationary and therefore dangerous, for it threatens to let in unwanted entities such as *heterological*, the property a property has if it does not instantiate itself. *Heterological* leads to paradox, to prevent which some sort of hierarchy of types may need to be posited. But in the context of a vector logic we do not need the dangerous abstraction principle, for we can take the semantic value of a complex predicate to be not a unitary entity, but simply a vector of the various objects named by the simple parts of the complex predicate. Taking the vector as the semantic value incurs no new ontological commitment, for on the schematic interpretation reference to a vector is not reference to a new sort of ordered object, but only a new sort of ordered reference to objects. Therefore vector reference brings with it no new entities, is not ontologically inflationary, and brings with it no new risk of paradox. A vector logic has therefore no need to invoke a theory of types, and can be free of type restrictions.

So just as we defined a Russellian proposition as not one thing, but a vector many, so we can define a Russellian property as not one thing but a vector many, as follows: some things are a Russellian property if they always make a Russellian proposition when completed by a suitable number of other things. The required number of other things is the *arity* of the Russellian property.

Definition of Russellian property: θ are a *Russellian property of arity*
$n =_{df} (\forall x_1) \ldots (\forall x_n)(\text{sense}(\theta, x_1, \ldots, x_n))$

A Russellian property can serve as the semantic value of a complex predicate; a Russellian proposition is a Russellian property of arity zero.

2.7 Complex Facts

A negative fact is an example of a *complex* fact, i.e., a fact one of whose constituents is the referent of a 'logical constant'. But does Reality actually contain complex facts? Wittgenstein denied it in the *Tractatus*:

40312 My fundamental idea is that the 'logical constants' do not stand for anything.

54 There are no 'logical objects' or 'logical constants' (in Frege's and Russell's sense). (1961b: 43, 89)

Wittgenstein found it hard to believe that whenever the fact p exists, then there exists also the doubly negative fact $\neg\neg p$, the doubly doubly negative fact $\neg\neg\neg\neg p$, etc., etc. It seems that once we admit the objective existence of a referent for the logical negation sign, we are obliged to admit for every atomic fact the existence of an infinite collection of further doubly negative facts, which all seem to amount to more or less the same thing; the existence of these further facts seems not to make the slightest difference to the world. The same point arises in the case of conjunction. Suppose the facts p and q exist. If there are complex facts, then there exists also their conjunction $p \wedge q$, which is a third fact different from them both. Similarly, there also exist the further facts $q \wedge p, p \wedge p, q \wedge q, p \wedge p \wedge p$, etc., etc., all of which are different.

However, it is not clear that this is much of a difficulty. Compare the case of set theory. If there really are any sets, then there are infinitely many, since every set has a fresh singleton. It may make no empirical difference to the world, to have not only Socrates and his singleton, but also his singleton's singleton, his singleton's singleton's singleton, and so on, but that is no objection to set theory. Similarly if there are any complex facts there are infinitely many, but that does not seem a deep reason for scepticism about complex facts.

Wittgenstein had a deeper reason, which was his rejection of *a priori* knowledge in the philosophy of logic. In Wittgenstein's view, the conclusion of a logically correct argument is already 'contained in the premisses'. The advance from premisses to conclusion is not an epistemic advance; there is no new and previously unknown fact which we come to know as a result of the deduction. Since deduction does not lead to new knowledge, there can be no such thing as the epistemology of deduction, and the problem of *a priori* inference is dissolved. Similarly, logical axioms do not state logical facts, on Wittgenstein's view. There are no logical facts, for any such would be complex, and there are no complex facts. The sentences that give the 'logical axioms' turn out to be 'tautologies' that 'say nothing'. Since the axioms state no facts, there can be no such thing as the epistemology of logical axioms, which dissolves the problem of how logical knowledge can be primitive *a priori*.

The doctrine of the *Tractatus* is that the atomic facts are all the facts there are. There exists the fact p, so we may say truly that A. There exists the fact q, so we may say truly that B. There does not also exist the conjunctive fact $p \land q$. Nevertheless, we may still say truly that $A \land B$. The sentence '$A \land B$' does not need a new conjunctive fact to make it true, for it is already made true by two simple facts, viz., the fact p and the fact q. No further conjunctive fact is needed. Wittgenstein therefore declined to undertake the project of offering a metaphysics of conjunction. Instead he treated it as a pragmatic or psychological matter. As he puts it (1961b: 63):

44 A proposition is an expression of agreement and disagreement with truth-possibilities of elementary propositions.

His suggestion is that we should regard a complex sentence (i.e., one that contains a logical constant) not as representing a complex fact, but as expressing a complex pattern of agreement and disagreement with the truth-possibilities of its simpler sentential parts. This opens up the possibility of a radically new account of deduction, as follows. Atomic sentences, which have no sentential parts, 'disagree with' the absence of the fact they represent. So in an inference of Conjunction Introduction, the first premiss A disagrees with the absence of p, the second premiss B disagrees with the absence of q, and so between them the two premisses jointly disagree with every line except the first of the following 'truth-table' for the conclusion $A \land B$:

A	B	$(A \land B)$	
T	T	T	—not disagreed with.
T	F	F	—disagreed with by 'B'.
F	F	F	—disagreed with by 'A'.
F	F	F	—disagreed with by both 'A' and 'B'.

Thus if we have already asserted A and asserted B, then when we assert $A \land B$ at the end of a deduction, we are not narrowing down our description of the world at all; for the conclusion $A \wedge B$ disagrees only with what has already been disagreed with by the two premisses.

Wittgenstein's account has the advantages of providing a justification for deduction while at the same time dispensing with the need for an account of *a priori* logical knowledge. (1961b: 75, §§511–5121) But it has the disadvantage of not giving any account of the usefulness of deduction. What is the point of it? Why all this agreeing and disagreeing? His account seems to present deduction as nothing more than 'simply taking out of the box again what we have just put into it' (Frege 1968: 101ᵉ, §88). If that is what deduction is, then it is clear why it is logically legitimate, but obscure why it is so fruitful. As Dummett puts the difficulty:

> When we contemplate the simplest basic forms of inference, the gap between recognising the truth of the premisses and recognising the truth of the conclusion seems infinitesimal; but, when we contemplate the wealth and complexity of number-theoretic theorems which, by chains of such inferences, can be proved from the apparently simple set of Peano Axioms, we are struck by the difficulty of establishing them, and the surprises they yield. We know, of course, that a man may walk from Paris to Rome, and yet that a single pace will not take him appreciably closer: but epistemic distance is more puzzling to us than spatial distance. (1978: 297)

Wittgenstein's rejection of complex facts can be no more persuasive than his account of deduction. That account does indeed work smoothly enough for Sentence Calculus, because the truth-conditions of any complex sentence of sentence calculus can be given in terms of a finite number of atomic sentences. But the account runs into trouble with sentences whose truth condition involve an infinity of elementary facts. For example, consider the inference:

$$\frac{(\forall x)Fx}{Fa}$$

Wittgenstein denies that the logical constants stand for anything. The quantifier '$\forall$' has no referent, so there are no general facts, and there is no metaphysics of generality. Instead we are offered a pragmatic or psychological account of generality. Wittgenstein treats the general proposition $(\forall x)Fx$ as the possibly infinite conjunction of all the atomic propositions Fa, Fb, Fc, etc. Given his account of conjunction, it follows that 'agreement' with $(\forall x)Fx$ requires (distributive) agreement with infinitely many atomic sentences, if the domain of discourse is infinite. Set aside the difficulty that perhaps not everything in the infinite domain has a name in our language; in any case, it is clearly impossible for a human being to agree or disagree individually with each of an infinity of atomic facts. Thus Wittgenstein's account of generality cannot be correct.

Because there can be no psychologistic account of generality, there can be no psychologistic account of conjunction either, for conjunction can occur within the scope of generality, as for example in '$(\forall x)(Fx \wedge Gx)$'. Therefore there can be no hope of explaining by Wittgenstein's methods the correct deduction:

$$\frac{(\forall x)Fx \wedge Gx)}{Fa}$$

It follows that Wittgenstein's account of conjunction cannot be correct, since at best it covers only the special case where the conjunction does not occur within the scope of a quantifier. In the same way, his account of negation cannot deal with negation within the scope of a quantifier.

Conjunctive Facts

Suppose we reject Wittgenstein's scepticism about complex facts. In that case we should acknowledge the existence not only of negative facts, but also of conjunctive and general facts.

If the conjunctive fact $p \wedge q$ exists, what are its constituents? The fact $p \wedge q$ exists only if p exists and q exists, so the existence of $p \wedge q$ requires the existence of the constituents of p and the constituents of q. But since we are rejecting Wittgenstein's view that the logical constants do not 'stand for' anything, we shall also need whatever it is that the conjunction sign 'stands for'. What can that be? I suggest that conjunction is the multigrade relation that obtains between some things θ and some other things ϕ if and only if a fact combines θ and a fact combines ϕ. Letting '$\wedge$' name this relation, we may define it as follows:

   Conjunction: $\underline{\wedge} \, (\theta, \, \phi) =_{df} (\exists p)(\exists q) \, (p \cdot \theta \wedge q \cdot \phi)$

Conjunction is governed by the following axiom:

   Conjunction Axiom: $(\exists p)(p \cdot (\underline{\wedge}, \, \theta, \, \phi)) \leftrightarrow (\exists q)(\exists r)(q \cdot \theta \wedge r \cdot \phi)$

The truth of this axiom guarantees the correctness of the familiar rules of inference for conjunction, viz., Conjunction Introduction and Conjunction

Elimination. Our *a priori* knowledge of the correctness of these rules is just our knowledge, under a different mode of presentation, of the fact stated by the Conjunction Axiom.

General Facts

Since the *Tractatus* account of deduction is unsatisfactory, it gives us no reason to reject general facts, and we should form an opinion on whether or not they exist by taking into account broader metaphysical considerations. Of these by far the most important is that the existence of general facts is required if we are to give a realist account of laws of nature: for a law is a general fact, which can hold at different possible worlds, even if the particular objects that exist at the two worlds are not the same. For this reason, and for the sake of uniformity with our account of negative and conjunctive facts, I believe we do best to reject Wittgenstein's account, and to recognise general facts as a third category of complex facts.

What are the constituents of a general fact? If we treated generality as infinite conjunction, then we should have to suppose that every entity in the domain of quantification is one of the constituents. But there is no need for such complexity: we can follow Frege, and treat generality as a property of properties, namely that property which a property has, if everything instantiates it (Frege 1891, 1968: 65^e, §53). But since we are taking 'properties' to be Russellian properties, i.e., vectors, this conception of generality need not give rise to a Fregean hierarchy of levels. We simply posit a multigrade relation of *generality*, which is the relation in which a monadic Russellian property stand to each other, if everything instantiates them. Writing '$\underline{\neg}$' for the generality relation, we have:

Generality: $\underline{\neg}(\theta) =_{df} (\forall x)(\exists p)(p \cdot (\theta, x))$

Thus the general fact will have the constituents $(\underline{\forall}, \theta)$. We can give the following axiom:

Axiom of Generality: $(\exists p)(p \cdot (\underline{\neg}, \theta)) \leftrightarrow (\forall x)(\exists q)(q \cdot (\theta, x))$

This Axiom justifies the familiar Rules of Inference for Quantifier Introduction and Quantifier Elimination.

2.8 'Variables Explained Away'

The apparatus developed so far gives the constituents of atomic facts, namely particulars and universals. It also recognises *negation, conjunction* and *generality*, which are the constituents of some of the complex facts that can be expressed in Predicate Calculus. But it does not deal with the variables that play such an important part in logical notation. Without variables it would not be possible to express in the predicate calculus all the facts that English can express. For example, consider the following four English sentences, and their predicate calculus equivalents:

1.	Everyone loves someone	$(\forall x)(\exists y)Lxy$
2.	Everyone is loved by someone	$(\forall x)(\exists y)Lyx$
3.	Someone loves everyone	$(\exists x)(\forall y)Lxy$
4.	Someone is loved by everyone	$(\exists x)(\forall y)Lyx$

None of these are logically equivalent. Adding the variables has allowed us to express the full range of possibilities, for the difference between 'Lxy' and 'Lyx' has semantic significance in the above formulas. In combination with the ordering of the other logical signs, the ordering of the variables allows Predicate Calculus to attain its full expressive power.

This point about the symbolism applies also to the facts symbolised. The symbolism of predicate calculus allows for the representation of four different facts here, but if the only logical relations available in our theory of facts are $\forall$ and $\exists$, then we have available only these two combinations or possible facts:

$\langle \forall, \exists, L \rangle$ = 'the fact that everyone loves someone'
$\langle \exists, \forall, L \rangle$ = 'the fact that someone loves everyone'

With the building blocks so far available, our theory of facts can construct only two of the four possible facts that the full Predicate Calculus can represent. The other two are absent because we have nothing to correspond semantically to the predicate calculus variables. We must find constituents of reality to reflect the semantic significance of the variables. But surely there are no variable objects!

In the formulas $(\exists x)(\forall y)Lxy$ and $(\exists x)(\forall y)Lyx$, we see that what matters is not so much the variables themselves, as the order in which they occur. The fact that one variable is the letter 'x' and the other the letter 'y' has no semantic significance. But there is a difference between *Lxy* and *Lyx* that would persist even if we substituted other variables for *x* and *y*; the difference is in the *arrangement* of the variables. We need only find a constituent of reality to correspond to the arrangement of the variables; we need not find a constituent corresponding to the variables themselves.

A constituent corresponding to an arrangement will be an additional logical constant; its inclusion in a fact will have the same effect that permuting the order of variable objects would have, if there were any variable objects to permute. An example of a logical constant of this sort is *inverse*. It is another multigrade property, namely the property that θ, *x* and *y* have, if they are a Russellian proposition and there exists a fact that combines θ, *y* and *x*.

Definition of Inverse: inverse $(\theta, x, y) =_{df} sense\ (\theta, x, y) \wedge (\exists p)(p \cdot (\theta, y, x))$

Thus *inverse* obeys the following axiom:

Axiom of inverse: $(\exists p)(p \cdot (inverse,\ \theta, x, y)) \leftrightarrow (\exists q)(q \cdot (\theta, y, x))$

If *R* is a binary relation, the above axioms for *inverse* justify the following Introduction and Elimination Rules:

Rt_1t_2 *inverse* Rt_2t_1
_____ (*inverse* Introduction)   _____ (*inverse* Elimination)
inverse Rt_2t_1 Rt_1t_2

Thus 'harmonious' introduction and elimination rules exist for *inverse*, just as they do for the more familiar logical constants. This gives support to the claim that *inverse* is indeed a logical constant. It surfaces in natural language as the passive voice; for example, '*inverse* loves' is expressed in English by 'is loved by'. Thus 'Romeo loves Juliet, therefore Juliet is loved by Romeo' is a correct deduction, by the above rule of *inverse* Introduction.

We could not previously give the constituents of the fact represented by $(\forall x)(\exists y)(y$ loves $x)$. But if we have *inverse* available as an additional logical constant, we can give its constituents as follows:

$(\forall, \exists, inverse, love)$

Applying our axioms, we see that:

$(\exists p)(p \cdot (\forall, \exists, inverse, love))$
$\leftrightarrow (\forall x)(\exists p)(p \cdot (\exists, inverse, love, x))$
$\leftrightarrow (\forall x)(\exists y)(\exists p)(p \cdot (inverse, love, x, y))$

$\leftrightarrow (\forall x)(\exists y)(\exists p)(p \cdot (love, y, x)$

$\leftrightarrow (\forall x)(\exists y)(y \text{ loves } x))$

We have arrived at the correct condition for the existence of the fact, i.e., we have arrived at the correct 'truth-condition'. Recognising *inverse* as an additional logical constant allows us to distinguish the constituents of the fact *that everyone is loved by someone*, (∀, ∃, *inverse*, *love*) from the constituents of the fact *that everyone loves someone*, (∀, ∃, *love*). These two lists of constituents have nothing corresponding to variables, but they do have something corresponding to the arrangement of the variables, viz., the presence or absence of *inverse* as a constituent.

Inverse on its own is not of course sufficient to allow us to give constituents for all the facts that predicate calculus can express. For example, we are not yet in a position to give the constituents of 'everything loves itself', '$(\forall x)(x \text{ loves } x)$'. Since *love* is a binary relation, the vector (∀, *love*) are a Russellian property of arity one, and not the constituents of the required Russellian proposition. Therefore we need to find yet another logical constituent of facts. We must recognise the further logical constant *self*, which is the multigrade property that θ and x have, if there exists a fact that combines θ, x and x.

Definition of self: $self(\theta, x) =_{df} (\exists p)(p \cdot (\theta, x, x))$

Self obeys the following axiom:

Axiom of self: $(\exists p)(p \cdot (self, \theta, x)) \leftrightarrow (\exists q)(q \cdot (\theta, x, x))$

It follows that *self* is subject to the following harmonious Introduction and Elimination Rules:

$$\frac{Rtt}{self\ Rt} \quad (self \text{ Introduction}) \qquad \frac{self\ Rt}{Rtt} \quad (self \text{ Elimination})$$

We now give the constituents of the fact represented by $(\forall x)(x \text{ loves } x)$ as:

(∀, *self*, love)

From our axioms we see that:

$(\exists p)(p \cdot (∀, self, love))$

$\leftrightarrow (\forall x)(\exists p)(p \cdot (self, \; love, \; x))$

$\leftrightarrow (\forall x)(\exists p)(p \cdot (love, \; x, \; x))$

$\leftrightarrow (\forall x)(x \; loves \; x)$

We have arrived at the correct existence-condition, so recognising the new logical constant *self* allows us to give the correct constituents for the fact represented by '$(\forall x)(x \; loves \; x)$'. Like *inverse, self* surfaces in natural language. *Self* is the English reflexive; for example, 'Cato killed Cato, therefore Cato killed himself', is a correct deduction by the Rule of *self* Introduction.

Inverse and *self* are still only the merest beginning on what is needed to match the full expressive power of predicate calculus. The difficulty is that we have to deal with properties of every arity. Even if universals themselves were all either qualities or binary relations, logical combinations would still give rise to Russellian properties of every arity. For example, the Russellian property expressed by the open sentence '$Bxy \land Czw$' is of arity 4, although the predicates B and C are themselves each of adicity only 2. Thus *inverse* and *self* are insufficient on their own, because we need to be able to find constituents to correspond to all the possible arrangements of the predicate calculus variables in complex sentences.

Given any k things, if a Russellian property θ are of arity n, then in terms of the 'slots' metaphor there are k^n ways to fill the property's n 'slots' from the k things, allowing for repeats. Let $\pi = (\pi(1), \ldots, \pi(n))$ be a vector of numbers selected from the numbers from 1 to k. For each such π, we could posit the existence of a corresponding logical constant, namely the *arrangement* Π. In terms of the 'slots' metaphor, we can think of the selection function π as assigning the ith thing in a vector $(x_1, \ldots, x_k)$ to fill the jth 'slot' in a Russellian property θ of arity n. The arrangement Π associated with the selection function π is then the corresponding multigrade property, namely the property that θ and $x_1, \ldots, x_k$ have, if they are a Russellian proposition, and there exists a fact that combines θ and $x_{\pi(1)}, \ldots, x_{\pi(n)}$. So:

Definition of the arrangement associated with π: $\Pi(\theta, x_1, \ldots, x_k) =_{df}$ sense$(\theta, x_1, \ldots, x_k) \land (\exists p)(p \cdot (\theta, x_{\pi(1)}, \ldots, x_{\pi(n)}))$

We can give the following axiom:

Axiom of arrangement: $(\exists p)(p \cdot (\Pi, \theta, x_1, \ldots, x_k) \leftrightarrow (\exists q)(q \cdot (\theta, x_{\pi(1)}, \ldots, x_{\pi(n)}))$

With all these different *arrangements* available, we certainly now have enough entities to give the constituents of any fact expressible in predicate calculus. (This is proved in the Appendix to this chapter.) This shows that what has semantic significance in the sign '$x_{\pi(1)}, \ldots, x_{\pi(n)}$' is not the individual variables, but their arrangement.

But although this solution is formally adequate, it may seem ontologically unsatisfactory to have to recognise a new multigrade relation Π corresponding to each and every possible arrangement π of the variables. The theory of facts threatens either to cease to be finitely axiomatisable, or to require an excessive quantity of auxiliary mathematical apparatus. But here we can use a device of Quine's (1995). Instead of single occurrences of any of the infinitely many individual logical constants Π of arrangement, we can make do with multiple occurrences of just three logical constants, which can serve as a basis for all possible arrangements. Two of these we have already met, namely *self* and *inverse*. The third is the new constant *cycle*, which corresponds to a sort of rotation of the variables from the ordering $x_1, \ldots, x_n$ to the new ordering $x_n, x_1, \ldots, x_{(n-1)}$. The effect of the rotation of variables on the list of a predicate's arguments is to make what was the last variable the first, and to move all the other variables up one place in the order, in effect cycling the whole list. We therefore define the logical constant *cycle* as the multigrade property that $(\theta, x_1, \ldots, x_n)$ have, if they are a Russellian proposition, and there exists a fact that combines $(\theta, x_n, x_1, \ldots, x_{(n-1)})$:

$$cycle\ (\theta, x_1, \ldots, x_n) =_{df} sense(\theta, x_1, \ldots, x_n) \wedge (\exists p)(p \cdot (\theta, x_n, x_1, \ldots, x_{(n-1)}))$$

Thus *cycle* obeys the following axiom:

Axiom of cycle: $(\exists p)(p \cdot (cycle,\ \theta, x_1, \ldots, x_n)) \leftrightarrow (\exists q)(q \cdot (\theta, x_n, x_1, \ldots, x_{(n-1)}))$

It follows that *cycle* is subject to the following harmonious Introduction and Elimination Rules:

$Rt_1 \ldots t_n$		$cycle\ Rt_n t_1 \ldots t_{(n-1)}$	
———	(*cycle* Introduction)	———	(*cycle* Elimination)
$cycle\ Rt_n t_1 \ldots t_{(n-1)}$		$Rt_1 \ldots t_n$	

Every permutation of the variables can be obtained by some combination of *cycle* and *inverse*; if any repetitions are needed we can permute to the required arrangement and apply *self*. Thus these three logical constants serve as a basis to generate all possible arrangements. So if one is uncomfortable about the existence of an infinity of logical constants, one can use Quine's device to shrink the infinity of arrangements to just these three basic combinations. This is analogous to the situation with the truth functions: there are an infinity of truth functions, but they can all be reduced to combinations of '∧' and '¬'; similarly, there are an infinity of arrangements, but they can all be reduced to combinations of *self, inverse* and *cycle*. These three, together with the three more familiar logical relations of *negation, conjunction* and *generality*, are all the logical constants required for predicate calculus. *Pace* Wittgenstein, it is not the case that the 'logical constants' do not stand for anything. Each 'stands for' a multigrade relation, i.e., for a universal. This makes the logical constants quite unmysterious. Each is simply a predicate; if it is the 'main operator' in a sentence, it attributes the universal it stands for to the referents of the other terms in the sentence, in the order indicated by the syntax of the sentence. Contrary to the teaching of Frege and Russell, we can therefore regard every sentence of predicate calculus, without exception, as of subject-predicate form.

2.9 The Adequacy Condition

According to Realism, the metaphysical theory we have been advocating, the totality of all things divides into two natural kinds, the particulars and the universals. The totality of particulars divides in turn into two further natural kinds, the individuals and the facts: an individual is a particular that combines no vector, and the facts are the particulars that are not individuals. The universals include the logical constants, which are all multigrade universals. The relation of combination, itself a universal, provides the link between facts, particulars and universals, since facts can combine universals and particulars. I now wish to suggest that this ontology is an adequate basis upon which to build all the possibilities that can be represented by formulas of first order predicate calculus. It would follow that this ontology is a suitable foundation for a theory of how thought represents the world, at least for those thoughts that can be expressed in predicate calculus.

To show that the present ontology is indeed adequate for predicate calculus, what is needed is an 'Adequacy Theorem'. The concept of such a theorem is due to Tarski (1983: 187–8), who laid it down as a condition on the adequacy of a semantic theory that the theory should entail every instance of the following schema:

A is true $\leftrightarrow \underline{A}$

Here the schematic variable A is to be replaced by the name of any sentence, and the variable $\underline{A}$ is to be replaced by the sentence itself.

On the approach to representation adopted in this book, the concept of truth has no explanatory role to play. The work that the concept of truth does in other philosophical theories is instead done here by the concepts of knowledge and fact. But even if truth is not central to a theory of representation, the need remains for at least an analogue of an adequacy theorem. For it is a constraint on an ontology that it should provide for a range of possibilities no richer than the possibilities our language can describe. Conversely, the background ontology of a semantic theory must be rich enough to permit the construction from its building blocks of all the possibilities our language can describe. To verify that our Realist ontology of particulars, universals and facts is appropriately rich, it is necessary to prove it can meet an analogue of Tarski's adequacy condition.

Before we can prove an adequacy theorem, we need a semantics. In the context of metaphysical Realism, the obvious suggestion for a semantic theory for predicate calculus is a *picture theory*. A correspondence exists between the syntactic categories of the predicate calculus and the ontological categories of metaphysical Realism, as follows; the individual constants correspond to any entity, the predicate letters of fixed adicity correspond to universals of fixed arity, and the logical constants correspond to multigrade universals. If a sentence concatenates signs in a certain order, the sentence pictures a fact that combines the referents of the signs in the corresponding order. A closed formula of predicate calculus can therefore be regarded as in effect a list; the referents of this list are a certain vector; if the formula is well-formed, the vector are a Russellian proposition. Similarly, an open formula also has a vector as referents; if the open formula is well-formed, the vector are a Russellian property. According to this picture theory, a speaker who asserts a sentence states the existence of the fact that combines the constituents of the Russellian proposition 'expressed' by the sentence—the sentence is a logical picture of the fact whose existence it represents. Thus to each formula A of predicate calculus, a picture theory assigns a vector $h(A)$, comprising the referents of the symbols of A in an order determined by the syntax of A. If the formula A is a sentence, then according to the picture theory it asserts that there exists the fact whose constituents are $h(A)$.

I shall use the following notational conventions. Since by the axiom of fact identity there can be no more than one fact with the constituents θ, I shall use the sign '$\langle\theta\rangle$' to abbreviate the following definite description: 'the fact whose constituents are θ'. In this notation, the picture theory says that the sentence A is a logical picture of $\langle h(A)\rangle$: to assert A is to state that $\langle h(A)\rangle$ exists. Similarly to deny A is to state that $\langle \neg, h(A)\rangle$ exists, i.e., it is to state that there is a negative fact that combines *negation* and $h(A)$; in which case the definite description '$\langle h(A)\rangle$' does not denote anything. I shall also adopt a convention of underlining to distinguish object language and metalanguage: symbols without underlining, e.g. 't', name symbols of the object language; underlined symbols, e.g. '$\underline{t}$', name in our metalanguage the referent of the symbol underlined: thus it will always be the case that t refers to $\underline{t}$.

The task of a semantics based on a picture theory is to identify for each sentence the fact $\langle h(A)\rangle$ which the sentence pictures. Such a semantics can be given straightforwardly as follows. First, we assign to each simple sign a referent:

Sign	Referent
individual constant	any object
predicate letter of adicity n	universal of arity n
logical constant	multigrade universal
variable sequence	arrangement

We next define the semantic value $h(A)$ of any atomic sentence A. If A is an atomic sentence, then A consists of a predicate letter followed in order by some names; its semantic value is the vector that comprises the universal the predicate stands for, followed in order by the things that the names stand for. For example, if $A = Fabc$ then $h(A) = \langle F, \underline{a}, \underline{b}, \underline{c}\rangle$ is the vector comprising the referent of F followed in order by the referents of a, b and c. Then $Fabc$ is true if $\langle \underline{F}, \underline{a}, \underline{b}, \underline{c}\rangle$ exists, i.e., if $\underline{Fabc}$, where '$\underline{Fabc}$'

is the term-by-term translation of '*Fabc*' into the metalanguage. In case A is a logically complex sentence, $h(A)$ is defined recursively in terms of the vectors assigned to the subformulas of A. Thus to each sentence A there is assigned a vector $h(A)$ as its semantic value; the Appendix sets out in detail how this is to be done.

The semantics assigns to each predicate calculus sentence A a fact $\langle h(A) \rangle$ that A pictures. If the semantic theory is correct, then the sentence A and the statement that there exists the fact $\langle h(A) \rangle$ will be equivalent, since both will represent the existence of the same fact. So if the semantic theory is correct, it will entail every instance of the following schema:

Adequacy: $\langle h(A) \rangle$ exists $\leftrightarrow$ $\underline{A}$

The instances of this schema are obtained by putting the name of a sentence in place of A, and the sentence itself in place of $\underline{A}$. This is the analogue, for a theory that does not give a central role to truth, of Tarski's Adequacy Condition. In the Appendix it is proved that the picture–theory semantics, together with the axioms of fact existence, do indeed entail every instance of this schema.

Suppose a picture–theory semantics failed the adequacy condition, so that for some sentence A of the language, the semantics fails to entail that $\langle h(A) \rangle$ exists if and only if $\underline{A}$. Then the semantic theory is definitely unsatisfactory. Perhaps the theory is just mistaken about which fact A pictures. But there is also the possibility that the theory does not itself have the resources to describe the fact that A states. For example, if our background ontology had not included the arrangements as the referents of variable lists, and as potential constituents of facts, we would not have been able to give the correct constituents for the fact pictured by '$(\exists x)(\forall y)(Lyx)$'. In that case the semantic theory would not have been adequate to the expressive power of predicate calculus, since it could not have dealt with the semantics of multiple generality.

Conversely, if a semantic theory is proved to meet its appropriate adequacy condition, we can be confident that the entities presupposed in the background metaphysics of the semantic theory do provide an adequate basis for any possibility the language can describe. Therefore the adequacy theorem for the picture–theory semantics allows us to feel more confident that the background metaphysics of particulars, universals, facts and multigrade properties is indeed a satisfactory foundation for the theory of representation.

Although the picture-theory semantics given here conforms to an analogue of Tarski's Adequacy Condition, it is very different from the sort of semantics given by Tarski. For Tarski subscribed to Reism, the metaphysical doctrine that only individuals exist; he therefore wished to dispense with the entire apparatus of metaphysical Realism. Tarski did believe in the existence of sets, which are permissible under Reism, for a set is metaphysically an individual. Since Tarski's ontology included no non-individuals, he was not in a position to construct a picture-theory semantics. Nor could he say that the function of language is to classify things, for lacking universals he had no way of distinguishing the natural classes from classes generally; he could offer no substantive account of predication, since he had no explanation to offer of why assigning things to classes serves any useful purpose. Since his ontology admitted neither facts to picture, nor universals to attribute, Tarski had little choice but to take *truth* as the central primitive concept in semantics; in this he has been followed by many contemporary authors.

In the context of Tarski's metaphysical Reism, there is of course no such property as truth, since Reism denies that there are any properties. However, Reism allows that there is such a thing as the set of true sentences. Tarski held that we can define this set by the following schema:

Disquotational Truth Schema A is true if and only if *A*

Tarski argued that this schema is sufficient to define the set of true sentences. For example, it entails that 'snow is white' is a member of the set of true sentences, if snow is white. Since snow is white, it follows that 'snow is white' is a member of the set. Thus the schema, together with the empirical facts, determines for each sentence whether it is in the set; since a set is determined by its members, it follows that the schema defines the set.

A drawback of the Disquotational Truth Schema as a 'definition' of truth, however, is that it has infinitely many substitution instances, so that we are not actually able to state the definition. It would not help if the definition were stated for us by a helpful infinite being; we should not be able to comprehend the statement. What finite beings would like is a finitely stateable definition; Tarski provided the next best thing, a definition by recursion on the syntactic complexity of sentences. In order to deal with sentences containing quantifiers, it is technically easier to carry through the definition not by a direct recursion on truth, but instead to use the concept of satisfaction of a formula by an (infinite) sequence s of objects from the domain. Truth is then defined in terms of satisfaction: A is true if and only if every sequence s satisfies A. For 'formalised' languages, Tarski's definitions of satisfaction and truth jointly entail each instance of the Disquotational Truth Schema, thus satisfying the adequacy condition.

In Tarski's theory, the link with the Disquotational Truth Schema makes *satisfaction* a concept of semantics proper. By means of the concept of satisfaction, he appears to finesse all talk of properties, facts and thoughts. For example, he is able to side-step the question of referents for the logical constants, without Wittgenstein's psychologism, by giving recursive clauses for them:

s satisfies $\neg A$ iff s does not satisfy A;

s satisfies $A \wedge B$ iff s satisfies A and s satisfies B;

s satisfies $(\forall v_i)A$ iff every sequence that differs from s at most in the ith place satisfies A.

In the interests of a picture theory of atomic sentences, Wittgenstein had retained at least facts in his ontology, and also universals, or at any rate 'objects' with differing 'logical forms' (Wittgenstein 1961b: 7–11, §§201–20141). But Tarski uses satisfaction to dispense with facts, and with universals too. Whereas a metaphysical Realist will say that 'is wise' refers to the universal *wisdom*, Tarski avoids such ontological commitment by instead giving the semantic 'axiom' for 'wise' in terms of satisfaction:

s satisfies 'x_i is wise' iff the ith element of s is wise.

Is a Tarskian approach the right way to do semantics? Satisfaction is supposed to be a relation between sequences and formulas; since Tarski is a Reist, what he means by 'relation' is not a universal, but a set of ordered pairs. So 'satisfies' has as its extension a set of ordered pairs of sequences and formulas. Tarski's problem, as he saw it, was to provide a recursive definition of this set, in such a way as to conform to the adequacy condition of entailing every instance of the Disquotational Truth Schema. This problem is indeed elegantly solved by his recursive definition of satisfaction. But although the definition takes us to a set, it does not follow that it takes us to a unitary kind, i.e., to a set unified by a property that is shared by its members, and which is of explanatory or theoretical significance in the science of semantics. Given the language, and given our knowledge of what its sentences mean, we do arrive at a correct mathematical characterisation of the set that is the extension of 'satisfies'; but it is unclear how this does anything to assist our scientific understanding of how language works.

A Tarskian semantics makes no claim to offer a substantive philosophical account of the nature of language. In this respect it is less ambitious than a picture theory. For a picture-theory semantics sets itself the task of identifying, for each sentence, the fact which the sentence pictures. The theory of facts is a substantive metaphysical theory: the theory of picturing belongs to the theory of thought, a substantive account of which can be hoped for from the philosophy of mind. Thus a picture-theory semantics gives, or at any rate has the potential to give, a substantive philosophical theory of how language works. In contrast, a Tarskian theory sheds little light on the nature of language. A symptom of this is the fact that Tarskian 'truth' has to be defined afresh for each new language we study: for example, a knowledge of the extension of 'true-in-English' is of no help in determining the extension of 'true-in-French'. Tarski has shown us how to define, for every language, its set of true sentences, but he has certainly not shown us how to define truth. To define a predicate, one must state a condition, such that if anything x satisfies the condition, then x falls under the predicate; for example, one defines 'bachelor' by saying that if x is an unmarried man, then x is a bachelor. Tarski does not do this with respect to the predicate 'true'. Certainly for every x he states a condition such that if x satisfies that condition, then x is true; but he does not state a condition, such that for every x, if x satisfies the condition then x is true. Tarski does not give us the same condition for every x; so he does not tell us what the true sentences have in common, and therefore he does not define truth.

The only constraint Tarski allows on the definition of 'is true' is that it must entail every instance of the Disquotational Truth Schema. Can this one constraint really be enough on its own to tell us all there is to tell about the essence of truth? That seems scarcely credible—after all, the Disquotational Truth Schema is not even a correct schema, for it has instances that are not true, as the Liar paradox shows. The Liar Sentence is:

(L) L is false.

Taking 'L is false' as a substitution instance of the Disquotational Truth Schema, we obtain:

'L is false' is true $\leftrightarrow$ L is false.

By inspection we see that $L = $ 'L is false.' So:

L is true $\leftrightarrow$ L is false.

But that is absurd, so at least one instance of the Disquotational Truth Schema is not true. But once we have found one exception to the schema, we can find infinitely many, e.g.:

(L^*) snow is white and L^* is false.

A schema with infinitely many untrue instances cannot be a sound foundation for semantic theory.

Obviously if anything is to be rescued from Tarski's approach to semantics, something must be done to block all these counterinstances. But it is far from obvious what to do. Tarski has deliberately deprived himself of all guidance on the nature of language from metaphysics and the philosophy of mind. He has chosen to rely solely and entirely upon the Disquotational Truth Schema in building an account of truth. But the Disquotational Truth Schema is an incorrect schema, so Tarski's account of truth would appear to be without resource.

In fact Tarski himself was quite relaxed about this difficulty. It arises, he said, because a natural language is 'semantically closed', i.e., it contains 'semantic terms' such as the term 'true' (Tarski 1944: 348, §8). He thought a concept of truth for 'formalised languages', from which semantic terms have been excluded, is all that we need. We can give an account of truth for the formalised language, which is the only language we need for the purposes of science. Those parts of a natural language that lie outside the domain of the formalised language are of no concern to scientific semantics and cannot be used to make statements that are true or false in the strict sense, according to Tarski.

But what are the 'semantic terms'? If they are defined by their ability to generate paradoxical counterexamples to the Disquotational Truth Schema, then they will include not only 'truth', but also 'knowledge' and 'necessity', which are both truth-entailing. Presumably if the paradox of the Liar makes 'truth' a semantic term, then the paradox of the Knower makes 'knowledge' a semantic term, and Montague's necessity paradox makes 'necessary' a semantic term. But in that case nothing we can say about truth, knowledge or necessity comes within the part of language whose sentences are strictly speaking true or false. Few philosophical beliefs can be expressed without the use of any of these three concepts; it would follow that most philosophical beliefs are not true, and not false either. Thus if we follow Tarski in adhering to the Disquotational Truth Schema we shall be forced to say that philosophy is not a fit topic for rational inquiry, since there can be no question of philosophical beliefs being true (McGee 1991: 78–9). But since it was a philosophical argument that led us to accept the Disquotational Truth Schema in the first place, Tarski's whole programme appears self-defeating. A better policy is to reject the Disquotational Truth Schema, and to rely instead on some more substantive account of semantics.

Defenders of the Tarskian approach may reply with a *tu quoque*. Are not the semantic paradoxes a difficulty for every theory, substantive or not? For example, Frege's is a substantive semantics, but it only avoids semantic paradox by imposing a theory of levels. This forbids a property being predicated of another property at the same level; thus it rules out as not well-formed a formula such as '$F(F)$'. That makes it impossible—nonsense—to attempt to give the following definition of the property 'heterological':

$$\text{heterological } (F) =_{df} \neg F(F)$$

The property *heterological* is paradoxical: for if heterological is heterological, it follows that it is not heterological, and *vice versa*. Therefore it would be good to be able to block the above definition. But the theory of levels is not a satisfactory way to block it, for it is impossible to state the theory of levels without making statements that are 'nonsense' according to the theory of levels. For example, one would like to say that the concept *horse* is a first-level concept, but that would transgress against the theory of levels; Frege was therefore obliged to say, self-defeatingly, that because the concept *horse* is a concept, one cannot say it is a concept (Frege 1892a).

Russell's difficulties with the paradoxes led him to the Theory of Types (1908), which pronounces the paradoxical sentences to be 'nonsense' since they contravene type restrictions. The Theory of Types rules out the Russell set of all non-self-members. There is no paradox, according to the Theory of Types, for '$x \in y$' is 'nonsense' unless x is of lower type than y. Therefore we cannot even ask the question whether a set is a member of itself, or whether a function applies to itself. But this too is not a satisfactory way to block paradox, for again the difficulty is that any attempt to state the theory violates the theory's own type restrictions—any statement of the Theory of Types is nonsense, according to the Theory of Types. Graham Priest puts the difficulty as follows:

[T]he very theory of orders cannot be explained without quantifying over functions, and hence violating it. For to explain it, one has to express the fact that *every propositional function* has a determinate order. Hence, the theory is self-refuting. (Priest 1995: 152, original emphasis)

Wittgenstein was indeed willing to embrace this self-defeat; his picture theory incorporates level restrictions which it is necessary to break in order to state his theory; accordingly he ended the *Tractatus* by saying that anyone who understood him would eventually recognise his propositions as nonsensical. Thus it is perfectly true that the paradoxes present great difficulty for many semantic theories, and not just Tarski's.

Is the version of the picture theory presented in this chapter subject to semantic paradox? The theory has no analogue of Frege's theory of levels, and it allows universals to be applied to universals; for example, it asserts that although it is false that *red* is red, still it is not 'nonsense'. Nor has the theory any analogue of the Theory of Types; it allows a type-free version of predicate calculus. It therefore completely lacks the standard means of defence against paradox. But in their place it has two other lines of defence. The first is ontological circumspection; the second is the use of vector logic, on its modest, schematic, interpretation.

The first line of defence is ontological circumspection. Set theoretic paradoxes such as Russell's do not trouble the present theory, since it is silent about what sets, if any, exist. The Theory of Types is needed in set theory only if one subscribes to the false abstraction principle that for every description of some things, there exists a set that has exactly those things as its members. Better to follow Zermelo and reject this principle; then we can deny the existence of the Russell set of non-self-members, without having to add that this very denial is 'nonsense'. Circumspection also helps with the heterological paradox and the Liar paradox. The present theory is silent about which universals exist, leaving that as a matter for scientific inquiry. Devices such as the Theory of Levels are needed only if one accepts the false abstraction principle that for every predicate, there is a universal instantiated by all and only those things that satisfy the predicate. Better to follow Plato and reject this principle. Then nothing in the theory entails that 'heterological' stands for a universal: quite the contrary—we can take the 'heterological' paradox as proof that there is no such universal. The theory can allow the existence of a Russellian property corresponding to the definition of 'heterological'; but this Russellian property are a vector, which is to say that they are several things referred to in order. Hence they cannot serve as argument to a unary property, and do not give rise to paradox.

Since we are rejecting the abstraction principle that every meaningful predicate stands for a universal, it is also open to us to argue that 'true' as applied to sentences stands for no universal; for if it did, then on the principles of the picture theory, the Liar paradox would be unavoidable. For on the picture theory, we say that truth is correspondence with fact, so we assert the following principle (writing **E** for existence):

Correspondence Principle: $(\forall \theta)(\forall A)(h(A) = \theta \rightarrow (\mathrm{truc}(A) \leftrightarrow \mathbf{E}(\theta)))$

So consider this version of the Liar sentence:

(L) L is not true

Assume, for *reductio*, that 'true' expresses a universal. Then presumably L expresses the Russellian proposition whose constituents are:

$h(L) = \langle \neg, true, L \rangle$

Assume L is true. Then by the Correspondence Principle, $\langle \neg, true, L\rangle$exists. By the Adequacy Condition, for any A, $h(A)$ exists if and only if $\underline{A}$. So since $\langle \neg, true, L\rangle$exists, we deduce that L is not true. But if L is not true, then by the Correspondence Principle again, $\langle h(L)\rangle = \langle \neg, true, L\rangle$does not exist. So by the meaning of *negation*, $\langle true, L\rangle$ exists. So L is true after all. We have arrived at a contradiction, which we can regard as a proof by *reductio ad absurdum* that 'true' does not stand for a universal.

Still, even if 'true' does not stand for a universal, our picture theory may succumb to paradox in some other way. According to the theory, sentences are false in virtue of expressing false propositions. So perhaps a more dangerous Liar sentence would be the following:

(L1) $(\exists x)(x$ is the proposition expressed by $L1$, and x is false)

This is where the present theory's second line of defence comes into operation, namely its use of vector logic. In $(L1)$ we have ordinary objectual quantification, in which the variables range over single entities. But on the present theory Russellian propositions are not single entities: they are vectors, so the Liar cannot be expressed as $(L1)$. But it cannot be expressed with the vector quantifier either:

(L2) $(\exists\theta)(\theta$ are the Russellian proposition expressed by $L2$, and θ are false)

This is not permitted on the schematic interpretation of the vector quantifier, which disallows existential quantification over vectors. Thus vector logic provides additional protection against the Liar paradox.

Is the following a version of the Liar that might trouble the picture theory?

(L3) $L3$ does not correspond with fact

The Correspondence Principle says:

$$(\forall\theta)(\forall A)(h(A) = \theta \rightarrow (\text{true}(A) \leftrightarrow \mathbf{E}\langle\theta\rangle))$$

Then we might understand $(L3)$ as wishing to express the following: 'For any θ, if θ are the Russellian proposition expressed by this very sentence, then no fact has θ as its constituents.' This might be symbolised as:

(L4) $(\forall\theta)(h(L4) = \theta \rightarrow \neg\mathbf{E}\langle\theta\rangle)$

But here again the vector logic stops the paradox—$(L4)$ is not a Liar sentence either. The reason is that, on the schematic interpretation of the vector quantifier, $(L4)$ is not a single sentence at all, but rather a schema for all the many sentences of the following form:

(L4n)$(\forall x_1) \dots (\forall x_n)(h(L4n) = (x_1, \dots, x_n) \rightarrow \neg\mathbf{E}\langle x_1, \dots, x_n\rangle)$

Each substitution instance $(L4n)$ of the schema $(L4)$ receives an interpretation $h(L4n)$, and none of the $h(L4n)$ are paradoxical. But $(L4)$ itself, being infinitely many sentences, does not receive an interpretation $h(L4)$. Therefore a sentence $(L4)$ with the proposed paradoxical properties does not in fact exist.

It may be objected that the present version of the picture theory buys its immunity from paradox at the price of having no account to offer of the nature of truth. The theory denies that truth is a universal; but the predicate 'true' is perfectly meaningful, and no semantic theory can be regarded as satisfactory if it does not have anything to say about what 'true' means. And certainly the picture theory slogan that 'truth is correspondence to fact' cannot be the whole of the theory of truth. For any sentence that does not contain 'true' or kindred terms the Correspondence Principle says:

$$(\forall\theta)(\forall A)(h(A) = \theta \rightarrow (\text{true}(A) \leftrightarrow \mathbf{E}\langle\theta\rangle))$$

But being an infinite schema, this cannot be turned into an explicit definition of truth. Thus if truth is not a universal, we have no guidance from the picture theory as to the constituents of the Russellian proposition expressed by 'true(A)'.

The Correspondence Principle tells only part of the truth about truth. As was noted earlier, the application of the predicate 'true' to a sentence we can describe but not state is one of its most important uses. For example, suppose I tell you that everything S will tell you is true. S tells you that not everything S^* will tell you is true. S^* tells you that $2 + 2 = 4$, and that the earth is flat. Because you trust me and are good at arithmetic, you deduce that the earth is not flat. This sort of reasoning is a normal part of our everyday use of the word 'true'. The Correspondence Principle does nothing to explain the correctness of this reasoning.

It is possible to extend the theory of truth beyond the Correspondence Principle, to cover the use of 'true' to endorse described sentences and sets of sentences, for example by the methods of Kripke (1975) and Gupta (1982). Their axiom systems are adequate to capture the pattern of most of our actual reasoning about truth. But each of these axiom systems leaves the truth conditions of some sentences unsettled; we call such sentences *ungrounded*. The systems never assign them a truth-value, because in the case of ungrounded sentences the rules for determining truth-value do not issue in a definite answer but lead round in a circle, or generate an infinitely descending chain.

It may seem that such a theory of truth still harbours paradox, because of the Strengthened Liar. This is the sentence:

(L6)   *L6* is false or ungrounded.

According to groundedness theory, (L6) is ungrounded. Therefore ground-edness theory entails that (L6) is false or ungrounded. But that (L6) is false or ungrounded is exactly what (L6) asserts, so (L6) would appear to be true after all. Therefore groundedness theory entails both that (L6) is true, and that (L6) is ungrounded, i.e., not true. But this conclusion can be resisted by observing that strictly speaking a theory of truth is given not for sentence types, but only for sentence tokens. The theory of groundedness can say that the first token of (L6) above is ungrounded, because it refers to itself. The second token, which occurs in the commentary on the first token, is not ungrounded but true, since it refers to the first token and not to itself. Since it is only the second token that is asserted by groundedness theory, we can reject the argument that the theory issues in a contradiction. Thus there is still no paradox.

It remains however that we are forced to say that ungrounded sentences are neither in the extension, nor in the anti-extension, of 'true': from which it follows that truth is not a property. This conclusion would be disastrous if we had been supposing that truth is the fundamental property upon which the theory of representation must be built. But it is possible to found the theory of representation not on the supposed property of truth, but instead on the genuine relations of knowledge and combination in a fact. To do so will be the project of the next chapter. With knowledge and combination available, truth itself need play no foundational role in the theory of thought and language. We can be perfectly comfortable with the idea that the predicate 'is true' does not after all attribute a property: in our account of truth, we can follow Strawson (1950) and treat 'is true' pragmatically, as a mere conversational device of endorsement. The predicate 'is true' is convenient in our reasoning about people's propositional attitudes, and is indeed indispensable in the practical business of life, but the fact that it is unsuited to a foundational role in semantics need cause us no alarm.

Appendix: Adequacy of the Semantics

Notation

(i) '$\langle \theta \rangle$' for 'the fact whose constituents are θ'.

(ii) '$\mathbf{E}(\theta)$' for '$\langle \theta \rangle$ exists', i.e. $(\exists p)(p \cdot \theta)$.

(iii) In the proofs that follow we shall be working in a semi-formal metalanguage. If σ is any symbol of the object language, $\underline{\sigma}$ is the corresponding symbol of the metalanguage that directly translates it. If R^n is an n-adic predicate of the object language, I shall use the symbol '$\underline{R}^n$' for two purposes: first, as a predicate, to attribute the property $\underline{R}^n$, and secondly as a name, to name the property $\underline{R}^n$. Thus in the metalanguage sentence '$\underline{R}^n x_1 \ldots x_n$' the symbol '$\underline{R}^n$' is occurring as a metalanguage predicate, but in '$\mathbf{E}\langle\underline{R}^n, x_1, \ldots, x_n\rangle$' it is occurring as a metalanguage name of the property $\underline{R}^n$. (The two purposes are differentiated lexically in English, e.g., 'is wise' and *wisdom*.)

(iv) If α is a variable, then '$A[\alpha|\beta]$' is the formula that comes from A by replacing each free occurrence of α by β. If α is a constant, then '$A[\alpha|\beta]$' is the formula that comes from A by replacing each occurrence of α by β.

(v) If θ and ϕ are vectors, $\theta = (x_1, \ldots, x_m)$, $\phi = (y_1, \ldots, y_n)$, then (θ, ϕ) is the vector $(x_1, \ldots, x_m, y_1, \ldots, y_n)$.

(vi) '0' is the empty vector name, i.e., it is a vector name that fails to name anything. N.B. it is not the name of 'the empty vector' (there is no such thing).

(vii) The symbols 'x_1', x_2'..., 'x_m', ..., etc., are reserved as metalanguage variables.

(Metaphysical) Axioms of Fact Existence and Identity

Identity   Different constituents, different fact; same constituents, same fact.

$(Axiom\ 1)\ (p_1 \cdot \theta_1 \wedge p_2 \cdot \theta_2) \rightarrow (p_1 = p_2 \leftrightarrow \theta_1 = \theta_2)$

Negation   Negation is the multigrade relation. $\neg$. It obeys the following two axioms:

(Axiom 2a: Double Negation) $\mathbf{E}\langle\theta\rangle \leftrightarrow \mathbf{E}\langle\neg, \neg, \theta\rangle$
(Axiom 2b: Contradiction) $\neg(\mathbf{E}\langle\theta\rangle \wedge \mathbf{E}\langle\neg, \theta\rangle)$

Definition of Arity   For each n we define arity n by the following definition schema:

θ have arity $n =_{df} (\forall x_1) \ldots (\forall x_n)(\mathbf{E}\langle\theta x_1, \ldots, x_n\rangle \vee \mathbf{E}\langle\neg, \theta, x_1, \ldots, x_n\rangle)$

Definition of Russellian Property, Russellian Proposition

θ are a *Russellian property of arity n* $=_{df}$ θ have arity n.
θ are a *Russellian proposition* $=_{df}$ θ have arity zero.

Law of Excluded Middle   If θ are a Russellian proposition, then by axioms (2a) and (2b):

(*Law of Excluded Middle*) $\mathbf{E}\langle\theta\rangle \leftrightarrow \neg\mathbf{E}\langle\neg, \theta\rangle$

Definition of Universal of Arity n

(A single entity) x is a *universal of arity n* $=_{df}$ x has arity n.

Definition of Property of Arity n

R^n is a *property of arity n* $=_{df}$ $\underline{R}^n$ is a universal of arity n, or $\underline{R}^n$ are a Russellian property of arity n.

Arrangement   Let $\pi = (\pi(1), \dots, \pi(n))$ be a vector of numbers such that for each i, $1 \leq \pi(i) \leq k$. Then the *arrangement* $\underline{\Pi}$ *corresponding to* π is a multigrade relation such that $\underline{\Pi}(\phi)$ if $\phi = (\theta, x_1, \dots, x_k)$ and the fact $\langle\theta, x_{\pi(1)}, \dots, x_{\pi(n)}\rangle$ exists.

(*Axiom 3*) $\mathbf{E}\langle\underline{\Pi}, \theta, x_1, \dots, x_k\rangle \leftrightarrow \mathbf{E}\langle\theta, x_{\pi(1)}, \dots, x_{\pi(n)}\rangle$

Conjunction   *Conjunction* is a multigrade relation $\underline{\wedge}$ such that $\underline{\wedge}(\theta)$ iff $\theta = \langle\theta_1, \theta_2, \xi_1, \xi_2\rangle$ and the fact $\langle\theta_1, \xi_1\rangle$ exists and the fact $\langle\theta_2, \xi_2\rangle$ exists.

(*Axiom 4*) $\mathbf{E}\langle\underline{\wedge}, \theta_1, \theta_2, \xi_1, \xi_2\rangle \leftrightarrow (\mathbf{E}\langle\theta_1, \xi_1\rangle \wedge \mathbf{E}\langle\theta_2, \xi_2\rangle)$

(Note that this definition is slightly more complex than that given in section 2.7, to allow for the interaction of conjunction and quantification in what follows.)

Generality   *Generality* is a multigrade relation $\underline{\forall}$ such that $\underline{\forall}(\theta)$ if for every x, the fact $\langle\theta, x\rangle$ exists.

(*Axiom 5*) $\mathbf{E}\langle\underline{\forall}, \theta\rangle \leftrightarrow (\forall x)(\mathbf{E}\langle\theta, x\rangle)$

Axiom Schema of Atomic Facts   Let R^n be any n-adic predicate of the object language, and let $\underline{R}^n$ be the property it attributes. Then:

(Axiom 6) $\mathbf{E}\langle \underline{R}^n, x_1, \dots, x_n\rangle \leftrightarrow \underline{R}^n x_1 \dots x_n$

Definition of Interpretation

Let L be a standard predicate-calculus language. The interpretation assigns to each individual constant c_i of L the entity $\underline{c}_i$, and to each predicate letter R^n of L the property $\underline{R}^n$. To each wff A of L the interpretation assigns a pair of vectors $h(A)$ and $t(A)$: $h(A)$ is a vector of entities of any sort; $t(A)$ is a vector of variables of the language L, i.e., it is a vector of *symbols*. We define $h(A)$ and $t(A)$ recursively. First we treat the special case that A contains no individual constants.

(I0) A is Atomic   Let $A = R^n v_1 \dots v_n$. Let the free variables of A be $v_{a(1)}, \dots, v_{a(k)}$. Define π as follows: if $v_i = v_{a(j)}$ then $\pi(i) = j$. Let $\underline{\Pi}$ be the arrangement corresponding to π. Then:

$$h(A) = (\underline{\Pi}, \underline{R}^n)$$
$$t(A) = (v_{a(1)}, \dots, v_{a(k)})$$

(I1) A is a Negation   Let $A = \neg B$. Define:

$$h(A) = (\underline{\neg}, h(B))$$
$$t(A) = t(B)$$

(I2) A is a Conjunction   Let $A = B \wedge C$. Let the free variables of A be $v_{a(1)}, \dots, v_{a(k)}$. If $t(B) = (v_{\beta(1)}, \dots, v_{\beta(m)})$, and $t(C) = (v_{\gamma(1)}, \dots, v_{\gamma(n)})$, define π as follows. For $1 \leq i \leq m$, if $v_{\beta(i)} = v_{a(j)}$, then $\pi(i) = j$; for $(m+1) \leq i \leq (m+n)$, if $v_{\gamma(i-m)} = v_{a(j)}$, then $\pi(i) = j$. Let $\underline{\Pi}$ be the arrangement corresponding to π. Then define:

$$h(A) = (\underline{\Pi}, \underline{\wedge}, q(B), q(C))$$
$$t(A) = (v_{a(1)}, \dots, v_{a(k)}).$$

(I3) A is a Quantification   Let $A = (\forall v_j)B$. Let the free variables of A be $v_{a(1)}, \dots, v_{a(k)}$. If $t(B) = (v_{\beta(1)}, \dots, v_{\beta(k+1)})$, define m by $v_{\beta(m)} = v_j$. Define $\pi(i)$ as follows: if $i = m$, then $\pi(i) = k+1$; if $i = k+1$ then $\pi(i) = m$; otherwise $\pi(i) = i$.
Let $\underline{\Pi}$ be the arrangement corresponding to π. Then define:

$$h(A) = (\underline{\forall}, \underline{\Pi}, q(B))$$

$$t(A) = (v_{\beta(\pi(1))}, \ldots v_{\beta(\pi(k))}) = (v_{a(1)}, \ldots, v_{a(k)}).$$

(I4) A Contains Individual Constants   Suppose $c_1, \ldots, c_m$ are the individual constants of A, and that $v_{a(1)}, \ldots, v_{a(k)}$ are the free variables of A. Let $u_{a(1)}, \ldots, u_{a(m)}$ be fresh variables, and for $1 \leq i \leq k$, let $u_{a(m+i)} = v_{a(i)}$. Let $A^* = A[c_1|u_{a(1)}, \ldots, c_m|u_{a(m)}]$. Then define:

$$h(A) = (h(A^*), \underline{c}_1, \ldots, \underline{c}_m)$$
$$t(A) = (\underline{v}_{a(1)}, \ldots, v_{a(k)})$$

Proof of the Adequacy Theorem

We can now define *satisfaction* and *truth* on the interpretation.

Satisfaction

$$\theta \text{ satisfy } A =_{df} \mathbf{E}\langle h(A), \theta \rangle$$

Truth-definition

$$A \text{ is } true =_{df} 0 \text{ satisfy } A.$$

A is true if there is a fact that combines in order the vector $(h(A), 0)$, i.e. if $(\exists p)(p \cdot h(A))$.

To prove that the above truth-theory meets Tarski's Adequacy Condition, we first prove the following:

Lemma: The above truth theory entails every instance of

$$(x_1, \ldots, x_k) \text{ satisfy } A \leftrightarrow \underline{A}\, [\underline{v}_{a(1)}|x_1, \ldots, \underline{v}_{a(k)}|x_k]$$

where $\underline{A}$ is the direct symbol-by-symbol translation of A into the metalanguage, and $(v_{a(1)}, \ldots, v_{a(k)}) = t(A)$.

Proof: We may assume that the semi-formal metalanguage in which we are working is given its interpretation by clauses exactly corresponding to the clauses (I0) - (I4) we gave for the object language. We first prove by induction the special case where A contains no individual constants.

Case 0: A is Atomic   Let $A = R^n v_1 \ldots v_n$. If the free variables of A are $v_{a(1)}, \ldots, v_{a(k)}$, define π and Π as in (I0). Then by (I0), $h(A) = (\underline{\Pi}, \underline{R}^n)$ and $t(A) = (v_{a(1)} \ldots v_{a(k)})$. So:

$(x_1, \ldots, x_k)$ satisfy A

$\leftrightarrow \mathbf{E}\langle h(A), x_1, \ldots, x_k\rangle$

$\leftrightarrow \mathbf{E}\langle \underline{\Pi}, \underline{R}^n, x_1, \ldots, x_k\rangle$

$\leftrightarrow \mathbf{E}\langle \underline{R}^n, x_{\pi(1)}, \ldots, x_{\pi(n)}\rangle$ (Axiom 3)

$\leftrightarrow \underline{R}^n x_{\pi(1)} \ldots x_{\pi(n)}$ (Axiom 6)

Now $\underline{R}^n x_{\pi(1)} \ldots x_{\pi(n)}$ comes from $\underline{A}$ by replacing each $\underline{v}_i$ with $x_{\pi(i)}$. But for each i, $1 \leq i \leq n$, $\underline{v}_i = v_{a(\pi(i))}$, by definition of π. So:

$$\underline{R}^n x_{\pi(1)} \ldots x_{\pi(n)}$$
$$= \underline{A}[\underline{v}_{a(\pi(1))}|x_{\pi(1)}, \ldots, \underline{v}_{a(\pi(n))}|x_{\pi(n)}]$$
$$= \underline{A}[\underline{v}_{a(1)}|x_1, \ldots, \underline{v}_{a(k)}|x_k], \text{ since each } j \text{ is some } \pi(i), 1 \leq j \leq k.$$

So $(x_1, \ldots, x_k)$ satisfy $A \leftrightarrow \underline{A}[\underline{v}_{a(1)}|x_1, \ldots, \underline{v}_{a(k)}|x_k]$, as required. Now assume the result proved for formulas with N or fewer logical operators, and suppose A has $(N+1)$ logical operators.

Case 1: A is a Negation   Let $A = \neg B$. Then by (I1), $h(A) = \langle \underline{\neg}, h(B)\rangle$, and $t(A) = (v_{a(1)}, \ldots, v_{a(k)}) = (v_{\beta(1)}, \ldots, v_{\beta(k)}) = t(B)$. So:

$(x_1, \ldots, x_k)$ satisfy A

$\leftrightarrow \mathbf{E}\langle h(A), x_1, \ldots, x_k\rangle$

$\leftrightarrow \mathbf{E}\langle \underline{\neg}, h(B), x_1, \ldots, x_k\rangle$

$\leftrightarrow \neg\mathbf{E}\langle(h(B), x_1, \ldots, x_k\rangle$ (Law of Excluded Middle)

$\leftrightarrow \neg(\underline{B}(v_{\beta(1)}|x_1, \ldots v_{\beta(k)}|x_k))$ (Induction Hypothesis)

$\leftrightarrow \underline{A}[\underline{v}_{a(1)}|x_1, \ldots, \underline{v}_{a(k)}|x_k]$

Case 2: A is a Conjunction   Let $A = B \wedge C$. Define π, $\underline{\Pi}$, m and n as in (I2). Then by (I2), $h(A) = (\underline{\Pi}, \underline{\wedge}, h(B), h(C))$ and $t(A) = (v_{a(1)}, \ldots, v_{a(k)})$. So:

$(x_1, \ldots, x_k)$ satisfy A

$\leftrightarrow \mathbf{E}\langle h(A), x_1, \ldots, x_k\rangle$

$\leftrightarrow \mathbf{E}\langle \underline{\Pi}, \underline{\wedge}, h(B), h(C),$
   $x_1, \ldots, x_k\rangle$

$\leftrightarrow \mathbf{E}\langle \underline{\wedge}, h(B), h(C), x_{\pi(1)}, \ldots, x_{\pi(n)}\rangle$

$\leftrightarrow \mathbf{E}\langle h(B), x_{\pi(1)}, \ldots, x_{\pi(m)}\rangle \wedge \mathbf{E}\langle h(C), x_{\pi(m+1)}, \ldots, x_{\pi(m+n)}\rangle$
   (Axiom 4)

$\leftrightarrow ((x_{\pi(1)}, \ldots, x_{\pi(m)}) \text{ satisfy } B) \wedge ((x_{\pi(m+1)}, \ldots, x_{\pi(m+n)}) \text{ satisfy } C)$

$\leftrightarrow \underline{B}[\underline{v}_{\beta(1)}|x_{\pi(1)}, \ldots, \underline{v}_{\beta(m)}|x_{\pi(m)}] \wedge \underline{C}[\underline{v}_{\gamma(1)}|x_{\pi(m+1)}, \ldots, \underline{v}_{\gamma(n)}|x_{\pi(m+n)}]$

(Induction Hypothesis)

Now for each i, $1 \leq i \leq m$, we have $\underline{v}_{\beta(i)} = \underline{v}_{a(\pi(i))}$. So:

$\underline{B}[\underline{v}_{\beta(1)}|x_{\pi(1)},\ldots, \underline{v}_{\beta(m)}|x_{\pi(m)}]$
$= \underline{B}[\underline{v}_{a(\pi(1))}|x_{\pi(1)},\ldots, \underline{v}_{a(\pi(m))}|x_{\pi(m)}]$
$= \underline{B}[\underline{v}_{a(1)}|x_1,\ldots, \underline{v}_{a(k)}|x_k]$, since the free variables of B are included in the free variables of A.

Similarly,

$\underline{C}[\underline{v}_{\gamma(1)}|x_{\pi(m+1)},\ldots, \underline{v}_{\gamma(n)}|x_{\pi(m+n)}] = \underline{C}[\underline{v}_{a(1)}|x_1,\ldots, \underline{v}_{a(k)}|x_k]$.

So:

$(x_1, \ldots ,x_k)$ satisfy A
$\leftrightarrow \underline{B}[v_{a(1)}|x_1,\ldots, v_{a(k)}|x_k] \wedge \underline{C}[v_{a(1)}|x_1,\ldots, v_{a(k)}|x_k]$
$\leftrightarrow \underline{A}[\underline{v}_{a(1)}|x_1,\ldots, \underline{v}_{a(k)}|x_k]$.

Case 3: A is a Generalisation   Let $A = (\forall v_j)B$. Define π, Π and m as in (I4), so $h(A) = (\underline{\forall}, \underline{\Pi}, h(B))$ and $t(A) = (v_{\beta(\pi(1))},\ldots, v_{\beta(\pi(k))}) = (v_{a(1)},\ldots, v_{a(k)})$. Then:

$(x_1, \ldots ,x_k)$ satisfy A
$\leftrightarrow \mathbf{E}\langle h(A), x_1, \ldots ,x_k\rangle$
$\leftrightarrow \mathbf{E}\langle \underline{\forall}, \underline{\Pi}, h(B), x_1, \ldots ,x_k\rangle$
$\leftrightarrow (\forall x_{k+1})(\mathbf{E}\langle \underline{\Pi}, h(B), x_1, \ldots ,x_k, x_{k+1}\rangle)$
$\leftrightarrow (\forall x_{k+1})(\mathbf{E}\langle h(B), x_{\pi(1)}, \ldots, x_{\pi(k)}, x_{\pi(k+1)}\rangle)$
$\leftrightarrow (\forall x_{k+1})((x_{\pi(1)},\ldots, x_{\pi(k)}, x_{\pi(k+1)})$ satisfy $B)$
$\leftrightarrow (\forall x_{k+1})(\underline{B}[\underline{v}_{\beta(1)}|x_{\pi(1)},\ldots, \underline{v}_{\beta(k+1)}|x_{\pi(k+1)}])$ (Induction Hypothesis)

For $1 \leq \pi(i) \leq k$, $v_{a(\pi(i))} = v_{\beta(\pi(\pi(i)))} = v_{\beta(i)}$. And when $\pi(i) = k+1$, $i = m$, and $v_{\beta(i)} = v_{\beta(m)} = v_j$. So:

$\underline{B}[\underline{v}_{\beta(1)}|x_{\pi(1)},\ldots, \underline{v}_{\beta(k+1)}|x_{\pi(k+1)}]$
$= \underline{B}[\underline{v}_{a(\pi(1))}|x_{\pi(1)},\ldots, \underline{v}_{a(\pi(k+1))}|x_{\pi(k+1)}, \underline{v}_{\beta(m)}|x_{\pi(m)}]$
$= \underline{B}[\underline{v}_{a(1)}|x_1,\ldots, \underline{v}_{a(k)}|x_k, \underline{v}_j|x_{k+1}]$

So:

$(x_1, \ldots ,x_k)$ satisfy A
$\leftrightarrow (\forall x_{k+1})(\underline{B}[\underline{v}_{a(1)}|x_1,\ldots, \underline{v}_{a(k)}|x_k, \underline{v}_j|x_{k+1}])$

$\leftrightarrow (\forall \ \underline{v}_j)(\underline{B}[\underline{v}_{a(1)}|x_1,\ldots, \ \underline{v}_{a(k)}|x_k, \ \underline{v}_j|\underline{v}_j])$, (changing the metalanguage variable)

$\leftrightarrow (\forall \ \underline{v}_j)(\underline{B}[\underline{v}_{a(1)}|x_1,\ldots, \underline{v}_{a(k)}|x_k])$

$\leftrightarrow \underline{A} \ [\underline{v}_{a(1)}|x_1,\ldots, \underline{v}_{a(k)}|x_k]$

Case 4: A Contains Individual Constants   We have now proved the Lemma for the special case of formulas with no individual constants. Now suppose the constants of A are $c_1, \ldots, c_m$. Define A^* and the $u_{a(i)}$ as in (I4). Then $h(A) = (h(A^*), \underline{c}_1,\ldots, \underline{c}_m), t(A^*) = (u_{a(1)},\ldots, u_{a(m+k)})$ and:

$(x_1, \ldots, x_k)$ satisfy A

$\leftrightarrow \mathbf{E}\langle h(A), x_1, \ldots, x_k\rangle$

$\leftrightarrow \mathbf{E}\langle h(A^*), \underline{c}_1,\ldots, \underline{c}_m, x_1, \ldots, x_k\rangle$

$\leftrightarrow \underline{A}^*[\underline{u}_{a(1)}|\underline{c}_1 \ldots, \underline{u}_{a(m)}|\underline{c}_m, \underline{u}_{a(m+1)}|x_1,\ldots, \underline{u}_{a(m+k)}|x_k]$ (by the special case of the Lemma)

$\leftrightarrow \underline{A}[\underline{u}_{a(m+1)}|x_1,\ldots, \underline{u}_{a(m+k)}|x_k]$

$\leftrightarrow \underline{A}[\underline{v}_{a(1)}|x_1,\ldots, \underline{v}_{a(k)}|x_k]$ □

Adequacy Theorem   To prove that our truth-definition for language L meets Tarski's Adequacy Condition, we must prove the following:

Adequacy theorem: The above truth theory entails every instance of:

A is true $\leftrightarrow \underline{A}$

where A is any sentence, and $\underline{A}$ is the direct symbol-by-symbol translation of A into the metalanguage.

Proof: By our definition, A is true if 0 satisfy A. By the Lemma, for any wff A, the truth theory entails :

$(x_1, \ldots, x_k)$ satisfy $A \leftrightarrow \underline{A}[\underline{v}_{a(1)}|x_1,\ldots, \underline{v}_{a(k)}|x_k]$

If A is a sentence, $\underline{A}$ is the wff that comes from $\underline{A}$ by 'replacing' none of its zero free variables, so we can prove by the methods of the proof of the Lemma that 0 satisfies A iff $\underline{A}$. So the truth theory entails each instance of:

A is true iff $\underline{A}$.

'Variables Explained Away'

We can pass from the predicate calculus language L to a new language L' with no variables as follows. To obtain the class of symbols of L', first delete all variables from L, then add for each π a symbol 'Π' to name the arrangement corresponding to π. Now let A be any sentence of L. By the Adequacy Theorem, A is true if $\langle h(A) \rangle$ exists. Let $h(A)$ be $(x_1, \ldots, x_n)$. For each i, $1 \leq i \leq n$, let a_i be the symbol of L' that names x_i. By concatenating the a_i, we obtain a sentence $A' = a_1 \ldots a_n$ of L' that 'pictures' the fact that is truth-maker for A. The language L' is thus a 'picture-theory' language.

L' contains infinitely many symbols, since for each π it has a symbol Π for the corresponding arrangement. We can replace L' with a language L'' with finitely many symbols, by replacing each Π with an equivalent combination of *self*, *inverse* and *cycle*. Despite its finite vocabulary, however, a language such as L'' could not be an accurate model of human thought. There is a limit to the complexity of the sentences we can parse, so a more realistic model would be simply some finite fragment of L'.

3

Concept and Content

How are contents and concepts related? An answer often given is that a content is composed of the concepts it combines. According to Frege, a content, which he called a Thought, is a complex abstract object whose parts are concepts, which he called (simple) senses. According to Peacocke, concepts are abstract objects that can be 'combined into complex, structured contents'. According to Fodor, a content is a 'sentence' of the 'Language of Thought', and a concept is one of its constituent 'words'. (Frege 1918: 390; Peacocke 1992: 99; Fodor 1998: 25.)

In this Chapter I recommend a different picture. A content is neither an abstract object nor a sentence-like entity. Rather, it is a universal: it is that property of a mental act that is its power of contributing to the getting of knowledge. Similarly, a concept is not an abstract object, nor yet a mental symbol. It too is a universal, a mental property of a mind; the mind's 'grasp' of the concept is just its instantiation of the property which the concept is.

On this account, concept and content are related as follows. A concept is a mental property of a mind, which in cooperation with other such properties confers on its possessor a certain power: namely, the power to think thoughts with a certain range of contents. So whereas Frege and Fodor would say that the concept is part of the content itself, on the present account possession of the concept is rather a part of understanding the content, i.e., it is part of the basis of the ability to think a thought with the given content.

In the right circumstances, thinking a thought can cause knowledge. Therefore epistemology needs a way of classifying thoughts in accordance with the facts they enable us to know. That is what contents do: to assign a content to a thought is to classify it in respect of its Fregean *Erkenntniswert* (1892b: 78), i.e., its 'apprehension value', or value-for-the-getting-of-knowledge. Thus a content is an epistemological property of a thought. We can individuate contents by an epistemological criterion of identity: if

x and y are contents, then $x = y$ if in any course of reasoning substituting a mental act with content x for a mental act of the same type with content y preserves justification—i.e., if it never turns knowledge to ignorance. As well as defining sense, epistemology can define reference. The concepts involved in making a judgement with a given content can be correlated one for one with the constituents of the fact the judgement enables the subject to know; from this the referent of each concept is determined. Thus the theory of knowledge is sufficient to found the theory of reference.

The plan of this Chapter is as follows. In Section 1 I present a theory of mental acts. In Section 2 I suggest that some mental acts are apprehendings, which is to say that they non-mediately cause one to acquire knowledge. In Section 3 I define the content of a mental act by the contribution it makes to apprehending, i.e., to the getting of knowledge. Section 4 defines concepts as powers of the mind to be the subject of mental acts with a certain range of contents. Section 5 defines reference, and deduces Russell's 'Principle of Acquaintance'. Section 6 gives further argument for the Principle of Acquaintance, in the context of the epistemology of definitions. Section 7 notes connections between content, truth and language.

3.1 Mental Acts

A standard account of content, deriving from Frege and Russell, is that contents are the objects of propositional attitudes. On this account, when S believes that A, a relation of *belief* obtains between S and a certain particular, the content κ, which is the content expressed by the sentence A. The logical form of 'S believes that A' is thus Rab, where R is the relation of belief, a is the mental subject, and b is the content κ. Thus contents are simply the particulars in which it is possible to stand in the *believes* relation. The account continues by supposing that there are other propositional attitudes—other psychological relations—in which one might stand to the content κ. For example, one might also stand in the *desire, hope* or *fear* relation to the content κ. According to the analysis, all of these have the same logical form Rab.

A difficulty for the propositional attitude theory is the metaphysics of content: what are these particulars to which one is related by one's beliefs and desires, by one's hopes and by one's fears? On a Fregean conception, a content is an abstract particular outside of space and time. (1918: 363.) But we should prefer, if possible, an account of content that does not require peculiar entities not needed in other areas of metaphysics.

Another difficulty for the propositional attitude theory is that it seems to deal only with mental states, whereas much of our mental life consists of conscious events, or what Geach (1971) calls 'mental acts', such as perceiving, willing and judging, which have content too. The relational analysis *Rab* does not seem the right logical form for reports of such mental acts, for it is too simple. Following Ramsey's suggestion with respect to event reports generally, it seems better to take e.g. '*S* perceives that *A*' as reporting 'the existence of an event of a certain sort'. (Ramsey 1927: 37.) Then instead of taking a content to be a particular to which one stands in a certain mental relation, we can more naturally take it to be a universal: it is a property of a mental act of which one is the subject.

Events

An event is an occurrence, which happens at a time. The *occurs-at* relation has a role with respect to time that is analogous to the role of the *occupies* relation with respect to space. If a body exists, then necessarily it occupies some point; just so, if an event exists, then necessarily it occurs at some moment. The *occupies* relation defines physical objects and spatial points: if x occupies y, then x is a physical object and y is a point. Similarly, the *occurs-at* relation defines events and moments of time: if x occurs at y, then x is an event and y is a time.

The metaphysics of events is contentious, so here I shall simply assume a straightforward account that fits conveniently with the metaphysics of facts of the previous Chapter. I assume that a substance is a temporally enduring particular, and that a (simple) event is a temporal fact, i.e., a fact that combines a universal, one or more substances, and a time. We can then explain the *occurs-at* relation as the relation that holds between the event and a time t, if the event is the fact *that x has U at t*, i.e. the fact $\langle U, x, t \rangle$. On this account, a universal that is a constituent of an event must always have at least two 'argument-places', since a fact combines it with a substance and a time. Lewis has concluded that those who say there are substances are obliged to deny that there are any 'temporary intrinsics', i.e., qualities a thing can have at one time and not have at another time. (1986: 202–205.) This seems to presuppose that the criterion of whether a universal is a quality or a relation is the number of its argument-places: since the universals that occupy predicate position in events all have at least two argument-places, they must all be relations and not intrinsic qualities. But when temporal facts are in play there is no reason why the substance theorist should accept this arity criterion. For the true test of whether a universal is a quality or a relation is not its arity, but whether it is a respect of resemblance of things taken singly, or taken in pairs, or in trios, etc. Now resemblance itself can be a temporal fact. Therefore a temporary intrinsic is a universal that is a respect in which substances taken singly can resemble each other at a time; a temporary binary relation is a universal that is a respect in which substances taken in order in pairs can resemble each other at a time; and so on.

I shall assume that a complex event is a number of suitably related single events; those of its component events that have the same time of occurrence comprise a *stage* of the complex event. This plural account of complex events is an alternative to the more familiar mereological account, which takes events to be not facts but individuals with temporal parts. The metaphysics of facts of the previous Chapter dispensed with the part-whole relation, so here we can replace the mereological account of events with one that needs only the resources of the theory of facts and plural logic: instead of saying that a simple event e is 'part' of a complex event E, we say E is some simple events (temporal facts), and that e is one of them.

Whether simple or complex, events can resemble other events, and so events must themselves have properties. Since complex events are pluralities, some properties of events will be collective or plural properties. Any plurality of events is itself an event on the present account, so officially there are therefore a great many 'events'; but in practice we are usually interested only in events of certain special kinds. A (possibly collective) property of events is an *event sortal* if it picks out events that belong to a natural kind. Each natural kind of event has its own characteristic features, usually including characteristic spatial, temporal, material and causal continuities.

An important natural kind of events are the *acts*, which are a kind characterised by their causes and effects. An act is a complex event caused by an exercise of the powers of some substance, called the subject of the act; the subject is not necessarily a person. If acts of a given kind cause in a characteristic way a change in the state of something, the act-kind is said to be transitive, and the thing changed is called the object of the act. Thus an act-kind is individuated partly by the causal relations in which acts of the kind stand to other things, and it carries with it argument-places for the subject and perhaps also for the object of the act.

Verbs

Verbs are the words we use to report acts. For example, we report a certain act by saying 'The stone broke the window.' What is the logical form of this report, and how should we represent it in the predicate calculus? One suggestion is that we have here an instance of the relation of *breaking*, i.e., the supposed relation in which x stands to y if x breaks y. But if a sentence really does report a straightforwardly relational fact, the verb used is usually only the anodyne English copula 'is'; for example 'the stone is to the left of the window,' 'the stone is above the window,' etc. Our copula is only a vestigial grammatical form, not a genuine 'doing word' verb; many languages dispense with the copula altogether.

A genuine verb implies an act, and a subject of the act. When the stone broke the window, a complex event occurred, a *breaking*, which took a little time and had several stages, from the initial contact of the stone with the glass, through the deformation of the glass, to its final separation into shards. Following Ramsey and Davidson, we should therefore take the true logical form to contain an existential quantifier: the fact that the stone broke the window is the fact that there was in the past an event of a certain sort, namely a breaking, in which the breaker was the stone, and the thing broken the window. (Ramsey 1927: 36–7; Davidson 1966.)

'The stone broke the window' $=_{df}$
$(\exists x)(x$ is an event $\wedge$ x is past $\wedge$ x is a breaking $\wedge$ subject(x) = the stone $\wedge$ object(x) = the window)

Here the verb 'broke' in the surface form has given way at the level of logical form to a corresponding verbal noun, viz., 'breaking', which is an event sortal. The grammatical subject of the verb is the subject of the event; it is the stone that is the subject, because it was the exercise of a power of the stone that caused the window to break. The stone possessed the power in virtue of its intrinsic structure, momentum, etc.: these caused the breaking in just the manner characteristic of breakings; which is why the breaking is the act of the stone.

The grammatical object of the verb, the window, is the *object* of the act. The window is the object, because it was the window in which the act wrought the change characteristically produced by events of its kind. A breaking is a kind of event which in a characteristic way changes an intact thing by causing it to be separated into parts, and the thing changed in this way is the object of the breaking. The same holds generally: the grammatical object of a transitive verb is the thing in which is wrought the change characteristic of the act-kind reported by the verb. Not every act has an object, of course; the grammatical distinction between transitive and intransitive verbs marks the distinction between acts that have objects, and acts that have none.

The mental events that are of interest in attitude attributions, and which Geach called 'mental acts', are acts in the present sense. A mental act need not be an action; it is called an act because it is the 'actualisation' or exercise of a power of its subject; it is a mental act because (1) it is the exercise of a power of a mind and (2) it is conscious.

3.2 Apprehending a fact

How is knowledge related to mental acts? The Causal Thesis of Chapter 1 said that knowledge is a direct, unmediated mental relation to the world. If knowledge were nothing over and above the mental act in the context, for example if it reduced to a perceptual experience or a belief which in a favourable case is embedded in the world in the right way, then mental acts would be intermediaries between mind and world, and we should discern the world only through 'the veil of ideas'. But according to the Causal Thesis, knowledge is a simple relation in its own right, so it can relate mind and world directly, without intermediaries and their attendant veils and shadows. If we wish to dispense entirely with intermediaries, we must insist that what is known is the fact itself. This the Causal Thesis allows us to do: it says the contentful mental act is only the cause of the knowledge of fact; it is a causal intermediary, certainly, but not an epistemic intermediary. The mental act causes the mind to be in direct epistemic contact with the world, but is not itself a middle term mediating the contact.

If knowledge is indeed a relation, then we might expect the verb 'knows' simply to state the fact that the relation obtains; this particular verb would therefore not admit of a Ramsey-style analysis. The logical form of 'Pharaoh knows that Hesperus is shining' would be *Kap*, where *a* is Pharaoh, and *p* is the fact *that Hesperus is shining*. But as was argued in Chapter 1, knowledge attributions indicate not only the fact known but also the content of the mental act of apprehending which caused the fact to be known.

A mental act is an *apprehending* if it causes knowledge in the manner characteristic of the faculty that produced it. For example, a visual experience is an apprehending if it causes knowledge, in the manner characteristic of the faculty of vision, of some visible fact about one's environment. Thus an apprehending is a kind of act, so for the logical form of '*S* apprehends that *A*' we need the Ramsey analysis again:

S apprehends that $A=_{df}$
$(\exists x)(x$ is an event $\wedge x$ is an apprehending $\wedge$ subject$(x) = S \wedge$ object$(x) =$ the fact *that-A*)

The reason a fact can be regarded as the object of an act of apprehending is as follows. We said the object of an act is the thing which the act changes in a characteristic way. One apprehends a fact by some mental act that causes one to know the fact; the act of apprehension changes the fact in a characteristic way, for in consequence of it the subject stands in the knowledge relation to the fact. Just as a touched thing is changed by the creation of a new (spatial) relation between the subject and the thing touched, so an apprehended fact is changed by its new epistemic relation to the subject of the mental act.

The Ramseyan analysis of mental acts gives due recognition to the episodic nature of our mental life. The analysis allows us to take mental acts as the primary bearers of content; non-episodic mental states such as belief, desire etc., can be explained as dispositions to mental acts, which inherit their content from the mental acts to which they dispose. For example, a belief is a mental state that disposes one to a certain judgement; therefore the content of a belief *B* is that content κ such that *B* disposes one to a judgement with content κ. Similarly a desire is a mental state that disposes one to action: for any desire *D*, its content is that content κ such that for any content ρ that one can will, if one believes that if ρ then κ, then the desire *D* disposes one to will that ρ. Here the desire inherits its content κ from the content of all the conditional beliefs 'if ρ then κ' with which it cooperates in disposing one to will that ρ. Thus we may take contents to be in the primary sense properties of mental acts: and we may suppose that a mental state that is not a mental act inherits its content from the mental acts with which its functional role connects it.

3.3 Content

What is the criterion of identity for contents? One suggestion is that we should define content in terms of synonymy, and synonymy in terms of truth. Then two words are *synonyms* if the one can be substituted for the other in any sentence *salva veritate*; two sentences are *synonymous* if the one comes from the other by substitution of synonym for synonym. The suggestion is that if sentence A_1 expresses the content κ_1, and sentence A_2 expresses the content κ_2, then $\kappa_1 = \kappa_2$ if and only if A_1 and A_2 are synonymous.

The trouble with this is that a definition of synonymy that relies on substitution *salva veritate* must allow for substitution within oblique contexts, else it will fail to detect the difference in sense between e.g. 'Hesperus' and 'Phosphorus'. If we allow oblique contexts, there seems no principled reason to disallow doubly oblique contexts. But as Mates (1952) observed, such a test is far too stringent, for then no two sentences can be synonyms. For whatever A and B may be, the following will be true:

No one doubts that anyone who believes that A believes that A.

Yet if A and B are different, substituting B for the second A will yield something false:

No one doubts that anyone who believes that A believes that B.

For example, it is true that no one doubts that anyone who believes that Ralph is an eye-doctor believes that Ralph is an eye-doctor. However, it is false that no one doubts that anyone who believes that Ralph is an eye-doctor believes that Ralph is an oculist—certainly some philosopher of belief doubts that. Thus 'oculist' and 'eye-doctor' are not everywhere substitutable *salva veritate*, and therefore they are not synonyms by this test. It therefore appears that no words whatever will be synonyms by the test, so this proposed criterion of identity for content fails.

Evans' 'Intuitive Criterion of Difference' (1982: 18–19) for contents is for two reasons an improvement on the synonymy test. First, it operates at the level of complete contents, rather than individual words. Secondly, it goes beyond truth, and takes account of rationality: according to the Intuitive Criterion, contents κ_1 and κ_2 are identical if it is not coherently possible to take different attitudes to κ_1 and κ_2. But this 'Intuitive Criterion' fails to allow for mere differences of Fregean tone: for example, if there can be such a thing as rational pride, Ralph might coherently take pride in being an oculist, yet not take pride in being an eye-doctor, even though the difference is only one of tone. A second objection is that whenever $A \leftrightarrow B$ is immediately obvious *a priori* it will not be coherently possible to take different attitudes to A and B, yet they may not have the same content. For example, one cannot coherently take different attitudes to 'ABC is triangular' and 'ABC is trilateral,' for these are obvious *a priori* equivalents, but they differ in content.

The difficulties with Evans' criterion suggest that we need to define content by a test that looks not just at individual mental acts, but at their relations to each other in a 'course of reasoning'. The content of a mental act determines which inferences involving it are correct, so contents are different if substitution of one for the other in a course of reasoning can affect its rational correctness. That was Frege's criterion for sameness of content:

It may, or it may not, be the case that all inferences that can be drawn from the first judgement when combined with certain other ones can also be drawn from the second when combined with the same other judgements. ... Now I call the part of the content that is the same in both the *conceptual content*. *Only this* has significance for our symbolic language; we need therefore make no distinction between sentences that have the same conceptual content. ... In my formalised languages only that part of judgements which affects the *possible inferences* is taken into consideration.' (*Begriffsschrift* §3, original emphasis.) (Frege 1966: 2–3.)

Frege's claim is that the content of two judgements is the same if substitution of the one for the other makes no difference to the possible inferences. We might also put it like this: two contents are the same if the one can be substituted for the other in any proof *salva demonstratione*—'saving the proof'. We can generalise Frege's criterion to cover not only proofs in the narrow mathematical sense, but any course of reasoning (sequence of mental acts) that allows a conclusion to be drawn. The generalised criterion is that mental acts of the same psychological type have the same content if in every context either can replace the other in any course of reasoning without affecting the rational correctness of the reasoning.

I propose to adopt this Fregean criterion of identity for contents in what follows. But what is rational correctness? A complete account of thought cannot be merely descriptive; there is a right way to reason, so the theory of thought needs something that provides a standard of correctness. According to Frege, thought aims at truth, which he held to be something absolutely primitive and indefinable; logic is the study of the laws of truth, and we reason correctly only when we reason logically, i.e., in accord with the laws of truth. (Frege 1967: 13.)

Frege insisted on the norm of truth to secure the objective correctness of right reasoning. But for this purpose knowledge will serve just as well as truth. For knowledge is factive, so the demand that thought aim at knowledge is also effective in safeguarding objectivity. And indeed the norm of knowledge is superior to the norm of truth, for we need to bring epistemic considerations to the theory of correct reasoning. A norm of truth cannot define rational correctness.

The two standard notions of validity that can be defined in terms of truth are *modal* validity and *logical* validity. We already noted in Chapter 1 that neither of these is coextensive with rational correctness. Thus the following argument is modally valid, but not rationally correct:

Hesperus is beautiful.
Phosphorus shines.
Therefore, something beautiful shines.

It is impossible for the premises to be true and the conclusion false; but despite its modal validity, this is obviously an incorrect deduction. Logical validity serves us no better. An argument is logically valid if its conclusion is true in any model in which its premises are true, but that is not a necessary condition of the correctness of arguments. Consider:

Some oculists are tall.
All eye-doctors are wise.
Therefore, someone tall is wise.

This argument is rationally correct but not logically valid, for interpretations that assign different extensions to 'oculist' and 'eye-doctor' will generate counter-models. It may be replied that the argument becomes logically valid if synonym is substituted for synonym, since 'oculist' means the same as 'eye-doctor'. But the reply is unavailing in the present context, since we have as yet no definition of synonymy. We are forced to conclude that neither modal validity nor logical validity is the right test of the correctness of a deduction. The notion of content with which we are concerned is therefore not definable in terms of truth.

Rational correctness cannot be defined in terms of truth, but it can be defined in terms of knowledge. An argument is rationally correct if one is epistemically justified in advancing by its means from believing its premises to believing its conclusion. We can therefore state our Fregean criterion for identity of contents as follows:

> If x and y are contents, then $x = y$ if in any course of reasoning, epistemic justification is preserved if a mental act with content x is substituted for a mental act of the same type with content y.

In Chapter 1 we defined justification in terms of knowledge, so we could equally say that contents x and y are the same if substituting x for y never turns knowledge into ignorance.

It is a consequence of the Fregean criterion that if a thought is to have a definite content, then it must potentially occur in some verification, i.e., in some course of reasoning that results in knowledge. Does this make the criterion itself verificationist—must we say that an undecidable statement is meaningless, since neither it nor its negation can be proved? No: the criterion requires only that a statement or its negation be capable of appearing *somewhere* in a proof—it need not figure as the last line. A statement has content if it has Fregean *Erkenntniswert*, i.e., apprehension-value; and it can have this value even if it is unknowable whether what it itself states is a fact or not. The reason is that for the Fregean, though not perhaps for the verificationist, the Law of Excluded Middle is valid. Thus a statement or its negation might have an indispensable occurrence in a proof as an instance of Excluded Middle. This is sufficient to ensure a content for the undecidable statement, even though neither it nor its negation can occur as the *last* line of a proof. The verificationists were quite right to take as the test of contentfulness the occurrence of a statement or its negation in some verification; their only mistake was to suppose that the occurrence has to be in the last line.

3.4 Concepts

Frege was the first to observe the importance of concepts in connection with the phenomenon of compositionality. He argued that our ability to understand a complete content derives compositionally from our grasp of the associated concepts; for this reason, one can understand even an unfamiliar sentence, provided one is familiar with the concepts expressed by its constituent words. Frege conjectured that the concepts must be part of the content; one understands the content in virtue of one's grasp of its parts. (1918: 390.)

But can concepts literally be *parts* of contents? It is not clear exactly what notion of part and whole Frege can have had in mind here. Not the spatial or temporal relation of part and whole, where the part occupies some of the spatial or temporal region occupied by the whole; for a Fregean concept is a non-spatiotemporal particular. Nor can it have been the part-whole relation of extensional mereology, where the same parts determine the same whole regardless of order. For in the case of concept and content, order matters; the content *that Romeo loves Juliet* is different from the content *that Juliet loves Romeo*, though both deploy the same three concepts, viz. *Romeo, love,* and *Juliet*. Thus the relation between concept and content is not the relation of part and whole of extensional mereology. Frege must have had in mind some ordered structuring, but now it is unclear what the relation is that induces the structuring, or how the mind is sensitive to it. Frege tells us, somewhat obscurely, that the mind 'grasps' the concept; but he is silent on how the mind is responsive to the relation that supposedly structures the concepts in a content.

If we set these difficulties to one side for the moment, the form at least of Frege's account is clear enough: for each content κ, there are concepts $a_1, \dots, a_n$, such that κ stands in some semantically important relation to $a_1, \dots, a_n$. Let us call this relation, which is somehow connected with part and whole, the *activation relation*. I shall use the symbol "*" for the activation relation. If a content κ activates concepts $a_1, \dots, a_n$ I write:

$$\kappa^* (a_1, \dots, a_n)$$

I shall assume that, like the combination relation between a fact and its constituents, the activation relation between a content and its concepts is multigrade. This as usual is to avoid the need for auxiliary apparatus such as sequences, etc.

I make the assumption that the activation relation is functional, in the sense that a content activates a unique vector of concepts. In *Foundations of Arithmetic*, Frege himself seems to have made the opposite assumption, for he claimed that the same content could be 'analysed' into different conceptual parts: for example, he says that '*a* is parallel to *b*' has 'by definition' exactly the same content as 'the direction of *a* is identical with the direction of *b*.' (Frege 1968: 74–5, §64) But this is not consistent with his own *Begriffsschrift* definition of sameness of content. For from '*a* is parallel to *b*' there follows immediately that something is parallel to *b*, whereas this does not follow from 'the direction of *a* is identical to the direction of *b*,' unless we insert the definition as an additional line in the proof. Thus the two sentences must have different contents by our Fregean criterion, since they are not intersubstitutable in every proof.

What is the activation relation between a content and its concepts? Any satisfactory account of the relation will have the same starting point as Frege's; namely, the fact that one's ability to understand a content has one's grasp of the appropriate concepts as in some sense its parts. Thus something like a part-whole relation does indeed obtain between grasp and understanding. But it by no means follows that a part-whole relation must also hold between the concept which is grasped and the content which is understood. We need not assume that concepts are literally parts of contents, if in some other way we can ensure that grasp is part of understanding.

We must enquire what understanding is. Suppose that one understands the content expressed by the sentence 'Socrates is wise,' but that one does not understand the content expressed by the sentence 'Noumena are unintuitable.' In what does the difference consist? A natural answer is that although one can *say* the second sentence, one cannot *think* it; no relevant judgement, supposition, or experience goes on in one's mind as one says it. More precisely, there is no event *e* and content κ, such that *e* is one's mental act, κ is the content expressed by the sentence, and the content of *e* is κ. On the assumption that the sentence is meaningful and does actually express a content, it follows that there is a content κ, such that some people are able to express thoughts with the content κ, but that one is not oneself able to think thoughts with that particular content. Thus understanding is an ability: to understand the content κ is to be able to be the subject of mental acts with the content κ.

An ability is a power of acting. Powers are relational properties: for example, the power of a key to open a lock is a relation in which the key stands to all locks of a certain design. But such a relational property is not metaphysically fundamental; it is grounded in intrinsic properties of the key and the lock. If an intrinsic property grounds a power it is said to be a *basis* of the power; for example, the shape of the key is a basis of the key's power to open the lock, because in any instance of the exercise of the power, the key's having that shape is a cause of the opening of the lock. My suggestion is that grasp of a concept is similarly a basis of understanding a content: understanding the content is the power of thinking a thought with that content, and in any exercise of the power, the subject's grasp of the concept is a cause of the subject thinking a thought with the given content.

What is it to 'grasp' a concept? To answer this question, we must first ask what a concept is. The Fregean doctrine that concepts are parts of contents stands in the way of taking concepts and contents to be universals, for contents are universals, and universals do not have parts. But if we abandon the Fregean doctrine, we can take a concept to be simply a property of the mental subject. 'Grasp' of a concept can then be very simply explained—a mental subject 'possesses' or 'grasps' a concept just if the subject instantiates the property which the concept is.

If the suggestion that concepts are universals is correct, then compositionality does not force us to regard the relation of concept to content as that of part to whole. Rather, concept is to understanding as basis is to power: whenever a thought occurs with the given content, it is because the concept entered into the causation. This allows us to make progress towards saying what the activation relation is: the content activates the concept if a mental act with that content always relies on the concept in its causation. Then given any class of concepts, there will be a corresponding class of contents, namely those that activate only the given concepts. These are the contents an understanding of which is conferred by a grasp of the concepts in question. Of course concepts alone do not cause mental acts; it is some faculty of the mind that is the prime mover. However, the faculty on its own would be unable to cause the mental act, if the subject did not possess the appropriate concepts.

Activation, as we defined it, is an order-sensitive relation, for the content *that Romeo loves Juliet* activates the same concepts as the content *that Juliet loves Romeo*, but in a different order. The notion that a concept is a basis of a power allows us to say which concepts are activated by a content: they are the concepts without which one would be unable to think compositional thoughts with the content in question. But that is not the whole story, for it does not tell us the order of activation. For that, we need to bring in a new relation, namely the relation of reference.

3.5 Reference

In the theory of a compositional language, the term 'reference' usually names the relation between a name and its bearer. The relation is not usually regarded as a fundamental one, but is taken to be constituted by further relations between the name, the bearer and some third thing. Different accounts of language invoke a different third thing: according to Locke, the intermediary is the idea in the mind of the user of the name; according to Kripke, it is the social practice to which use of the name belongs; according to Frege, it is the sense of the name. (Locke 1979: 405; Kripke 1980: 91–5; Frege 1892b: 61.)

Here I follow Frege, and take the name-bearer relation to be the product of two more fundamental relations, namely the *expression* relation between a name and the concept that is its sense, and the *presentation* relation between the concept and the thing itself; the bearer of a name is the thing presented by the concept expressed by the name. Since in this Section language is not under discussion, I shall use the term 'reference' here to name what Frege calls the 'presentation' relation; the referent of a concept is then intuitively the thing one is thinking of when one deploys the concept.

Our problem was to define the order in which the content of a mental act activates the concepts involved in the causation of the mental act. I shall suggest that a related problem is the definition of the reference relation between a concept and the thing of which it is a concept. The single solution I shall recommend to both problems is a picture theory of compositional thought, according to which the two relations of activation and reference are to be defined jointly.

The fundamental idea of the picture theory is that there is an isomorphism between thought and fact, in virtue of which the content of a compositional thought can be seen as a picture of the fact whose existence it represents. Suppose a thought or other mental act e has content κ, and suppose κ activates concepts $a_1, \ldots, a_n$ in that order. Suppose the concepts $a_1, \ldots, a_n$ have respectively the referents $x_1, \ldots, x_n$. Then the picture theory says that the fact represented by κ is the fact whose constituents are the vector $(x_1, \ldots, x_n)$; i.e., it is the fact whose constituents are in order the referents of the concepts activated by the content κ.

> *Picturing Assumption*: Let e be a compositional thought with content κ. Suppose that κ activates the concepts $a_1, \ldots, a_n$, and that the referents of $a_1, \ldots, a_n$ are respectively the things $x_1, \ldots, x_n$. Then e represents the fact p whose constituents are $(x_1, \ldots, x_n)$.

Thus according to the picture theory, the activation and reference relations are jointly defined by the connection between them and the representation relation.

To define the two relations further, what we now need is a way of determining the representation relation, i.e., of determining what fact a given mental act e represents. Our Fregean criterion of identity suggested that the content of a mental act is the property it has which determines what facts it enables one to know in consequence of a course of reasoning. Consider a course of reasoning which ends with a mental act e with content κ, and suppose that e represents the fact p. Suppose that the context is epistemically favourable, so that in the manner characteristic of its originating faculty, e causes one to know the fact p. Then it must be p that is the fact which e represents. So:

> *Representation Assumption*: If in a given context a mental act e with content κ is the apprehension of a fact p, then in that context e represents the fact p.

The Picturing Assumption and the Representation Assumption together constrain the relation of activation and the relation of reference. Suppose that in a given context a_i is the ith concept activated by the content κ of e, that e is the apprehending of p, and that x_i is the ith constituent of p: the constraint is that in that context x_i must be the referent of a_i. That is, if

$$\kappa^*(a_1, \ldots, a_n)$$

and

$$p \bullet (x_1, .., x_n)$$

then the referent of each a_i is the corresponding x_i. Thus we have the relation diagram shown in Figure 3.1.

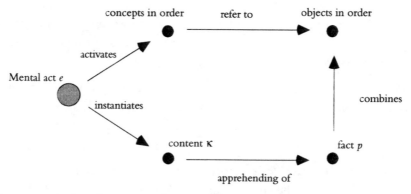

Figure 3.1. Activated concepts picture a fact

   The picture theory may be summed up in the statement that if a mental act causes knowledge, then this relation diagram is commutative: starting from the given mental act e, one eventually arrives at the same objects in the same order whether one takes the upper or lower branch; the activation and reference relations are jointly constrained by the requirement that they carry us to the constituents of the fact apprehended.

   The picture theory supposes that the human capacity for judgement is articulated in a way that corresponds to the logical articulation of facts. It takes the relation between content and concept to be not a mind–independent part–whole relation between abstract objects, but to be constituted by a psychological reality. The claim is that there is a relation R between contents and concepts, such that for any given subject S with a capacity for compositional thought, there is a permutation ρ such that if S is the subject of a mental act e with content κ, and κ stands in R to $a_1, \ldots, a_n$, then the order in which the concepts enter the causation of e in S is the order $a_{\rho(1)}, \ldots, a_{\rho(n)}$. This postulated relation R is the *activation* relation: it does not belong to pure metaphysics, but is rather a postulate of a special science, namely the psychology of compositional thought. The fact that activation is a psychological reality plays an important role in the interpretation of a subject's language, as I discuss in Chapter 7.

Russell's 'Principle of Acquaintance' says:

'Every proposition which we can understand must be composed wholly of constituents with which we are acquainted.' (Russell 1959: 58.)

Evans famously complained that 'the difficulty with Russell's Principle has always been to explain what it means'. (1982: 89.) Evans suggested that we should think of acquaintance as discriminatory knowledge, i.e., 'the capacity to distinguish the object of judgement from all other things'. Russell himself took acquaintance to be a matter of direct presentation to consciousness. On either of these understandings of acquaintance, Russell's Principle does not look very plausible: one can certainly think about things which one cannot discriminate from all other things, and which are not immediately present to consciousness. But if we define acquaintance with a thing just as knowing something about it, i.e., knowing some fact of which the thing is a constituent, then for conceptual thought at least Russell's Principle will be true according to the picture theory. For if one's thought is to represent a fact whose constituents are a certain Russellian proposition, then the concepts activated by the content of the thought must have as their referents the constituents of the proposition. But according to the picture theory, in a given context a concept can be assigned a determinate object as its referent only if some thought that activates the concept is the apprehending by the subject of a fact about the object. Russell's Principle follows: one can have a conceptual thought only about an object of which one has some knowledge, i.e., with which one is acquainted. For if in a given context one's concept has a referent and is not empty, the relation diagram of the picture theory entails that one must know something about the referent. In a context where the concept figures in no knowledgeable judgement, the picture theory assigns it no referent; the concept is empty, and thoughts that activate it are merely fictions.

3.6 Epistemology of Definitions

In this section I offer further argument for the Principle of Acquaintance, on the grounds that it is needed in a correct account of the epistemology of definitions. Suppose someone utters the sentence '$a =$ the F' as a definition. Then the definer does not use the sentence with the force of a statement:

rather, it has the force of a command—we are to use the word 'a' in the future to refer to the F. Later someone may utter a token of the very same sentence '$a =$ the F' in accordance with the definition, but now with the force of a statement. There is now the following puzzle. The sentence occurs perhaps as a line in some proof, and in this occurrence it states a fact, for example, a mathematical fact. It must be a known fact, since it is stated in a correct proof. But how is one's knowledge of the mathematical fact *that a is the F* guaranteed by one's mere compliance with a command about the use of a word?

A solution sometimes proposed is that a definition does not after all express a fact, still less a known fact; it gives rise only to a 'tautology' that 'says nothing', or at least, nothing substantive. The tautology theory says that if a is defined as the F, then 'Fa' and 'F(the F)' have the same content, and '$Fa \leftrightarrow F$(the F)' is a tautology. But this solution cannot be right, for 'Fa' expresses a singular proposition, whereas 'F(the F)' expresses a general proposition. So the sentences 'Fa' and 'F(the F)' have different truth–conditions, and hence they have different contents, contrary to the tautology theory.

But Russell had a manoeuvre here to protect the tautology theory. 'Fa' and 'F(the F)' can still be synonymous 'by definition', if the sign 'a' is not a genuine proper name. Not every grammatically proper name is a logically proper name, according to Russell: some signs with the syntactic characteristics of proper names are not proper names at all, but are introduced by definition as mere abbreviations of denoting phrases. (Russell 1959: 54; 1918: 243.) On Russell's account, there can be no problem in such a case about how we know 'by definition' that $a =$ the F. We know it because the surface sentence does not express a singular proposition; rather, it abbreviates the general proposition 'the $F =$ the F', which is a triviality supposing the F exists. Thus there is no interesting epistemology of definitions on Russell's account.

We can read Russell as in effect endorsing the following Rule of Inference for definitions:

> *Rule 1*: If 'a' is an uncommitted name, you may stipulate that 'a' is to abbreviate 'the F', and you may infer 'by definition' that if the F exists, then $a =$ the F.

But Russell's abbreviation theory is refuted by its failure to account for the role of definitions in concept-formation. We often acquire new concepts from a genuine definition, whereas no one can learn a new concept from a mere abbreviation. The difficulty was pointed out by Wittgenstein in connection with Russell's philosophy of mathematics. (1967a: 65–72.) In *Principia Mathematica*, Russell and Whitehead (1970) had provided definitions of the numbers; the decimal notation can then be defined in the primitive notation of pure logic. But if these definitions are mere abbreviations, then a textbook proof of an arithmetical theorem is not really a proof, since it is only an abbreviation of the much longer proof we arrive at when all the definitions are expanded into primitive notation. But the longer proof when fully written out in primitive notation is far too long to be taken in! Admittedly it is a sequence of signs that is valid in the modal sense that it is impossible for its premisses to be true and its conclusion false. But this sign-sequence is of no use to us epistemically, since it is too long to take in; it is not really a proof at all. In contrast, the unexpanded proof in the arithmetic textbook really is a proof, since it does indeed lead to new mathematical knowledge. Since thoughts are the same whether their expression in written symbols is abbreviated or not, a mere abbreviation cannot transform a non-proof into a proof, and therefore the definitions must contribute something that goes beyond mere abbreviation. We must therefore reject Russell's theory of definitions.

According to Kripke (1980: 53–60), we can 'fix the reference' of a proper name by a definite description; the name is a genuine singular term, and not merely an abbreviation of the description. For example, one can simply stipulate that the name 'one metre' is to refer to the length of a certain stick. Then the mere fact of the stipulation is supposed to be in and of itself an adequate explanation of how we know 'by definition' that, if the F exists, then $a =$ the F. The stipulation theory endorses the following revised Rule of Inference for definitions:

> *Rule 2*: If 'a' is an uncommitted name, you may stipulate that 'a' is to refer to the F, and you may infer 'by definition' that if the F exists, then $a =$ the F.

If Rule 2 were correct, then once one has made the mere verbal stipulation, one could infer the following sentence 'Carnap Sentence' for 'a':

> If the F exists, then $a =$ the F.

Can we indeed know the Carnap Sentence on the basis of a mere definition? We may concede that, having defined *a* as the *F*, one has arrived at a new concept: and one has attached the new concept to the term '*a*' as its sense. But it does not follow that the new concept has a referent for one, as the following counterexample shows. Let *F* be the description Conan Doyle gave of his famous fictional detective. We can imagine Doyle introducing the name 'Holmes' by the definition:

Holmes = the *F*.

Anyone who understands this definition is in a position thereby to grasp the *Holmes* concept. But the definition does not cause one to know the associated Carnap Sentence:

If anyone is the *F*, Holmes is the *F*.

This is not something one can know, for since Holmes is a fictional character, the name 'Holmes' is empty, so the Carnap Sentence does not state a fact. The name 'Holmes' would still have been empty even if, unknown to Doyle, there really was someone, call him Schmidt, who did all the things Doyle described Holmes as doing. When Doyle wrote his stories, he was not referring to Schmidt. 'Holmes' is still an empty name even on this scenario, and the Carnap Sentence still does not state a known fact. The name 'Holmes' would have a reference only if Doyle had told his stories as known fact. (Lewis 1978: 266.) In that case the Carnap Sentence would have been true, and the fact it would have stated would have been known to Doyle, and hence known to his readers in virtue of Doyle's testimony. Thus Carnap Sentences are not in themselves knowable by stipulation, as it were 'by definition' or *a priori*. Definitions do not generate knowledge—they presuppose knowledge. If a definition is to succeed in giving a term not only a sense but also a reference, the definer must already be in possession of relevant knowledge.

What is the relevant knowledge, that is needed if a definition is to secure reference? It might be proposed that the definer is required to know that the *F* exists. We might interpret this as an endorsement of the following Rule of Inference for definitions:

Rule 3: If '*a*' is an uncommitted name, and if you know that the *F* exists, then you may stipulate that '*a*' is to refer to the *F*, and you may infer 'by definition' that *a* = the *F*.

What might be interpreted as a 'proof' of Rule 3 is to be found in some contemporary logic texts, e.g. Mendelson (1987: 80–1). However, Rule 3 is not a correct rule, as the following counterexample shows. Suppose that in a certain lottery the rules ensure that one and only one ticket will win. Suppose there are a million tickets in the lottery, and that the lottery is fair. Suppose S know all this, and that S knows that the draw will in fact take place next week. S knows that one ticket and no more will win, so S knows that the winning ticket exists. So by Rule 3, S can define 'Lucky' as the winning ticket. Despite Rule 3, however, S certainly does not know that Lucky is the winning ticket. There are a million tickets, so S knows that the present objective chance that any given ticket will win is one in a million; so S knows that the present chance that Lucky will win is one in a million. Therefore S's present degree of belief that Lucky will win cannot rationally exceed one in a million; in other words, S cannot rationally have more than a vanishing degree of belief that Lucky will win. Therefore S does not know that Lucky will win, since one does not know what one cannot rationally believe. So even if one knows that something is the F, a mere definition does not for any x allow one to arrive at knowledge of the singular fact that x is the F.

It therefore appears that if the definition '$a =$ the F' is to succeed in making the name 'a' refer to something x, then one must already know of x that it is the F. Naturally one does not already know this fact under the mode of presentation 'a is the F', but one must already know it under some mode of presentation or other. We are forced to conclude that the value of a definition cannot lie in any new knowledge it gives one, for of itself it does not give one new knowledge. Rather, its value lies in its enabling one to form a useful new concept of an object with which one is already acquainted. The new concept does not cause one to know the fact that a is the F, for one already knew that under the other mode of presentation. But it may lead to new knowledge of other facts, arrived at not 'by definition' but by the ordinary method of honest toil. Therefore the correct Rule of Inference for definitions is as follows:

> *Rule 4*: If 'a' is an uncommitted name, and if for some x you know that x is the F, then you may stipulate that 'a' is to refer to the F, and you may infer 'by definition' that a is the F.

Whereas Rule 3 required only *de dicto* knowledge of the *F*, Rule 4 demands actual acquaintance with the *F*; only given *de re* knowledge of *x* that it is the *F* does the definition make '*a*' refer to *x*.

Definitions have an epistemically useful role in concept-formation, which explains why they are so useful in mathematics. But they are useful in other contexts too. For example, one might wish to introduce a new individual concept of *x*, if one had previously been thinking of *x* only as 'that *F*', i.e., only under a demonstrative mode of presentation. If the demonstrative mode of presentation depends on a perceptual experience, it will no longer be available after one has ceased to remember the experience. By forming a new individual concept of *x*, the definition '*a* = the (demonstrated) *F*' gives one the capacity to continue to think about *x* even when the perceptual–demonstrative mode of presentation is no longer available.

Our Rule 4 entails that a successful definition demands more than a merely verbal stipulation: the thing that is to be the referent of the *definiendum* must be something with which one is acquainted. That this is indeed a requirement may be concealed by the fact that someone can come by the needed knowledge simply by being the audience of a verbal definition. The circumstances of the definition may themselves suffice to make the audience acquainted with the referent of the *definiendum*, for example by showing the referent in an ostensive definition, or by implicitly telling of the referent by testimony. Another instance is where a definition is given in the context of an abductive hypothesis. For example, if I hear squeaks and scuttlings from behind the skirting board, I know by an inference to the best explanation that a mouse lives there. I am acquainted with the mouse, because the evidence for my abductive inference consists of actual sounds and traces of that very mouse. Therefore I can give myself the definition '*a* = the mouse behind the skirting board', and thereby make '*a*' refer to that particular mouse. Always the definition successfully assigns a referent to a new concept only if at the time of the definition the audience is actually acquainted with the referent.

3.7 Thought and Language

So far we have not needed to make any appeal to a primitive notion of the truth of a content. No such appeal to truth is needed; we can define truth in terms of reference, and hence ultimately in terms of knowledge, activation and combination. We can give a piecemeal definition in the spirit of Ramsey, with a separate clause for each atomic logical form, and recursive clauses for logically complex judgements. (Ramsey 1927: 38–9) To this a theory of groundedness will need to be added, to guard against the Liar Paradox, as noted in Chapter 2.

We define truth for contents as follows. Let κ be a content that activates $a_1, \ldots, a_n$. Suppose that in context C the referents of $a_1, \ldots, a_n$ are respectively $x_1, \ldots, x_n$. Then κ is true in the context C if in C there is a fact p whose constituents are $x_1, \ldots, x_n$. Or in vector notation, in a given context C:

$$(\kappa^* \phi \wedge \text{reference}(\phi) = \theta) \rightarrow (\text{true}(\kappa) \leftrightarrow (\exists p)(p \bullet \theta))$$

We cannot turn this implicit definition into an explicit definition, because of the Liar paradox.

As noted in Chapter 2, there are infinitely many ungrounded sentences that are neither in the extension nor in the anti-extension of 'is true'. It follows that truth is not a property: *a fortiori*, it is not the theoretically central property in the theory of thought. Nor is language theoretically central, for our treatment of concepts was entirely at the level of thought. There was no need to mention language, and no reason to suggest that language is essential for concepts. But concepts are essential for a compositional language, which requires a map from words to concepts, i.e., a *lexicon*, together with a syntactic convention for representing logical forms, i.e. a *grammar*. The grammar allows us to pass from the vector of words in a sentence to a corresponding vector of concepts, and hence to the unique content that activates this vector. Thus lexicon and grammar jointly determine a map from sentences of a language to the contents that are their meanings. In Chapter 7 I suggest that a language is the actual language of a population if and only if they use sentences of the language to give testimony with the corresponding meaning as its content.

However, even if language is not the essence of thought, it would certainly be very difficult to learn the contents of a person's thoughts without taking into account their language. Our knowledge of the thoughts of others does clearly depend on a process of interpretation, in which assigning a meaning to a person's utterances plays an indispensable part. Quine and Davidson have suggested that the task of the interpreter is to build a holistic theory which makes overall good sense of the interpretee.

They argued that building a semantic theory of the interpretee's language will be an indispensable part of the interpretative task. No doubt that is correct; but if we set verificationism aside, then even if it is true that knowledge of thought requires knowledge of language, still it does not follow that thought requires language. No doubt one human being cannot have detailed knowledge of the thoughts of another without a working knowledge of the other's language, but that is only an epistemological point, from which no firm conclusion can be drawn about the relation between thought and language themselves.

4

Necessity

Previous chapters have defined truth in terms of the mental relation of knowledge. According to Russell, it is in fact impossible to define truth without the mental. 'A world of mere matter', he says, 'since it would contain no beliefs or statements, would also contain no truths or falsehoods' (Russell 1959: 121). But here Russell failed to anticipate modern modal realism, which says there are many possible worlds, that a proposition is a set of worlds, and that a proposition is true if it has the actual world as one of its members. Modal realism claims to reduce truth, and hence all mentality, to an ontology of possible worlds. Can a metaphysics of knowledge effect the converse reduction, and give a satisfactory account of modality without other possible worlds?

In this chapter I use the theory of the previous three chapters to attempt such a reduction. Chapter 1 suggested that knowledge is a metaphysically fundamental relation between mind and fact, Chapter 2 outlined a theory of facts, and Chapter 3 gave a theory of contents as modes of presentation, or ways of apprehending facts. In the present chapter I apply these ideas to defend a rationalist theory of modality, which has the following as its central claim:

> *Rationalist Thesis*: a fact is necessary if and only if it has an *a priori* mode of presentation.

It is widely believed that there are many counterexamples to this claim that the necessary is the *a priori*. Kripke (1980) has influentially argued that apriority is a concept of epistemology, and that necessity is a concept of metaphysics; since the concepts are different, we have no reason to think they should be coextensive. Kripke proposed counterexamples to coextensiveness: it is necessary, but not *a priori*, that Hesperus is Phosphorus; it is *a priori*, but not necessary, that the Standard Metre is one metre long.

Following Kripke, a number of other counterexamples have also been proposed.

I do not find these counterexamples persuasive. I discuss several of them in this chapter, and I argue that all of them fail. If they do, a rationalist theory can still be a viable account of modality. Apriority is admittedly an epistemic concept, but it does not follow that it cannot be of service in metaphysics, provided it is defined in a way that is not psychologistic. We should not define the *a priori* as, for example, that which can be known independently of experience, for that brings in too many psychological matters. The correct rationalist definition is that the *a priori* comprises all the primitive truths, and all their logical consequences; it is not claimed that every logical consequence can be known. But since the primitive can be defined in terms of knowledge, and the logical consequence relation can be defined in terms of knowledge too, it follows that by identifying the necessary with the *a priori*, we do reduce modality to the metaphysics of knowledge.

An alternative to the rationalist theory is the ontic conception, which postulates other possible worlds, besides the actual world. On the ontic conception, facts about what is possible are facts about possibilities, which are taken to be objectively real entities. For example, according to David Lewis (1986) a possibility is something that really happens in a parallel universe; according to other theorists, it is something that merely represents a happening. A maximal possibility is a possible world, determining an entire course of history, complete in every detail. For Lewis, a possible world is a real parallel universe; other theorists take it to be an entity that merely represents an entire universe.

The rationalist theory postulates only the one real or actual world: other possible worlds are the proprietary property of the ontic conception. However, this does not mean that the discourse of possible worlds is also proprietary to the ontic conception. The rationalist theory can speak of worlds too, but without ontological commitment. There exists only the one real world, but we can *describe* other worlds, for to describe something is not to presuppose its existence. Just as the phrase 'the King of France' is a perfectly good definite description, despite the non-existence of the King of France, so a description of another possible world is perfectly meaningful, despite the non-existence of that world.

Therefore we can use the discourse of possible worlds in philosophical analysis, while understanding the discourse in a way that is ontologically non-committal. We can define a 'world' as a complete totality of facts. There is only one such totality, namely the actual world; a description of a totality describes a 'possible' world if it is not *a priori* that the described totality does not exist. We can define 'truth at a world': a description describes a world at which *A* is true if the existence of the described world entails the truth of *A*. We can define 'closeness' of worlds: descriptions describe close worlds if the worlds are described as closely resembling each other. Definitions such as these allow us to speak of worlds while staying comfortably within the modest ontology of a metaphysics of knowledge.

The plan of this chapter is as follows. In section 1 I give the rationalist definition of the *a priori*, and propose that the necessary is the *a priori*. In section 2 I discuss which modal logic is correct, on the rationalist conception of necessity. Then in the following five sections I discuss various supposed counterexamples to the rationalist thesis that the necessary is the *a priori*. Section 3 discusses 'Cartesian' counterexamples, section 4 mathematical counterexamples, and section 5 counterexamples involving singular and plural identity and non-identity; section 6 discusses descriptive names, and section 7 counterexamples involving 'actually'. Finally in section 8 I discuss how the rationalist theory can use the discourse of possible worlds in philosophical analysis.

4.1 The *A Priori*

The rationalist theory is that the necessary and the *a priori* coincide. Leibniz says:

There are two kinds of truth, those of *reasoning* and those of fact. Truths of reasoning are necessary and their opposite is impossible, while those of fact are contingent and their opposite is possible. (Rescher 1991: 120)

Kant agrees:

If we have a proposition which in being thought is thought as necessary, it is an *a priori* judgement. (Kant 1929: 11, Axv)

Any knowledge that professes to hold *a priori* lays claim to be regarded as absolutely necessary. (1929: 43, B3)

We can read the same kind of view into Frege. He says a judgement is *a priori* if 'its truth can be derived exclusively from general laws, which themselves neither need nor admit of proof' (1968: 4, §3). And what makes a judgement apodeictic or necessary is, he says, 'the existence of general judgements from which the proposition can be inferred' (1966: 4).

The rationalist conception of the *a priori* presupposes that different kinds of knowledge arise from different faculties of the mind. The rationalists posited special faculties that give rise to *a priori* knowledge. Leibniz posits a faculty of reason or understanding, which he says distinguishes the minds of rational beings from the minds of beasts, and which gives us knowledge of necessary truth (1982: 50–1). Kant says it is the faculty of reason which supplies the principles of *a priori* knowledge (1929: 58, A11/B25). Frege includes among his 'sources of knowledge' a 'logical source' and a 'geometrical and temporal source' (1979: 266). Thus the concepts of reason and the *a priori* are interdependent on the rationalist view, for *a priori* truths are defined as those that are apt to be known by pure reason, and reason is the faculty which enables us to know *a priori* truths. It is however not quite ideal to define the *a priori* in terms of truth, for neither apriority nor necessity are essentially connected with anything linguistic. I shall therefore prefer to use the terminology of facts; a fact is *a priori* if it is apt to be known by reason alone. The definition of the faculty of reason can be filled out in accordance with the general form of the definition of a faculty, as discussed in Chapter 1.

Some philosophers have used alternative definitions of the *a priori* that are intended to admit the desired species of fact, without presupposing the faculty psychology of the rationalists. For example, the *a priori* is sometimes defined as that which can be known 'without recourse to experience'. But this definition puts too much strain on the concept of 'experience'. For example, it does not seem definitely right to count clairvoyance as *experiential* knowledge, so the proposed definition would perhaps class clairvoyance as *a priori*. However, on the rationalist conception, clairvoyance is definitely not *a priori* knowledge; for whether or not clairvoyance is experience, it is not knowledge by pure reason.

Another common definition is that a proposition is *a priori* if someone who considers it is on that account in a position to know that it is true. But we must add something to say how the proposition is known. For a proposition might have a feature that causes it to be known as soon as it is considered, but by a deviant causal chain. For example, it might be pleasing to the gods if human beings consider a certain proposition. If anyone does consider it, the gods are so pleased that they appear in person to give authoritative testimony that the proposition is true. One only needs to consider the proposition to be in a position to know it is true, but it is not *a priori*, for one knows it by testimony and not by pure reason.

A rationalist account of the *a priori* will define it in terms of the epistemic faculties that enable us to know *a priori* facts. The definition begins by postulating a base class of *a priori* facts, namely the *primitive*, and a corresponding power of the mind which we may call *intellect*. The primitive and intellect are defined jointly: the primitive facts are those that are disposed to be known by intellect, and intellect is the power of the mind that enables it to know the primitive facts. This definition is not circular, because we complete it by giving examples of primitive facts; for example, the law of identity, that everything is identical to itself, is a primitive fact.

The *a priori* facts are the primitive facts and all their logical consequences, so the next step is to define the *logical consequence* relation. According to the rationalist theory, some facts have some other facts as a logical consequence, if it is primitive that, if the former facts exist, then so do the latter. For example, if p and q are not *a priori* facts, then $(p \land q)$ is not *a priori* either, but $(p \land q)$ is a logical consequence of p and q, because it is primitive that if they exist then it exists also. We define logical consequence by the following chain of definitions. Define a *logical condition* on facts as a purely formal condition on their constituents: a formal condition is one that is 'completely general' in the sense of Frege, i.e., it is not restricted to any special subject matter. A *logical generalisation* says that whenever there exist some facts that meet a certain logical condition, then there exist some further facts that are related by a logical condition to the former facts. A logical generalisation is a *law of logic* if it is both true and primitive. For example, the Rule of Inference *Modus Ponens* corresponds to the following law of logic:

$$p \cdot \theta \land q \cdot (\underrightarrow{\rightarrow}, \theta, \phi) \rightarrow (\exists r)(r \cdot \phi)$$

The logical consequence relation can now be defined: some facts have another fact as a logical consequence if the existence of the former facts requires the existence of the latter fact by a law of logic. So for example, if $p = \langle \theta \rangle$, $q = \langle \underrightarrow{\rightarrow}, \theta, \phi \rangle$ and $r = \phi$, we say that r is a logical consequence of p and q, by the above law of logic for *Modus Ponens*.

The rationalist account defines the *a priori* as the primitive facts and their logical consequences. Since primitiveness defines both the base class of *a priori* truths and the laws by which the remainder follow, and since primitiveness is defined by its relation to an epistemic faculty, this conception of the *a priori* is thoroughly epistemic. However, it is not psychologistic, for there is no suggestion that every *a priori* truth is humanly knowable; on the contrary, the limitations of our cognitive powers restrict the *a priori* truths we can come to know. Just as rationalists posit *intellect* as the power of the mind which enables us to know the primitive truths, so they posit *deduction* as the power that enables us to trace the consequences of laws; deduction is thus a further way in which knowledge can be extended by reason alone. The actual deductive powers of human beings are restricted by our cognitive limitations. For example, our ability to discern chains of instances of laws is limited by the length and complexity of the chain; thus we may fail to draw a conclusion that does in fact follow objectively because the chain of logical relations in virtue of which it follows is too long for us to discern. A second limitation arises because it is not enough just to know a law; we need also to be able to recognise its instances, which calls for good judgement and may not be easy.[1] A third limitation is that a logical law may require a great many premises: if it requires too many for us to survey them all, for example because it requires infinitely many premises, then we shall never advance to knowledge of any conclusion by means of our knowledge of this particular law.

The rationalists seem to have held that any rational being can come to know any primitive truth by intellect. However, they would certainly have conceded that individual rational beings will vary in their deductive powers, according as they vary in capacity to discern chains of logical relations, in logical judgement, and in ability to encompass multiple premises in a single survey. Therefore the *a priori* must not be defined in terms of what any given thinker can actually deduce: for the thinker might have been able to deduce more had their deductive powers been greater. Instead we should focus on the property that makes a fact *apt* for being intuitively or

---

[1] A physician, a judge, or a ruler may have at command many excellent pathological or legal rules, even to the degree that he may become a profound teacher of them, and yet, none the less, may easily stumble in their application. For although admirable in understanding, he may be wanting in natural powers of judgement. He may comprehend the universal *in abstracto*, and yet not be able to recognise whether a case *in concreto* comes under it. (Kant 1929: 178, A134/B 173)

deductively known, supposing the deductive powers of the thinker are great enough. That is the property of being either primitive or following from primitive facts by primitive laws, which is therefore the proper rationalist definition of the *a priori*.

4.2 The Strongest Modal Logic Consistent with Rationalism is S4

In the sections that follow, I will be considering counterexamples that have been suggested to the rationalist thesis that the necessary is the *a priori*. Obviously it would beg the question against rationalism, if a proposed counterexample to the rationalist thesis presupposed a modal logic that is inconsistent with rationalism. So in this section, as a preliminary, I discuss which modal logic best fits the rationalist conception of necessity.

How are we to decide which is the correct modal logic? Before the development for modal logic of the model theory of worlds and their accessibility relations, logicians debated the correctness of modal formulas such as '$\Box A \rightarrow \Box\Box A$' by appeal to intuitions. Since the intuitions were neither clear nor robust, many issues remained unresolved. The discovery of the model theory brought order to the subject, elegantly systematising the various modal logics, and making it possible to correlate suggested axioms with accessibility relations in the model. For example:

T: $\vdash \Box A \rightarrow A$

Axiom **T** is valid in all models where the accessibility relation is reflexive.

B: $\vdash \Diamond\Box A \rightarrow A$;

Axiom **B** is valid in all models where the accessibility relation is symmetric.

4: $\vdash \Box A \rightarrow \Box\Box A$;

Axiom **4** is valid in all models where the accessibility relation is transitive.

On the ontic conception of modality, it is usually held that the modal logic **S5** has the best claim to be the correct modal logic. The reason is as follows. The axioms of **S5** are valid in any model in which the accessibility relation is symmetric, transitive and reflexive; in other words, they are valid in any model in which the accessibility relation partitions the worlds into equivalence classes. The trivial accessibility relation makes each world accessible to every world; in effect it makes the whole of logical space a single equivalence class, and so it gives a model of **S5**. On the ontic conception it seems natural to suppose that the possibility 'in the broadest sense' of a state of affairs consists in the mere existence of a possible world at which the state of affairs obtains; 'accessibility' relations are relevant only when some more restricted sense of 'possible' is in question. This suggests that if we wish to axiomatise necessity in the broadest sense, we must treat all possible worlds as accessible to each other. Thus we are led to assign a primacy to the modal logic **S5**, and to regard other modal logics as giving axioms for only some more restricted sense of 'possible'.

However, this line of argument in support of **S5** seems odd, and indeed self-defeating. The argument begins by laying great stress on the importance of the accessibility relation as evidence for the correctness of the model theory; but it ends by insisting on the ultimate irrelevance of accessibility, so far as necessity in the broadest sense is concerned. If accessibility can be so easily set aside as irrelevant to genuine necessity, its usefulness elsewhere cannot be regarded as strong evidence for the correctness of the model theory. And in any case there must be serious doubts about whether the model theory is correct. For the semantics for the modal object language is being carried through in a non-modal metalanguage; so it may be doubted whether the metalanguage is capable of exact translation of every object language sentence.

The rationalist theory of modality will therefore attach little weight to an argument for **S5** from model-theoretic considerations alone. It will feel free to endorse whichever modal logic best fits its own conception of the necessary as the primitive facts and their logical consequences. On this conception, if a fact is necessary, it will have a 'proof'. Logicians think of a proof as a sequence of sentences, each of which either is an axiom or follows from earlier sentences in the sequence by a 'Rule of Inference'. The rationalist theory's conception of proof is structurally similar to this, but it takes a proof to be a sequence of facts, not sentences. A logician's proof needs a language, but on the rationalist conception a proof is not language-dependent; so we define a proof as a sequence of facts, each of which is either primitive or a logical consequence of earlier facts in the proof. (This notion of proof is idealised: it is not suggested that human beings can follow every such 'proof'.)

Every *a priori* fact has a proof. For we defined the *a priori* as the primitive facts and their logical consequences, so every *a priori* fact is a descendant under the *logical consequence* relation of some primitive facts. If it is a descendant, there is a family tree of its descent; this 'tree', itself a complex fact with facts as constituents, is a 'proof' of the fact. The *a priori* fact that is the conclusion of the proof is the 'root' of the proof-tree, and each leaf of the proof-tree is a primitive fact.

In light of the connection between the *a priori* and proof, we can examine some standard axioms and Rules of Inference of modal logic, to test their acceptability from the point of view of the rationalist conception of necessity. All normal modal logics have the following Rule of Inference:

RN (Rule of Necessitation) If you have proved A, you may infer $\Box A$

If A is a theorem, then there is a proof of the fact p which combines the constituents of the Russellian proposition expressed by A. Since p has a proof-tree it is *a priori*, hence necessary according to the rationalist theory, so $\Box A$ is true. Note that we can assert this only for formulas A that do in fact express Russellian propositions; when we consider supposed counterexamples to rationalism later it will be important that the rationalist theory does not underwrite application of **RN** to 'open sentences', i.e., to formulas that contain free variables. If such formulas are understood as implicitly prefixed by universal quantifiers, then **RN** is applicable to them of course; but otherwise such a formula cannot be regarded as stating a determinate fact, so on the rationalist conception it does not express a necessary truth.

We also need to consider which axioms are acceptable on the rationalist conception. Axiom **T** is acceptable:

T $\vdash \Box A \rightarrow A$

Justification: assume $\Box A$ is true. Then some *a priori* fact combines the constituents of the proposition expressed by A. Since a fact combines them, A is true.

The following Axiom **K** is also acceptable:

K (Modal Modus Ponens) $\vdash \Box(A \rightarrow B) \rightarrow (\Box A \rightarrow \Box B)$

Justification: assume that $\Box(A \rightarrow B)$ and $\Box A$ are both true. Then some *a priori* fact p combines the constituents of the proposition expressed by A, and some *a priori* fact *q* combines the constituents of the proposition expressed by $A \rightarrow B$. So the law of logic corresponding to *Modus Ponens* requires that there exist a fact *r* that combines the constituents of *B*. The fact *r* is a logical consequence of the *a priori* facts *p* and *q*, so since they have proofs, *r* has a proof. So *r* is *a priori*, and hence $\square B$ is true.

The Rule of Inference **RN**, and the axioms **T** and **K** seem clearly correct on the rationalist conception of necessity. Thus on the rationalist conception, the modal logic **KT** (which includes **RN, K** and **T**) is clearly correct. **KT** is quite a weak modal logic. To reach the stronger logic **S4** we need the following axiom:

$$\mathbf{4} \vdash \square A \rightarrow \square\square A$$

To reach **S5** we require in addition the 'Brouwerian axiom':

$$\mathbf{B} \vdash \Diamond\square A \rightarrow A$$

I shall argue that the axiom **4** is probably correct on the rationalist conception, but that the axiom **B** is not correct. Thus on the rationalist conception, the modal logic **KT4** (i.e., **S4**), which adds the axiom **4** to **KT**, is probably correct, but the logics **KTB**, which adds **B** to **KT**, and the logic **KTB4** (i.e., **S5**) which adds **B** to **KT4**, are not correct.

The axiom **4** can be justified on the rationalist conception only if we make the following two assumptions:

(i) If a fact *p* is primitive, then it is primitive that *p* is primitive;
(ii) If *p* is a direct consequence of *X*, then it is *a priori* that *p* is a direct consequence of *X*.

Assumption (i), that the primitive is primitively primitive, is a special case of the **KK** principle, that if one knows, one knows that one knows. The **KK** principle is clearly not correct in general, but may seem plausible in the case of knowledge that is primitive *a priori*. Assumption (ii) is that for any instance of the direct consequence relation, it is *a priori* that it is an instance. Since the direct consequence relation is purely formal, it can be coded arithmetically; it can therefore be argued that when it obtains, there is an arithmetical proof that it obtains. So it seems that a case can be made out for the second assumption also. Granted assumptions (i) and (ii), axiom **4** can be justified as follows. Assume $\square A$ is true. Then some *a priori* fact *p* combines the constituents of the proposition expressed by *A*. Since *p* is *a priori* it has a proof, so by assumptions (i) and (ii), we can construct from the proof of p a parallel proof of $\Box p$, by replacing each fact q in the original proof by its necessitation $\Box q$. This replacement process results in a proof of $\Box p$, so $\Box p$ is necessary, so $\Box\Box A$ is true.

The Brouwerian Axiom **B**, '$\vdash \Diamond\Box A \to A$', is a different matter. On the ontic conception of modality, the axiom is valid for possibility 'in the broadest sense', i.e., where we assume that the accessibility relation is the trivial relation. For assume $\Diamond\Box A$ is true. Then there is a world w accessible from the actual world at which $\Box A$ is true; hence A is true at every world accessible to w, and hence in particular at the actual world, if the accessibility relation is symmetric. The trivial accessibility relation for 'metaphysical necessity' is symmetric, of course, so axiom **B** will be correct on the ontic conception.

But is the Brouwerian Axiom really correct? The principle $\vdash \Diamond\Box A \to A$ certainly seems rather doubtful. For example, consider the following 'proof' of the existence of God. By definition, God is a necessary being; it is conceivable that God exists; what is conceivable is probably possible; so probably it is possibly necessary that God exists; therefore by the Brouwerian axiom, probably God exists. It would be extremely surprising if God's probable existence could be so easily proved, but the only questionable assumption in the proof seems to be the Brouwerian Axiom, which must therefore fall under suspicion.

It does not appear to be possible to justify the axiom **B** on the rationalist conception of modality. An equivalent form of **B** is $\vdash A \to \Box\Diamond A$. On the rationalist theory, that would amount to the claim that if A, then it is *a priori* that it is not *a priori* that $\neg A$. But that does not seem to be correct. If A is true and p combines the constituents of A then certainly $\neg p$ cannot be *a priori*, so there can be no proof of $\neg p$. It does not follow that it is *a priori* that there is no proof of $\neg p$. For to establish *a priori* that no proof proves $\neg p$, we would need to examine every proof, to check that it did not prove $\neg p$. After that we would have to combine our knowledge about the individual proofs into knowledge of the single general fact that no proof proves $\neg p$. Of course all of this is beyond the powers of finite beings; but even if an infinite being could examine every proof, still the being could not conclude *a priori* that no proof proves $\neg p$, unless it knew *a priori* that the examined proofs are all the proofs there are. But no reason has been given to think that it could ever be known *a priori* that a given collection of primitive facts included every primitive fact without exception, or that a given collection of laws of logic included every law of logic. Hence from the rationalist perspective the axiom **B** does not appear very plausible.

The characteristic axiom of **S5** is the axiom:

$$5 \vdash \Diamond A \rightarrow \Box \Diamond A$$

This is a theorem if the axiom **B** is added to the modal logic **KT4** (i.e., **S4**). But since the rationalist theory does not endorse the Brouwerian Axiom, then since **5** and **T** entail **B**, it follows that the rationalist theory cannot endorse **5**. Thus the rationalist theory will be unwilling to assert that every possibility is necessarily possible. This unwillingness seems not unreasonable. For example, Socrates is wise, but the possibility exists of Socrates being foolish. This possibility is not a necessary existent, for it is ontologically dependent upon the existence of Socrates, who is a contingent being. In a world in which Socrates does not exist, the possibility of Socrates being foolish does not exist either.[2] (For the distinction between existence 'in' and 'at' a world, see section 4.8.) Thus the existence of the possibility of Socrates being foolish does not entail its necessary existence; therefore that Socrates is possibly foolish does not entail that it is necessarily possible that Socrates is foolish. From the perspective of the rationalist theory, the axiom **5** cannot be asserted.

It therefore appears that, on the rationalist conception, the correct modal logic can be no stronger than **KT4**, with the Rule of Necessitation **RN** restricted to closed formulas. With this background modal logic in place, we are now in a position to examine the supposed counterexamples to the rationalist identification of the necessary and the *a priori*. In the next five sections I shall examine several of these supposed counterexamples: I shall argue that they are not successful in undermining the rationalist theory.

---

[2] (Here I am grateful to a referee.) This is not to deny that there are things such that, if they had not existed, still their existence would have been possible. Perhaps Socrates is one of them. A clearer case is this pickaxe, which might not have existed, if its head and its handle had never been fitted together. But even it they had not been fitted together, still the possibility of their being fitted would have existed, and so the possibility of this very pickaxe would still have existed, or so it could be argued. However, this does not show that the possibility of the existence of the pickaxe *a* exists at every world. There are worlds at which neither *a* nor its head nor its handle exist; there seems no compelling reason to suppose that according to such a world it is possible that this very pickaxe *a* exists.

4.3 Cartesian Counterexamples to the Rationalist Thesis

The Cartesian 'I exist' is often supposed to be an example of the contingent *a priori*, since it was something Descartes could know even when he was placing no trust whatever in the senses. It is indeed contingent, but is it *a priori* on the rationalist conception? Descartes was surely correct to think that his own existence was not immediately evident to the intellect; so it is not a primitive fact. We therefore have grounds to count his 'I exist' as *a priori* only if we can point to *a priori* premisses of which it is a logical consequence. Descartes' famous proof, the *cogito*, started from the premiss 'I think'. His knowledge of this premiss was independent of experience; moreover, he only had to consider the premiss to know that it was true. However, these facts are not sufficient to make his knowledge *a priori* on the rationalist conception. Descartes' knowledge that he is thinking is an example of a person's knowledge of their own conscious states. Such knowledge is admittedly not perceptual, but it is not *a priori* either: for example, if someone has toothache, they know they have toothache; this is not perceptual knowledge, but neither is it *a priori*. In the context of a theory of faculties, self-knowledge of one's own conscious states is most plausibly attributed to introspection, not to pure reason. Thus the premiss 'I think' ought not to be accounted *a priori*, and we have so far no reason to suppose that the *cogito's* conclusion 'I exist' is *a priori* either.

David Kaplan has half-suggested that we can bypass the *cogito*, since the contingent sentence 'I exist' is a 'logical truth of the logic of demonstratives' (Kaplan 1977: 540). I know *a priori* that every token of 'I exist' is true, so in particular I can know of what is in fact my own token that it is true. But to deduce from this that I exist, I need to know that my token was uttered by me and not by someone else. I do know that, of course, but it is ordinary empirical knowledge, not something I can know by pure reason. Therefore it has not been shown that 'I exist' is *a priori* in the sense of the rationalists, and I do not think it can be shown; the same applies, of course, to variants such as 'I am here now'. The supposed Cartesian counterexamples to the rationalist theory are therefore unconvincing.

4.4 Mathematical Counterexamples

Goldbach's Conjecture is the proposition that every even number greater than two is the sum of two primes. At the present time no one knows whether it is true. For all we know at present, the Conjecture could be true yet have no humanly graspable proof; its truth might be just a kind of infinite coincidence, with no reasonably uniform finite mathematical explanation that we can grasp. In that case it may seem the Conjecture is not *a priori*. However, if the Conjecture is true it is 'presumably' necessary, Kripke says, and so it will be a counterexample to the thesis that necessity and apriority coincide (1980: 36–8).

Is Kripke correct to 'presume' that Goldbach's Conjecture is necessary if true? Let $G(n)$ mean that n is Goldbachian, i.e., that if n is even and greater than two then it is the sum of two primes. For any given number, if it is Goldbachian, there is a proof that it is by simple arithmetic. So if we assume that every number is Goldbachian, it follows that every number is provably Goldbachian, and therefore necessarily Goldbachian according to the rationalist theory. Therefore:

(1) $(\forall n)\, G(n) \rightarrow (\forall n)\square G(n)$

We could advance to the conclusion that Goldbach's Conjecture itself is necessary if we were assured of the truth of:

(2) $(\forall n)\square G(n) \rightarrow \square(\forall n)\, G(n)$

But (2) is an instance of the Barcan Formula. In the modal logic **KT4**, which I suggested is the strongest modal logic consistent with the principles of the rationalist theory, the Barcan Formula is not valid. So the rationalist theory cannot directly infer (2) from (1).

But there is a different way to prove Goldbach's Conjecture necessary if true. We appeal instead to the 'ω-rule':

ω-*rule*: infer $(\forall n)A(n)$ from all (the infinitely many) statements expressed by sentences of the form $A(\underline{n})$, where $\underline{n}$ is a numeral.

The ω-rule is simply an extension to the infinite case of the primitive law of logic that Susan Stebbing (1930: 244) calls *perfect induction*:

$S_1, S_2, \ldots, S_n$ are F.

Every S is either S_1 or S_2 or...S_n.
Therefore every S is F.

We can represent the ω-rule as an (infinite) case of perfect induction, as follows:

(1) 0, 1, 2, ... are F
(2) Every number is either 0, or 1, or 2, or ...
(3) Therefore every number is F.

Line (2) is justified *a priori*, because from the (plural) Peano Axioms, which are *a priori*, the following can be proved:

> If there are some things, such that 0 is one of them, and every successor of one of them is one of them, and nothing else is one of them, then every number is one of them, and every one of them is a number.

From this line (2) follows, i.e., every number is either 0, or 1, or 2, ... Now suppose Goldbach's conjecture is true. Then each of the infinitely many statements $G(0)$, $G(1)$, $G(2)$, ... is true, hence provable and therefore *a priori*. So it is *a priori* that 0, 1, 2, ... are Goldbachian. Hence by Perfect Induction, i.e., by the ω-rule, it follows *a priori* that every number is Goldbachian. So Goldbach's Conjecture is *a priori* if true; so whether or not it is true, it is not a counterexample to the rationalist theory.

Gödel's theorem shows not only that there might be arithmetical truths that cannot be proved by ordinary logic, but that there actually are. But the analysis given in the case of Goldbach's Conjecture can be generalised. The Peano Axioms are primitive, and every truth of arithmetic is 'provable' from the Peano Axioms in ω-logic, the logic that comes from Predicate Calculus by adding the ω-rule (Boolos 1993: 189). So since the ω-rule is *a priori*, it follows that every truth of arithmetic is *a priori*: therefore Gödel's theorem does not entail that arithmetic generates any counterexamples to the rationalist thesis. Of course the ω-rule requires infinitely many premises, so it is not a rule that human beings can use. But what makes a fact *a priori* is the objective logical relations in which it stands to primitive facts; these relations obtain or not, whether or not human beings can know they obtain.

Set Theory

Set theory may provide another potential source of mathematical counterexamples to the rationalist theory. A proposition of set theory purports
to state a fact about the realm of abstract objects; so it may seem plausible
that such a proposition is necessary if it is true. But it may not seem
plausible that every truth of set theory is *a priori*. For not all the 'axioms'
of set theory command general acceptance, and certainly they are not all
primitive truths. For example, the Axiom of Choice says that whenever
there is a set of pairs of things, there is another set which contains exactly
one member of each pair. Call this set the choice set. The Axiom has been
debated because it may not be possible to given an explicit definition of
the choice set, so its existence is not guaranteed by an abstraction axiom
or an axiom of separation. Russell's example: if there is an infinite set of
pairs of matching boots, we do not need the Axiom of Choice to tell us
that there exists a set containing all the left boots; but the choice set from
an infinite set of pairs of matching socks is a different matter. Therefore
not all mathematicians regarded the Axiom of Choice as self-evident. It
therefore seems implausible that it is primitive. Moreover, it is known that
neither the Axiom nor its negation can be proved from the other axioms
of current set theory. The Axiom may therefore be undecidable *a priori*,
if neither it nor its negation is *a priori*. Suppose we assume that either it
or its negation must nevertheless be true. Suppose we further assume that
whichever of them is true is necessarily true. On these assumptions we shall
have a counterexample to the rationalist theory.

It would of course be possible to question some of these assumptions.
Not all philosophers believe that there are any sets; of those that do, not
all believe that sets are abstract objects; of these, not all believe sets are
necessary rather than contingent beings. But even if we grant all these
assumptions for the sake of argument, it is still not clear that set theory
really is a counterexample to the rationalist theory.

For set theory is an epistemological oddity. The Peano Axioms for arithmetic strike everyone as self-evident and primitive *a priori*, but the 'axioms'
of set theory do not strike anyone as self-evident in the same way. But they
do not seem to be empirical either, for we know that set theory is conservative over empirical phenomena; this means that there can be no empirical
evidence for or against set theory. Why then do mathematicians believe the

'axioms' of set theory? I would suggest that the reason is that the so-called 'axioms' are not really axioms at all, in the sense of primitive first principles. Rather, they should be regarded as set-theoretical *laws*, i.e., as postulates of a powerful mathematical theory arrived at by induction from an *a priori* evidence base. Set theory systematises the previously known mathematics of arithmetic, geometry and analysis. Thus the evidence for set theory is all *a priori*. Moreover, the evidence is complete, in the sense that it is not possible that in the future contrary evidence will come in from arithmetic, geometry or analysis. So set theory is *a priori*, and therefore necessary.

Admittedly most truths that we arrive at by induction are contingent, but that is only because the evidence from which they are inferred may be contingent; or the evidence may be incomplete, in the sense that evidence yet to come in may disconfirm a hypothesis, since in the realm of concrete things there is no *a priori* guarantee that the future will resemble the past. But the correctness of the inductive method itself is primitive, so what is inferred inductively from evidence that is complete and *a priori* is itself *a priori*. It follows that the Axiom of Choice is not a counterexample to the rationalist theory. For although neither the Axiom nor its negation is self-evident, still we may suppose that either it or its negation is a consequence of whichever version of set theory best systematises the whole of mathematics. In that case either the Axiom, or its negation, counts as a truth of reason, since it is an inductive consequence, and hence a logical consequence, of complete *a priori* evidence. This position is consistent with our not being able to tell at the present time whether the axiom or its negation is true: it may require much further work in the mathematical sciences before we know which system of set theory, if any, is indeed objectively the best systematisation of the whole of mathematics.

4.5 Identity Statement Counterexamples

A third type of supposed counterexample to the rationalist theory is the true identity statement; Kripke's example is the statement that Hesperus is Phosphorus (1980: 100–5). Our giving one planet two names cannot create for it the possibility of being non-identical with itself, so it may seem necessary that Hesperus is Phosphorus. But it may seem there is no case for saying it is *a priori* that Hesperus is Phosphorus, since this major scientific discovery could not have been anticipated *a priori*.

This type of supposed counterexample, which turns on identity, can be dealt with by appeal to Frege's distinction between sense and reference. The rationalist theory says a fact is necessary if it is has an *a priori* mode of presentation—it does not say the fact must be *a priori* under every mode of presentation. Now the fact stated by the sentence 'Hesperus is Phosphorus' is the same fact as that stated by the sentence 'Hesperus is Hesperus.' Therefore if the fact that Hesperus is Hesperus is necessary and *a priori*, then the fact that Hesperus is Phosphorus is also necessary and *a priori*, which dissolves the counterexample.

However, on the rationalist theory it is certainly not either necessary or *a priori* that Hesperus is Hesperus. If it were, it would be necessary and *a priori* that something is Hesperus, and hence necessary and *a priori* that Hesperus exists; which is not the case, since Hesperus is a contingent being. Why then do many philosophers assert the necessity of identity? One reason is that in some systems of modal logic, the necessity of identity can be 'proved' as follows:

$$\vdash x = y \rightarrow (\Box(x = x) \rightarrow \Box(x = y)) \text{ (Leibniz' Law)}$$
$$\vdash x = x \text{ (Law of Identity)}$$
$$\vdash \Box(x = x) \textbf{ (RN)}$$
$$\vdash x = y \rightarrow \Box(x = y) \text{ (Predicate Calculus)}$$

The step that is open to question here is the application of the rule of Necessitation **RN** to the open sentence '$x = x$'. This formula is admittedly a logical truth, for it is true on any assignment to the variable x; but it is not logically necessary, for if the object assigned to x fails to exist at a possible world, then '$x = x$' is not obviously true at that world, and hence '$\Box x = x$' is not obviously true. The proof does succeed if we assume that the quantifiers range over the same objects at every world; but this requires us either to adopt 'possibilist' quantifiers, so that we include non-existent objects in the domain of quantification; or it requires us to say that everything that exists, exists necessarily. Neither of these options is very attractive philosophically. We can avoid them by remaining within the modal logic of the rationalist theory, which as noted above does not permit the application of the Rule of Necessitation **RN** to open sentences. The Rule **RN** applied to closed sentences is justified because every proved fact is *a priori*, but an open sentence does not state a fact, so the Rule does not apply. (Of course, if the formula '$x = x$' is understood with an implicit universal quantifier, then it does express a (general) proposition, from which however the next line of the above 'proof' does not then follow.)

Still, there does seem to be something necessary about the identity of Hesperus and Phosphorus. Since 'Hesperus' and 'Phosphorus' are rigid designators, we can at least claim that if they are actually identical, then it is impossible that they exist without being identical. Therefore if they were not identical, Hesperus would not exist:

$\Box$(Hesperus $\neq$ Phosphorus $\rightarrow$ Hesperus does not exist)

This is equivalent to:

$\Box$(Hesperus exists $\rightarrow$ Hesperus = Phosphorus)

We may therefore retreat from the claim that 'Hesperus is Phosphorus' is necessary, to the more modest claim that 'If Hesperus exists, then Hesperus is Phosphorus' is necessary. But this is no counterexample to the rationalist theory, for it has the following *a priori* mode of presentation: 'If Hesperus exists, then Hesperus is Hesperus.'

Plural Counterexamples

A related type of possible counterexample arises in plural logic. A natural language has referring expressions that refer collectively and are plural rigid designators. Because of rigidity, it seems a plausible principle that if something is one of a plurality, then necessarily if they exist, it is one of them:

(3) $(\forall x)(\forall Y)(x$ is one of $Y \rightarrow \Box(Y$ exist $\rightarrow x$ is one of $Y))$

Thus if a sentence 'a is one of C' is true, and the individual constant 'a' and the plural referring expression 'C' are both rigid designators, then it would appear necessary that if C exist, then a is one of C. But this may seem to generate counterexamples to the rationalist theory. Suppose that we see from a distance a crowd of people coming this way. As it happens, Socrates is one of them, though we are unable to recognise him individually from this distance. Then necessarily, if these people exist, Socrates is one of them; but that scarcely seems *a priori*.

If a is one of C, is there a mode of presentation under which it is *a priori* that, if C exist, then a is one of C? Suppose the plurality C are the individuals $c_1, \ldots, c_n$. If our language does not already contain names 'c_1', $\ldots$,

'c_n' for these individuals, suppose these names added to the language. Now define the new plural term 'C^*' by:

$$C^* =_{df} [\text{the } X: x \text{ is one of } X \leftrightarrow (x = c_1 \lor \ldots \lor x = c_n)]$$

Now if a is one of C, then for some i, $a = c_i$. The fact stated by 'If c_i exists, then $a = c_i$' has the mode of presentation 'If c_i exists, then $c_i = c_i$'. Hence 'If c_i exists, then $a = c_i$' is *a priori*. So assume C^* exist. It then follows *a priori* that $c_1 \ldots c_n$ all exist, so c_i exists, so since $a = c_i$, a is one of [the $X: x$ is one of X iff $x = c_1 \lor \ldots \lor x = c_n$] $= C^*$. So it is *a priori* that if C^* exist, then a is one of C^*. Since $C = C^*$, this is the needed *a priori* mode of presentation of the fact that if C exist, then a is one of C. Plural inclusion is therefore not a counterexample to the rationalist theory.

Plural terms that refer to an infinity of things may seem to present more of a difficulty for the rationalist theory. For a plural logic is very powerful, and allows for plural reference to an infinite, and indeed a numberless plurality. For example, 'the numbers' denotes infinitely many things, and according to set theory 'the sets' denotes numberless things. So the case can arise when 'a is one of C' is true, and C are infinite or numberless. To prove that a is one of C by the method just given, we would require an infinite disjunction to specify individually each of C. The difficulty is that we human beings cannot speak an infinitary language. However, we can describe such a language, and we can state the rules of inference that apply to its sentences, and this is sufficient to allow us to resolve the counterexamples, even in the infinite case.

The discussion can parallel the finite case. Let L be an infinitary language in which infinite and indeed numberless disjunctions are allowed. The syntax of L is just like Predicate Calculus, except that if Γ are some formulas of the language, then their disjunction $V(\Gamma)$ is a sentence of the language also. $V(\Gamma)$ is true if at least one of Γ is true. Then we have the following rule of inference: if A is one of Γ, then from A one may infer $V(\Gamma)$. This is the analogue for the infinitary language of the usual rule for Disjunction Introduction; we finite beings can know that the infinitary rule is primitively correct, even though we cannot ourselves apply the rule in practice.

We now proceed as before. Let $\Gamma(x)$ be all the formulas '$x = c_\lambda$', where each c_λ is the name of one of C. (If L does not already contain names for each one of C, then as before suppose the required names have been added.) Then define C^* by:

$C^* =_{df} [\text{the } X: x \text{ is one of } X \leftrightarrow V(\Gamma(x))]$

Assume that 'a is one of C' is true. Then for some κ, '$a = c_\kappa$' is true, so it is a priori that if c_κ exists, then $a = c_\kappa$. Then by the above infinitary Introduction Rule, it follows a priori that if C^* exist, then a is one of C^*. Thus since $C = C^*$, in the infinite case also there is a mode of presentation under which it is a priori that if C exist, then a is one of C. It is necessary, but it is also a priori, so it is not a counterexample to the rationalist theory.

There is a simpler way to arrive at the same conclusion, if we use the plural list-forming operator 'and', which must be distinguished from 'and' used as a conjunction. The list-forming 'and' takes two terms to make a plural term, whereas conjunctive 'and' takes two sentences to make a conjunctive sentence. It is the list-forming 'and' that occurs in the sentence 'D'Artagnan and the three musketeers were friends.' This does not mean that D'Artagnan was a friend, and the three musketeers were friends. It means that D'Artagnan, Athos, Porthos and Aramis were friends: 'one for all, and all for one'.

If a is one of C, we can use list-forming 'and' to find an a priori mode of presentation of 'If C exist, a is one of C'. Let D be a plural proper name of all the referents of C except a. Then $C = a$ and D, where 'and' is list-forming 'and'. Then 'If a and D exist, then a is one of a and D' is the required a priori mode of presentation of 'If C exist, then a is one of C'.

Necessity of Difference

Another possible counterexample to the rationalist theory is the alleged necessity of difference. It has been argued that just as one thing cannot be possibly two (Necessity of Identity) so two things cannot be possibly one (Necessity of Difference). For example, if the planet Venus is not the planet Mercury, then necessarily Venus is not Mercury. This if correct seems a counterexample to rationalism, since it does not seem guaranteed that there is a mode of presentation under which it is a priori that Venus is not Mercury.

The Necessity of Difference can be deduced from the Necessity of Identity as follows:

$\vdash x = y \rightarrow \Box(x = y)$ (Necessity of Identity)
$\vdash \Diamond(x = y) \rightarrow \Diamond\Box(x = y)$ (**T, K**)
$\vdash \Diamond\Box(x = y) \rightarrow (x = y)$ (**B**)
$\vdash (x \neq y) \rightarrow \Box(x \neq y)$ (Sentence calculus, definition of '$\Diamond$')

Use of the Brouwerian Axiom here is essential, for the Necessity of Difference cannot be proved without it in standard modal logic. But as we noted earlier, the correctness of the Brouwerian Axiom is not attested on the rationalist conception of necessity. Indeed, even on the ontic conception of necessity, the principle '⊦ $\Diamond\Box A \to A$' seems doubtful, as shown by our earlier 'proof' of the probable existence of God.

The Brouwerian Axiom is true if the accessibility relation of relative possibility between worlds is symmetric. Therefore if we deny the necessity of difference, we must also deny symmetry. Let w_1 be a world at which a and b exist and are non-identical. Let w_2 be a world where a and b both exist, but are identical to c. Then if w_2 is accessible to w_1, then w_1 is not accessible to w_2. (See Figure 4.1).

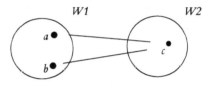

Figure 4.1. Asymmetric accessibility

From the point of view of world w_1, we can say that it is possible that a is identical to c, and that b is identical to c. For from the point of view of w_1 there is no contradiction in asserting this possibility:

$$a \neq b \land \Diamond(\exists x)(x = a \land x = b)$$

Thus relative to w_1, it is possible that $a = b$; so w_2 can be 'accessible' to w_1. But from the point of view of w_2, we may certainly not assert that c is possibly identical to two different things a and b. That would require there to be a possible world where a contradiction is true, for it requires the truth of:

$$\Diamond(\exists x)(\exists y)(x \neq y \land x = c \land y = c)$$

Thus although w_2 is possible relative to w_1, w_1 is not possible relative to w_2. The merging of the entities a and b at world w_1 into c at world w_2 is an irreversible process; once distinctness has gone, the very possibility of distinctness goes with it. Thus we can certainly make sense of the idea that the accessibility relation is not symmetric. Therefore we need not find the Brouwerian Axiom compelling, so we do not as yet have a proof of the necessity of difference.

Williamson (1996) has given a derivation of the Necessity of Difference without using the Brouwerian Axiom, but in an enriched language that includes the operator 'actually'. A crucial step in his proof is the following line (Williamson uses the symbol '@' for 'actually'):

$$@(x \neq y) \rightarrow (x \neq y) \vdash \quad \Box(@(x \neq y) \rightarrow (x \neq y))$$

Here again we have the application of the Rule of Necessitation to an open sentence, something to which we have already seen reason to object in our discussion of the 'proof' of the necessity of identity. Indeed Williamson does not claim that his derivation proves the necessity of difference; he claims only that anyone who accepts the argument for the necessity of identity ought for similar reasons to accept the necessity of difference. Williamson's argument therefore does not compel the rationalist theory to accept the necessity of difference. For as I argued earlier, the (unconditional) necessity of identity cannot be proved if the rule **RN** is restricted to apply only to closed sentences, in accordance with rationalism.

It seems the Necessity of Difference is not provable. It might be suggested that it needs no proof, on the grounds that it deserves to be adopted as an axiom in its own right, as part of the logic of identity. Certainly the Necessity of Difference seems to follow from the usual model theory for modal logic. For suppose that an assignment assigns a to x and b to y, and that $a \neq b$. On that assignment '$x = y$' cannot be true at any world, from which the Necessity of Difference appears to follow. But this only reflects the fact that the usual model theory is being formulated in a non-modal metalanguage. In a non-modal language one cannot of course consistently assert that two things are one; so if an assignment assigns different things to x and to y, then '$x = y$' will always be false on that assignment, hence false 'at every world'. But sceptics about the Necessity of Difference can reply that a non-modal metatheory, whatever its mathematical virtues, is simply inadequate to capture the expressive power of a modal object language. In a genuinely modal language, such as a natural language, we can say truly, without committing ourselves to *possibilia*, that there could have been more things than there actually are, and that there could have been fewer; perhaps we can also truly say that two things could have been one. Perhaps you could have been Napoleon!—this possibility may seem slightly unnerving at first, but one soon gets used to it. So it is possible to question the Necessity of Difference; but then if it is not necessary that

Venus is different from Mercury, the fact that it is not *a priori* either is not a counterexample to the rationalist theory.

4.6 Descriptive Name Counterexamples

Appeal to Frege's distinction between sense and reference allows the rationalist theory to resolve the supposed counterexamples about the necessity of identity. But it may seem that this very manoeuvre only leads to a fresh crop of counterexamples. For we are counting a fact as *a priori* if it has even one *a priori* mode of presentation, and it may seem only too easy to find an *a priori* mode of presentation for certain contingent facts. For example, consider the fact expressed by:

(4) Aristotle if anyone was the pupil of Plato and teacher of Alexander the Great.

This is surely contingent. But the sense of the word 'Aristotle', according to Frege, 'might be taken to be the following: the pupil of Plato and teacher of Alexander the Great' (1892b: 58n). If the word 'Aristotle' really has the sense Frege says it has, then it may seem that anyone thinking of Aristotle under this mode of presentation can know the fact expressed by (4) *a priori*.

It is customary to call a name a *descriptive name* if it is introduced into the language in the way Frege appears to have thought 'Aristotle' could have been introduced. The literature discusses several examples of descriptive names with the corresponding predicates that introduce them: for example, 'one metre' and 'is the length of the standard metre' (Kripke 1980: 54−7); 'Julius' and 'invented the zip' (Evans 1979); and 'Shorty' and 'is the shortest spy' (Kitcher 1980: 200). Each of these has been claimed to give rise to corresponding contingent *a priori* truths of the form of sentence (4): for example, that one metre if anything is the length of the Standard Metre, that Julius if anyone invented the zip, and that Shorty if anyone is the shortest spy. Descriptive names may therefore seem to yield an extensive class of contingent *a priori* truths.

Closer inspection shows that the introduction of a descriptive name does not on its own lead to a contingent *a priori* fact: at most it produces only a sentence such that it is *a priori* that the sentence is true, and which states a contingent fact. For example, suppose S stipulates that 'Julius' is to refer to the inventor of the zip if there is a unique inventor, and that otherwise it is to refer to the number zero. Then if S is a sufficiently reflective thinker:

(5) S knows *a priori* that 'Julius if anyone invented the zip' is true.

Moreover, the fact stated by 'Julius if anyone invented the zip' is contingent. But we do not yet have an example of the contingent *a priori*, unless it can be shown that:

(6) S knows *a priori* that Julius if anyone invented the zip.

Does (6) follows from (5)? We may deduce (6) from (5) only if there is a way to advance from knowledge that a sentence states a fact to knowledge of the fact the sentence states. Philip Kitcher, discussing the example of 'Shorty', suggests that disquotation is such a way. He writes:

[S]peakers of English apparently know (?a priori) that 'If Shorty exists then Shorty is a spy' is true if and only if, if Shorty exists then Shorty is a spy. So it is hard to see why I can't at least come to know that if Shorty exists then Shorty is a spy, on the basis of the knowledge I obtained through my reference-fixing. (1980: 200)

Kitcher here uses the disquotation principle, that 'A' is true if and only if A. If the disquotation principle is *a priori*, and if it is *a priori* that 'A' is true, then Kitcher thinks it cannot fail to be *a priori* that A. So if Kitcher is right, then descriptive names will indeed yield examples of the contingent *a priori*.

In considering Kitcher's argument, it will be useful to consider the 'theoretical terms' of science, which are semantically similar to descriptive names. Here I shall follow the account in Lewis (1970a) of theoretical terms. Lewis considers a theory T that introduces new theoretical terms 'c_1', ... , 'c_n'. We can conjoin all that T has to say about the entities named by the terms in a single sentence, which we call the *Postulate* of theory T:

Postulate: $Rc_1 \ldots c_n$

The Postulate contains the whole of the theory. We can distinguish two separate items of information that it conveys: first, it tells us that some entities exist which (uniquely) satisfy the (complex) predicate $Rx_1 \ldots x_n$; secondly, it tells us that these entities are named 'c_1', ... , 'c_n' respectively.

The first piece of information will often be an empirical discovery made through scientific investigation. The second depends only on a convention to assign to the postulated entities the names 'c_1', ... , 'c_n'. So we regard any term–introducing theory T as dividing without residue into an empirical part, the 'Ramsey sentence' of the theory, and a conventional part, its 'Carnap Sentence':

> *Ramsey sentence*: $\exists! x_1 \ldots \exists! x_n (Rx_1 \ldots x_n)$
>
> *Carnap sentence*: $(\exists! x_1 \ldots \exists! x_n (Rx_1 \ldots x_n)) \rightarrow Rc_1 \ldots c_n$

This division can be justified as follows. The term-introducing theory T extends the original language L to a new language L'. It can be shown that the logical consequences of the Ramsey sentence in the unextended language L are identical with those of the Postulate. So if we are thinking of L as the 'observation' language, we can put this by saying that the Ramsey sentence has precisely the same 'observational' warrant and predictive power as has the Postulate itself. It is therefore natural to regard the Ramsey sentence as expressing the whole of the empirical knowledge the theory purports to convey. Contrast the Carnap sentence, which has no logical consequences in the original language L (except logical truths); it is therefore a conservative extension of the original language L. Because it has no 'observational' consequences, it has no observational warrant. Why then is it included in the theory? The reason is the second of the Postulate's two tasks, namely the introduction of the terms 'c_1', ... ,'c_n' as the names of the postulated entities. As these terms were not already in use in the language, we were free to assign to them by convention whatever referents we pleased. By stipulating that the Carnap sentence is true, we make them denote the entities posited by the Ramsey sentence, if such entities exist. (Mendelson 1987: 80–1.) Stipulating that the Carnap sentence is true just is the act of implicitly defining the theoretical terms. So the presence of the Carnap sentence in the theory is justified by (knowledge of) convention alone.

On this analysis, whenever there are implicitly defined terms, we can expect there to be a term-introducing theory complete with its Postulate, Ramsey sentence, and Carnap sentence. A descriptive name will fit this pattern, so we can see each descriptive name as embedded in its own term-introducing theory. Of course the 'theories' associated with descriptive names are usually degenerately simple; but despite the simplicity of its theory, a descriptive name is formally a theoretical term. For example, for the descriptive name 'Julius' we have the following 'theory':

> *Postulate*: Julius invented the zip.
>
> *Ramsey sentence*: $\exists! x$ (x invented the zip)
>
> *Carnap sentence*: $(\exists! x)$ (x invented the zip) $\rightarrow$ Julius invented the zip.

We see that the allegedly contingent *a priori* sentence associated with a given descriptive name is just the Carnap sentence of the theory that introduced the name; for example, in the case of 'Julius', it is the sentence 'Julius if anyone invented the zip.' What therefore needs to be investigated is the epistemic status of Carnap sentences. I will argue that it is not true in general that the fact stated by a Carnap sentence is something we know, whether *a priori* or otherwise.

A Carnap sentence is sometimes said to be 'true by convention', for by laying down that the Carnap sentence is to be true, we supposedly fix the reference of the theoretical term. Carnap himself called the Carnap sentence the 'analytic postulate' of the theory. However, it is certainly not in general the case that Carnap sentences are analytic. For every logical truth is necessary, so every analytic truth is necessary, since it becomes a logical truth on replacement of synonym by synonym. But Carnap sentences can be contingent. For example, the Carnap sentence for 'Julius' is:

$$(\exists! x)(x \text{ invented the zip}) \rightarrow \text{Julius invented the zip}$$

This is false at possible worlds where someone other than Julius uniquely invented the zip. Therefore it is not true in general that Carnap sentences are analytic *a priori*: indeed, if all there is to go on is a mere linguistic stipulation, the fact expressed by the Carnap sentence, so far from being *a priori*, need not be known at all, or even believed by the stipulator *S*. At the end of the previous chapter I gave arguments from the theory of content for Russell's 'Principle of Acquaintance'. On the given assumptions, *S* is not acquainted with Julius; therefore according to the Principle of Acquaintance, it is impossible for *S* to have any beliefs about Julius. So in particular, it is impossible for *S* to have the belief that Julius if anyone invented the zip; hence this is not something *S* knows.

This conclusion is supported by general considerations about the nature of belief. A belief is internally realised by some intrinsic state of the believer; if the state is to represent that a certain fact exists, a suitable relation must obtain between the state and the fact. Robert Stalnaker calls this the *indication* relation:

What I want to suggest is that belief is a version of the propositional relation I called *indication*. We believe that *P* just because we are in a state that, under optimal conditions, we are in only if *P*, and under optimal conditions we are in that state because *P*, or because of something that entails *P*. (Stalnaker 1987: 18)

But in the case of S's alleged belief that Julius if anyone invented the zip, we find no suitable relation of indication. Let a be S's intrinsic state just before stipulating that the Julius sentence is to be true, and let β be S's intrinsic state immediately afterwards. By assumption the prior state a contains no part that is sensitive under any conditions, optimal or otherwise, to whether it was specifically Julius who invented the zip. But then exactly the same appears to be true of the state β that S enters upon making the stipulation. What β indicates is only that S has stipulated that the sentence 'Julius if anyone invented the zip' is to be true; there are no 'optimal conditions' under which β is any more sensitive to facts specifically about Julius than was a. So β does not indicate that Julius if anyone invented the zip, and therefore β is not a realiser of a belief that Julius if anyone invented the zip.

The same conclusion is supported by Bayesianism. Assume that for each rational agent there is a subjective probability function $P(X)$ giving for each proposition X the agent's degree of belief or credence that X is true. Assume that rational agents revise their opinions by conditionalising: if they learn that A, then their new credence function should come from their old credence function by conditionalising on A:

$$P_{new}(X) = P_{old}(X|A)$$

Here '$P(X|A)$' denotes the conditional probability of X given A. It is possible to make a Dutch Book against agents who revises their beliefs on some other plan. Since *ceteris paribus* it is not rational to agree to a series of bets that cannot gain and may lose, we may conclude that it is at least a necessary condition of rationality that agents revise their beliefs by conditionalising. (Lewis 1999b.)

Suppose that at the outset of deliberation S has no particular opinion about who if anyone invented the zip. Later S stipulates that the Julius sentence is to be true. Is it rational for S on that account alone now to have a high revised credence for the proposition that Julius if anyone invented the zip? Not according to Bayesianism: the new credence ought to equal the old credence conditional upon the stipulation, and this on calculation turns out not to be high.

The calculation is as follows. Prior to stipulating that the Julius sentence is true, S has no evidence bearing on the question of who invented the zip, so S ought to distribute credence fairly evenly across all the worlds where someone or other invents the zip. Since worlds where specifically

Julius invents the zip are a small proportion of these, and since credence is additive, if S is rational then S's credence that someone invented the zip must greatly exceed S's credence that Julius invented the zip, i.e.:

(7) $P((\exists!x)(x$ invents the zip$)) \gg P$ (Julius invents the zip)

Now let A be the proposition *that S stipulates that the Julius sentence is true.* There are many A-worlds (worlds where A is true) where someone other than Julius invents the zip (and hence where the stipulation makes 'Julius' denote this other person). S ought to distribute credence evenly across all the A-worlds, so we conclude that:

(8) $P((\exists!x)(x$ invents the zip$) \wedge A) \gg P$ (Julius invents the zip $\wedge A$)

Therefore:

(9) $P((\exists!x)(x$ invents the zip$) \,|A) \gg P$ (Julius invents the zip $|A$)

So if J is the material conditional that Julius if anyone invented the zip, S's conditional probability $P(J|A)$ is:

(10) $P(J|A) = 1 - P((\exists!x)x$ invents the zip $|A) + P($Julius invents the zip $|A)$

(9) and (10) together tell us that S's conditional probability for J given A is low unless S regards it as unlikely given A that anyone invented the zip, which we may presume is not the case. Therefore according to Bayesianism, S's knowledge of S's own stipulation does not alone make it rational for S to give much credence to the proposition that Julius if anyone invented the zip. Therefore the Bayesian account of rational belief is telling us that it is unreasonable for S to believe that Julius if anyone invented the zip. It is telling us that this is not something S knows.

The Disquotation Argument

Still, someone who sympathises with Kitcher (1980) may find it 'hard to see' why S, having stipulated that 'Julius if anyone invented the zip' is to be true, cannot know by disquotation that Julius if anyone invented the zip. For the following 'disquotation argument' might be given:

(11) S knows *a priori* that 'Julius if anyone invented the zip' is true.
(12) S knows *a priori* that if 'Julius if anyone invented the zip' is true, then Julius if anyone invented the zip.
(13) Therefore, S knows *a priori* that Julius if anyone invented the zip.

But this argument is mistaken. The nature of the mistake is most easily seen if we examine the second premiss. On the assumption that the disquotation principle is *a priori*, the second premiss (12) has a reading on which it is true. However, it has another reading on which it is false, as follows. For suppose that Schmidt and not Julius had invented the zip, and suppose that S had still made the same stipulation. Then the sentence 'Julius if anyone invented the zip' would still have been true, but it would have meant that Schmidt if anyone invented the zip. Now if the Julius sentence can be true even if someone other than Julius invented the zip, it can scarcely be *a priori* that if 'Julius if anyone invented the zip' is true, then Julius if anyone invented the zip. Thus the second premiss has a true reading and also a false reading. The explanation of the two readings is that the word 'true' carries with it an argument place for a language: 'true' means 'true in the language S speaks'. Therefore a scope ambiguity arises with respect to this implicit definite description, and in fact a scope ambiguity is present in both premisses.

In discussing the scope ambiguity, I shall make use of the notion of an *epistemic alternative*: a world w is an epistemic alternative for S at w' iff everything S knows at w' is true at w. The notion is useful in proofs of ignorance: if S has an alternative at which A is false, i.e., if there is there is a possible world w such that everything S actually knows is true at w, yet A is false at w, then S does not actually know that A. The converse is false, of course: every necessary truth is true at every world, hence true at every epistemic alternative of S; it does not follow that S knows every necessary truth.

Using the notation for definite descriptions of Neale (1990), premiss (11) has the following narrow scope reading:

(11a) S knows *a priori* that [the L : S speaks L] ('Julius if anyone invented the zip' is true in L)

Suppose we concede for the sake of argument that the narrow scope reading is true. Then S's stipulation has brought it about that S knows that S speaks some language or other in which the Julius sentence is true. It does not follow that the language L which S actually speaks is such that S knows that the Julius sentence is true in L. For in S's actual language 'Julius' denotes Julius and not Schmidt, so the Julius sentence 'Julius if anyone invented the zip' is true in S's actual language only if Julius invented the zip. But S has an epistemic alternative at which it was Schmidt not Julius who invented the zip, so S has an alternative at which the Julius sentence is false in S's actual language. Thus the following wide scope reading (11b) of the first premiss is false:

(11b) [the L: S speaks L] S knows *a priori* that ('Julius if anyone invented the zip' is true-in-L)

Thus premiss (11) is true only when read with narrow scope.

There is the same scope ambiguity in the second premiss. The narrow scope reading is:

(12a) S knows *a priori* that [the L : S speaks L] ('Julius if anyone invented the zip' is true-in-L → Julius if anyone invented the zip)

The wide scope reading is:

(12b) [the L: S speaks L] (S knows *a priori* that ('Julius if anyone invented the zip' is true-in-L → Julius if anyone invented the zip))

This time at most the wide scope reading (12b) can be true. The language L which S actually speaks is such that the Julius sentence is true in L if Julius if anyone invented the zip. This fact about the abstract language L is arguably a necessary truth, and hence it is true at all of S's alternatives. But S has an alternative at which Schmidt invented the zip. At that alternative, S's stipulation that the Julius sentence is to be true brings it about that 'Julius' denotes Schmidt; so S has an alternative where S speaks a language in which 'Julius if anyone invented the zip' is true if Schmidt if anyone invented the zip. It follows that (12a) is false. The second premiss can be true only when read with wide scope.

So if the disquotation argument is to have true premisses, the definite description must have narrow scope in the first premiss, and wide scope in the second. But then the argument is clearly fallacious. We can symbolise the argument with '*Sx*' for '*S* speaks *x*,' '*Cx*' for ' "Julius if anyone invented the zip" is true in *x*,' and '*A*' for 'Julius if anyone invented the zip:'

(11*) **K** [the *x*: *Sx*] *Cx*
(12*) [the *x*: *Sx*] **K** (*Cx* → *A*)
(13*) Therefore, **K***A*

This is invalid in epistemic logic. Counterexample: let '*Sx*' mean '*x* is the shortest spy', let '*Cx*' mean '*x* is a spy', and let '*A*' mean 'Ortcutt is a spy'.

The shortest spy is Ralph's neighbour Ortcutt. Ralph (of course) knows that the shortest spy is a spy, so (11^*) is true. Ralph (of course) also knows that if Ortcutt is a spy, then Ortcutt is a spy; so Ralph knows concerning the shortest spy that if *he* is a spy, then Ortcutt is a spy, i.e., (12^*) is true. But Ralph does not know that Ortcutt is a spy, so (13^*) is not true.

Once we see that the premisses have scope ambiguities, we should no longer be persuaded by the disquotation argument. On a disambiguation of its premisses on which they are both true, the argument is not valid. On a disambiguation on which the argument is valid, its premisses are not both true. *Pace* Kitcher, we see we cannot know by disquotation that Julius if anyone invented the zip. Therefore descriptive names do not provide any convincing contingent *a priori* counterexamples to the rationalist theory.

4.7 Counterexamples with 'Actually'

The last class of supposed counterexamples involve 'actually'. The function of 'actually' is to allow us, when discussing a hypothetical situation, to cross-refer back to the actual situation. If we say that some people who are poor might have been rich, we do not mean that there is a possible world where some poor people are rich; we mean there is a possible world where some people who are poor in the actual world are rich in that world: so we say that some who are actually poor might have been rich.

The first counterexample with 'actually' is supposedly necessary *a posteriori*:

(14) Actually the Earth moves.

In the terminology of Kaplan (1977), a semantics for 'actually' needs to keep track of the 'context of utterance', as well as the 'circumstance of evaluation'. Standard semantics says that 'actually A' is true in context u at circumstance v iff 'A' is true in context u at circumstance u. So on standard semantics (14) is true in context u at circumstance v iff 'the Earth moves' is true in context u at circumstance u, i.e., if the Earth moves at circumstance u. So the proposition expressed by (14) in the actual context is true in any circumstance if the Earth moves at the actual world; since the Earth does move at the actual world, the proposition expressed by (14) is true in every circumstance, and so it is necessary. But it is suggested that it is not *a priori* that actually the Earth moves.

It would be possible, following Dummett (1981: 447), to distinguish between the 'content sense' and the 'ingredient sense' of the sentence (14). We could say that when (14) occurs as a complete sentence on its own, the word 'actually' is semantically inert, so that its 'content sense' is merely that the Earth moves, a proposition that is neither necessary nor a priori. But although Dummett's seems a defensible strategy, the rationalist theory need not rely on it. For it is possible to defend the rationalist theory even on standard semantics, which treats 'actually' as an indexical expression. An indexical has the semantic role of referring to an entity or entities supplied by the context: for example, on an occasion of use, 'now' refers to the time of the context; similarly, according to standard semantics, 'actually' refers to the possible world of the context. So an actual utterance of 'actually the Earth moves' expresses a fact about the actual world. To defend the rationalist theory, we must find a mode of presentation of this fact that is a priori.

What fact is stated by the sentence (14)? Not the fact that the Earth moves, for that is contingent. Rather it is a fact about that fact, namely that it is one of the facts that exist, according to the actual world. So (14) is equivalent to (15):

(15) According to the actual world, the Earth moves.

I shall abbreviate 'according to the actual world' as 'at @'. So (16) is:

(16) at @, the Earth moves.

To defend the rationalist theory, we must prove that (16) is a priori. We proceed as follows. Let C be the totality of all facts. By definition of C, the actual world is the world according to which C are all and only the facts, so the following is a priori:

(17) at @, C exist.

Now let a be the fact that the Earth moves. If the Earth moves, then the fact a exists, so a is one of the totality of facts, so a is one of C. By our discussion of plural inclusion, it follows that it is a priori that if C exist, then a is one of C. And if a is one of C, then a exists. So the following is a priori:

(18) $\square(C$ exist $\rightarrow a$ exists$)$

What is true according to a world is closed under entailment. For if according to w it is the case that A, then if A entails B, it must be the case according to *w* that it is the case that *B*, else according to *w* a contradiction would be true. So the following is *a priori*:

(19) $((at\ w, A) \wedge \Box(A \rightarrow B)) \rightarrow at\ w, B$

Since (17), (18) and (19) are all *a priori*, we deduce that the following is *a priori*:

(20) *at @*, the fact *that the Earth moves* exists.

It follows that (14) is no counterexample to the rationalist thesis, for (20) is *a priori*, so we have shown that it is *a priori* that actually the Earth moves.

It might seem that this takes us from the frying-pan only to the fire. If it is *a priori* that actually the Earth moves, are we not forced absurdly to conclude that it is *a priori* that the Earth moves? This does not follow, as can be seen by consideration of (21):

(21) If actually the Earth moves, then the Earth moves.

According to Davies (1981: 224), (21) is an example of the contingent *a priori*. The antecedent of this conditional is 'actually the Earth moves,' which in the actual context expresses a necessary proposition, as we saw. Its consequent expresses the contingent proposition that the Earth moves. Therefore in the actual context, the conditional (21) expresses a proposition that is contingent, since it is true only if the Earth moves. But, according to Davies, (21) is *a priori*: indeed, he says, 'such knowledge is constitutive of mastery of the concept of actuality'.

It is indeed constitutive of mastery of the concept of actuality to know *a priori* that in any context (21) is true, but it does not follow that the fact stated in the actual context is itself something we know *a priori*. Indeed, it is easy to see that it cannot be, because for all we know *a priori*, it is false that the Earth moves. Therefore the right side of the conditional (21) is not *a priori*. But the left side is *a priori*, if I have been right in arguing that it is *a priori* that actually the Earth moves. Therefore the conditional as a whole cannot be known *a priori*: for if a conditional has a left side that is known *a priori* and a right side that is not known *a priori*, it follows that the conditional as a whole is not known *a priori*, in virtue of the following analogue for epistemic logic of the modal principle **K**:

$$\mathbf{K}(A \rightarrow B) \rightarrow (\mathbf{K}A \rightarrow \mathbf{K}B)$$

Therefore (21) is not *a priori*; so it is not a counterexample to the rationalist thesis.

Horizontal and Diagonal

We now have a whole collection of sentences that some authors have claimed to be *a priori*. These include:

'I exist.'
'Julius if anyone invented the zip.'
'If actually the Earth moves, then the Earth moves.'

If I am right in saying that these sentences are not in fact *a priori*, there must be some explanation of why they have seemed to so many authors to be *a priori*.

The distinction between the 'horizontal' and 'diagonal' propositions expressed by a sentence can provide the needed explanation. Consider Kaplan's kidnapped heiress, who might say 'It is dark here now' in the trunk of the kidnap car. (1977: 536.) She speaks truly, but does she speak knowledgeably? From one point of view, we should be reluctant to say she does. The proposition expressed by her sentence in context is true only at worlds where her actual location is dark. But she has no idea where she is. She has epistemic alternatives where she is at a different dark location and, for all that has been said, at some of these her actual location is light. The proposition expressed by her sentence is false at these alternatives, so it seems it is not something she knows. But from another point of view we may hesitate to reach this conclusion: after all, the heiress does know that, wherever she is, it is dark at that place. Since her sentence seems exactly right for expressing that knowledge, perhaps we must say she does speak knowledgeably after all.

This is an example of a general phenomenon that arises with context-dependent sentences. Taken one way, the heiress's words express a proposition she does not know; taken another way, they express a proposition she does know. Stalnaker (1978) distinguishes a 'horizontal' and a 'diagonal' proposition associated with a context-dependent sentence. The horizontal proposition is true at a world if the sentence in the actual context is true at that world, whereas the diagonal proposition is true at a world if the sentence in the context of that world is true at that world. The rule of pragmatics of 'conversational accommodation' tells us that when a sentence can bear more than one meaning, we should prefer the interpretation that treats a speaker's utterance as expressing something the speaker knows, rather than something the speaker does not know. So if the diagonal proposition is known, and the horizontal proposition is not known, we interpret the speaker's utterance as expressing the diagonal proposition.

This explains the case of the heiress. She has alternatives at which the horizontal proposition associated with her 'It is dark here now' is false, for she does not know where she is. But she has no alternatives at which the associated diagonal proposition is false, for at each of her alternatives it is dark where she is in that alternative. She knows the diagonal proposition, so the rule of conversational accommodation tells us to interpret her words as expressing the diagonal proposition. This also explains why we are willing to count (22) as true:

(22) S knows *a priori* that if actually the Earth moves then the Earth moves.

S has (*a priori*) epistemic alternatives at which the horizontal proposition expressed by (22) is false. But S has no alternatives at which the diagonal proposition is false. The rule of conversational accommodation tells us to interpret the speaker as expressing the diagonal proposition. That is the explanation of why we are inclined to endorse (22).

Evans (1979) suggested that people at a world where someone other than Julius invents the zip would still be speaking English when they used 'Julius' to refer to this other person. The suggestion would appear to be that we should treat 'Julius' as context-dependent: in a given context it refers to the inventor of the zip at that context. In that case we should expect there to be distinct horizontal and diagonal propositions associated with the content sentence in the following:

(23) S knows that Julius if anyone invented the zip.

The horizontal proposition will be true at a world w if either no one invented the zip at w, or the actual inventor did. The diagonal proposition will be true at w if either no one invented the zip at w, or the inventor at w did. Obviously S can know *a priori* that this latter condition is satisfied. The rule of conversational accommodation tells us to interpret the speaker as expressing the diagonal proposition; that is the explanation of why we are inclined to endorse (23).

Thus attributions of *a priori* knowledge like (22) and (23) have a sense in which they are true after all, because the diagonal proposition associated with each content sentence is indeed *a priori*. But still there is no counterexample to the rationalist theory, for the associated diagonal proposition is itself necessary in each case.

4.8 Possible Worlds Discourse with Only One World

Because the rationalist theory explains the necessary as the *a priori*, it has no need to appeal to possible worlds in its account of necessity. Still, possible worlds figure usefully in many areas of philosophical inquiry. What should the attitude of the rationalist theory be to the discourse of other possible worlds? Are there really any other possible worlds, in addition to the actual world?

Realism about other possible worlds became more popular following the development of a semantics for modal logic in terms of worlds and an 'accessibility' relation between them. It was then noticed that if possible worlds are taken with full ontological seriousness it is possible to develop fruitful applications not only in logic, but also in metaphysics and semantics. In *The Plurality of Worlds*, David Lewis (1986) makes a case for possible worlds in view of their theoretical fruitfulness in metaphysics. He identifies four major areas in which he thinks worlds can contribute to metaphysical theory:

1. Worlds give an analysis of modality—they tell us what it is for something to be possible. '$\Diamond A$' is true if there is a world at which A is true.

2. Comparative overall similarity between worlds provides a foundation for the theory of *closeness*, needed in discussions of counterfactuals.

3. Worlds can found the theory of content—a proposition is a set of worlds.

4. Worlds can found the theory of properties—a property is a set of *possibilia*.

According to Lewis, possible worlds provide the ontological basis for a comprehensive and systematic metaphysical theory. The theory can dispense with universals, for it replaces them with classes of *possibilia*. It can dispense with facts: a proposition is true, not if it corresponds to a fact, but if it is a class of worlds that includes the actual world. It can dispense with unreduced mental relations such as knowledge: a creature has a mind, not if it knows something, but if its functional states can be ascribed propositional contents, i.e., sets of worlds, in such a way as to make the creature interpretable.

On Lewis's own theory, possible worlds are parallel universes. But that is by no means the only way to be a realist about possible worlds. One might instead take a world to be a way for things to be, i.e., a complex property of all the things there are; or one might identify a world with a set of propositions that represent how things are; etc., etc. Thus there are a variety of candidates to fill the theoretical role of possible worlds. It would appear that any theory with worlds in its ontology can dispense with facts and unreduced mentality.

This book seeks to go in exactly the opposite reductive direction, how-ever, and to dispense with worlds in favour of facts and the unreduced mental relation of knowledge. I therefore wish to acknowledge the exis-tence of only one possible world, namely the real world. But dispensing with other worlds does not require us to dispense with talk of other worlds, for we can talk of them if we can describe them, and describing them does not presuppose their existence. So I shall rely on the Theory of Descriptions to underwrite the discourse of other possible worlds, without ontological commitment to any world but the real world.

To give an account of the discourse, without the worlds, we need an account of 'Possibly A' that does not require the real existence of a world at which A. The rationalist theory of modality provides such an account, allowing us to define 'necessary' and 'contingent', 'possible' and 'impossible' in terms of a priori knowledge. We take the bearers of necessity and contingency to be facts: a fact is necessary if it is a priori, contingent otherwise. We take the bearers of possibility to be Russellian propositions: a proposition is possible if no a priori fact combines the constituents of its negation, impossible otherwise. 'Possibly A' is true if it is not a priori that $\neg A$.

Given these definitions, we can give an account of the discourse of possi-ble worlds. We have the symbol '$< x_1, \ldots, x_n >$' as a definite description of the fact whose constituents are $(x_1, \ldots, x_n)$. We can introduce an individual constant 's' to denote the fact thus described; the constant 's' is not a logically proper name; it is a 'term' in the sense of Free Logic, since it denotes something if the fact described exists, and denotes nothing otherwise. Thus we give the meaning of s by the definition:

$$s =_{df} \; < x_1, \; \dots \; , x_n >$$

Since we are working in a plural logic, we are not restricted to singular terms. We can introduce plural definite descriptions, which denote plurally if they denote at all. We shall adopt the convention that a plural description denotes some facts only if *all* the described facts exist. For example, the definite description 'the facts that Plato is wise and that Socrates is foolish' does not denote according to this convention, since the required facts do not both exist. Given any condition $A(X)$ on facts, we can form a plural definite description of the facts that meet the condition, and introduce a plural denoting term 'S', in the sense of Free Logic, to denote them:

$$S =_{df} [\text{the } X: X \text{ are facts} \land A(X)]$$

Thus the situation term 'S' denotes the A-ish facts, if they exist, and denotes nothing otherwise. Now whenever the discourse of possible worlds speaks of a certain possible situation, we can interpret this as follows. We introduce a situation-term 'S', which we take to denote not a situation (for there are no such things) but a class of facts that satisfy the condition $A(X)$ implicit in the description of the situation. The statement that the situation obtains is to be understood as an assertion of the situation's *characteristic proposition* $(\exists X)(X = S)$. The situation's being actual, possible, or impossible corresponds to its characteristic proposition being respectively true, possibly true or necessarily false.

According to the ontology of possible worlds, a situation that is possible but not actual is something which does not exist but which might have done. This threatens to enmesh us in the metaphysics of Meinong. To escape, what we need is the Theory of Descriptions. If we say that a certain situation S is possible but not actual, what we **should** mean is that the situation-term 'S' does not denote, though it might have done. 'S' possibly denotes some facts, but it does not follow that it denotes some possible facts. Unlike the ontology of possible worlds, this interpretation has no tendency to underwrite the Meinongian thesis that there are things that do not exist.

Given the paraphrase for situations, it is straightforward to extend it to worlds. A class w of facts is said to be *complete* iff every fact is one of w. According to the rationalist theory, there exists only one complete class of facts, so there is only one complete class of facts to which we can *refer*. However, we can certainly *describe* other complete classes of facts, simply by including completeness in the description. Define a *world-term* as any term for a class of facts described as satisfying a condition $A(X)$ on facts, and as being complete. Thus we might define a world-term 'w' as follows:

$$w =_{df} [\text{the } X : X \text{ are facts} \wedge X \text{ are complete} \wedge A(X)]$$

Then whenever the discourse of possible worlds speaks of a definite world w, we understand it as introducing at this point a corresponding world-term 'w'. We understand the expression 'the actual world' to denote the complete class of facts, i.e., all the facts there actually are. Since a description of a possible world is a description of a situation, we understand a world w as being actual, possible or impossible according as its characteristic proposition $(\exists X)(X = w)$ is true, possibly true or necessarily false. As with situations, so with worlds: a world that is possible but not actual is not something which does not exist, but which might have done. The world under discussion gives way to a world term 'w', which does not denote but which might have done.

The discourse of possible worlds has many fruitful applications in philosophical inquiry. We shall wish to be assured that these applications are still available to us if we understand talk of possible worlds in terms of the theory of descriptions. One important application is Bayesian decision theory, where possible worlds are needed as points in a structure that represent an agent's credences and values. The points must form a space on which it is possible to define for the agent a credence function and a valuation function. But Bayesianism requires only that there be some structure or other of points; it does not determine the nature of the needed points. Since the structure is to represent only the agent's mental states, it need provide no more points than the agent can actually discriminate in thought. So we can take the points to be not Meinongian worlds, but descriptions of worlds, our 'world-terms'. The descriptions of worlds can all be drawn from the agent's language, or 'language of thought', which will provide enough 'points' for this particular application.

In all applications of the discourse of possible worlds, central use is made of the notion of a proposition being true '*at*' a world. Can this be defined without ontological commitment to other worlds? The idea is intuitive enough if we are thinking of a world as one of Lewis's parallel universes, but on any other conception of possible worlds it conceals some difficulties, and is even ambiguous. We must distinguish between a ('Russellian') proposition's being true 'in' a world, and being true 'according to' a world. It is true 'in' a world, if the fact it represents is one of the facts that exists in that world:

$(x_1, \ldots, x_n)$ is true 'in' $w =_{df}$
$\Box((\exists X)(X = w) \rightarrow (\exists p)(p \cdot (x_1, \ldots, x_n) \land p$ is one of $w))$

A proposition is true 'according to' a world, if the existence of the fact it represents is entailed by the existence of that world:

$(x_1, \ldots, x_n)$ is true 'according to' $w =_{df} \Box((\exists X)(X = w) \rightarrow (\exists p)$
$(p \cdot (x_1, \ldots, x_n)))$

'According to' is weaker than 'in': a proposition can be true 'according to' a world, even if it is not true 'in' that world. For example, the *a priori* proposition 'If Hesperus exists, then Hesperus is Hesperus' is true 'according to' every world, for since it is *a priori*, it is entailed by every proposition, hence in particular by the proposition that a given world w exists. But it is not true 'in' every world, for Hesperus is a contingent being, so there are worlds in which Hesperus does not exist, hence worlds where the proposition does not exist, hence worlds none of whose facts combines its constituents. Since we wish to say that if 'A' is necessarily true, then 'A' is true at every possible world, we must accordingly interpret truth '*at*' a world as truth 'according to' a world. Otherwise we shall be obliged to adopt the system of Williamson (1998), which regards all beings as necessary beings.

In the discourse of possible worlds, a proposition is possible if there is a possible world at which it is true. We cannot interpret this to mean:

(25) $\Diamond A =_{df} (\exists x)(x$ is a possible world $\land$ *at* $x, A)$

For on our view, there is only one possible world, the real world. Therefore we must not say 'There is a possible world at which...' but rather 'It is possible that there is a world at which...,' i.e.:

(26) $\Diamond A \leftrightarrow \Diamond(\exists x)(x$ is a world $\land$ *at* $x, A)$

Similarly we should understand the claim that necessity is truth at all possible worlds as follows:

(27) $\Box A \leftrightarrow \Box(\forall x)(x$ is a world $\rightarrow$ at $x, A)$

In the modal logic **KT4** we can prove (27) as follows. For the left-to-right direction, suppose that $\neg\Box(\forall x)$ (x is a world $\rightarrow$ at x, A). Then it is possible that there is a world whose existence does not entail A. So it is possible that it is not necessary that A. But in **KT4**, $\Box A \rightarrow \Box\Box A$. So $\neg\Box A$. For the converse, assume $\neg\Box A$. Then $\{\neg A\}$ is consistent, so by the reasoning of Lindenbaum's Lemma (Mendelson 1987: 61–2), it is possible that there is a complete class of facts that includes $\neg A$. So it is possible that there is a world in which $\neg A$, and hence at which $\neg A$. So $\neg\Box(\forall x)(x$ is a world $\rightarrow$ at x, A).

Closeness

An important application of the discourse of possible worlds is the analysis of 'closeness'. Given closeness, we can say that a counterfactual conditional '$A \,\Box\!\!\rightarrow B$' is true if B is true at the closest world to the actual world at which A is true. But how can a merely possible world resemble the real world? Must we give a Meinongian account of such similarities?

One can imagine something that does not exist, but which resembles something that does. For example, looking at one's hand, one can imagine a duplicate of it. By definition, the merely possible duplicate exactly resembles the fully actual original. The Meinongian will say here that there is an x, such that x is a duplicate of one's hand, and one imagines x. But the imaginary object can be avoided by saying, with more careful attention to scope, that in this situation one is simply imagining that there is an x which is a duplicate of one's hand. The predicate 'is a duplicate' is employed within the scope of 'imagines': it is part of the description of the imaginary thing. Similarly, resemblance between worlds is not a relation between two entities, the actual world and one that is merely possible. Rather we must think of the property of resembling the actual world as being included in the description of the possible world: the facts described are described as resembling the actual facts.

This can be spelled out as follows. First we explain the 'trans-world resemblance' of individuals and facts in terms of the truth of propositions at worlds. For example, Socrates is wise but Cyrus is foolish. Had Socrates been unwise and Cyrus wise, then Socrates as he would have been would have resembled Cyrus as he actually is. What this means is explained as follows. We have already defined what it is for a 'Russellian' proposition to be true at a world, so now we simply say that there is a resemblance in respect U between x as it would be at w_1 and y as it would be at w_2, if the proposition (U, x) is true at w_1 and the proposition (U, y) is true at w_2. We can conceive of some weighted similarity metric that takes account of all the various respects in which the things 'at' one world severally and collectively resemble the things 'at' another world.

In this way we can conceive of assigning a sense to phrases like 'the world closest to the actual world at which A is true'. Indeed, we can regard such a phrase as defining a possible world by the method of 'specific difference'. This old-fashioned method of biological classification takes a particular species as representative of a genus, and defines other species of the genus by its 'specific difference' from the representative species. For example, if we took the tawny owl as the representative species of the genus *owl*, then we could describe the barn owl as the species of bird that is most similar to the tawny owl, except that it is white and lives in barns. The same method can be used to describe a possible world. As the representative world we take the one and only real world. Then we can describe other worlds by giving their specific difference from the actual world: for example, the world that is most similar to the actual world, except that at it kangaroos have no tails. In general, given any condition $A(X)$ on facts, we can form the definite description:

'the complete class of facts X which are most similar to the actual facts, except that $A(X)$.'

This is sufficient to allow the rationalist theory to give essentially Lewis and Stalnaker's analyses of counterfactuals. (Stalnaker 1968; Lewis 1986b.) We are therefore able to carry over these analyses, formally unchanged, into a rationalist conception of modality.

For example, according to Lewis, '$A \,\square\!\!\rightarrow B$' is true if at every world closest to the actual world at which A is true, B is true also. We translate this as follows:

'$A \,\square\!\!\rightarrow B$' is true if it is *a priori* that if X are any complete class of facts which are most similar to the actual facts except that the fact A is one of X, then the fact B is one of X.'

For example, consider the counterfactual 'If kangaroos had no tails, they would fall over.' Let A be 'kangaroos have no tails' and let B be 'kangaroos fall over'. Let Γ be the totality of facts. Suppose Γ includes the (derived) laws of nature L_1 and L_2, that creatures with off-centre centres of mass fall over (L_1), and that the centre of mass of a tail-less kangaroo is off-centre (L_2). Then on our suppositions about Γ, and on standard assumptions about similarity of worlds, it is *a priori* that if X are a complete collection of facts as much like Γ as possible, except that X include the fact that kangaroos have no tails, then since X will include L_1 and L_2, X will include the fact B, that kangaroos fall over. Thus B is 'true at every closest A-world', and so we can reproduce the Lewis-Stalnaker account within the rationalist conception of modality.

Conclusion

Lewis (1986a) recommended the metaphysics of possible worlds for its capacity to address the four problems of modality, closeness, content and properties. But the rationalist theory seems able to address the four problems equally well. It has an account of what modality is, for it says a fact is necessary if it is either primitive, or a consequence of primitive facts by primitive laws. It preserves the discourse of possible worlds, and of closeness of worlds, without ontological commitment to any world but the real world. Its background metaphysics of knowledge and facts can do just as well as possible worlds theory in providing a theory of content; indeed it can do better, for as I argued in Chapter 3, it can take account of the Fregean aspects of content. Finally the rationalist theory has a background metaphysics of universals, which is a better account of properties than Lewis's class nominalism. I conclude that the rationalist theory gives a workable foundation for the discourse of possible worlds, without presupposing any world but the real world.

5

Consciousness

So far I have said little about the mind *relatum* of the knowledge relation. I suggested earlier that knowledge is the essence of mind; some consequences of that claim will be under investigation in the rest of the book. In this chapter I discuss the relationship between consciousness and knowledge. I advocate a thesis, the Identity Thesis, which defines consciousness in terms of knowledge: it says that all and only those mental acts are conscious that are identical with knowledge of themselves.

A version of the Identity Thesis is to be found in the *De Anima*, 425:12–19. Aristotle writes :

Since it is through sense that we are aware of seeing or hearing, it must be either by sight that we are aware of seeing, or by some sense other than sight. But the sense that gives us this new sensation must perceive both sight and its object, viz., colour, so that either (1) there will be two senses both percipient of the same sensible object or (2) the sense must be percipient of itself. Further even if the sense which perceives sight were different from sight, we must either fall into an infinite regress, or we must assume somewhere a sense which is aware of itself. If so, we ought to do this in the first case. (Aristotle 1941: 583)

A 'sense that is aware of itself' would conform to the Identity Thesis.

In the form in which I shall defend it here, the Identity Thesis exploits the notion of *qualia*:

Identity Thesis: A mental act is conscious if and only if it is identical with knowledge of the *quale* it itself has.

In this form, the Identity Thesis does not derive from Aristotle but from Thomas Reid. Translated into contemporary terminology, Reid's view is that a conscious mental act is identical with knowledge of its own qualitative character.

Reid's Identity Thesis addresses three main problems of consciousness. First, there is the problem of how introspective self-knowledge is possible of one's own conscious states; the Identity Thesis tells us that these conscious states just are knowledge of themselves and their own qualitative character. Secondly, there is the problem of what consciousness is; the Identity Thesis tells us that one is conscious if and only if one is the subject of a mental act that is identical with knowledge of its own qualitative character. Thirdly, there is the problem of how to define *qualia*, and whether there are any; the Identity Thesis allows us to define a *quale* as a universal, each instantiation of which is identical with knowledge of that very instantiation; it entails that there really are such universals, and that they are the qualitative characters. The Identity Thesis thus completely resolves our perplexity about the mystery of consciousness—but only by replacing it with perplexity about the mystery of knowledge.

The plan of this chapter is as follows. Section 1 discusses the problem of introspective self-knowledge, and section 2 introduces the problem of consciousness. Section 3 discusses the considerations that might lead us to posit *qualia* as real universals. Section 4 discusses the problem of the necessary co-occurrence of a conscious state and the consciousness of it. Section 5 introduces Reid's Identity Thesis and restates it in terms of the metaphysics of this book. Section 6 suggests that the Identity Thesis has some important advantages, and section 7 argues that it is an objection to functionalism that it is inconsistent with the Identity Thesis.

5.1 Self-knowledge by Consciousness

At the moment I am facing a table. Also, it looks to me as if I am facing a table. These are two different facts, both of which are known to me. It is by visual perception that I know I face a table. But how is it that I know that it looks to me as if I face a table? Let us call *introspection* this power we have of knowing how we experience things to be.

Is introspection the same thing as consciousness? I am of course conscious of its looking to me as if I face a table, but that is only to say that the experience is one of which I am conscious. I am conscious of the experience; the experience is of its looking to me as if I face a table; but it does not follow that I am conscious that it looks to me as if I face a table. Therefore we cannot simply assume that introspective self-knowledge and consciousness are identical. And indeed it seems plausible that they are not identical, for introspection seems to require more concepts than consciousness. For example, one might lack the concept of a visual appearance: then one would be unable to judge that it looked to one as if one faced a table, even though it did in fact look to one that one was facing a table, and one was conscious of it looking to one as if one faced a table. (For the distinction between 'knowing that' and knowing of', see Section 1.2.)

But although introspection is not simply consciousness, it must certainly be closely connected with consciousness, for only conscious states are introspectible. For example, there is nothing it is like for me to believe that I face a table. A belief is not a conscious state, so beliefs are not introspectible. I believe that I face a table, but to know I believe that, I must observe what I do; since beliefs guide actions, by observing my actions I can infer my beliefs. Another way to know what I believe is by introspection of the judgements I make. For example, Evans gave the following test: 'I get myself into a position to answer the question whether I believe that p by putting into operation whatever procedure I have for answering the question whether p.' (1982: 225.) Evans' test exploits introspection of the conscious judgement, but it is not direct introspection of the belief. That it is indirect is proved by the way it can fail in certain cases. For example, it may be that one cannot bear to acknowledge explicitly to oneself in conscious judgement some unpalatable truth that one nevertheless knows and believes, as all one's actions prove. Such examples shows that Evans' test is not introspection, but only a potentially fallible inference from introspection.

Introspection is a kind of 'privileged access' one has to facts about oneself, which is based on one's awareness of one's own conscious states. Other people can have knowledge of one's conscious states; for example, if one is in pain, other people can be aware of the fact by observing one's behaviour. But one's knowledge of one's own conscious states does not rely on external observation of one's behaviour: one has privileged access to one's own experience, in the sense that one has a way of knowing of it that is not available to other people.

If S is in pain, S knows of S's being in pain, for S could scarcely be in (excruciating) pain and not be aware of it. The rest of us may be aware of it too, because we see S wincing. But S does not rely on seeing S wincing; S

knows of the pain by a different epistemic route. What is it that is privileged in Privileged Access? Some suppose that S is privileged with respect to the fact of S's pain, as if S alone really knows of its existence, whereas the rest of us are reduced to surmise and conjecture. But this 'Sole Access' version of Privileged Access is false—we often know of other people's pain. It is not that there are certain facts to which only S is privileged to have access, but rather that there is an access to these facts which only S is privileged to have. This special way of knowing 'from the inside' about S's pain, which only S is privileged to have, is what I shall refer to as *consciousness*.

Although consciousness is knowledge of what is in fact a state of oneself, I do not mean to imply that it requires one to think of oneself as oneself, i.e., by means of the 'I'-concept. That would restrict consciousness to thinkers sophisticated enough to grasp the concept of the self. But there are many creatures that are conscious, even though they lack a concept of the self —human infants, perhaps, and certainly many animals. Even if one lacked a concept of oneself, one could be consciously aware of pain, without necessarily knowing that it was oneself who was in pain. For example, suppose that Descartes' problems at the start of the second of his *Meditations* had been compounded by a bad toothache. He would have been aware of his toothache by consciousness, but he would perhaps not have known that he himself had toothache, since he had not yet hit upon the *cogito*. Thus consciousness does not require knowledge of the Self.

But consciousness is self-knowledge, in the minimal sense that it is knowledge of what is in fact a state of oneself. The problem of this species of self-knowledge is this: how can there can be any, if it does not rely on observation of one's own behaviour? A number of unsatisfactory solutions have been proposed. One unsatisfactory solution is what Daniel Dennett disparagingly calls the 'Cartesian Theater. (Dennett 1991: 134). This solution says that the mind is a kind of mental theatre, with seats for an audience of only one. The events of S's mental life are an inner drama enacted in S's theatre, and the only seat is always already taken by S's Ego, which has a privileged view of the proceedings by means of inner sense, i.e., by a kind of quasi-perception of mental events. This solution is unsatisfactory because consciousness of 'inner' events is not at all like perception of outer events by a genuine sense like vision. And the 'solution' does not even begin to address the main problem of Privileged Access, which is why there is only one seat in this particular 'Theater'.

A version of functionalism offers a second unsatisfactory account of how there can be self-knowledge without self-observation. Functionalism says a system is a mind if it has inner states that cause and are caused in a certain characteristic pattern. Thus state s_1 will be pain if the characteristic pattern includes e.g., s_1 being caused by bodily damage, and avoidance behaviour being caused by s_1. Similar functional specifications can be given of states of belief; in particular there is a state s_2 that has the functional role of the belief that one is in pain. David Lewis noted that it is open to the functionalist to stipulate that the specification of what it is for a system to have a mind is incomplete unless it is required that s_2 never occurs without s_1. Lewis explains the suggestion, which he himself neither endorses nor rejects, as follows:

> Two states cannot be pain and belief that one is in pain, respectively, if the second *ever* occurs without the first. The state that *usually* occupies the role of belief that one is in pain may, of course, occur without the state that *usually* occupies the role of pain; but in that case (under the suppositions above) the former no longer is the state of belief that one is in pain, and the latter no longer is pain. Indeed the victim is no longer in any mental state whatever, since his states no longer realise (or nearly realise) common-sense psychology. Therefore it is impossible to believe that one is in pain and not be in pain. (1996: 261)

According to this suggestion, if S ever believes S is in pain, S will in fact be in pain, so S's belief reliably tracks the truth with respect to S's pain. Since the rest of us are not hard-wired in the same way to S's pain, we do not have the privileged access that S has.

This suggestion solves the problem by brute force. It says that it is constitutive of pain that having the belief that one is in pain entails that one is in fact in pain. So a state cannot be pain if one can believe one is in the state but not be in it. But in that case most normal human beings are never in genuine pain. For it is certainly not true of human beings that always when they believe they are in pain, they really are in pain; they can succumb to post-hypnotic suggestion, or mistake an itch for a pain. The requirement of exceptionless entailment is clearly too draconian. If the belief that one is in pain can sometimes occur without the pain itself, then we need to know what makes the belief knowledge on the occasions when it does happen to co-occur with the pain.

Perhaps the functionalist will invoke some version of reliabilism. For example, we might posit an introspective belief-fixing mechanism whose task is to write the 'Language of Thought' sentence 'I am in pain' in one's belief box when and only when one is in pain. It can be conceded that other causes, such as post-hypnotic suggestion or an itch, may cause the same sentence to be written when it is false. But this does not detract from the reliability of the introspective belief-fixing mechanism: when it is the mechanism that writes the sentence, the belief so formed is reliably based. The difficulty with this is that the bare reliability of a belief-fixing mechanism is not in general sufficient for a true belief to be knowledge; we are therefore owed an account of why reliability is supposed to be sufficient for knowledge in the special case of introspective self-knowledge.

A second difficulty with the suggestion is concerned with defeasibility. Usually when a belief is formed by a reliable mechanism, rationally convincing but misleading evidence that the mechanism is unreliable will defeat knowledge. For example, suppose I usually fix my beliefs about whether it will rain today by consulting my barometer. My barometer is working perfectly and correctly predicts rain, so my true belief that it will rain today is produced by a reliable mechanism. But if a barometer expert mistakenly tells me that my barometer is faulty, my evidence is defeated and I cease to know that it will rain. In contrast, if a consciousness expert mistakenly tells me I have a disorder of consciousness that causes me to seem to feel pains that are not really there, a different situation seems to arise. If later I am in pain, what the expert misleadingly told me may or may not affect my belief that I am in pain, but it will scarcely stop me *feeling* the pain. But if I still feel the pain, I am still aware of it and my knowledge of its existence is undefeated. Thus perception and consciousness differ with respect to defeat by analogously misleading evidence. Since reliabilism does not explain the disanalogy, it seems we must regard its account of self-knowledge as incomplete.

There seems in any case to be some mistake in the very idea that consciousness is to be explained by the operation of a belief-fixing mechanism, or even a faculty. When the operation of a faculty causes knowledge, the faculty causes a mental act in the mind, and the mental act in turn causes knowledge of the fact. For example, one knows by looking, or by inferring, or by remembering; in each case we can distinguish between the mental act produced by the faculty and the fact which the mental act causes the thinker to know; the mental acts are 'distinct existences' from the facts known, and each can exist without the other. For example, a visual experience can exist without the scene it represents existing, and conversely a scene can exist without being represented in any visual experience. But consciousness seems different; it seems impossible for that of which one is conscious to exist, without consciousness of it existing also. Thus the relation between the fact known and the consciousness of it cannot be causal. It seems that we acquire knowledge by consciousness in a different way from other kinds of knowledge, and I will be suggesting that there is in fact no faculty of consciousness.

5.2 What is Consciousness?

Wittgenstein wrote:

The feeling of an unbridgeable gulf between consciousness and brain-process. I turn my attention in a particular way on to my own consciousness, and, astonished, say to myself: THIS is supposed to be produced by a process in the brain! - as it were clutching my forehead. (Wittgenstein 1967b: 124^e, § 412)

Wittgenstein is certainly right to say that it is obscure how a material substance can be conscious. However, it is equally obscure how an immaterial substance can be conscious. The Cartesian account of consciousness is that we are conscious because we are, or are in part, mental substances: consciousness is the 'essence' of mental substance, just as extension is the essence of material substance; the difference between conscious and non-conscious is the difference between material and immaterial. But this distinction cannot be the heart of the matter. Suppose scientists of the future do indeed discover that humans are not entirely material beings, and that we have an immaterial part, or at least are in causal contact with something immaterial. How would that shed any light on the nature of consciousness? We do not understand how material substance can think, it is true; but it is just an illusion to suppose that we have any better understanding of how an immaterial substance can think (Locke 1979: 539−43, IV.iii.6).

Can functionalism solve the problem of consciousness? One functionalist account is the Higher Order Thought theory, or HOT. According to Rosenthal (1993: 199), for example, a mental state's being conscious just is its being accompanied by a suitable higher-order thought, such as the belief that one is in the state. An obvious difficulty is that this seems to set too high a standard for being in conscious pain. According to the theory, it is possible for an animal that lacks beliefs to be in pain, but its pain will not be conscious, since it lacks the ability to believe that it is in pain. It follows that being in pain makes no difference to what it is like to be that animal, even if the pain is excruciating. That might seem to common sense to be a *reductio ad absurdum* of the theory, though the difficulty is brushed aside by some HOT theorists (Carruthers 1996: 222–3).

A second difficulty with the HOT theory is that it is liable to count too many mental states as conscious. Beliefs are never conscious, for a belief is merely a disposition to judgement and other action, and the disposition itself is not a conscious state. But one can certainly believe that one believes that *A*, and according to the HOT that should make one's belief that *A* a conscious belief. This consequence of the HOT is therefore an objection to it.

It might be suggested that the scope of the HOT should therefore be restricted to experiences rather than beliefs. Further difficulties remain, however. For example, it is necessary to take account of the mode of presentation. Suppose, as HOT thinks possible, that you are in excruciating pain, but that you are not consciously in pain, since for some reason you do not believe you are in pain. Suppose you now catch sight of yourself in a mirror, without recognising yourself. You notice that the person in the mirror is wincing, so you naturally come to believe that that person is in pain. You believe of that person, i.e., of yourself, that they are in pain; according to the HOT, it should follow that your excruciating pain has now become conscious, with dramatic effects on your experience. But that is absurd. How could noticing what you take to be someone else wincing have such a dramatic effect on your own experience? The HOT must therefore specify some special mode of presentation, under which one must believe one is pain, if the pain is to be conscious. Surely that can only be the mode of presentation under which one has privileged access to one's own mental states, i.e. the mode of presentation characteristic of consciousness. But that just returns us to our first problem of self-knowledge by consciousness. Since we lack an adequate functionalist account of self-knowledge, the HOT is not an adequate account of consciousness.

5.3 The Problem of *Qualia*

It looks to me as if I face a table. There are three features of this conscious state that are of theoretical interest here. First, the state belongs to a certain psychological type, namely, it is a visual experience. Secondly, it has a certain content, namely *that I face a table*. Thirdly, the experience has a certain phenomenal character, since there is something it is like for me when it looks to me as if I face a table. Here I distinguish 'phenomenal' character from 'qualitative' character or *qualia*. Phenomenal character is supposed to be a neutral term defined, without presupposing *qualia*, as follows: mental acts have the same phenomenal character if and only if they are subjectively indiscriminable. States q_1 and q_2 are subjectively indiscriminable for S if and only if whenever S is in state q_1, S is aware by consciousness of the fact of S's being in state q_1, but S is not aware by consciousness that S is not in state q_2; and *vice versa*.

The debate about *qualia* is not about whether experiences have phenomenal character—that ought to be uncontroversial on any view. Rather the issue is whether an experience's having a certain phenomenal character is anything over and above its being of a certain psychological type and having a certain content. The advocates of *qualia* say that *qualia* are a distinct third class of universals that are not exhausted by the experience's psychological type and content: they hold that an experience has its particular phenomenal character in virtue of instantiating the *quale* it does, and that experiences are subjectively indiscriminable if and only if they instantiate indiscriminable *qualia*. Some advocates of *qualia* make many further claims about *qualia*; for example, that they are 'subjective' properties, or non-physical properties, or that they are 'intrinsic' or 'non-representational'; I shall not be concerned with any such claims here. I shall simply assume that *qualia* are hypothesised to be the distinctive universals that give experience its phenomenal character

One argument for the existence of *qualia* is the 'inverted spectrum' (Locke 1979: 389, II.xxxii.15). It is suggested that it is a perfectly intelligible possibility that two people might have their colour *qualia* inverted with respect to each other, in a way that could not be detected in behaviour. One might object to this on verificationist grounds, since there is by hypothesis no way of verifying that the spectrum is inverted. A better objection is that it has not been shown that this is not just a case of *concept* inversion: since the contexts are different (different agents) the inverted colour concepts can yield knowledge of exactly the same facts, resulting in indiscernible behaviour. In any theory that has concepts in play, the inverted spectrum does not appear to enforce belief in *qualia*.

A second argument is Frank Jackson's (1982). It concerns a hypothetical person Mary who lives in a black-and-white environment. Mary has never had the experience of seeing colour. She knows what *red* is, for she has a comprehensive knowledge of the physics of colour and the objective science of colour vision. But there is one fact about *red* she has still to learn. When she first has the experience of seeing something red, she will come to know the *quale* of the experience of seeing something red. But Jackson's argument does not force us to posit *qualia*. For if concepts are in play we can say that the new experience does not cause Mary to encounter a new property. Rather, it causes her to form a new experiential concept of an old property, namely the property *red*, of which she already has a theoretical concept from her scientific knowledge (Papineau 2002: 47–72). The new concept, and the new skills it makes possible, sufficiently explain everything in the Mary story that requires explanation.

A third argument for *qualia* is more promising than the first two, since it cannot be evaded by appeal to new concepts. This argument appeals to phenomenal resemblance. Where some properties are determinates of a determinable, we can speak of the distance of two of the properties in the quality space of that determinable; for example we say that a red thing and an orange thing are closer in *colour space* than are a yellow thing and a violet thing. The degree of resemblance depends on how far the colours are from each other in colour space. Now experiences can resemble each other more or less, and in different respects. Sometimes a resemblance is a matter of closeness of psychological type, sometimes of closeness of content. If *qualia* are a distinct third determinable under which experiences fall, then it is possible that experiences that lie far from each other in psychological-type space and far from each other in content space might lie close to each other in *qualia* space. And it seems very plausible that this is in fact how things are. For example, Locke reports a certain 'studious blind man' as follows: 'Upon his friend demanding what scarlet was, the blind man answered it was like the sound of a trumpet.' (1979: 425, III.iv.12.) Locke uncharitably took the blind man to mean that the colour scarlet resembles the sound of a trumpet.

But it seems more likely that what he meant was that the visual experience of seeing scarlet resembles the aural experience of hearing a trumpet, which it does. The experiences are far from each other in psychological-type space, and far from each other in content space, yet there is a real resemblance between them. The *qualia* theorist can explain the resemblance by saying that the experiences lie close in *qualia* space; *qualia* are real universals, and are a distinctive respect in which experiences can resemble.

A fourth argument concerns imaginary beings—Martians, perhaps— who look and behave just like us, but have no *qualia*. I shall argue that such a being cannot be a true functional analogue of ourselves. To see why, consider the phenomenal character of experiences of pain. Noception, the sense of pain, is a specialised sense for the perception of bodily injury; for example, to have a pain in one's foot is to perceive by this specialised sense that there is damage to one's foot. For human beings, mental acts of noception have a characteristic unpleasant phenomenal character. Now imagine two patients who need surgery to their feet; one patient is a Martian, the other a normal human. The Martian will be content to have the needed surgery without an anaesthetic; it will sense by noception the temporary bodily injury done to its foot by the surgery, but it doesn't mind the injury, for it knows it is temporary and needed for health. Nor does the Martian object to nocecepting the injury—on the contrary, it is pleased to know that it has a working faculty of noception, which it knows is also needed for health. The Martian experiences no *qualia*, so it has no objection to the noceceptive experience, and no objection to the surgery being performed without anaesthetic. But the human patient does object. Like the Martian, the human doesn't mind the injury to their foot that they nocecept, nor do they mind knowing by introspection that they nocecept. But they do mind the noceceptive experience itself, because of its unpleasant phenomenal character. It is so unpleasant that without an anaesthetic they would refuse to agree to the surgery. The Martian and the human behave differently, so they are not functional duplicates, though the psychological type and the content of their noceceptive experiences are the same. Therefore a being who lacked *qualia* would not behave like a human being; and therefore *qualia* are something over and above the psychological type and content of our experiences.

These arguments for *qualia* of course do nothing to show that *qualia* are not physical properties. They do not even show that *qualia* have anything specially to do with consciousness. But I will now argue that *qualia* are indeed linked to consciousness, since they are needed to help explain the necessary connection that seems to exist between one's experience and one's consciousness of it.

5.4 The Necessity of Co-occurrence

A striking feature of certain mental events is that the event and one's consciousness of it necessarily co-occur—it is metaphysically impossible to have the one without the other. For example, let p be the fact that one is in pain, and let Cp be the fact that one is conscious of being in pain. Then the one fact cannot exist, unless the other does also. For if one is in (excruciating) pain, how could one fail to be conscious of it? And conversely if one is conscious of pain, then one really is in pain. So the fact of pain and the fact of consciousness of pain are mutually entailing:

Consciousness Co-Occurrence $\Box(Cp \leftrightarrow p)$

All and only the mental events that satisfy this co-occurence property are conscious.

Functionalist theories of consciousness usually treat consciousness as a species of belief. In view of co-occurrence, such theories must say that pain and the belief that one is in pain are mutually entailing. So if p is the fact that one is in pain, functionalists must endorse:

Belief Co-occurrence $\Box(Bp \leftrightarrow p)$

This separates into the following two entailments:

Reliability entailment $\Box(Bp \to p)$
Awareness entailment $\Box(p \to Bp)$

As noted, Lewis suggested that functionalists might explain introspection by proposing that the Reliability entailment $\Box(Bp \to p)$ is an analytic truth about the belief that one is in pain. The HOT theory endorses the Awareness entailment $\Box(p \to Bp)$ as an analytic truth about conscious pain. But as I argued earlier, both these suggested entailments are incorrect. The claim that belief has the co-occurrence property therefore cannot be sustained, so the thesis $C = B$, i.e., that consciousness is belief, cannot be sustained either.

A better idea is the thesis that $\mathbf{C} = \mathbf{K}$, i.e., that for conscious mental states, consciousness is knowledge. That requires knowledge of conscious states to have the co-occurrence property:

Knowledge Co-occurrence $\Box(\mathbf{K}p \leftrightarrow p)$

The left-to-right direction of this is true of course, for '$\Box(\mathbf{K}p \rightarrow p)$' is just the factiveness of knowledge. The right-to-left direction, '$\Box(p \rightarrow \mathbf{K}p)$' is also true, for pain is a feeling, so one can be in pain only if one feels pain; but one cannot feel a pain without being aware of the pain, i.e., without knowing of it.[1] Thus the co-occurrence property of consciousness, that $\Box(\mathbf{C}p \leftrightarrow p)$, rules out identification of consciousness with belief, but it does not rule out the identification of consciousness with knowledge.

5.5 The Identity Thesis

If consciousness is knowledge, what is the explanation of the necessary connection between pain and knowledge of pain? Why is it a metaphysical impossibility to have the one without the other?

According to the theory of necessity presented in Chapter 4, a fact is metaphysically necessary only if it is *a priori* under some mode of presentation. So there must be modes of presentation of my present pain and my present awareness of that pain, under which it is *a priori* that either both or neither exist. Now if the pain and the knowledge of it are two different things, it is unlikely to be *a priori* that if the one exists, then so does the other. That would require the laws of psychology that deal with human sensation to be not only true, but primitive, or at least provable *a priori*. A more plausible explanation of the apriority of '$\mathbf{K}p \leftrightarrow p$' is that the pain and the knowledge of it are the same thing. Wherever there is identity, there is a mode of presentation under which it is *a priori* that you cannot have the one thing without the other: for example, you cannot have Hesperus without Phosphorus, because it is *a priori* that you cannot have Hesperus without Hesperus. Thus if the theory of necessity of Chapter 4

---

[1] For a persuasive defence of this, see Shoemaker (1996: 226–9). The distinction between 'knowing that' and 'knowing of' again assumes some importance; I could not be in excruciating pain without being aware of it, but I might not be aware that it was excruciating, if for example I lacked the concept expressed by 'excruciating', or if the pain was a borderline case of excruciating pain.

is accepted, the simplest explanation of the co-occurrence property is the Identity Thesis that the pain and the knowledge of it are identical.

If the theory that necessity is apriority is not accepted, then necessity must be explained some other way. Suppose we explain it as truth at all possible worlds. Then the co-occurrence property means that the pain and the knowledge of it are present or absent together at exactly the same possible worlds; we never get the one without the other. Why should that be? Realists about possible worlds should be willing to endorse Hume's Principle that, at least for contingent beings, there are no necessary connections between distinct existences. Given Hume's Principle, the necessary connection between pain and the knowledge of it entails that they are not distinct existences. The simplest way for things to be not distinct is to be identical, so on this account of necessity too we are led to the Identity Thesis.

We find the Identity Thesis in Thomas Reid. He writes:

Consciousness is that immediate knowledge we have of our present thoughts and purposes, and in general of all the present operations of our minds.

When I am pained, I do not say that I perceive pain, but that I feel it, or that I am conscious of it. When I am pained, I cannot say that the pain I feel is one thing, and that my feeling it is another thing. They are one and the same thing, and cannot be disjoined, even in imagination.

What we have said of pain may be applied to every other sensation. The feeling and the thing felt are one and the same. (Reid 1846: 222, I.i.7; 222, I.i.6; 229, I.i.12)

According to Reid, pain is identical with feeling pain, which is identical with being conscious of pain, which is identical with knowledge of pain.

How exactly should we understand Reid's claim? Reid is clearly denying that there needs to be a distinct mental act by which one learns of one's pain. He is concerned to draw a sharp distinction between conscious self-knowledge and knowledge that comes from a faculty. For example, in perceptual knowledge, e.g., visual knowledge of a seen fact, the visible fact causes one's faculty of vision to cause in one a mental act of visual experience, which in turn causes one to know the fact. In consciousness, by contrast, there is no distinction between the event of which one is conscious, for example one's pain, and the mental act by which one is conscious of this event. One's pain and one's awareness of one's pain are the very same thing.

How should we represent Reid's Identity Thesis in the notation for facts that I have been using? Let q be the fact S is aware of, when S is conscious of S's pain. Let e be S's pain at time t. The pain e is an event, so by the metaphysics of events of section 3.1, e is a temporal fact. By Reid's Identity Thesis, the pain e is identical with S's consciousness of the fact q: so we must identify e with the temporal fact that S knows q at t. Letting '**K**' denote the knowledge relation, we have:

Reid's Equation: $e = \langle \mathbf{K}, S, q, t \rangle$

Supposing Reid's Equation is correct, which is the fact q that one is aware of when one is conscious of pain? I shall consider five candidate 'solutions' to Reid's Equation.

A first suggestion is that q is the fact that is given to noception. For example, if one has a pain in one's foot, q is the fact which one is aware of under a noceptive mode of presentation, namely, that there is injury to one's foot. But this solution cannot be right. For one can be in pain even when no fact is given to noception: phantom limb pain is real pain, but it is not the noception of injury to a real limb. The fact of which one is aware in conscious pain concerns the noceptive experience itself, not what the experience represents. So we must reject the first solution.

A second solution is that what one is conscious of is the type and content of one's experience; in the present case, that e is a noceptive experience with the content that one's foot is injured. But this suggestion does not seem very plausible. A simple animal can be consciously aware of its pain; it seems unlikely that the fact q of which it is aware is that it is having a noceptive experience that represents bodily injury. Moreover, pain is a feeling, as Reid says, and the feeling is something over and above the type and content of the experience. Our imaginary Martian had the same noceptive experience with the same content as the human being, but was not conscious of the same thing the human was conscious of, since the Martian did not mind the experience of the surgery without anaesthetic. We should therefore reject the second solution.

It looks as if we must bring *qualia* into the story, so a third suggestion is that the fact q is 'what it is like' for the subject of the experience e. The suggestion would be that a *quale* is a property of the subject of the experience; what one is conscious of is one's instantiation of the *quale*. This fits well, at least superficially, with what Reid himself says:

Sensation, taken by itself, implies neither the conception nor the belief of any external object. It suppose a sentient being, and a certain manner in which that being is affected; but it supposes no more. (1846: 312, II.xvii)

We may be tempted to identify the 'certain manner' in which the 'sentient being' is affected with 'what it is like' for the subject of the experience. Let λ be 'what it is like' to be the subject of the pain. Then our third 'solution' to Reid's equation will be that the fact q of which S is conscious is S's instantiation of λ:

Solution (3): $q = \langle \lambda, S, t \rangle$
$e = \langle \mathbf{K}, S, q, t \rangle = \langle \mathbf{K}, S, \langle \lambda, S, t \rangle, t \rangle$

But the fact $\langle \lambda, S, t \rangle$ is not identical with the fact e, for it has different constituents; and it is not a fact about e, for e is not a constituent of $\langle \lambda, S, t \rangle$. So $\langle \lambda, S, t \rangle$ is not a fact about one's pain e, and so e is not consciousness of e, contrary to the Identity Thesis. So we must reject solution (3).

A fourth solution is that the fact q just is the fact e that is the experience itself. Then:

(Solution 4) $q = e$
$e = \langle \mathbf{K}, S, e, t \rangle$

An initial concern about solution (4) is that it entails that the relation of combination in a fact is not well-founded. It says e is a constituent of itself, i.e., that:

$e \cdot \langle \mathbf{K}, S, e, t \rangle$

This entails that we may not assert an axiom of 'foundation' for the combination relation, which might suggest an increased danger of self-referential paradox in the theory of facts. However, since there is a consistent theory of non-well-founded sets, we may reasonably hope that there can also be a consistent theory of non-well-founded facts.[2] If so, then

---

[2] See Aczel (1988) for non-well-founded sets. I discussed at the end of Chapter 2 how the metaphysics of facts can avoid paradoxical sentences and paradoxical (Russellian) propositions. In the absence of an axiom of well-foundedness for combination we might worry about the possibility of paradoxical facts. For example, the fact *that this very fact is not known*, if it existed, would give rise to paradox. An axiom of foundation would prevent this troublesome fact from existing, but in the absence of that axiom the law of contradiction can do the job just as well. Paradox would arise only if some other axiom demanded the existence of the troublesome fact; but nothing in the theory of Chapter 2 does demand its existence, so far as I can see.

having *e* as a constituent of itself is actually quite an attractive feature of solution (4), for it fits well with the apparently 'self-referential' character of consciousness, that pain is consciousness of pain, which is consciousness of consciousness of pain, and so on. So I think we need not reject this solution merely because it conflicts with the well-foundedness of facts.

However solution (4) does not tell the whole story about consciousness of pain. Conscious states come in great variety, and we wish to know what distinguishes the varieties from each other. According to Reid:

A small degree of reflection may satisfy us that the number and variety of our sensations and feelings is prodigious; for to omit all those which accompany our appetites, passions and affections, our moral sentiments and sense of taste, even our external senses furnish a great variety of sensations, differing in kind, and almost in every kind an endless variety of degrees. (1846: 311, II. xvi)

There is nothing in solution (4) to tell us which 'variety' of sensation the event *e* is: indeed, there is nothing even to tell us that it is a sensation. Therefore the fact *q* that is given to consciousness when one is in pain is left undetermined by the bare identity $q = e$, and we must reject solution (4).

A fifth solution again invokes *qualia*, and agrees with the third solution that we need to recognise *qualia* as genuine properties. But it takes a *quale* to be a property not of the subject of experience, but of the experience itself. It says that the fact *q* that *S* is conscious of is the painful qualitative character of *S*'s current experience. So if *e* has the *quale* μ, then *q* is the fact that *e* has μ at *t*, i.e.:

Solution (5): $q = \langle \mu, e, t \rangle$
$e = \langle \mathbf{K}, S, q, t \rangle) = \langle \mathbf{K}, S, \langle \mu, e, t \rangle, t \rangle$

Solution (5) is fully consistent with the criterion of identity for facts. It is inconsistent with well-foundedness, it is true, for it makes the event *e* a constituent of a constituent of itself; but as I suggested earlier, I do not think we need regard that as a compelling objection. I therefore propose to adopt this as the right way to formulate Reid's Identity Thesis: one's pain is identical with one's awareness of the qualitative character of the pain.

The Identity Thesis thus formulated allows us to distinguish consciousness from other kinds of knowledge. Bystanders who observe one's behaviour may judge correctly that one is in pain: the judgement gives them knowledge of one's pain, but their knowledge of the pain is not identical with the pain itself, and hence it is not knowledge by consciousness. One may oneself have a present memory of past pain: the time constituent of the fact of the pain is different from the time constituent of the memory; therefore memory knowledge of past pain is not identical with the remembered pain, and hence it is not consciousness. The knowledge is consciousness only if the pain and the knowledge of it are one and the same fact.

Reid himself applied the Identity Thesis for consciousness only to sensation, but Brentano generalised it by advocating an Identity Thesis that extended to every conscious mental event. According to Brentano, each conscious state is identical with consciousness of its own occurrence; he claims that this is in fact the criterion of whether an event is conscious. (1995: 101–37.) The Identity Thesis of Brentano includes every event which is part of 'what it is like' for a subject at a time. If we do extend the Identity Thesis to all conscious mental events, we can define *qualia* as follows: a unary property μ is a *quale* if and only if every instance of μ is identical with knowledge of itself.

μ is a *quale* $=_{df}$
$(\forall e)(\mu(e) \rightarrow (\exists S)(e$ is a mental act $\wedge$ subject$(e) = S \wedge e = \langle \mathbf{K}, S, \langle \mu, e, t \rangle, t \rangle))$

Given this definition of phenomenal character, we can define what it is for an event to be 'conscious':

Definition of 'conscious': e is *conscious* $=_{df} (\exists \mu)(\mu$ is a quale $\wedge \mu(e))$

According to these definitions, an event is conscious if and only if it is identical with knowledge of its own *quale*. Conscious states are self-intimating, since each is identical with knowledge of its own qualitative character: if one is in such a state, one is aware of its occurrence. Of course that is not to say that one knows of it under every description. For example, if one hallucinates a dagger, one need not know one is hallucinating. One is conscious of the occurrence of a visual experience; the experience is a hallucination; it follows that one is conscious of the occurrence of a hallucination; it does not follow that one is conscious that it is a hallucination.

'Primary' and 'Secondary' Content of a Mental Act

Suppose that S imagines that Socrates sits. The imagining is a conscious mental act with the content *that Socrates sits*. S's mental act is an imagining, not an apprehending, so it does not require the existence of the fact ⟨*sits*, Socrates, *t*⟩. Indeed, the act of imagining has no fact as its object. But it does have a content, for it can play a role in inference, for example in reasoning about counterfactual situations. So imagining that Socrates sits is a mental act with a content but no object, an 'intransitive' mental act. The Ramsey-style logical form is:

'*S* imagines that Socrates sits' $=_{df}$
$(\exists e)(e$ is an event $\wedge$ *e* is an imagining $\wedge$ subject $(e) = S \wedge$ content$(e) =$ *that Socrates sits*)

According to the Identity Thesis, however, this is not the whole story, for imagining is conscious, so it is identical with knowledge of its own qualitative character. So the Identity Thesis entails that one and the same mental act of imagining is related to more than one state of affairs. *Qua* imagining, it has the content *that Socrates sits*. *Qua* consciousness, it is knowledge of its own qualitative character μ. Since necessarily every act of imagining is conscious, we have:

S imagines that Socrates sits $\leftrightarrow$
$(\exists e)(\exists \mu)(e$ is an event $\wedge$ μ is a *quale* $\wedge$ *e* is an imagining $\wedge$ subject $(e) = S \wedge$ content $(e) =$ *that Socrates sits* $\wedge e = \langle K, S, \langle \mu, e, t \rangle, t \rangle)$

With one and the same mental act, *S* both imagines that Socrates sits, and is conscious of the *quale* of that very mental act.

What if instead of imagining that Socrates sits, *S* looks at Socrates and sees that he sits? In that case *S* will have a visual experience as of Socrates sitting, and in the circumstances this experience will cause *S* to know that Socrates sits. The visual experience is conscious, so by the Identity Thesis it will also be knowledge that it itself is occurring. Then the visual experience will involve knowledge of two different facts. First, it *causes* knowledge of the fact that Socrates sits, and secondly it is *identical* with knowledge of the fact that it itself has a certain *quale*. There is therefore no difficulty in the idea that the same experience can give knowledge of two different facts.

This conclusion accords well with Brentano's ideas, for in Brentano's scheme experience has both a 'primary' object, e.g. the seated Socrates, and also a 'secondary' object, viz. the experience itself. Discussing the experience of hearing a sound, Brentano writes:

[W]e have to answer the question of whether there is more than one presentation affirmatively, if we determine them according to the number of objects; with the same certainty, however, we have to answer this question negatively if we determine these presentations according to the number of mental acts in which objects are presented. The presentation of the sound and the presentation of the presentation of the sound form a single mental phenomenon; it is only by considering it in its relation to two different objects, one of which is a physical phenomenon and the other a mental phenomenon, that we divide it conceptually into two presentations. In the same mental phenomenon in which the sound is present to our minds we simultaneously apprehend the mental phenomenon itself. ... We can say that the sound is the *primary object* of the *act* of hearing, and that the act of hearing itself is the *secondary object*. (1995: 128)

5.6 Advantages of the Identity Thesis

Is the Identity Thesis a fruitful theory? Does it shed any light on the three problems about consciousness that I mentioned at the start of this chapter?

Problem 1: How is Conscious Self-knowledge Possible?

The Identity Thesis is the simplest possible solution to the problem of self-knowledge. One cannot introspect all one's mental states; e.g., one cannot introspect one's beliefs or desires. But if a state is conscious, for example if it is an experience or a volition, then the Identity Thesis says the occurrence of the state is identical with knowledge of its own qualitative character. That entails the co-occurrence property $\Box(\mathbf{K}p \leftrightarrow p)$. The Identity Thesis therefore provides a simple explanation of how one's self-knowledge of one's own conscious states is possible.[3]

The Identity Thesis solves the Privileged Access problem of why there is only ever one seat in the 'Cartesian Theater'. Necessarily, only I can have my pain. But according to the Identity Thesis, my pain and my conscious knowledge of my pain are identical. Therefore, since necessarily only I can

---

[3] The Knowledge Equivalence entails that the condition that one is in a given conscious state is luminous in the sense of Chapter 4 of Williamson (2000), i.e., if it obtains, one is in a position to know of its obtaining. Williamson there argues that there are no non-trivial luminous conditions. However, his argument is not applicable to a condition the obtaining of which is identical to knowledge of its obtaining. The reason is the same as for other exceptions, noted at Williamson (2000: 108–9).

have my pain, necessarily only I can have my conscious knowledge of my pain, since these are the same thing.

The Identity Thesis also explains why self-knowledge through consciousness is indefeasible. Since conscious knowledge of pain is identical with the pain itself, the knowledge must last while the pain lasts, whatever misleading evidence may turn up to the contrary in the meantime. That is not to say I could not be misled into judging that I am not in pain, even though I am in pain. I can mistakenly judge that I am not in pain, but it does not follow that I do not then know I am in pain. Conscious knowledge is quite independent of judgements and beliefs. It therefore rests on no evidence, which is why there is no possibility of undermining the evidence on which it rests. The consciousness is the pain, so it exists whenever the pain exists, and is absolutely indefeasible.

Thus the Identity Thesis underwrites the Cartesian claims that there is such a thing as consciousness, that it is characterised by Privileged Access, and that it is proof against even a Cartesian deceiver. But it does not underwrite a further claim, which I shall label First-Person Authority, which is also often called Cartesian, though I myself have not been able to find it in Descartes. This is the claim that first person judgements are authoritative; necessarily, what one believes about one's own mental state is correct. First-Person Authority is an infallibility claim with respect to one's beliefs about one's conscious states; for example, it entails that, necessarily, if one believes one is in pain, then one's belief is true. But this claim is certainly mistaken, as post-hypnotic suggestion and itches prove. It is not even plausible as a 'default' assumption, contrary to Shoemaker (1996: 65–6) and Wright (1989: 250–4). The Identity Thesis of course entails that if one is conscious of pain, then one is in pain. But it is completely silent about what follows if one merely believes one is in pain, so it gives no support to First-Person Authority.

Nor does the Identity Thesis entail First-Person Omniscience, the even stronger claim that for each of one's possible conscious states, one is always in a position to know whether one is in that state or not. This claim is also false. Suppose one has an itch q_1 that one cannot discriminate from a pain q_2. Then one is not omniscient with respect to q_2. One does not know one is in q_2, because one is not in q_2. One does not know one is not in q_2, for one is in q_1, and by hypothesis one cannot discriminate q_2 from q_1. Contrary to First-Person Omniscience, one does not know whether or not one is in q_2: one is not in pain, but one does not know one is not in pain. The Identity Thesis says pain is identical with knowledge of pain, which entails that if one is not in pain, one does not know one is in pain; however, it does not entail that if one is not in pain, one knows one is not in pain. The Identity Thesis says nothing about what one knows in the case that one is not in pain, so it does not entail First-Person Omniscience.

Problem 2: What is Consciousness?

A creature has consciousness if and only if it instantiates a conscious state. According to the Identity Thesis, a conscious state is a state such that instantiating it is identical with knowledge of its qualitative character. To that extent the Identity Thesis illuminates the nature of consciousness: indeed, in a sense it solves the problem of consciousness completely. But the solution it provides is only slightly illuminating, since it does not tell us what knowledge itself is: it merely assimilates the mystery of consciousness to the mystery of knowledge. Wittgenstein is left 'as it were clutching my forehead' at the suggestion that knowledge 'is supposed to be produced by a process in the brain'.

Problem 3: What are Qualia, and are there Any?

There is a close interplay between the theory of *qualia* and the Identity Thesis. In the absence of the Identity Thesis, it is a nice question whether *qualia*, if they exist, are properties of the mental subject of experience, or properties of the experience itself. The Identity Thesis makes a contribution here, in favour of the view that *qualia* must be properties of the experience. In the context of the theory of facts, the Identity Thesis makes sense only if *qualia* are self-intimating properties of the experience itself; of the various ways of understanding the Identity Thesis that we examined, only the solution that invoked *qualia* as properties of experience succeeded.

A further connection between the Identity Thesis and the theory of *qualia* concerns the essentiality of qualitative character. If a mental act, such as a pain e, has a particular *quale* μ, must e have the *quale* μ at every world at which it exists? Kripke emphatically thinks so: 'Can any case of essence be more obvious than the fact that *being a pain* is a necessary property of each pain?' (1980: 146.) The Identity Thesis has a ready explanation. For if e is a pain, and μ is its painful *quale*, then according to the Identity Thesis:

$$e = \langle \mathbf{K}, S, \langle \mu, e, t \rangle, t \rangle$$

It follows that the event e is essentially a pain: for at any world w at which e exists, e is identical with S's knowledge that e has the painful *quale* μ, and hence by the factiveness of knowledge e does indeed have the painful *quale* μ at w, i.e., e is a pain at w. The Identity Thesis entails the essential painfulness of pain. But it only does so if it is a thesis about knowledge. Belief is no substitute. Suppose we modify the Identity Thesis to assert that a conscious mental act is identical, not with one's knowledge of its *quale*, but with one's belief about its *quale*. Then the identity would become:

$$e^* = \langle \mathbf{B}, S, \langle \mu, e^*, t \rangle, t \rangle$$

Then the following difficulty arises. Pain is essentially pain. But the hypothetical event e^* need not be essentially a pain. At any world w at which e^* occurs S will indeed believe e^* has the painful character μ, but since belief is not factive, it does not follow that e^* really does have μ at w, and hence it is possible that e^* exists without being a pain. Thus it is essential to the account of *qualia* given by the Identity Thesis that it is based on knowledge, not mere belief.

5.7 Are Functionalism and the Identity Thesis Compatible?

The Identity Thesis says that every conscious mental act is knowledge. It puts knowledge at the centre of the mind. But functionalism does not put an account of knowledge at the centre of its account of the mind. Some functionalists seem to assume that there must exist some analysis of knowledge in terms of belief, so that the theory of knowledge need be no more than an afterthought to the theory of belief. Others accept that knowledge cannot be precisely defined functionally: but they say that the problem lies not with functionalism, but with the concept of knowledge, which they regard as unsuitable for precise scientific work, and therefore not worth defining. Thus Lewis writes:

If you doubt that the word 'know' bears any real load in science or metaphysics, I partly agree. If I am right about how ascriptions of knowledge work, they are a handy but humble approximation. They may yet be indispensable in practice, in the same way that other handy but humble approximations are. (Lewis 1996:440)

Standard functionalism gives no special theoretical place to knowledge. Instead it assumes there is a correct theory of the mind, call it theory T, which has *experience, action, belief* and *desire* as its theoretical terms. Theory T says that x has a mind if and only if x satisfies certain axioms; the axioms do not mention knowledge, but can rely on e.g., Bayesianism instead. Thus the axioms of T might include:

(i) x always performs the *action* with the highest expected value in relation to x's *beliefs* and *desires*.

(ii) x always updates x's *beliefs* by conditionalising on x's *experiences*.

We can imagine these axioms conjoined with many others in a single Postulate:

(iii) x has a mind $=_{df} \Psi(x, experience, action, belief, desire)$

Here the complex predicate Ψ is supposed not itself to contain any irreducibly psychological terms.

There need be no conflict between the Postulate (iii) and the Identity Thesis. But the Postulate is one thing, and standard functionalism another. Functionalism says not only that the Postulate is a truth, but that it is the whole truth about experience, action, belief, and desire. Functionalism says having a mind does not require instantiation of the states that in human beings constitute experience, action, belief and desire; all that is required is that one instantiate some states or other that jointly satisfy the predicate Ψ, and which therefore have the requisite functional roles. Thus we may replace the Postulate with its Ramsey Sentence in the definition of mind:

(iv) x has a mind $=_{df} (\exists Y)(\exists Z)(\exists U)(\exists V)\Psi(x, Y, Z, U, V)$

Thus functionalism is consistent with quite inhuman minds; even an electronic computer could have a mind, according to functionalism, provided its internal states are causally related to each other in exactly the way that human experience, action, belief, and desire are causally related to each other; for in that case they satisfy the predicate Ψ, and that is sufficient to endow the computer with a mind.

Here there is certainly potential for conflict with the Identity Thesis! If S satisfies the Postulate (iii) then S experiences and acts, and so, according to the Identity Thesis, S instantiates the epistemically peculiar conscious states which are identical with knowledge of their own occurrence. But if S satisfies only the existential generalisation (iv), we have no guarantee that S experiences and acts, for we have no guarantee that suitable epistemically peculiar states play in S the role that experience and action play in humans. Nothing standard functionalism says rules out *a priori* the possibility of states which have the causal role of experience, but which fail to be identical with knowledge of their own qualitative character; but according to the Identity Thesis, such states cannot genuinely be experience or action. Thus functionalism and the Identity Thesis will come into conflict, because functionalism will assert what the Identity Thesis denies, that satisfying the existential generalisation (iv) is enough to guarantee having a mind.

Would it be possible to modify functionalism by incorporating the Identity Thesis within it? Shoemaker has indeed proposed a partial identity thesis: he has suggested that the states that realise pain and the corresponding introspective belief might be part-identical. He writes:

One possibility is that while two states have different core realisations, their total realisations overlap in a certain way. ... [Or] it might be that the total realisation of the first-order state is a proper part of the total realisation of the first-person belief that one has it. (1996: 243)

But Shoemaker's partial identity relates pain and belief, not pain and knowledge, so it is subject to the various difficulties noted earlier. To go any further in the direction of the Identity Thesis would require functionalism to make explicit theoretical room for knowledge itself. That requires the functionalist to claim that there exists a correct and exact functionalist definition of knowledge. If that were true, functionalism could use the definition to incorporate the Identity Thesis into functionalism, and thereby take the mystery out of consciousness. But if knowledge is an absolutely indefinable and primitive concept, as I believe it to be, then the Identity Thesis implies that functionalism is never going to help much with the problem of consciousness.

6

Persons

The mind is that which knows. That defines the mind by a relation in which it stands to other things. However, it leaves its intrinsic nature an entirely open question. Can we deduce anything about the intrinsic nature of the mind from features of the relation that defines it? In particular, can we deduce anything about whether it is material or immaterial? In the previous chapter I brushed aside the suggestion that the hypothesis of an immaterial mind could help explain consciousness. But several writers have made the converse suggestion, that if we reflect on the nature of consciousness we shall find insuperable difficulties in the view that a conscious mind could be a wholly material being, at least in the case of those minds that are persons.

An intuition that is widely shared by dualists and non-dualists alike is that consciousness does not admit of borderline cases. Thus McGinn writes:

[I]n the case of consciousness its possession is a matter of there being something 'inner', some way the world appears *to* the creature; and we cannot imagine the position of a creature for whom it is indeterminate whether there is such an 'inner' subjective aspect... The emergence of consciousness must rather be compared to a sudden switching on of a light, narrow as the original shaft must have been. (1982: 14)

This intuition can be the first premiss of an argument for substance dualism. The second premiss is that for complex material beings, statements of identity are vague, as the Ship of Theseus proves. So if persons are complex material beings, it follows that borderline cases of personal identity are possible. But, it is suggested, we cannot make sense of such a possibility, because we cannot imagine 'from the inside' what it would be like. Suppose someone will be in excruciating pain tomorrow, and that it is borderline today whether you are identical with that person. Then although the pain will be excruciating, it is borderline whether you will be conscious of it. It is suggested that this is baffling, indeed absurd, and we are invited to conclude that vague personal identity is inconsistent with the determinateness of consciousness. Therefore we should reject vague personal identity; so we must reject materialism's thesis that persons are complex material beings.

In this chapter I examine this 'Bafflement Argument'. By analysing the concept of a person, I conclude that the argument does not succeed. I define a person as a mind that is aware of itself under the 'I'-concept: since mind is defined as that which knows, and since concepts are individuated by an epistemic criterion, this subsumes the metaphysics of persons within the metaphysics of knowledge. I argue that the 'I'-concept combines a subjective and an objective mode of presentation of the Self. The subjective 'first-person' mode of presentation is expressible in Lichtenberg's subjectless language: for example, I will be in pain tomorrow only if the Lichtenbergian sentence 'It pains tomorrow' is true. If one could think of one's own states only in the solipsistic Lichtenbergian way, it would indeed be baffling how it could be borderline whether one would be conscious of the excruciating pain tomorrow. But here the objective mode of presentation needs to be taken into account. I argue that the 'I'-concept combines the Lichtenbergian subjectless way of thinking of one's conscious states with an objective conception of oneself as part of the objective order; it is the objective component that ensures that borderline personal identity need not baffle non-solipsists. I conclude that if the intuition of the determinateness of consciousness does support any version of dualism, then at most it supports property dualism (or, more exactly, relation dualism). We cannot extend it to draw any conclusion about the intrinsic nature of the conscious mind itself.

The plan of the chapter is as follows. Section 1 introduces the 'Bafflement Argument', that from the first-person perspective we can make no sense of borderline personal identity. Section 2 discusses logical features of the 'I'-concept. Section 3 describes Lichtenberg's subjectless language, and introduces the 'Lichtenbergian' solipsist, who not only doubts the existence of 'other minds', but doubts his own existence also. Section 4 discusses how the Lichtenbergian solipsist could become an expert physicist and acquire the '*my-body*'-concept, without thereby acquiring the 'I'-concept. Section 5 discusses how the solipsist could become a rational agent, section 6 how he could become an expert psychologist in the sense of functionalism, and section 7 how he could at last arrive at the 'I'-concept by merging the objective functionalist conception of a psychological agent with the Lichtenbergian way of thinking of conscious states. Section 8 suggests that this undercuts the Bafflement Argument, and section 9 concludes that at the present time we are simply ignorant about the intrinsic nature of minds.

6.1 Unclarity of Personal Identity

If someone journeys by matter transfer booth, or undergoes a brain fission, it can seem unclear whether they will survive the adventure. The well known thought-experiments about personal identity raise questions which we cannot see clearly how to answer.

What is the explanation of irresoluble unclarity about personal identity? We might say that sometimes there is no precise fact of the matter about identity of persons; that would be to explain the unclarity as a case of objective indefiniteness. We might instead say that in every case of unclarity there is always a precise fact, but that in some cases we do not know how to discover it; that would be to explain the unclarity as simply our own ignorance.

If materialism is true then probably the explanation of the unclarity is objective indefiniteness. One version of materialism says that persons are biological beings. We already know enough about biology to know that probably nature draws no sharp boundaries in the biological realm; that means there can be borderline cases where there is no fact of the matter whether a particular animal has survived, or whether a particular biological organ such as a brain has survived. A different version of materialism identifies a person's life with a psychological process sustained by an underlying physical mechanism. Again, we already know enough about mechanisms to know that, whether natural or artificial, probably there are no sharp boundaries in the realm of mechanisms. So standard versions of materialism seem committed to the view that personal identity can be objectively indefinite.

Cartesian dualism, in contrast, standardly denies that there can be borderline cases of personal identity: in the realm of the soul, dualists think, the relevant boundaries are always sharp. Dualism explains unclarity about personal identity as due to our own ignorance, not objective indefiniteness. Historically, dualism has been motivated less by abstract metaphysics than by issues in ethics and the philosophy of religion. For example, Kant held that it is a requirement of pure practical reason that moral agents be able to hope that if they so act as to be worthy of happiness, then they will in fact attain happiness. But happiness and worthiness of happiness seem uncorrelated in this present life, so Kant argued that belief in a future life is practically necessary. (1929: 645–51, A820–31.) But this seems to require that the person who is to enjoy happiness in the future life be definitely the one who had made themselves worthy of happiness; presumably it would be unsatisfactory if was indefinite whether the right person was enjoying the happiness. Dualist resistance to indefiniteness of identity is the reason that Reid and others were led to the initially odd-seeming doctrine that a person is a *monad*, i.e., a simple thing that has no parts.[1] The motivation is that if we replace enough parts of a complex thing like the ship of Theseus, it can seem indefinite whether it survives; whereas a simple thing is not subject to this kind of indefiniteness.

The epistemic theory of vagueness of Williamson (1994) invokes ignorance to explain unclarity even in borderline cases. A dualist and a materialist who subscribes to the epistemic theory will therefore be in agreement that unclear cases of personal identity are cases of ignorance. Where they will differ is over whether the unclear cases are ever *borderline* cases of personal identity, for the dualist will deny it, but the materialist will affirm it. According to Williamson, vagueness and borderline cases are due to a special kind of ignorance which arises because of limitations of our powers of conceptual discrimination. (1994: 237.) Williamson says that if a concept is vague, it is because we are unable to discriminate it from other concepts we might have used instead, which draw the line in a slightly different place from where we actually draw it. This inability of ours, itself epistemic, reflects something ontological, namely the absence of a natural division where the line would naturally fall: in the absence of a natural division, there is nothing to 'stabilise' the extension of the concept; that is why the concept is vague. (1994: 231.) Thus even on the epistemic theory, the materialist will say that personal identity can be objectively indefinite, because of an absence of natural boundaries; whereas the dualist will deny this.

The question whether personal identity is determinate therefore seems a central issue in the debate between materialism and dualism. But can we

---

[1] 'A part of a person is a manifest absurdity. A person is something indivisible, and is what Leibniz calls a monad'(Reid 1846: 344, III.iv)

even make sense of objectively indefinite identity in the case of persons? Bernard Williams has suggested that there is something baffling in the very idea of it.

Williams (1970) invites you to imagine you have fallen into the clutches of a mad surgeon. The surgeon tells you that he will bring it about that tomorrow there will be two human persons A and B, each with a plausible claim to be yourself. A will be bodily continuous with you; B will be psychologically continuous with you; and either A or B will be tortured tomorrow. You naturally wonder whether you will still be surviving tomorrow, and if so whether you will be in pain. In normal cases bodily and psychological criteria of personal identity go together, but the point of Williams' example is to oblige us to consider a case where they come apart. It may seem tempting to say there is no fact of the matter whether you will be A or B; for example, on the grounds that our concepts are simply not designed to cover such situations. But Williams thinks this would encounter an 'extraordinary difficulty'. He writes:

[T]here seems to be an obstinate bafflement in mirroring in my expectations a situation in which it is conceptually undecidable whether I occur. (1970: 196)

The reason is as follows:

Central to the expectation of [situation] S is the thought of how it will be for me, the imaginative projection of myself as participant in S. Suppose it is for conceptual reasons undecidable whether it involves me or not. The subject has an incurable difficulty about how he may think about S. If he engages in projective imaginative thinking (about how it will be for him) he implicitly answers the unanswerable question; if he thinks that he cannot engage in such thinking, he answers it in the opposite direction. (1970: 194)

If the supposition of indefinite personal identity really faces an 'incurable difficulty', we might think we could develop Williams' point into an argument against materialism generally. Since there can be borderline cases of bodily continuity, and borderline cases of psychological continuity, it follows that standard versions of materialism imply that there can be borderline cases of personal identity, and hence that there can be indefiniteness of personal identity. But if indefinite personal identity is so baffling as to be incoherent, a version of materialism that implies it must itself be incoherent.

I shall call this the Bafflement Argument against materialism. Richard Swinburne states it as follows:

An awkwardness for any such empiricist theory is that there will inevitably be borderline cases. But there seems no intermediate possibility between a certain future conscious being being that person, and not being that person. (1974: 240)

Geoffrey Madell also endorses it. He writes:

What I fear about the future pain is simply its being felt by me. We, rightly, find unintelligible the idea that there could be a pain in the future which is in part mine and in part not. I claim, then, that the empiricist view of personal identity is incoherent in itself. (1989: 32−3)

The Bafflement Argument is open to the reply that it is not at all baffling to learn that a person vaguely identical with oneself will be tortured tomorrow; one knows exactly what to expect, for one knows how to describe it from the third-person perspective, and what one must expect is *that*. If it is insisted that bafflement remains because one cannot effect the imaginative projection of oneself into the situation, the reply is that this is just false. One can project oneself quite vividly into the pain that the person who may or may not be oneself will feel tomorrow. So one can imagine the torture tomorrow 'from the inside', and one can conceive of its being indefinite whether that will happen to oneself. So why should it be insisted that we still cannot really make sense of indefinite personal identity?

Despite this reply, it seems to me that the Bafflement Argument retains a residual ability to puzzle us. What seems so hard to imagine is not just the situation tomorrow, but one's whole course of experience between today and tomorrow. Consider a variant of the mad surgeon's experiment, where he permits only A to be alive tomorrow. One is told today that it is objectively indefinite whether one is identical with A, and that A will be tortured tomorrow. How is one to imagine one's future course of experience? If one is definitely not identical with A, one will not survive until tomorrow, and so one will have a course of experience that will end before tomorrow. If one is definitely identical with A, one will have a course of experience that extends through today into torture tomorrow. Either of these courses of experience is imaginable, but it is not so easy to imagine 'from the inside' a course of experience that is somehow borderline between the two. To put it another way, what one would like to know is whether the light of one's own particular consciousness—*this* consciousness—will be on or off tomorrow, and what seems so baffling is the answer that it will not definitely be on, but it will not definitely be off either.

Here I attempt a diagnosis of this bafflement. I argue that the concept of a person is a theoretical concept of a theory that combines two distinctive components, namely a subjective conception of conscious states, and an objective conception of psychological agents. Exclusive concentration on the 'third-person' objective component is misguided, but it is equally wrong to overemphasise the subjective component. I suggest that the latter mistake is what underlies the Bafflement Argument: by focusing excessively on the subjective component it induces a solipsistic perspective from which indefinite personal identity is indeed baffling.

6.2 'I'—The 'Essential' Indexical

I shall assume that x is a person only if x has a mind, and x has a mind if x at some time knows something. One way to know something, and therefore to have a mind, is to be the subject of a conscious state; for as I argued in Chapter 5, a state is conscious only if its subject is aware of it, and hence is aware of what is in fact a state of itself. In that sense any conscious mind is conscious of itself. It does not follow, however, that such a mind is *self*-conscious, for it may lack a concept of its Self. Because of the possibility of such conceptual deficiency, awareness of what is in fact a state of itself need not give a mind self-awareness. There is no contradiction in supposing that an event of which a certain mind is the subject could be presented under a mode of presentation that failed to present the subject. More generally, if the fact p is the instantiation of F by x, and κ is a content that presents p, it need not follow that κ activates a concept that presents F and a concept that presents x. If there can be a simple mode of presentation of that kind of a mental event, it could fail to present separately either the instantiated mental state or the instantiating mental subject.

The distinction between mere consciousness and full self-consciousness was relied on by Locke to distinguish between minds generally and the special kinds of minds that are persons. According to Locke, a person is:

a thinking intelligent Being, which has reason and reflection, and can think of it self as it self, the same thinking being in different times and places. (1979: 335, II.xxvii.9)

Here 'it self' is occurring as the English indirect reflexive, i.e., the pronoun used in indirect speech to report the content expressed by speakers who refer to themselves as 'I'. Locke's definition then amounts to the claim that a being with a mind is a person if it is able to think of itself by means specifically of the concept that is expressed by the word 'I'. A concept is individuated by its cognitive role, which is a matter for epistemology. So on Locke's assumptions, the philosophy of the self is one of those rare cases where metaphysics is best done by epistemological methods; if a self is that which can think of itself under a self-concept, we study the Self best by studying the *'self'*-concept, and therefore by studying its cognitive role.

The cognitive role of the self-concept expressed by 'I' has at least the three following distinctive features:

(1) *Warrant*: My normal warrant for 'I am in pain' ceases to be a warrant if a co-referring expression is substituted for 'I'. I know by immediate introspection that I am in pain, but even if I am A, I cannot know by introspection that A is in pain—unless I know that I am A. The same applies to other contents warranted by introspection.

(2) *Desire*: 'Thank goodness I am not to be tortured!' This expression of relief will not be apt if a co-referring expression is substituted for 'I'. It is not the same to say 'Thank goodness A is not to be tortured!', even if I am A. I am not relieved that B is to be tortured and A is not—what's so good about that? Here is a characteristic kind of concern for oneself which is not contrastive, and which can only be properly expressed in English by the first-person and its cognates.

(3) *Action*: Substitution of another mode of presentation for the first-person can destroy the rationalisation of action. Suppose I desire that the race should start, and believe that if I wave my arm the race will start. The desire and belief jointly rationalise my trying to wave my arm, but they do not rationalise my trying to wave A's arm, unless I know that I am A.

Perry (1979) and others give a psychologistic account of this 'essential indexical' role of 'I'-thoughts, by appeal to the supposed causal powers of first-personal 'belief-states'. But we can give an account that is more Fregean in spirit if we regard conscious action as rationalised by a practical syllogism whose conclusion is the action. A practical syllogism is rationally correct if its action conclusion and its belief premiss formally entail its desire premiss, e.g.:

> (desire) the race starts
> (belief) if I wave my arm then the race starts
> (action) I wave my arm

A syllogism rationalises an agent's conscious action only if it describes it under that mode of presentation in which the action is given to the agent's consciousness. Now consciousness of waving my arm warrants my thought that I am waving my arm, but it does not warrant the thought that A is waving his arm, even if I am A. So the following practical syllogism is not rationally correct:

> (desire) the race starts
> (belief) if A waves his arm then the race starts
> (action) I wave my arm

Here the action and the belief do not formally entail the thing desired (Campbell 1994: 83–4). The action would get me what I want, but I do not know that, and cannot rationally act on this belief and desire. Rational correctness can be restored here only by adding as an extra premiss the belief 'I am A.'

6.3 How Do I Know I Exist?

To investigate the self-concept, we must investigate its cognitive role. This will include an investigation of what warrants one's judgements about oneself. A judgement I am inclined to make about myself is that I exist: what warrants that?

I cannot come to know of my existence by ordinary perception. I see my body, and thus have warrant for believing 'This body exists.' According to materialism, I now know concerning what is in fact myself that it exists. But I need not yet know that I exist, because the identity 'I am that body' would be informative for me. Nor can I do better by turning my mental gaze within. Even if there really were an inner gaze and, luckier than Hume, I managed to catch a glimpse of my cartesian Ego, still I would not know that I exist, for the judgement 'I am that Ego' would be informative for me.

I cannot know of my own existence *a priori*. It is perhaps *a priori* that any token of 'I exist,' including this one, is true. So I can know *a priori* of a token of 'I exist' which is in fact produced by me that it is true. But still I do not know *a priori* that I exist, for I do not know *a priori* that I produced that token.

I cannot know of my existence by introspection. Following Reid I will use 'consciousness' to denote the immediate knowledge one has of one's own conscious states. Then consciousness will be part of my warrant for such knowledgeable judgements as 'I am in pain', or 'I am thinking that snow is white'. But consciousness alone cannot warrant my judgement that I myself exist. For although consciousness informs me of the existence of a state of which I am in fact the subject, it does not follow that it informs me also of the existence of my self; as is shown by the existence of minds that are conscious but not self-conscious.

Descartes missed this point in his famous paralogism *Cogito, ergo sum*. But his critics such as Hume and Kant did not miss it; they correctly insisted that mere consciousness of a conscious state does not on its own warrant a belief in the existence of the subject of the state. As Lichtenberg put the point:

To say *cogito* is already to say too much, as soon as we translate it I think. (1990: 168)

According to Lichtenberg, all that is warranted on the basis of consciousness alone is a report of the conscious states in a subjectless style:

We should say it thinks, just as we say it lightens. (ib.)

Wittgenstein agreed. Discussing the word 'I' in *Philosophical Remarks* he says:

It would be instructive to replace this way of speaking by another in which immediate experience would be represented without using the personal pronoun. We could adopt the following way of representing matters: if I, L.W. have toothache, then that is expressed by means of the proposition 'There is toothache.' (1975: 88)

We can imagine constructing a Lichtenbergian language from our ordinary language. Whenever ordinary language contains a predicate which one is warranted in applying to oneself by consciousness together with knowledge that the conscious state is a state of oneself, we introduce into the Lichtenbergian language a corresponding subjectless sentence, for which the consciousness alone is warrant enough. Then we can replace 'I am thinking' by 'It thinks', 'I am in pain' by 'It pains', and so on. Each Lichtenbergian sentence expresses a content warrantable by consciousness alone; equivalently, it expresses a subjective mode of presentation of the relevant conscious state.

A Lichtenbergian language is of course the Wittgensteinian 'private language' which 'only I myself can understand' (1967b: 91, §256). Here I can side-step the question whether such a *language* is genuinely possible. All I require is the more modest assumption that there exist subjective modes of presentation of conscious states that are not modes of presentation of the Self. These are the modes of presentation which the Lichtenbergian 'private language' would express, supposing a private language were possible. Even if a private language is a fiction, it is a useful one here, since it provides a convenient means of discussing these modes of presentation.

A Lichtenbergian sentence is, by a convenient pun, subjectless in a double sense. First, it is subjectless because it is not a subject-predicate sentence. Instead it has the holophrastic logical form of a Quinean 'observation sentence'; the sentence calculus is adequate for its formal representation. (Quine 1990: 2–9.) Secondly, a Lichtenbergian sentence is subjectless because it expresses a conscious mental state without explicit mention of the owner or subject of that state. Thus someone could speak Lichtenbergian even if they had no concept of a mental subject. They could state the occurrence of states of affairs which were in fact states of a subject, without having a concept of the subject.

We can imagine someone following Descartes' method of doubt, believing only what he finds indubitable. He no longer believes in outer things. He can even doubt his own existence, and *pace* Descartes the doubt is not self-refuting—to say *dubito* 'is already to say too much'. This scepticism is extreme indeed. It goes beyond even what Russell called 'solipsism of the present moment', i.e., the belief that only I and my present experiences are real. Our sceptic goes further, for he lacks belief not only in the existence of other minds, but also in his own.

Imagine our sceptic has been sunk in his scepticism so long that it is no longer right to say he doubts his own existence; for he has now entirely lost the very concept of himself. I shall call such a sceptic a 'Lichtenbergian solipsist'. (I say 'solipsist' to accord with what I take to be Wittgenstein's usage, but the terminology is of course a little misleading: the Lichtenbergian solipsist does not think that he is the only person who exists, for he lacks so much as the concept of his own or other minds.) Our solipsist follows Lichtenberg's procedure, always saying 'It thinks' instead of 'I think,' and so on. Is he hopelessly stuck in his solipsism? Or is there a way he can rationally come to believe again that he exists? If we can discern such a way, that would throw light on the warrant we non-solipsists have for the belief 'I exist,' and hence would clarify the cognitive role of the self-concept.

6.4 Beyond Solipsism of the Present Moment

The Lichtenbergian solipsist arrived at his epistemological predicament by doubting all his *a posteriori* sources of knowledge other than consciousness. He can attain knowledge of his own existence again only if he starts to draw on the other sources of knowledge that he has.

If he is prepared to trust his memory, then he can have knowledge of the past. He can arrive at a conception of the future by remembering that in the past the present was not yet, i.e., was future. He can thus advance to a Lichtenbergian sentential language enriched with tense operators like *in the past* and *always*.

A second source of knowledge he might come to trust is induction, i.e., the ability to project a remembered regularity into the future. That enables him to know Lichtenbergian psychological laws. For example:

Always, if it pains, it is desired that it does not pain.

Compare the subjectless meteorological law:

Always, if it rains, it pours.

Knowledge of a Lichtenbergian psychological law is knowledge of a genuine law of subjective psychology, and as I shall suggest later, such knowledge plays a key role in our understanding of other minds. But no amount of such knowledge on its own will lead the solipsist to knowledge of the Self as one of the things that objectively exist, for the very conclusive reason that our solipsist may as yet completely lack the concept of a *thing*. The solipsist can arrive at this concept by trusting another source of knowledge—*abduction*, i.e., inference to the best explanation by means of a theory.

To think of himself as 'the same thinking thing at different times and places', our solipsist will need to have concepts of objective locations in time and space. Kant argued that one cannot have a conception of time and space without a conception of the physical objects that occupy time and space; this entails that Lockean self-consciousness requires concepts of physical objects. We arrive at the claim that (for human beings) there can be no conception of oneself without a conception of the physical world in which one is located.

Is the converse true, that one have no conception of the physical world without a concept of oneself as located within it? Strawson and others have argued that it is true, on the grounds that one could not regard one's experience as experience of independent objects without some rudimentary theory of perception which relates the content of one's experience to one's own location and the physical objects perceptible from that location.[2] If so, the transition from Lichtenbergian solipsism to knowledge of the physical world would necessarily bring with it knowledge of one's own existence.

The claim would appear to be that if our solipsist is to have experiential knowledge of material objects in space and time, he will need to develop at least a rudimentary physics in which physical objects, places and times are the theoretical entities. The solipsist's evidence for the theory will be the course of his own conscious experience, so to link the theoretical entities with his consciousness, he will need to supplement the physics with 'bridge laws' or 'correspondence rules' that amount to a rudimentary psycho-physical theory of perception. This theory must link physical states of affairs with states accessible to consciousness, and the key point is that in the case of human beings it must do so by linking conscious experience to physical impingements on the theorist's own body. Thus without something to play the role of their own body in the theory, there can be no prospect of a thinker having warrant for belief in physical objects.

If I have a concept of what is *my* body in this sense, do I have a concept of myself? Must I take the adjective '*my*' as the possessive case of the substantive 'I'? I think we must deny this if we wish to maintain a sharp division between mere mindedness and being a person. Example: it might not be definitely wrong to say that an animal can have the concept of *its* body, since it can acquire through perception knowledge that, for example,

---

[2] Strawson (1966). For a thorough discussion of this and the ensuing literature, see Cassam (1997).

there is food to *its* right; even so, it presumably remains definitely wrong to attribute to the animal a Lockean concept of itself.

Our solipsist's concept of *his* body will be embedded in a theory which posits physical objects as the 'theoretical entities' with the conscious experiential states of the theorist himself as the 'observation sentences'. I see no reason why this theory could not be developed by a solipsist who conceived of his own conscious states only in the subjectless style of Lichtenberg. The solipsist would acquire a concept of what is in fact his own body, and would think of it under the special mode of presentation it has in virtue of its central role in his theory of perception. We may suppose that the solipsist employs a special name to express this special mode of presentation of his own body; perhaps he adopts for it the name 'Centre' (Wittgenstein 1975: 88). Our solipsist has attained to a minimal physics, with an embedded theory of perception giving a special role to the material object Centre. But in view of the possibility of a Lichtenbergian 'observation language' his doing all this does not entail that he has formed a concept of himself; he might remain a solipsist.

In *The Blue Book*, Wittgenstein describes a solipsist who knows about the physical world, and is aware of his own conscious states, but lacks so much as the concept of his own or other minds.

[T]he man whom we call a solipsist, and who says that only his own experiences are real ... would say that it was *inconceivable* that experiences other than his own were real. (1958: 59)

Our Lichtenbergian solipsist seems to have arrived at the same situation as the solipsist of *The Blue Book*. Despite his extensive or even complete knowledge of the physical world and the psycho–physical laws relating his conscious states to the physical states of his body, our solipsist still lacks the concept expressed by the word 'I'.

6.5 The Solipsist as Rational Agent

Can this solipsist be a fully rational conscious agent, acting rationally upon his beliefs and desires, and learning rationally from his experience? We saw that 'I'-thoughts have an 'essential indexical' cognitive role, which is indispensable for our rationality. The solipsist has no self-concept, and therefore no 'I'-thoughts: but his Lichtenbergian sentences can play a corresponding 'essential indexical' role in his rational economy.

(1) *Warrant.* Consciousness is the salient warrant for self-attributions like 'I am in pain'. The solipsist has just the same warrant for the corresponding Lichtenbergian thought 'It pains'.

(2) *Desire.* There is a particular non-contrastive relief I feel when I learn I will not be tortured. The solipsist will feel the same non-contrastive relief when he learns that it is not Centre that will be injured, for from psycho-physical laws he knows he can infer 'It will not pain', and be relieved at that. His relief is non-contrastive, in just the required way: necessarily so, for he lacks the concepts of self and others, and so cannot draw the distinction that a contrastive relief would require.

(3) *Action.* Action normally requires intentional movement of one's body, so if a practical syllogism is to be rationally correct, its belief premiss must refer to the agent's body under the mode of presentation whereby one is conscious of it in voluntary movement. But that is the mode of presentation under which the solipsist thinks of his body when he refers to it as 'Centre'. So the solipsist's action can be properly rationalised by a Lichtenbergian practical syllogism. For example, if he waves his arm in order to start the race, we have:

> (desire) the race starts
> (belief) if Centre's arm is waved, then the race starts
> (action) Centre's arm is waved

So even in the absence of a self-concept, our solipsist can think thoughts with an 'essential indexical' rational role, and so he can be a rational agent.

6.6 A Functionalist Conception of Human Beings

At this stage about the only remaining difference between the solipsist and ourselves is the solipsist's continuing lack of a self-concept. Because the solipsist has no concept of a self, he lacks the concept of a person, and cannot be aware of other human beings as persons. However, he knows of their bodies and can predict how their bodies will move by using physics. Moreover there seems nothing to prevent the solipsist from acquiring a theory of objective psychology, which will allow him more easily to predict how human bodies will move.

An example of an objective psychology that is cognitively accessible to the solipsist is functionalism; for example, the functionalist 'folk psychology' that some say all normal human beings tacitly know. A functionalist theory says that human beings are functional agents with bodies; perhaps human beings are identical with their bodies, but this is a question functionalism need not settle. The psychological states of a psychological agent explain why their body moves as it does, in accordance with the functional role of each state. Such a functionalism would be fully cognitively accessible to a Wittgensteinian solipsist, but knowledge of the existence of psychological agents in the sense of functionalism is not yet knowledge of other minds. Functionalism treats pain as a psychological state, but as I argued in Chapter 5, it need not treat it as a conscious state, in the way that human pain is conscious. A fully developed functionalism may include functional analogues of introspection and qualitative character; for example, it may say that normally if x is in pain then x reliably believes that x is in pain and desires that x is not in pain, but this does not entail that the 'pain' is a state like the human conscious states. There need be nothing in a definition of functional pain that requires that pain is a conscious state.

6.7 Other Minds Theory

Although our solipsist is by now an expert physicist and an expert objective psychologist, he still does not know that there are any other conscious beings in the world. He does not know this because he still lacks the very concept of a conscious being or a conscious state. He is aware of what are in fact his own conscious states, but thinks of them only in the subjectless Lichtenbergian way.

To form a concept of the mental subject, the solipsist needs to conceive of his subjectless 'It pains' as being made true by a fact of subject-predicate form, i.e., by the instantiation of some property by some entity. He must posit the existence of a class of conscious states corresponding to each of his Lichtenbergian sentences, and then he can posit a type of entity that can instantiate these conscious states. Only then will he be able so much as to grasp the hypothesis that conscious entities exist, and that he himself is one of them.

How can the solipsist find evidence for this hypothesis? He must link the hypothesis in a theoretically fruitful way to the rest of what he knows. He already knows that each normal human body is associated with an agent in the sense of functionalism who 'owns' that body; in particular, he knows there is an agent that 'owns' Centre. Suppose the solipsist calls this agent the 'Ego'. The solipsist can now propose to identify the Ego with the entity that instantiates conscious pain when the Lichtenbergian sentence 'It pains' is true. Similarly, the solipsist knows there is a state that realises the functional role of pain in human beings. He can propose to identify this state with the state instantiated by the Ego when 'It pains' is true. He will propose corresponding property identifications for other sentences of the Lichtenbergian language.

A rich theory now emerges, in which the solipsist conceives of the Ego as both an agent in the sense of functionalism and as the conscious subject of the states of subjective consciousness expressed by Lichtenbergian sentences. Because the Lichtenbergian sentences are indexical, the solipsist's concept of the Ego is an indexical one. Thus the solipsist has attained to a self-concept at last, and he may as well start using the indexical word 'I' to express it. By 'I' he expresses a theoretical concept of the following theory: I am the 'owner' of Centre; I exist; whenever it pains, I am in pain, whenever it thinks, I am thinking, etc. Such an I-concept will have the proper 'essential indexical' rational role, since it will straightforwardly inherit that role from the corresponding Lichtenbergian sentences. It seems plausible that this is in fact the very concept expressed by the English indexical 'I'.

Our solipsist has now arrived at a psychological theory that is more powerful than functionalism alone. For by attributing *conscious* states to other human beings, he enables the Lichtenbergian psychological laws he knows to generalise to other minds. So now he has a new method of understanding other people: he can put himself in the other person's place by means of projective imaginative thinking. The Lichtenbergian psychological laws he knows from his own case can by this means be extended to apply to other people too, and thus he comes to understand other people better than he would if he were to rely on functionalism alone. The success of the method is evidence of the correctness of its assumptions; the solipsist is therefore warranted in believing in his own existence precisely because and to the extent that he is warranted in believing in the existence of other persons. This is the deep point of Wittgenstein's discussion of the problem of other minds: scepticism about other minds is an unstable position, because anyone seriously sceptical about the existence of other people will undermine the evidence they have for their own existence. Ontological commitment to self is inseparable from ontological commitment to others.

6.8 Is Personal Identity Indefinite?

Wittgenstein suggests in *The Blue Book* that 'as subject' uses of the first-person pronoun appear to be immune to error through mis-identification of the subject.

> There is no question of recognising a person when I say I have toothache. To ask 'are you sure it's you who have pains?' would be nonsensical. And now this way of stating our idea suggests itself: that it is as impossible that in making the statement 'I have toothache' I should have mistaken another person for myself, as it is to moan with pain by mistake, having mistaken someone else for me. (1958:67)

As Wittgenstein perhaps intended, if there is indeed such a phenomenon as immunity to error through mis-identification, it can be neatly explained in the light of the Lichtenbergian theory of the word 'I'. For a person can be mistaken in the 'as subject' belief 'I am in pain' only if they can be mistaken in what warrants it. But the warrant is their awareness of the pain under the introspective mode of presentation expressed by the Lichtenbergian sentence 'It pains'. Since the Lichtenbergian sentence is subjectless, there seems no possibility of mistakenly believing it as a result of mis-identifying its subject; therefore 'as subject' uses of 'I' are immune from error arising from error about the identity of the subject.

Keeping this point in mind, let us return to our consideration of the Bafflement Argument against materialism. The argument says it is hard to make sense of information that it is indefinite whether a person who will be in pain tomorrow will be me. The suggestion is that, from the first person perspective, there is something incoherent in the materialist claim that personal identity can be indefinite. There is an analogy here with immunity to error through mis-identification, which we can bring out by putting the suggestion of the anti-materialists in the following way: 'as subject' uses of 'I' are immune from indefiniteness arising from indefiniteness about the identity of the subject.

A neat Lichtenbergian explanation might again seem to be available. Consider again the situation where the mad surgeon is going to bring it about that the only candidate for being oneself tomorrow will be person A, who will be a borderline case of bodily and/or psychological continuity with oneself. One would like to know if one will still exist tomorrow. Since A will be tortured tomorrow, and one will exist tomorrow only if one is identical with A, then if one will exist tomorrow, one will be in pain tomorrow, and so one's corresponding Lichtenbergian sentence 'It will pain tomorrow' is true now. So a way to express what one would like to know about one's survival is this: if A is tortured tomorrow, will it pain tomorrow? Here I am expressing things from the Lichtenbergian perspective of a solipsist, but intuitively this does seem to be, at least in the present case, exactly 'what matters in survival' (Parfitt 1971). Now from a Lichtenbergian perspective, indefiniteness of identity and survival is indeed baffling; for the sentence 'If A is tortured tomorrow, it will pain tomorrow' seems immune from indefiniteness about the subject, since it does not employ a concept of the subject. Note that the Lichtenbergian sentence is not otherwise indefinite, for tomorrow's pain will be definite pain.

When an opponent of materialism feels bafflement about how their personal identity can be indefinite tomorrow, I suggest it is because they have slipped into thinking of things in this Lichtenbergian way. The subjectless sentence 'It will pain tomorrow' does indeed *appear* immune from indefiniteness about the subject. However, this appearance is misleading. For a vague object can make a sentence vague even if the sentence itself expresses no concept of the vague object. This can happen if the sentence concerned is indexical, for an indexical sentence may rely on the context to contribute an object that enters its truth-conditions, and if the context disobligingly contributes a vague object, then the indexical sentence itself will be vague.

Now non-solipsists know that Lichtenbergian sentences are indexical, so they understand that the subject does indeed enter the truth-condition of 'It will pain tomorrow':

A token of 'It will pain tomorrow' uttered by S at t is true if and only if S is in pain the day after t.

So non-solipsists understand that a token of 'It will pain tomorrow' will be indefinite if it is indefinite whether the person speaking at t is identical with the person who is in pain the day after t. Of course, the solipsist is baffled to understand this, for he lacks the concept of a person. But the fact that the solipsist is baffled does not mean that the rest of us ought to be.

6.9 Conclusion

The Bafflement Argument says that from the first-person perspective there is something incoherent in the materialist claim that personal identity can be indefinite. My suggestion has been that the anti-materialist's so-called 'first-person perspective' is not the genuinely first-person perspective of someone who conceives of themselves as part of the objective order. Rather it is the merely Lichtenbergian perspective of the solipsist, who does not conceive of himself at all. When an anti-materialist feels bafflement about how their personal identity can be indefinite tomorrow, I suggest it is because they are thinking of things from this subjectless point of view. They can escape the bafflement easily enough by going beyond solipsism and seeing Lichtenbergian sentences as indexical with respect to the subject of experience.

My account of the self-concept turned on the identification of states of the conscious subject with the properties that realise the functional properties of objective psychology. If the account is correct, it will follow that in our present state of knowledge we cannot answer the question whether personal identity can be indefinite. For our present concept of the self combines a functional with a subjective conception of conscious states, and neither of these can contribute any information on the question of the intrinsic nature of the conscious mind. For the time being at least, although we know what consciousness *does*, and although we know *what it is like* to be conscious, we lack an explanation of how it is possible.

It may turn out that a theory of consciousness can be completed within biology, or within the theory of physical mechanisms; if so, then personal identity will have turned out to be indefinite. But for all we presently know, the realm of consciousness may be one where nature does in fact draw sharp boundaries. If so, personal identity will not after all be objectively indefinite, and the most plausible versions of materialism will have been refuted. But this is not something we can decide in advance *a priori* by the Bafflement Argument.

Appendix: A Lichtenbergian Reconstruction of the Bafflement Argument

Assume the scenario of Williams (1970). Subject S is told today that tomorrow there will be a person A, who will definitely be the only person to suffer torture tomorrow, and who is such that it is objectively indefinite whether $S = A$. If materialism is true, what S is told is possibly true. But it is not possibly true, and so materialism is false.

'*Proof*': Use 'Δ' as the 'definitely' operator. What S is told is (1) and (2) below:

(1) $\neg\Delta\ (S = A) \wedge \neg\Delta\neg(S = A)$

(2) $\Delta\ (\forall x)(x$ will be in pain tomorrow $\rightarrow x = A)$

Assume you are definitely S.

(3) $\Delta\ (I$ am $S)$

(4) $\Delta\ (S = A \leftrightarrow I$ am $A)$ (from (3))

Now 'imaginatively project' yourself into A's situation tomorrow:

(5) $\Delta\ (I$ am $A \leftrightarrow I$ will be in pain tomorrow) (from (2))

In view of the connection between 'I' and your Lichtenbergian private language:

(6) $\Delta\ (I$ will be in pain tomorrow $\leftrightarrow$ It will pain tomorrow)

The pain in question is to be torture, i.e., definite pain. Since the Lichtenbergian sentence expresses no concept of the subject, it cannot be indefinite whether it will pain tomorrow. So:

(7) $\Delta\ (It$ will pain tomorrow) $\vee \Delta \neg(It$ will pain tomorrow)

We may assume that for the operator 'Δ' the following rule of inference is valid:

Definite Modus Ponens: $\Delta p, \Delta(p \rightarrow q) \vdash \Delta q$

Then we have from (4), (5) and (6)

(8) Δ (It will pain tomorrow) $\vdash \Delta$ $(S = A)$

(9) $\Delta \neg$(It will pain tomorrow) $\vdash \Delta \neg(S = A)$

And hence by (7) we may conclude:

(10) Δ $(S = A) \vee \Delta\neg(S = A)$

(10) contradicts (1), so either what S was told is not possibly true, and so materialism is false, or else the method of projective imagining (premisses (5 and 6)) is not possible in this case. But it would be 'baffling' to have a situation where projective imagining is not possible, since it is constitutive of the 'I'-concept. So materialism is false.

7

Language

What is the correct metaphysics of language? Some philosophers say that a language is an abstract object. Any humanly-used language, for example the language *English*, is they say only one of a great multitude of these abstract languages. There is the sociological or psychological or biological phenomenon of human use of a language, when a particular abstract language is adopted as the language of a particular community of speakers. But while a human community can make a language their own, they do not make their own language.

Opposed to the abstract conception of language are *use* theories, which say that a language is an artefact, a human construction for the purpose of communication. I call a use theory psychologistic if it conceives of communication as the mere exchanging of beliefs, without regard to the rationality of the beliefs exchanged. In this chapter, I advocate a use theory which is not psychologistic but epistemic. By treating knowledge rather than mere belief as the central explanatory concept in the account of language, it is possible to avoid psychologism while still regarding language not as an abstract entity but as a concrete phenomenon. On this account, language is to be explained in terms of the triadic relation of *use* which holds between a community of rational beings G, a content κ, and a sentence s if G use the sentence s to testify that κ. The account is epistemic if we assume, as I think we should, that to testify one must utter with the intention of causing to know.

We can define semantic meaning in terms of use. For example, there is a community E, the 'English-speaking community', such that if we hold E fixed we obtain a diadic relation, which holds between a sentence s and a content κ if the community E use s to testify that κ. So we can define:

's means in English that κ' $=_{df}$ E use s to testify that κ.[1]

---

[1] Notation: 's' is a variable that ranges over sentences of the object language, 'κ' is a variable that ranges over contents, and 'A' is a metalanguage substitutional 'variable' that takes object language

Given the *use* relation, we may define a sentence: *s* is a sentence if for some community G and some content κ, G use *s* to testify that κ. A sentence is an artefact whose design end is the giving of testimony; the language of G is their collection of such artefacts. Therefore we shall not understand language unless we understand testimony; and conversely we shall have no very satisfactory account of testimony unless we understand what a language is. Now testimony is a means whereby a speaker can pass on knowledge to a hearer, so testimony is the province of epistemology; it follows that language too must be studied from the point of view of epistemology.

How does a language facilitate the transmission of knowledge? A speaker who desires to communicate knowledge that κ to a hearer utters a sentence *s*, i.e., the speaker fashions an instance or token of the sentence *s*. Two models now compete to explain how the mere utterance of *s* can cause a hearer to know that κ. The first is the *Inferential Model* of testimony: this says that the transmission of knowledge occurs by an inference on the part of the hearer. The hearer knows the speaker would not utter an untruth in the context, so on hearing the speaker utter *s*, the hearer is able to infer that *s* is true. Moreover, the hearer knows that *s* is true only if κ, so the hearer can infer that κ. The Inferential Model and its variants have been advocated by a number of authors, from Hume onwards.

The Inferential Model of testimony is rejected here in favour of the *Faculty Model*, the central assumption of which is the hypothesis of the existence within the human mind of a language faculty. According to this hypothesis, the language faculty is the source of a certain characteristic conscious experience one has when one sees or hears a sentence *s* in a language one understands: if *s* means that κ, then seeing or hearing *s* causes one's language faculty to cause in one this characteristic mental act. I shall call the mental act *visual reading*, if it is prompted by seeing a written sentence; and *aural reading*, if it is prompted by hearing a spoken sentence.

The Faculty Model treats the acquisition of knowledge by testimony as similar to the acquisition of knowledge by perception. When one becomes aware of a fact κ by immediate visual perception, the seen fact causes one's visual faculty to cause in one a conscious mental act, namely a visual

sentences as its substituends. If Φ is a type of propositional attitude, 'S Φ that κ' means S is the subject of a propositional attitude of type Φ and content κ; 'S knows that κ' means that S knows that κ in virtue of a belief or mental act with content κ.

experience with the content that κ; if the context is suitable, the mental act in turn causes one to know the fact that κ. In just the same way, according to the Faculty Model, when one learns a fact κ by testimony s which means that κ in one's language, the speaker's uttering s causes one's language faculty to cause a conscious mental act of reading that κ; if the context is suitable this causes one to know the fact that κ.

In the sections that follow I develop this account. Section 1 gives an account of the grammar of a language. Section 2 introduces the mental act or 'propositional attitude' of reading that κ, and offers a definition of the ability to understand or speak a language in terms of reading-that. Section 3 criticises the Inferential Model of testimony, section 4 advocates the Faculty Model, and section 5 elaborates the analogy between testimony and perception. Section 6 discusses how to define use, and says it cannot be defined as a regularity of 'truthfulness and trust'; section 7 says it cannot be defined as a regularity of testimony. Section 8 proposes that a sentence is an artefact, and that its use can be defined as its design end or function, namely the communication of a certain content by testimony.

7.1 Grammar

Sentences

Meaning is a relation between sentences and contents. So far as sentences are concerned, it is customary, following Pierce, to draw a distinction between sentence types and tokens; this is the distinction between the property (type) and the particulars (tokens) which the type collects into a kind. The meaning relation, i.e., the relation that holds between s and κ if the community use s to testify that κ, is a relation between type and content, not token and content. A token sentence expresses a content if it is of a type associated by the meaning relation with that content.

A type is the defining property of some kind; a kind are some things all of which have the type property. A kind can be merely miscellaneous, if the defining property is some arbitrary principle of classification. Non-miscellaneous kinds include the natural kinds, members of which are natural productions, and artefact kinds, which are the products of design. The view that will be argued for here is that a sentence type is the defining property of an artefact kind whose design end is communication by testimony. Tokens of a sentence type are particular artefacts: a written sentence is a continuant artefact, and a spoken sentence is an event artefact. For example, 'Socrates is wise' is a sentence, and its tokens are artefacts, namely marks that look like 'Socrates is wise,' or sounds that sound like it. But it is not simply a question of possessing a characteristic shape or sound: the shape or sound must have arisen by design, for nothing but an artefact can be an instance of 'Socrates is wise.' The action of creating a token of a sentence is the action of uttering the sentence; for example, an utterance of 'Socrates is wise' is an action that produces the appropriate sounds or marks.

Words

If we were thinking of language in abstraction from the empirical facts about human minds, that would give an unduly wide choice of 'languages'. But in fact human beings only ever adopt *compositional* languages, in which the meaning of each sentence is built up from the concepts expressed by its constituent words. We therefore need an account of what words are, and how they are related to sentences. Now for a compositional language, if an artefact is an instance of one of its sentences, then typically the sentential artefact is complex; that is to say, it has various parts, which must occur in the right spatial or temporal order. The parts of a complex artefact may themselves be artefacts; for example, a bicycle is an artefact made of artefacts. Similarly, a complex sentence has artefacts as its parts; the parts are its component words. So a word is an artefact: e.g., the word 'Socrates' is an artefact type, any utterance of which is the making of a token of the type, i.e., a mark or sound that designedly resembles this one: Socrates.

Let us call the relation between a sentence and its words the *concatenation* relation. Then a sentence s concatenates the words $w_1, \ldots, w_n$ iff any token of s has as its parts tokens of $w_1, \ldots, w_n$ in that order. We write:

$$concatenates(s, w_1, \ldots, w_n)$$

to express that the sentence s concatenates the words $w_1, \ldots, w_n$; *concatenation* is a multigrade relation. One task of the theory of syntax is to provide a semantically revealing analysis of sentences into their constituent words, i.e., to discover for a given language L its concatenation function, the (possibly many-valued) function that maps each sentence of L to the words that the sentence concatenates.

Content and Concept

Frege was the first to attach central theoretical importance to the phenomenon of linguistic compositionality. According to Frege, our ability to understand the sense of a complete sentence derives compositionally from our grasp of the senses of its words; for one can immediately understand even an unfamiliar sentence if one is familiar with its component words. Frege concluded that the sense of the word must be part of the sense of the sentence; one understands the sense of the sentence by understanding the senses of its parts:

> [E]ven if a thought has been grasped by an inhabitant of the Earth for the very first time, a form of words can be found in which it will be understood by someone else to whom it is entirely new. This would not be possible, if we could not distinguish parts in the thought corresponding to the parts of a sentence, so that the structure of the sentence can serve as a picture of the structure of the thought. (1918: 390)

Frege called the sense of complete sentences *Thoughts*, which he conceived of as abstract objects outside of space and time. According to the account I offered in Chapter 3, however, the role played in Frege's system by Thoughts can instead be played by contents. A Thought is an abstract object, but a content is just a universal, the property of a mental act that is its cognitive value: if x and y are contents, then $x = y$ if in any context, in any course of reasoning, a mental act with content x can replace a mental act of the same type with content y without turning knowledge to ignorance.

Frege conceived of the *sense* of a word as also an abstract object: two words express the same sense if substitution of the one for the other in direct contexts never makes any difference to the Thought expressed. In Chapter 3 I suggested that the role played by Fregean (simple) senses can instead be played by *concepts*, which are not abstract objects but universals, namely properties of the mental subject that ground the subject's capacity to understand a range of contents. A mental subject 'possesses' or 'grasps' a concept if the subject instantiates the property which the concept is. The criterion of identity for concepts is that if x and y are concepts, then $x = y$ if in any mental subject, substituting a grasp of x for a grasp of y never makes any difference to the contents that the subject can understand.

Frege assumed that a sense is a part of a Thought, but as I argued in Chapter 3, we can make room for compositionality even if we do not assume that a concept is a part of a content. Where Frege would say that a Thought κ has as its parts the senses $a_1, \ldots, a_n$, we can say instead that the content κ activates the concepts $a_1, \ldots, a_n$. Like the relation between a sentence and the words it concatenates, the activation relation between content and concepts is multigrade. We define the *activation function* δ as the function which maps a string of concepts $a_1, \ldots, a_n$ to the unique content κ which activates them:

$$\delta(a_1, \ldots, a_n) = \kappa \leftrightarrow \textit{activates}(\kappa, a_1, \ldots, a_n)$$

Thus the theory of understanding can provide the materials for an account of compositionality. It is not necessary to appeal to the part–whole relation in the theory of content: it is sufficient to say that the concepts expressed by the words of a sentence are the basis of one's power to understand the content expressed by the sentence as a whole.

Are there Mental Intermediaries Between Words and Concepts?

We have defined words as artefacts, and defined a relation of concatenation between a sentence and the words it concatenates. We have defined concepts as mental properties, and defined a relation of activation between a content and the concepts it activates. We now wish to attach semantic values to individual words in such a way that the content expressed by a sentence as a whole depends on the semantic values of its words and the way in which they are concatenated: the guiding idea must be Frege's insight that 'the structure of the sentence can serve as a picture of the structure of the thought.'

It would be convenient if each word of a natural language expressed a corresponding concept, but empirically things are not quite so simple. A content that is expressed in one way in one natural language may in another natural language be expressed with a different number of words occurring in a different order. But does the bewildering variety of human natural languages conceal an underlying unity of structure? Fodor (1975) has suggested that human beings think in a *Language of Thought* (LoT), so we might see the grammar for a natural language as a function that carries sentences of the language to sentences of LoT. But how seriously are we to take the suggestion that the LoT is a language? Must we recognise symbols in the mind, that are akin to words of a public language, but are not themselves words? It is usually said that the 'words' and 'sentences' of the language of thought are syntactically defined mental states, which are causally efficacious when 'written' in one's belief box, desire box, etc., and which 'represent' in virtue of their causal connections to the world. But in the present theoretical context we do not need an extra layer of 'mental representations', and we do not need to conceive of the Language of Thought as extra symbols. We can identify the 'words' of the LoT with concepts, and the 'sentences' of the LoT with contents. Then the supposed syntactic relation between a 'sentence' of the LoT and its constituent 'words' gives way to the activation relation between a content and the concepts it activates. Instead of saying that a LoT sentence is 'written in one's belief box', it is sufficient to say that one has a belief with the given content. On this interpretation, the LoT hypothesis does not enforce the point of view that there is a level of purely mental representation that intervenes between the level of words and the level of concepts.

According to Chomsky (1986), it is an empirical fact that all human languages can be grammatically mapped onto a single 'language' *LF*, the level of logical form. Thus the grammar of the surface language is found by giving a transformational grammar which carries surface strings to their *LF* translations. On this view, it is at the level of *LF* that there is a connection between symbol and concept: the surface language does not connect with concepts directly, but only indirectly *via* the *LF* intermediaries. It may indeed be useful from the point of view of theoretical linguistics to treat the meaning function of a language as the product of two separate functions, a syntactic function that maps sentences to *LF* forms, and a semantic function that maps *LF* forms to contents. But it seems sufficient to regard the *LF* representation, if it does indeed have psychological reality, merely as indexing internal states of the language faculty. These states may be causally indispensable in the process whereby hearing a sentence causes us to think a thought with the corresponding content, but there seems no reason to insist that they themselves have content, or represent anything.

For present purposes we can regard the hypothesis of a universal representation *LF* as working at a level of empirical detail that is more refined than is necessary for a purely logical enquiry. To a first approximation, it would be enough to suppose that all human languages behaved in the following way. We may suppose that each language *L* has a *concatenation* function that splits sentences up into words, and also a *parser* function which expands logically complex expressions and then adjusts the order of the words in a sentence, putting them in that order in which the corresponding concepts will be activated; the parser in effect does the work of a Chomskian representation at the level of logical form. We may suppose that each language also has a *lexicon*, which maps words of the language to the concepts they express. By applying the lexicon to the output of the parser we obtain a string of concepts; the meaning of the sentence is the content activated by that string. If the similarity asserted by Chomsky really exists between all human languages, it can be represented here by the fact that all human languages have grammars of this sort, and that in particular their parsers are structurally very similar, so that any language can be carried into any other by one of a given family of fairly simple transformations. This way of putting the matter avoids the need to regard *LF* as a level of representation intermediate between word and concept.

Grammar

The task of a grammar is to define semantic relations which jointly specify the *means-that* relation for the language under study—i.e., the grammar must define appropriate semantic relations between sentences, words, concepts and contents such that the *means-that* relation is just the product of these semantic relations. For our (simplified) purposes, and to a first approximation, we can imagine a grammar Γ as having the following three components:

(1) The *concatenation function C* is a function that tells for each sentence of L the string of words that the sentence concatenates. (Here we may need to define the class of words and sentences somewhat generously, to include 'words' implied but not spoken, 'words' such as 'traces' that are recognised by grammarians but perhaps not explicitly by speakers, 'words' supplied by features of the context, etc., etc.)

(2) The *parser* Π is a function that takes the string of words concatenated by a (surface) sentence, expands its logically complex expressions, inserts new symbols as necessary, and rearranges the resulting strings of words as the corresponding 'deep structure' string.

(3) The *lexicon* Λ is a (possibly many-valued) function that gives for each word of the language the concept (or concepts) that the word expresses.

The grammar Γ is the triple of the above three relations, whose product when composed with the activation function δ maps a sentence s of L to its content $\kappa = \Gamma(s)$. Thus if s is a sentence of L, the concatenation function

$C(s)$ returns the string of words $(w_1, \ldots, w_n)$ that the sentence concatenates. If we apply the parser Π to these words we obtain the corresponding 'deep structure' string $(d_1, \ldots, d_m)$. From this we obtain a string of concepts by applying the lexicon Λ to each symbol in the string to obtain the corresponding string of concepts $(\Lambda(d_1), \ldots, \Lambda(d_m))$. Finally the activation function δ gives the unique content κ which activates these concepts. The content thus arrived at is the content expressed by the sentence according to the grammar Γ, i.e.:

> *Content according to the Grammar* Γ : '$\Gamma(s) = \kappa$' $=_{\mathrm{df}}$
> $\delta(\Lambda(\Pi(C(s)))) = \kappa$

A grammar Γ is extensionally correct if, considered as a relation, it is coextensive with the meaning relation, i.e., if:

> $\Gamma(s) = \kappa \leftrightarrow$ In L, s means that κ

But coextensiveness alone is not enough to determine the grammar, for there are many choices of the three relations Λ, Π and C whose products with the activation function will be coextensive. If we consider an individual human speaker, we may suppose that the three relations are somehow realised in the speaker's psychology, in the causal mechanisms that allow the speaker to understand the language; so there is a unique psychologically real grammar for that individual. That leaves room for the psychologically real grammar to vary between individuals, so long as the outputs of the idiolectal grammars of each overlap sufficiently to allow good communication in the 'public' language. Good communication requires that a speaker who desires a hearer to entertain the thought that κ can reliably achieve this purpose by uttering s. The speaker's purpose will be achieved if the utterance causes the hearer's language faculty to cause the hearer to be the subject of a suitable mental act, whose content activates the concepts expressed by the words of s, in the order in which the parser rearranges them. It is in this way that the 'correct' grammar of the language corresponds to a psychological reality.

7.2 Reading

A language L generates a meaning function that maps sentences to contents. But knowledge of the language cannot be taken to be knowledge of this function. For knowing the meaning of a sentence is more than the mere ability to *state* the content of the sentence. For example, suppose you are aware of the existence of the content *that noumena are unintuitable*, but find yourself unable to understand it. You know concerning the content *that noumena are unintuitable* that it is the content of the English sentence 'noumena are unintuitable'. But this knowledge is of no use to you in your efforts to follow what is being said when this sentence is asserted. You are in the position, with respect to this content, that Frege took himself to be in with respect to the content expressed by the sentence 'I am in pain' as uttered by Dr Lauban. Frege thought that while he himself could think about the content expressed by that utterance, he could not himself think it—only Dr Lauban could do that (1918: 358–9). And so generally: understanding a language requires that one can actually think the contents expressed by its sentences.

But understanding the content is not enough to understand the sentence. I perfectly understand the content *that Socrates is wise*, but if I know no French I will not understand the sentence 'Socrate est sage', for I do not know, concerning the content *that Socrates is wise*, that it is the content of 'Socrate est sage'. But even that may not be enough. There is a difference between merely hearing a sentence, and hearing it with understanding, in the sense of having something relevant go on in one's mind as one hears it. One's understanding of κ, and one's knowledge that s means that κ, are not in themselves sufficient to guarantee that on hearing s one will be the subject of a mental act with the content κ. Thus hearing with understanding still seems to require something more.

One model of how this something more might be supplied is the *Inferential Model*, according to which one is caused to arrive at the appropriate mental act by an inference from the fact that the speaker has uttered the sentence s. For example, one might reason as follows:

> S has uttered s. I trust S not to utter an untrue sentence. So s is true. But s is true only if κ. Therefore κ.

By the end of this course of reasoning one has inferred that κ, and so one is the subject of a judgement with the content κ. Moreover, one would not have been the subject of this mental act had one not known that s is true iff κ. The Inferential Model succeeds in explaining how hearing a sentence causes one to arrive at a mental act with the content κ, by invoking a process of reasoning that includes as a premiss one's knowledge that s is true only if κ.

A difficulty of the Inferential Model is that it seems quite remote from the actual phenomenology of hearing speech with understanding. No such reasoning process normally takes place in the mind of participants in ordinary human conversation! To meet this objection the inferentialist may say that the transition from hearing s to judging that κ is a rational habit: a 'habit' because it normally takes place automatically and unconsciously; 'rational' because it can be reviewed consciously if the need arises. But the account still faces serious difficulties. Unless farther elaborated it does not explain the difference in phenomenology between what it is like to hear speech one understands, as compared with hearing only the noise of speech one does not understand. Nor does it explain why this characteristic difference in phenomenology persists even if one does not believe what one hears, for example because one is watching a play and has 'suspended' judgement; one hears a sentence s which means that κ; one does not judge that κ; still the experience of hearing the sentence with understanding is phenomenologically unlike the experience of hearing only the noise of a sentence one does not understand.

A further difficulty of the Inferential Model is that the inferences it postulates rely on the premiss that s is true iff κ. But such a premiss is available only to a thinker who possesses the concept of truth. It is far from evident that one must possess an explicit concept of truth in order to understand a language: on the contrary, it appears quite plausible that truth is a concept one acquires only at a later and more reflective stage of language use.

To meet these difficulties, the inferentialist is obliged to say that the process of inference is unconscious, and that in the process concepts may be employed which do not figure in any conscious mental act of the hearer. Thus something goes on in the hearer, which may be entirely unconscious, such that on hearing the sentence s spoken by a trusted person, the hearer is disposed to judge that κ. And really the whole content of the inferentialist claim is that the causal process that goes on in the hearer is sufficiently like an inference to make it illuminating to describe the process as 'unconscious inference'. But I do not think the process has much resemblance to a genuine inference. I shall therefore instead be recommending the Faculty Model, according to which, if one understands the language L, and if in L

the sentence *s* means that κ, then merely seeing the written sentence *s* causes in one a special mental act with its own characteristic phenomenology, and with the content that κ. Similarly merely hearing the spoken sentence *s* causes a related mental act with a different characteristic phenomenology, but with the same content that κ.

What is this mental act? To take the visual case first, the English term for it is *reading*—one looks at the sentence *s*, and one reads that κ. For example, looking through the newspaper, one sees the sentence 'The Queen is in London' and reads that the Queen is in London. The experience of reading has its own characteristic phenomenal character. There is something it is like to read that the Queen is in London; if the content read is different, what it is like is different too. Moreover what it is like to read a sentence is different from what it is like to see the same sentence but not read it. So we may advance the hypothesis that reading is a distinctive kind of propositional attitude, a conscious mental act which we report by the locution '*H* reads that κ,' and which resists analysis into simpler propositional attitudes. The 'reads that' locution is not factive: from *H* reads that κ, one may not infer that κ. In this respect, 'reads' differs from 'sees', for if one sees that κ, it does follow that κ.

Reading is the conscious mental act of seeing a written sentence with understanding. There is a corresponding conscious mental act of hearing a spoken sentence with understanding, but this time English has no special term for it; there is no special English verb that stands to hearing as 'read' stands to seeing. Instead English makes do with an ambiguous use of the verb 'to hear'. In its first sense, 'hear' is used to report simple auditory perception: used in this sense, 'hears' is factive, since if *H* hears that κ, it follows that κ is the case. But 'hears' also has a non-factive sense of 'hearing with understanding'. One looks at a sentence *s* and reads that κ; just so, one listens to a sentence *s* and hears that κ, in this second sense of 'hears'. For example, one listens on the radio to the sentence 'The Queen is in London' and hears that the Queen is in London. Like 'reads', 'hears' in this second sense is not factive, for the radio report might be false. To avoid ambiguity, I shall use '*S aurally reads* that κ' to report that *S* hears that κ, in the non-factive sense of hearing-with-understanding.

Aural reading has its own phenomenal character, just as visual reading does. There is something it is like to aurally read that the Queen is in London; if the content were different, what it is like would be different too. And aural reading is phenomenologically quite unlike simple auditory perception of spoken sentences which one hears but does not understand. So aural reading like visual reading appears to be a distinctive kind of conscious mental act. There is also a characteristic difference in phenomenology between reading even a single word of one's own language, and merely seeing an inscription of a word in an unfamiliar language or script.[2] Presumably this difference too is attributable to the activity of the language faculty. English uses the verb 'to read' indifferently for both words and sentences; but I shall restrict it to the mental act which I posit to have as its content the content of the sentence read.

The ability to listen to s and hear that κ is a learned ability that requires training and practice, especially if one is learning a new language as an adult. There is an intermediate stage where one understands what is said in the new language by mentally translating it back into one's usual language. But eventually a stage is reached where one 'thinks in' the new language: if one hears the sentence s^* of the new language, and s^* means that κ, then one hears that κ; and this is phenomenologically different from first mentally translating s^* into a sentence s of one's usual language. There is a similar learning process when one is learning to visually read a written language, even if the language one is learning to visually read is one's own first language. At an intermediate stage, the learner 'reads' the sentence s by sounding its letters and so speaking s aloud; by uttering the sentence, the learner hears it and so is able to aurally read that κ. But at the end of the learning process the fluent reader reads silently, and by merely looking at the written sentence can directly visually read that κ. This shows that human beings have the ability to acquire new capacities for new mental acts. Visual and aural reading are not innate and need to be learned, but that should not prevent us from recognising them as genuine and distinctive species of conscious mental acts.

What is the logical form of 'H reads that κ'? I argued in Chapter 3 for a Ramseyan analysis of mental act reports. If we did not recognise a special mental act of reading, we would have to construe reading that κ as something like having a visual experience the content of which is that κ is written here. The logical form might be as follows:

'H reads that κ' $=_{df}$

---

[2] Here I am grateful to a referee.

$(\exists e)$(event $(e) \land$ subject$(e) = H \land$ visual-experience$(e) \land$ content$(e) =$ *that-κ-is-written-here*)

But this seems to require that H possess the concept of *being written*, since this concept is activated in the content of the supposed seeing. The implication is that one could not read if one lacked the concept of writing, which seems open to doubt. Another problem is that the content clause contains $κ$ in an indirect context, which creates difficulties of logical analysis. These problems are avoided if we acknowledge the existence of a distinctive mental act of *reading*. The logical form is then simplified, as follows:

'H reads that $κ$' $=_{\text{df}}$
$(\exists e)$(event $(e) \land$ subject $(e) = H \land$ reading$(e) \land κ(e)$)

We may now state the main hypothesis of the Faculty Model of understanding. The hypothesis is that understanding the spoken language L is the ability, if one hears a sentence s, to aurally read that $κ$, i.e., to be the subject of a mental act of aural reading with the content $κ$, where s means that $κ$ in L. Similarly, understanding the written language is the ability, if one sees the written sentence, to visually read that $κ$; understanding Braille is the ability, if one touches the Braille sentence, to tactually read that $κ$. So according to the Faculty Model, understanding a language is not the ability to *state* for each s its content $κ$. Nor is it knowing that s is true if and only if $κ$; understanding is not propositional knowledge at all, but simply a disposition on perceiving a sentence s to respond with a special mental act whose content is $κ$. The Faculty Model treats understanding a language L as understanding of the sentences of L:

H *understands* the spoken language $L =_{\text{df}}$ For enough sentences s of L, if H hears the sentence s, then H aurally reads that $κ$, where s means that $κ$ in L.

Understanding the written language is defined in the same way, *mutatis mutandis*.

Speaking a Language

Understanding a language is the capacity to have the appropriate experiences of reading when sentences of the language are seen or heard. In contrast, the ability to speak a language is a capacity for action. Speaking and writing are intentional actions, under conscious voluntary control. To be able to speak a language, it is not enough that one can utter its sentences: the utterance must be an intentional act. And not just any intention will do: to utter a sentence because, for example, one likes the sound of it is not yet to demonstrate a capacity to speak the language. One only speaks a language if one can speak with the intention of being understood by one's hearer. Therefore any model of the ability to speak a language must attribute to speakers some communicative intentions.

On the Inferential Model, the speaker counts as intending to be understood by the hearer if the speaker's intention in uttering the sentence is to induce a belief in the hearer. For example, if S utters s for H to hear, S's motivation might be as follows:

> I desire H to believe that κ. If I utter s, H will believe I would not utter s if it were not true. H knows s is true iff κ. So, if I utter s then H will believe that κ. Therefore I will utter s.

The Inferential Model succeeds in attributing to the speaker beliefs and desires sufficient to underwrite the claim that the speaker intends to be understood by the hearer. But the same difficulties arise as before. First, the phenomenology is wrong—one is not aware of any such intention in speaking, but simply says what one feels prompted to say. Secondly, it is again necessary to give a central role to the propositional knowledge that s is true iff κ, whereas it seems one might be a speaker even if one lacked an explicit grasp of the concept of truth. So we arrive at the conclusion that if any inference mediates the transition from the desire that H believe that κ to the uttering of s, it is a wholly unconscious one. The desire causes the utterance, but it seems doubtful that the causal process really involves the very sophisticated kinds of inference proposed by the Inferential Model.

The Faculty Model dispenses with the need for these sophisticated inferences. All it requires is that for enough of the contents κ expressible in L, one should be able intentionally to testify in L that κ. And for that it is enough if some pro-attitude one has towards testifying that κ should rationalise one's uttering a sentence s that means that κ in L. Thus one can speak the language if for sufficiently many contents κ one has the capacity to be moved by some such practical syllogism as the following:

Desire premiss	I desire that H know that κ.
Belief premiss	I believe that if I utter s, then H will know that κ.
Action Conclusion	Therefore, I utter s.

It is not required that one conceive of oneself as uttering a sentence s that means that κ in one's language; it is enough that the action one voluntarily performs does in fact fall under that description. Thus one will have the capacity to testify that κ if one's volition to cause H to know that κ causes one's language faculty to cause one to utter a sentence s, where s means that κ in one's language. So according to the Faculty Model:

S can speak the language $L =_{df}$ For enough contents κ in the range of L, S can testify that κ by uttering s, where s means that κ in L.

On this account the speaker never has any need for semantic knowledge, explicit or implicit, that s is true only if κ. The speaker is not required to grasp the concept of truth, or indeed to think any thoughts about language at all; it is sufficient that the speaker has for enough contents κ the capacity to testify in L that κ.

The capacity to speak a language is the capacity to testify, but not all speech is rationalised by a desire to cause knowledge. After we have learned to testify we soon learn to lie, by uttering a sentence with the intention of causing false belief. We can introduce the notion of 'telling' to cover the disjunction of either testifying, or representing oneself as testifying. In view of the fact that lies are not rare, we might alternatively say that the capacity to speak a language L is the capacity, for enough contents κ, to tell that κ in L.

A minor issue that is of some interest here is the content of the volition that controls speech. In speaking consciously one need not be consciously aware of the beliefs and desires that prompt one, but nevertheless the speaking is certainly a voluntary action under one's conscious control. Since the act is voluntary, some volition or act of the will causes it. Is the content of one's volition always that one say that κ? Or is the content that one utter s? The answer appears to depend on how practised the speaker is in the language. For the unfluent speaker learning to speak a second language, it is necessary to think how to put one's thought into words. One desires to say that κ but one needs consciously to consider how to do so; eventually one works out consciously that one must utter s. Thus for the unfluent speaker, the content of the volition is that one utter s. But for the fluent speaker, who is 'thinking in the language', it is not necessary to do this. The language faculty of a fluent speaker confers effective volition with respect to saying that κ in the language: one's volition to say that κ causes one's language faculty to cause one to utter s. The situation is similar to a learned motor skill. When one first learns a skilled action such as playing the piano, one has at first to think exactly how to move one's hands and fingers; the content of one's volition is that one's hand move in a certain way. Later one simply wills to play the notes; that has become the content of the volition. One still plays by moving one's hand and fingers in the right way, but here the volition is with respect to the end not the means: one's volition to play causes one's acquired motor skill to cause one's hand to move in the right way. Similarly, the skilled speaker says that κ by uttering s, but when 'thinking in the language' the content of their volition is simply to say that κ.

The Faculty Model of understanding is incomplete without an explanation of why the speaker should wish the hearer to be the subject of these experiences of aural and visual reading. What is so valuable about such experiences, that we constantly and rationally try to create them in each other? The explanation lies, I believe, in the role of reading in the giving of testimony. If we had no language—if we could not at will cause each other to read-that and to hear-that—then we could still exchange knowledge with each other, but the process would be slow, laborious and very prone to error. By using language we are able to exchange testimony quickly, easily and accurately. Thus a complete account of language requires an account of testimony.

7.3 The Inferential Model of Testimony

Testifying that κ is an intentional action, but it is not a basic action, for we testify that κ by speaking or writing, i.e., by an utterance. So to define testimony we must specify the purpose of the utterance, and the manner in which it is intended that it accomplish its purpose. In this section and the next I shall consider the respective accounts of testimony given by the Inferential Model and the Faculty Model.

According to the Inferential Model, the purpose of all saying, including saying which is testimony, is to induce a belief through an inference of the hearer H. The language faculty has only the minor and theoretically dispensable task of automating these inferences, making it possible for H to do rapidly what otherwise H could do only slowly. The Faculty Model, in contrast, says the purpose of testimony is to impart knowledge that κ by causing in the hearer an experience of reading that κ. The hearer's language faculty has the central and indispensable role of causing what is said to cause the experience of reading, by means of which it is possible for the speaker to impart knowledge to the hearer.

In order to say what I take to be wrong with the Inferential Model, I will in this section criticise the views of Grice, as a representative inferentialist. Grice (1957) gave an analysis of what he variously calls 'speaker meaning', 'non-natural meaning', or 'meaning$_{NN}$'. He proposed to analyse semantic meaning in terms of this, as conventions to speaker-mean: for example, the words 'Socrates is wise' have the semantic meaning they do because there is a convention to use these words to speaker-mean *that Socrates is wise*. Grice offered an account of speaker-meaning which we may summarise as follows:

S by doing x meant$_{NN}$ that κ' $=_{df}$ S did x intending:

(I1) that H believe that κ;
(I2) that H recognise S's intention I1;
(I3) that H believe that κ at least in part because H recognises S's intention I1.
(Grice 1969: 92)

Grice's account gives a picture of the speaker as in effect manipulating the beliefs of the hearer. S intends to get H to believe that κ by manifesting the intention that H believe that κ, and allowing H to make the appropriate inferences. But I shall suggest that Grice's account fails for two reasons. First, because he attempts to analyse speaker-meaning in terms of belief, when he should have analysed it in terms of knowledge. And secondly, because semantic meaning cannot be analysed in terms of conventions to speaker-mean; instead it must be analysed in terms of testimony.

The first objection is that, although Grice was certainly right that what he calls speaker-meaning is an important mechanism whereby a speaker can get a message across just by manifesting an intention to get that very message across, he was wrong to think that the relevant notion of getting one's message across is getting one's hearer to believe the message; rather it is a question of communicating knowledge. An epistemic analysis would therefore have been better. Grice's account is inferior to an epistemic analysis because it gets the extension of 'means$_{NN}$' wrong. Because Grice avoids the use of the concept of knowledge, he leaves room for it to be intended that the hearer's belief should be produced by reasons that are not evidential reasons. For example (Schiffer 1987: 246), suppose the belief that Zeus exists is an article of religious faith with S. S sincerely believes that Zeus exists, but S knows S does not know that Zeus exists. Still S is anxious that H believe that Zeus exists, so S gives H a beseeching look intending that H believe that Zeus exists because H recognise S's intention that H believe that Zeus exists. The beseeching look is motivated by exactly the three Gricean intentions, but it does not mean$_{NN}$ that Zeus exists. Thus Grice's account wrongly includes the beseeching look amongst things that have meaning$_{NN}$. In contrast an epistemic account does not make this mistake. S does not intend to cause H to know that Zeus exists, for S believes it is not possible to know that Zeus exists, but only to believe it by faith, so S is not testifying to H that Zeus exists. An epistemic account will therefore say correctly that the beseeching look does not mean$_{NN}$ that Zeus exists.

Counterexamples arise even if it is for evidential reasons that the Gricean intentions I1, I2, I3 produce the desired belief. There will be no speaker-meaning if there was no intention to communicate knowledge, if the plan was to produce belief by an inference of the hearer that the speaker knows will have a 'false lemma'. In such a case the speaker's plan can be entirely fulfilled, but since the plan was neither to transmit knowledge nor even to represent oneself as intending to transmit knowledge, we do not in such a case have any meaning$_{NN}$.

For example, H's husband is being unfaithful to H. S wants H to believe this, but for reasons of delicacy does not wish to tell H so explicitly. So S forms the following plan. Knowing that H is watching, but pretending not to know that H is watching, S puts lipstick on the collar of H's husband's shirt. H reasons as follows.

> Why is S putting lipstick on the collar of my husband's shirt? S does not know I am watching her. She intends that when I see the lipstick, I will not know that S put it there. So she intends that I will believe that the lipstick got there because my husband is unfaithful. But S is my friend.

She would not want me to believe that my husband is unfaithful unless she knew that he is unfaithful. So *S* knows my husband is unfaithful. So, my husband is unfaithful.

At this point *S*'s desire to cause *H* to believe that her husband is unfaithful is fulfilled according to plan. Yet intuitively the action of putting lipstick on the collar in these circumstances does not mean$_{NN}$ anything (Strawson 1964: 156; Schiffer 1987: 245).

The diagnosis is that *H* cannot use the above reasoning to arrive at knowledge, for it relies on the false premiss that *S* does not know that *H* is watching *S*. Since *S* fully intends *H* to rely on a premiss *S* knows to be false, *S* has no intention of causing *H* to know that her husband is unfaithful, and therefore *S* neither testifies to *H* nor does *S* appear to testify, which is why we do not have a case here of meaning$_{NN}$. Thus Grice's account fails to draw correctly the boundaries of meaning$_{NN}$. Of course it is possible for Griceans to bar this sort of counterexample by adding further conditions to supplement the list of intentions I1, I2 and I3. But a principled reason for adding further conditions is lacking, unless we require that the speaker intends to impart knowledge and not mere belief. Grice himself suggested that the higher-order counterexamples of this sort can be barred by adding to his analysis the condition that *S* does not intend *H* to be deceived about any of *S*'s relevant intentions (1969: 99–100); no principled reason was given for this suggestion, however. The epistemic account can explain that Grice needs the extra condition to avoid 'false lemma' counterexamples.

My second objection to Grice is that his theory that semantic meaning is constituted by conventions to speaker-mean leads to a mistaken epistemology of testimony. Grice's model of speaker-meaning is a doxastic one, according to which *S*'s plan is to cause *H* to believe that κ by exploiting a conventional device for manifesting an intention to cause *H* to believe that κ. But *H*'s knowledge that *S* intends that *H* believe that κ need have no tendency in and of itself to cause *H* to believe that κ. Therefore Grice proposes an inferential mechanism: from the premiss that *S* desires that *H* believe that κ, together with further premisses about the sincerity and knowledgeableness of *S*, *H* is to infer as conclusion that κ is indeed the case. On Grice's account, an assertion succeeds in its aim of inducing a belief in the hearer only as a consequence of an inference on the part of the hearer. Contrary to Grice, however, casual introspection does not seem to support the idea that any such course of reasoning goes on in hearers. Of course one does reason and make inferences when there is reason to doubt a speaker's testimony; but in a normal case one simply takes what a speaker says at face value. For example, if one listens to someone giving one directions or telling one the news, usually one is not conscious of making any inferences: one simply listens to the testimony and apprehends the facts stated. Straightforward introspection gives us no reason to believe that the Gricean inferences occur.

By making testimony rely on an inference of the hearer, the Gricean account makes transmission of knowledge by testimony too difficult. As I shall show, it often happens that knowledge of the premises needed for such an inference is simply not available to the hearer. Despite this, knowledge transmission by testimony occurs. I conclude that knowledge transmission is not always the result of any inference by the hearer, so Grice's account of semantic meaning must be wrong.

It seems plain that if S's testimony is to cause H to know that κ in the manner characteristic of testimony, then:

(1) S must be sincere in asserting that κ;
(2) S must be knowledgeable about κ.

S is sincere in asserting that κ if when S asserts that κ, S believes that κ. S is knowledgeable about κ if when S believes that κ, S knows that κ. If H arrives at the belief that κ on the basis of an assertion by S, then H's belief that κ will be reliable if and only if S is sincere and knowledgeable.

The condition (2), that S is knowledgeable about κ, is a necessary condition for successful testimony. Testimony that is not knowledgeable cannot give rise to knowledge in a hearer; at least, it cannot do so in the way characteristic of testimony. For example, it is not enough that S's belief that κ be true, for if the speaker's belief that κ is without justification, then the hearer's belief that κ will be unreliable, since it relies on unjustified testimony. Nor is it enough that the speaker's belief that κ is justified; if the speaker's belief is false, the hearer's belief will be false also, and hence not knowledge. It is not even enough that the speaker's belief is both true and justified: in a Gettier case, the speaker may have a true justified belief that falls short of knowledge because it could easily have been mistaken; a hearer who relies on the speaker's testimony acquires a true and justified but unreliable belief; so the hearer does not acquire knowledge.

Conditions (1) and (2) must therefore both obtain, if testimony is to cause the transmission of knowledge. But the Gricean model imposes the much more stringent requirement that they not only obtain but are known by the hearer to obtain. For according to the Gricean model, the mechanism by which a belief is formed from testimony is always an inference, with the conditions (1) and (2) as premisses. But an inference cannot produce knowledge unless its premisses are known to be true. Yet how often does it happen, in everyday testimony, that a hearer really *knows* that the speaker is sincere? Does the hearer really *know* that the speaker is knowledgeable? Suppose you ask a chance stranger the way to the post office, and the stranger tells you it is straight ahead; the stranger may be sincere and knowledgeable, but it seems doubtful that these facts are known to you. Nevertheless you really do now know where the post office is, because the sincere and knowledgeable stranger has told you: the Inferential Model of testimony cannot reconcile one's ignorance of the premisses of the supposed inference with one's knowledge of its supposed conclusion.

The objection can be sharpened. If the Inferential Model of testimony is correct, it follows that if *H* learns from *S* that *κ*, then *H* knows that *κ* by a Gricean inference, so *H* knows the premisses needed to infer that *κ*, i.e., *H* knows that *S* is sincere and knowledgeable. But then *H* can deduce that *S* knows that *κ*, as follows: *S* asserts that *κ*, so by *S*'s sincerity *S* believes that *κ*, so by *S*'s knowledgeableness *S* knows that *κ*. The Inferential Model therefore entails that if *H* learns that *κ* by testimony from *S*, then *H* is in a position to know that *S* knows that *κ*. But if *H* is in a position to know that *S* knows that *κ*, then *S* too must surely be in a position to know it; for normally *H* will know no more about the matter than does *S*. We have arrived at a restricted version of the **KK** principle: if *S* can communicate knowledge that *κ* by testimony, then *S* must not only know that *κ*, but know that *S* knows that *κ*. And now the difficulty for the Inferential Model is clear: the **KK** principle is a wrong principle. I shall give counterexamples to show that we can know and successfully give testimony, without being in a position to know that we know.

It may be objected that we reached the strong **KK** requirement because we required that the speaker be knowledgeable, i.e., that if *S* believes that *A*, then *S* knows that *A*. Would it not be sufficient that *S* is just alethically reliable on the question whether *A*, i.e., if *S* believes that *A*, then the belief is reliably true? I think not, for if *H* arrives at knowledge that *A* by an inference from S's mere alethic reliability, then it seems to me that H is not learning that A in the manner characteristic of testimony, but rather is using S's belief as inductive evidence for A, so that we would be dealing here with Grice's 'natural' meaning, rather than meaning$_{NN}$. But even if I am wrong about this, it does not help the inferentialist. If H is to infer the truth of A, H needs to know that S is alethically reliable; but then S must know that S is alethically reliable. But often we can transmit knowledge by testimony when we do not know we are alethically reliable. This is proved by the same counterexamples that I will give against the **KK** requirement.

It may be suggested that we should require that the hearer knows neither that the speaker is knowledgeable nor even that they are reliable; all that is required is that H knows that if S believes that A, then A. An inference based only on such a premiss seems even further from genuine testimony than an inference based on reliability, but it still does not help the inferentialist. Admittedly it is now guaranteed that S is in a position to know that if S believes that A, then A; for S knows that A, from which that follows. But prior to the testimony H does not know that A, so unlike S, H does not know that if S believes that A, then A. This also is proved by the same counterexamples.

The sort of counterexamples I shall give to inferentialism arise whenever a fact is a cause of knowledge, without being a premiss for knowledge:

> *Causal Dependence*: Knowledge that κ is *causally dependent* on q if in the circumstances the existence of q is causally necessary for knowledge that κ.
>
> *Inferential Dependence*: Knowledge that κ is *inferentially dependent* on q if in the circumstances knowledge of q is a necessary premiss of inferential knowledge that κ.

If knowledge that κ is dependent on q only causally, q needs only to be the case. But if knowledge that κ is dependent on q inferentially, then q needs to be known to be the case. Now let q be a fact that is causally but not inferentially necessary for knowledge that κ. Suppose S knows that κ but that nothing S knows entails that q. Then S has an epistemic alternative w where κ is the case but q is not the case. Since q is a causally necessary condition of S's knowing that κ, it follows that at w, S does not know that κ; hence at the actual world, S does not know that S knows that κ. Suppose that H has no knowledge whether κ is true or not, except the testimony of S that κ, and that H has no knowledge about q. Then since S does not know that S knows that κ, it follows that H does not know it either. Therefore either H does not know that S is sincere, or H does not know that S is knowledgeable. So H lacks knowledge of one of the two premises of sincerity and knowledgeableness that are required for a Gricean inference. Nevertheless H does in fact learn that κ by the testimony of S. Thus the transmission of knowledge by testimony does not require inference, and therefore the Gricean model is wrong.

Counterexample 1: Knowledge by Estimation[3]

Suppose S is reasonably good at estimating the number of apples in a box by just looking. S is knowledgeable on such questions as whether there are more than n apples in the box; which is to say that for most m greater than n, if there are m apples in the box, then S knows there are more than n apples in the box. However, S requires a two-apple margin of error. If there are more than $(n + 2)$ apples, then S knows there are more than n. But if there are $(n + 2)$ apples or fewer, then S is unreliable on the question whether there are more than n. Thus we have:

(a) If there are more than $(n + 2)$ apples, S knows there are more than n apples.

(b) If there are not more than $(n + 2)$ apples, then S does not know there are more than n apples.

Now consider a case where there are exactly 53 apples. By (a), S knows there are more than 50 apples. By (b), S does not know there are more than 52 apples, so S has an epistemic alternative w where there are only 52 apples. At this alternative, again by (b), S does not know that there are more than 50 apples; so actually S does not know that S knows there are more than 50 apples. Suppose S now sincerely asserts to H that there are more than 50 apples. We see that the following conditions obtain actually:

(1) S is sincere in asserting that there are more than 50 apples.

(2) S is knowledgeable about whether there are more than 50 apples.

S knows there are more than 50 apples, so there seems nothing to prevent S passing on to H the knowledge that there are more than 50 apples. But

---

[3] Counterexamples of this sort against the **KK** principle were given by Williamson (1992).

clearly H cannot acquire this knowledge by a Gricean inference. For since the only information H has about how many apples there are is what H learns from S, it follows that if S does not know that S knows there are more than 50 apples, then H cannot know it either. Therefore although S is sincere and knowledgeable, H does not know that S is sincere and knowledgeable; therefore H's knowledge that there are over 50 apples is not inferential knowledge, contrary to Grice.

The suggested weaker premises for H's inference also succumb to the counterexample. First, H does not know that S's belief is reliably true; for S does not know it, so H does not know it either. For S has an alternative where there are 52 apples, and S is not alethically reliable there, by assumption. So although S knows there are over 50 apples, and although S is reliable about it, S does not know S is reliable; so H does not know it either.

The second suggestion was that the premiss 'if S believes that A, then A' would suffice for the inference. In the scenario of the counterexample there are 53 apples, so trivially it is true that if S believes there are over 50 apples, then there are over 50 apples. But H need not know this. Prior to the testimony, H has no information about how many apples there are. So H has alternatives where there are 50 apples. H knows that if there are only 50 apples, S is as likely as not to be mistaken about whether there are over 50 apples. So H has alternatives where S falsely believes that there are over 50 apples. So H does not know that, if S believes there are over 50 apples, then there are over 50 apples; so H cannot arrive by inference at the knowledge that there are over 50 apples.

Counterexample 2: Perception

S sees the blue cube, but H is not in a position to see it; S informs H that there is a blue cube here, so now H knows it too. A visual experience as of a blue cube causes S in the right context to know that S faces a blue cube. The right context is one which includes the fact that viewing conditions are good. Suppose that good viewing conditions with respect to blue cubes demand that illumination is at least 50 units, and that illumination actually is 50 units; but suppose S cannot discriminate illumination of 50 units from illumination of 49 units. Then S has an epistemic alternative w where illumination is only 49 units. At w, S does not know that S faces a blue cube, for viewing conditions at w are not good enough to see reliably. So although S knows there is a blue cube, S does not know that S knows that there is a blue cube. So *H* does not know it either. In the same way it can be shown that *H* does not know that *S* is reliable. Also it can be shown as in the previous example, that *H* does not know that, if *S* believes *S* faces a blue cube, then *S* faces a blue cube. So *H*'s knowledge that there is a blue cube here is not inferential knowledge. There are therefore any number of counterexamples to the Inferential Model of testimony. On Grice's account it should be impossible for us to succeed in passing on things which we know, but do not know that we know. But since we do succeed in passing on knowledge in such cases, a different account is required of how testimony transmits knowledge.

7.4 The Faculty Model of Testimony

Saying and Showing

The upshot of our discussion of Grice is that assertion cannot be defined in terms of causing belief. Instead it must be defined in terms of testimony, which is a species of causing to know by what I shall call *showing*. One shows *H* that *κ* by some more basic action; one's plan is that the more basic action will by a foreseen causal chain cause *H* to know that *κ*. As in all cases where we do something *A* by doing something else *B*, the causal connection must be reasonably direct and its various links must be foreseen in reasonable detail. We may define showing as follows:

> *S* by doing *x* *shows* *H* that *κ* (in way *M*) if *S* does *x* intending that *x* cause *H* to know that *κ* (in way *M*).

Since there is such a thing as showing, there can be such a thing as intentionally appearing to show. When the conjuror shows us an apparently empty hat, there is the appearance of showing; the conjuror appears to show us that the hat is empty. We may indeed be fooled into believing that the hat is empty. But the disjunctive classification 'either showing, or seeming to show' does not coincide with the intentional production of belief. It is possible to induce a belief that *κ* by hypnosis; but the hypnotist neither shows nor pretends to show the subject that *κ*. Conversely if an audience is sophisticated the conjuror neither produces not intends to produce a belief that the hat is really empty; it is all just entertainment, but the conjuror does really appear to show that the hat is empty.

There are many ways of showing, for there are many ways M whereby one's action can cause another to know. In *demonstrating*, S shows H that κ by directing H's attention to the fact that κ, which is visible in the scene. For example, if a car is approaching, S directs the attention of H to this fact by pointing to the car. If the fact that κ is not currently visible, then S can show H that κ by taking H to a place where the fact is visible, or by removing some obstruction to H's vision.

There can be *iterated showing*, where the act x whereby S causes knowledge that κ is itself an act of showing: S shows H that κ by showing H that q. *Inferential showing* is an example of iterated showing: S shows H that κ by showing evidence $q_1, \ldots, q_n$ from which the fact that κ is an immediate and expected inference. For example, S inferentially shows H that it will soon rain by drawing H's attention to looming rainclouds; or S inferentially shows H that the angle in a semicircle is a right angle by showing a diagram with the radius to the vertex drawn.

I argued that testimony does not rely on inference, so contrary to Grice's view it is not inferential showing. But there is another species of iterated showing which I think is a better candidate: *showing by signs* is iterated showing where S shows H that κ by showing H a sign that κ. For example, we often show each other our state of mind by doing something that is a natural sign of the state of mind. Facial expressions are natural signs of the emotions; for example, if S is disappointed, S's face may take on the characteristic shape that a human face has if its owner is experiencing disappointment. This shape causes anyone who sees it to have a characteristic visual experience; H not only sees that S's face is shaped that way; H sees that S 'looks disappointed'. Someone can show their disappointment by showing their face: H sees that S 'looks disappointed' because H can read disappointment in S's face.

The existence of signs gives rise to the possibility of showing by signing, i.e., showing that κ by showing a sign that κ. This type of showing exploits the hearer's ability to read the signs. Some signs are human universals; for example, the facial expressions that express emotions appear to be human universals. Linguistic signs are not universal but still they are signs that can be read. If s means that κ in the idiolect of H, then S can show H that κ by showing H the sign s; for H will read that κ on seeing s, and can thereby be caused to know that κ. This is the Faculty Model of testimony: it treats testimony as causing knowledge by showing a sign: by reading the sign the audience is caused to know the testified fact.

If one understands a written language, one's language faculty may cause one to understand the content of a seen sentence by causing one to read it. If sentence s expresses the content κ then seeing s will cause one to visually read that κ; that is what it is for a sentence s in one's idiolect to mean that κ. We may define the idiolect of a given person as a relation between words and sentences that is established by the propensities of the person's language faculty:

> *Idiolect*: The *idiolect* I_H of H is the relation that obtains between s and κ if when H perceives s then H's language faculty is disposed to cause H to read that κ.

The suggestion of the Faculty Model is that testimony is a kind of showing that essentially exploits the hearer's ability to read signs. If S wishes H to know that κ, and if S can speak the idiolect of H, then S can find s such that $I_H(s) = \kappa$; by fashioning a token of s, S can cause H to read that κ, and in the right context this can cause H to know that κ, in the manner characteristic of testimony. We can therefore define testimony as precisely this kind of showing.

> *Testimony*: 'S by doing x *testifies* to H that κ' $=_{df}$ S does x intending to show H a sign that will cause H to know that κ, by causing H to read that κ.

7.5 The Analogy Between Testimony and Perception

Suppose one has a visual experience as of a blue cube before one, and thereby comes to know that there is blue cube before one. What is the relation between the experience and the visual knowledge? An inferentialist about perception will say that one's awareness of the experience leads one to infer that one faces a blue cube, as follows:

(1) I am having a visual experience as of a blue cube before me.
(2) My senses are working correctly and conditions are favourable for seeing.
(3) Therefore there is a blue cube before me.

If the premises are known, the conclusion is known, and so one has visual knowledge that there is a blue cube before one. Now one's seeing that there is a blue cube before one is one's apprehending of this fact. According to the inferentialist, one apprehends the fact only as the conclusion of one's inference; the visual experience is not the visual apprehension of the seen fact, but only a precursor of it, for the apprehending depends on an inference.

As in the case of testimony, there is a phenomenological objection and an epistemological objection to inferentialism about perception. The phenomenological objection is that we are not normally conscious of any inference in perception. When we know by seeing, usually the only mental act that occurs is the visual experience itself. As with testimony, the inferentialist is obliged to suppose that the inference is an unconscious one. But then the epistemological objection can be pressed, just as before, that if perceptual knowledge rests on an inference, then one could not know the conclusion without knowing the premises, so that one could not have visual knowledge that a blue cube was before one, unless viewing conditions were not only good but known to be good. Counterexample (2) above refutes that claim. Therefore we should reject inferentialism for perception.

An alternative epistemology of perception is the Faculty Model, according to which perceptual knowledge arises immediately by the activity of the faculty of perception. For example, a visible fact causes one's faculty of vision to cause a visual experience which if the context is suitable causes one immediately to know the visible fact. In this context, the experience itself, and no further act of inference or judgement, causes one to know the visible fact—the experience and the apprehending are one and the same event. Of course, whether an experience is the apprehension of a fact depends on the context in which it occurs; one's senses must be working properly and conditions must be favourable for seeing: but one's knowledge is dependent on the conditions only causally, and not inferentially.

The case of testimony is exactly analogous. I argued above that knowledge can be transmitted in testimony even if H does not know that S is sincere and knowledgeable. The speaker's utterance of s causes H to have an experience as of reading that κ, and according to the Faculty Model, this experience non-inferentially causes H to know that κ. Of course, reading is apprehending only if contextual conditions are right, which requires that one's informant is sincere and knowledgeable. But it is not required that contextual conditions are known to be right, for H's knowledge depends on the conditions only causally, not inferentially. According to the Faculty Model, it is no more necessary for H to carry out an inference in testimony than it is in perception. For example, suppose S testifies to H that S faces a blue cube. Then H has an experience of aurally reading that S faces a blue cube. If S is sincere and knowledgeable, H thereby apprehends that S faces a blue cube. The Faculty Model of testimony says the reading and the apprehending are the same thing, just as the Faculty Model of perception says that the visual experience and the visual apprehending are the same thing.

When Descartes proposed to doubt the 'testimony' of his senses, he was close to the Faculty Model of testimony, for he was taking perception to be an analogue of testimony. On Descartes' way of thinking, our senses are just like our witnesses. The Faculty Model reverses the Cartesian analogy, saying our witnesses are just like our senses. The analogy may be spelled out as follows. The proper function of a sense is to inform one of facts the sense detects by causing one to have an appropriate experience that represents the fact. For example, if one's visual faculty has detected that κ, it causes one to have an experience of seeming to see that κ, and in the right context this causes one to see that κ, i.e., to know visually that κ. Analogously, the office of a witness is to inform one of a fact κ that the witness has learned, by causing one to have an appropriate experience that represents that κ. The words of the witness cause one to have an experience of reading that κ, and in the right context this causes one to be apprised that κ, i.e., to know by testimony that κ.

It may be objected that the Faculty Model for testimony seems to be in obvious conflict with daily experience. When people tell us things, we do not always take what we are told uncritically and at face value. We ask ourselves whether we can trust the speaker – are they sincere, or do they perhaps have a deceptive intention? Is the speaker reliable on the topic – are they likely to be knowledgeable about it? And so we weigh the evidence on these matters. If we do arrive through this process at knowledge of the fact stated by the speaker, the knowledge depends on a more or less elaborate process of inductive inference, quite unlike the immediate apprehension of fact that is characteristic of perception. The objection is that testimony characteristically relies upon inference in a way that perception does not. In both perception and testimony, however, it is necessary to distinguish the case where one has in mind the possibility of defeaters from the case where things are being taken at face value. If one is aware of a potential defeater then neither testimony nor perception can be taken at face value, unless the defeater can first be defeated. Processes of inference surrounding testimony and perception have to do with the search for defeaters, defeaters of defeaters, etc.: these processes can occur equally with both testimony and perception, and therefore do not spoil the analogy between them.

To deny inferentialism, with respect either to perception or to testimony, is not to say that either is indefeasible. Even in a context that is in other respects favourable, the presence of a defeater can undermine knowledge from perception and testimony alike. For example, you see a blue cube in front of you, your vision is perfect and seeing conditions are good. Still you do not know there is a blue cube in front of you, for a doctor you trust has told you that you are subject to hallucinations as of blue cubes. The doctor's statement is a defeater of your visual experience because it entails that you may be currently experiencing a hallucination. The context is one in which you have an undefeated defeater, and so it is not a context in which you can know. Similarly, you may read that κ in a context where a writer is testifying sincerely, and the writer knows that κ. The context is in these respects favourable for the gaining of knowledge by testimony. But an expert you trust states that the writer was mistaken. The expert's statement is a defeater of the writer's testimony. It creates a context in which you have an undefeated defeater, and so you are unable to derive knowledge from the writer's testimony.

In the presence of defeaters, the rational thing to do if the topic is important is to pass your evidence in rational review, in what now really is a genuine process of inference. For example, if you persistently see the blue cube, and others say they see it too, then you may experiment to test your vision; if your vision seems to be working properly you may conclude that you are not hallucinating at the moment. The doctor's statement is itself defeated by your new evidence of the current reliability of your vision. By a process of evidence-gathering and inference you have found a defeater of the defeater and can now after all come to know that there really is a blue cube before you. The case is similar for testimony. You pass in review what you know both of the writer and of the expert, and you recall that the writer is widely regarded as reliable, whereas you remember the expert to have made many errors in the past. The expert's statement defeated the writer's testimony, but your recollection of the expert's past errors defeats this defeater. You discount what the expert told you and decide to trust the writer's testimony. By a process of inference and weighing of evidence you do after all come to know.

Thus there certainly are cases where one needs inference in order to arrive at knowledge both from perceptual experience, and from testimony. But we need not suppose it is so in every case; in the most common cases, in the absence of defeaters, no inference is involved. One has a perceptual experience, which one takes at face value, and thereby one apprehends a fact. One reads a writer; one takes the experience at face value, and thereby too one apprehends a fact.

However, we do seem to reason more frequently about testimony than about perception. A cynical explanation is that our witnesses are more likely to deceive us than our senses. A more interesting explanation is that testimony has by its nature a greater propensity for self-defeat than has perception. In a context in which S knowledgeably testifies that κ, it is quite likely that what S testifies is at least slightly surprising to H. There is a contrast here with perception: one may already know one faces a blue cube, but vision will continue to tell one this for as long as one continues to look at the blue cube; but speakers who keep telling conversational partners what they already know are soon partnerless. Therefore testimony in an interesting conversation is statistically more likely than perception to contain unexpected or even surprising information. But this entails that testimony also has a greater tendency to be prone to defeaters. S testifies that κ, and this surprises H, who had believed that $\neg\kappa$, perhaps for good reason. In such a case H's own existing evidence that $\neg\kappa$ is acting as a defeater to the testimony. As Hume pointed out, if we have strong evidence that $\neg\kappa$, then we shall be inclined to take testimony that κ not as evidence that κ but as evidence against the authority of the testifier, so that the testimony is defeated.

Thus we must distinguish two different types of evidential situations. The first type is where H has no opinion on the question whether κ, and there is no defeater to prevent S from passing on to H what S knows. H can take S's testimony at face value, and apprehend the fact S states without an inference. But if H had previously believed that $\neg\kappa$, H's evidence for $\neg\kappa$ is a defeater: so on receiving the testimony H will pass the total evidence in review, and embark on a process of inference. But exactly the same thing can happen with perception; it too can be subject to 'self-defeat', if we see something surprising or improbable. For example, if one saw a pink elephant, one would not believe one's eyes, because one has a firm prior belief that there are no pink elephants. Instead, one would initially assume that there was something wrong with one's vision. Thus in the perceptual case too we can draw a distinction between a type of situation where the experience is taken at face value, and a type where there is Humean 'self-defeat'.

7.6 Is Use a Regularity of Truthfulness and Trust?

Meaning is a relation between sentences and contents. But what sort of relation is it, and how is the relation to be defined? To answer this, I will appeal to the Wittgensteinian slogan that meaning is use. However, I shall not take this slogan, as Wittgenstein himself did, to express the doctrine that a sentence meaning, i.e., a content, is nothing over and above the use of the sentence in a language. Rather I shall be applying the slogan to the *means-that* relation that holds between a sentence s and the content κ if s means that κ. So applied, the slogan says that the obtaining of the *means-that* relation between s and κ in the language of G is nothing over and above the fact that G use s to say that κ. Thus we can define *means-that* if we can define what it is for a population to use a language. In the rest of this chapter I shall consider three hypotheses about the nature of the relation of *use*.

The first hypothesis is the regularity theory of David Lewis, which says that a population use a language L if there is a conventional regularity of behaviour among them of being truthful and trusting in L. According to Lewis (1972b), a language is an abstract mapping from sentences to propositions, whose existence does not depend in any way on human beings and their linguistic practices. Lewis set himself the task of defining the relation that obtains between a population G and an abstract language L, if L is the language used by G. His definition is that L is an actual language of G if a convention prevails among G of being 'truthful and trusting in L'. One is truthful in L if one tries never to utter a sentence of L that is not true; one is trusting in L if for each sentence s of L, one's conditional probability that s is true, given that s is asserted, exceeds one's unconditional probability that s is true. L is the language of G because a convention exists among G that sustains the following regularity: they are truthful and trusting in L.

Use cannot be defined by Lewis's methods in terms of truth alone, as the following counterexample of Schiffer's proves. Let L be the actual language of G, let s be a sentence which is not in L because e.g., it is too long to be conveniently uttered, and let $L^+ = L \cup \{s\}$. The sentence s is never uttered in G; *a fortiori*, it is never uttered untruthfully; suppose this is common knowledge in G. Then L^+ is a language in which there is a regularity of truthfulness sustained by concordant mutual expectation of truthfulness in L^+; so by Lewis's definitions, there is among G a convention of truthfulness in L^+, sustained by an interest in communication. If we required only truthfulness-in-L, then L^+ would be an actual language of G, which it is not. (Lewis 1972b: 187.)

In light of this counterexample, Lewis modified the account he gave in *Convention* (Lewis 1969) to include also the requirement of trust. Truthfulness in L, which is a condition only on speakers and which appeals only to truth, is insufficient to determine the actual language. Trust-in-L is a requirement on hearers and appeals to a Bayesian theory of the rational revision of belief. It amounts to this, that hearing a sentence of L asserted increase one's confidence that the sentence is true-in-L, so that as hearer one stands ready to count the assertion of any sentence s as evidence of its truth. This modification duly excludes unwanted languages like L^+. But it does not work for every sentence. Hume claimed, surely rightly, that a verbal report of a miracle raises one's confidence not that the report is true but that the reporter is mistaken. Call a *Hume sentence* any sentence such that the fact of its assertion only raises one's confidence that the speaker is under some misapprehension. There are a great many such sentences, and their existence defeats Lewis's criterion of trust. For example, any absurdity to which one has assigned probability zero is unlikely to have its subjective probability raised by being uttered; fluent speakers of English do not regard an utterance of, say, '$0 = 1$' as *prima facie* evidence that $0 = 1$. If we took Lewis's requirement of trust-in-L strictly, it would rule out English as the actual language of English speakers. I conclude that Lewis has not succeeded in accurately characterising the regularity of use. Indeed, I believe it cannot be characterised using just the notion of truth, by truthfulness-in-L, nor can it be characterised using belief revision, by trust-in-L. My diagnosis is that use needs to be characterised epistemically, not alethically or doxastically.

A second objection to Lewis's account is that his appeal to convention does not seem the right explanation of why it is that a regularity of language use prevails among G. Lewis follows Grice in thinking of a convention as a regularity that continues because everyone expects it to continue (1972b: 164–6). Specifically L is the language of G because everyone in G uses L, and all continue to use L because all believe all will continue to use L. According to Lewis, it is a 'platitude' that there are these conventions of language. But the claim that the regularity of use is sustained by convention does not appear to be true, for the ability of an individual human being to speak a language appears to be causally dependent on the configuration of the individual's language faculty. A population who all speak the same language do not do so merely by free choice. They cannot arbitrarily choose which language to speak, but must rely on the acquired capacities of their language faculties. People who speak the same language have attuned their language faculties to each other, often from childhood; the process of acquiring a different attunement, i.e., of learning a new language, is long and laborious for most people, and impossible for many. The language faculties of members of the same linguistic community are attuned, and that is the causal mechanism that underlies their concordant language use. Each speaks as they do because their language faculty enables them to speak fluently only that way; either they speak fluently that way, or they do not speak fluently at all; therefore all speak the same way. If the uniformity here is a conventional one at all, it is conventional to only a small extent; mostly it is sustained by a causal mechanism, namely the attuned language faculties of the population.

7.7 Use as a Regularity of Testifying—The Frequency Analysis

A second hypothesis characterises use epistemically rather than alethically or doxastically. It takes use to be a regularity of testimony, and appeals to the Faculty Model. Because Lewis attributed the regularity of use to a convention, he omitted the contribution of the language faculty: indeed, it might as well not exist, for all the role it plays in Lewis's theory. So he fails to raise the following interesting question—what is the function of the language faculty? If we knew what it is for, we could decide what words are for, and then we would be better placed to define the use of a word. The suggestion of the Faculty Model of testimony is that the function of the language faculty is the exchange of knowledge by speech; words are for giving testimony, so in an important sense that is their use.

According to the Faculty Model, all sayings can be defined in terms of testimony. We can define those sayings that are assertions as actions done with the intention either of testifying, or of appearing to testify. For example, a lie is the deliberately false appearance of testimony. Other sayings can all be explained in terms of assertion; an utterance on the stage is a pretend assertion; in a play within a play it is a pretend pretend assertion; in the language class it is a practice assertion, and so on. Thus all sayings can be reduced to assertion, and hence to testimony.

It may be objected that if the main verb of a sentence is not in the indicative mood, then usually the use of the sentence is not for assertion. For example, 'Shut the door' is a perfectly good sentence, but its verb is in the imperative mood, and it might be said that its use is not to assert that the door is shut, but to order that it be shut. However, that does not exclude the point of view that the use of the sentence is to testify that one orders that the door be shut; for the same utterance can be both an order and an assertion—one orders someone to shut the door by informing them that one orders them to shut the door. Indeed, if one fails to cause someone to know that one is ordering them to shut the door, then normally one would not count as having ordered them to shut the door (Lewis 1970b: 222—6).

Speech–act theorists such as Austin have said that verbs in the first-person present are often *performatives*, whose use is not testimony. Thus whereas 'You promised to come' is used to assert that you promised to come, 'I promise to come' is used to promise to come, i.e., to perform the speech act of promising, which is not testifying (Austin 1962: 1–11). The reply is the same: one can promise by testifying. Someone who utters 'I promise to come' testifies that they promise to come, thereby causing the promisee to know the promise has been given, which knowledge is a necessary condition of promising. Thus neither the non-indicative moods nor the performatives are compelling counterexamples to the general claim that we may analyse all saying in terms of testimony. So testifying can be taken to be the primary kind of speech act; orders, questions, deliberate falsehoods, stage speech and so on are all derivative and secondary. A use theory of meaning should therefore specify semantic meaning in terms of the primary speech act: s means that κ amongst G if G use s to testify that κ.

But how are we to analyse 'G use s to testify that κ'? Since G use s by uttering it, and since the tense of 'use' is present continuative, we might propose the *analysans* 'Usually, G utter s to testify that κ.' So the proposal of the Frequency Analysis would be:

> *Frequency Analysis*: 'G use s to testify that κ' =df Usually, G utter s to testify that κ.

But the Frequency Analysis as it stands is ambiguous. It has (at least) two disambiguations, depending whether the relevant actual or counterfactual comparison classes for 'usually' are those where a member of E is uttering s, or testifying that κ. Thus we might interpret the Frequency Analysis as either of:

> (A) Usually, if G utter s to testify, they testify that κ by uttering s.
> (B) Usually, if G testify that κ, they testify that κ by uttering s.

But neither of these disambiguations succeeds. The first is defeated by the phenomenon of ambiguity, the second by the phenomenon of synonymy.

Disambiguation (A) does not succeed. A sentence such as 'N went to the bank' has more than one meaning in English. However (A) entails it has no meanings. For let E be the English speech community. Then neither of the following is true:

> (1) Usually if E utter 'N went to the bank' to testify, they testify that N went to the (financial) bank.
> (2) Usually if E utter 'N went to the bank' to testify, they testify that N went to the (river) bank.

It does not improve matters if we substitute a disjunction such as (3):

> (3) Usually if E utter 'N went to the bank' to testify, either they testify that N went to the financial bank or they testify that N went to the river bank.

This will not do because such a disjunction can be true when there is only one meaning. For example:

> (4) Usually if E utter 'N went to the river bank' to testify, either they testify that N went to the financial bank or they testify that pigs have wings.

(4) is true, but 'pigs have wings' is not one of the meanings of '*N* went to the river bank'. It would be helpful if we had some criterion to distinguish wanted disjunctions like (3) from unwanted disjunctions like (4). But no criterion based only on what is usual comes to hand. For example, it does not help us to require that neither disjunct on its own gives the only usual use, because there are cases of genuinely ambiguous sentences where there is only one usual use, because the other uses are rare. Finally (5) will not help either:

(5) Usually if *E* utter '*N* went to the river bank' to testify, they testify that either *N* went to the financial bank or *N* went to the river bank.

'*N* went to the bank' has two non-disjunctive meanings, whereas (5) wrongly treats it as having one disjunctive meaning.

Disambiguation (*A*) is therefore not a satisfactory expression of the Frequency Model. But disambiguation (*B*) is not satisfactory either:

(*B*) Usually, if *G* testify that κ, they testify that κ by uttering *s*.

This fails, because it assumes that for each content κ there is only one sentence *s* that expresses that κ. But in a natural language there can be synonymous sentences that differ only in tone; for example, according to Frege, there is only a difference of tone between 'Fido is a dog' and 'Fido is a cur'. So for the disambiguation (*B*) we can now go through five analogous attempts $(1') \ldots (5')$ to give it a true reading; which will have exactly the same lack of success, for exactly the same reasons, *mutatis mutandis*. So neither (*A*) nor (*B*) is a satisfactory analysis of use. It seems the Frequency Analysis fails: the meaning of a sentence cannot be defined statistically in terms of actual or counterfactual frequencies of use.

7.8 Use as the Design End of an Artefact

The hypothesis about use that I wish to commend is the teleological theory of use, as follows: a sentence is an artefact, and its use is its design end. By regarding a sentence as an artefact we can respond to an objection by Wittgenstein to the very idea of a theory of meaning. Wittgenstein invited us to think of words as tools, which can be used for any of a number of purposes. He writes:

Think of the tools in a tool-box: there is a hammer, pliers, a saw, a screw-driver, a rule, a glue-pot, glue, nails and screws.—The functions of words are as diverse as the functions of these objects. (1967b: 6,§11)

The diverse tools can each be put to diverse uses:

'We name things, and then we can talk about them: can refer to them in talk.'—As if what we did next were given with the mere act of naming. As if there were only one thing called 'talking about the thing'. Whereas in fact we do the most various things with our sentences … (Thus for example, children give names to their dolls, and then talk about them and to them. Think in this connexion how singular is the use of a person's name to *call* him!) (1967b: 13, §27)

Since the uses are so diverse, language is a motley. No special order is discernible in the motley, so Wittgenstein encouraged us to give up the search for a single theory, and instead regard the use of words as simply a part of the natural history of our species.

As 'lateral thinkers' know, a brick has many uses. However, the fact that a token thing has many uses does not prevent a type of thing from having a single characteristic use. There is indeed such a thing as *the* use of an artefact, namely the design end of the artefact. Thus a brick is a kind of thing whose use (design end) is building; that is consistent with there being 'diverse' uses for an individual brick. Wittgenstein should have distinguished tools from artefacts: not every tool is an artefact, for an artefact is an artificial product designed for a particular purpose. For example, if a chimpanzee picks up a twig to fish for termites, it uses a tool; but if it has to break off a twig and strip the leaves, it uses an artefact. There is indeed no such thing, in general, as 'the use' of a tool: but tools that are artefacts have a design end, and that is 'the use' of the artefact type.

Of course, not every artefact is actually created for the design end of its kind. For example, the design end of a violin is to make music. But a violin might be made with the express intention that it be put in a museum and never played. It is still a violin because it is designed to be serviceable for the design end of a violin, even though it is not intended to be actually used for that purpose. If an alien visitor makes an exact copy for display in the aliens' museum, the copy if sufficiently accurate is also a violin, for it is designedly serviceable for the design end of a violin. The alien artificer did not know the design end, but it crafted the copy intending it to be serviceable for the actual design end, whatever that might be. If the alien makes its copy not by handcrafting it but by operating its matter-duplicator, it is still a violin. For the duplicator is a device whose design end includes making working copies of artefacts; hence to make things that are serviceable for the design end of the thing copied; hence the output of the duplicator is by design serviceable for the design end of the duplicated thing, whatever that might be.[4]

What does *serviceable* mean? To say that the violin is serviceable for making music is to say that a competent violinist could make music by playing it. The preposition 'by' here denotes the *by* relation:

Definition of 'by': 'S did A by B' $=_{df}$ S did B in the reasonable hope that B would cause A in way M, and B did in fact cause A in way M.

For example, S makes music by bowing the violin if S bows it in the hope that bowing it will in the violin's characteristic way cause music, and in fact the bowing does cause music in that way. Given the *by* relation, we can define *serviceability*: x is serviceable as an artefact of kind K if a competent user of K by employing x in the manner characteristic of K can effect the design end of K in the way characteristic of K. A necessary condition for x to be a member of the artefact kind K is that x is serviceable by design for the design end of K. It follows that for any artefact kind, the use of the kind is always well-defined, for the use is just the design end specified in the definition of the kind.

Artefacts like bricks and violins are continuants, but not every artefact is a continuant, for events can be artefacts too. Examples of artefact events include a party, a race and a wedding. Each of these kinds of artefact event has its own design end: the end of a party is conviviality; of a race, competition; of a wedding, marriage. Whatever the actual intentions of participants, no event is a party, a race or a wedding unless it is designedly serviceable for conviviality, competition or marriage; for example, an event is not a party unless party-goers could have been convivial by partying at it.

Therefore although Wittgenstein is right that a sentence token can be put to 'diverse' uses, there can still be such a thing as *the* use of a sentence

---

[4] Here I am grateful to a referee.

type, since a sentence is an artefact. The Faculty Model of testimony says the design end of a sentence is to convey knowledge of a certain fact, by actuating the language faculty of those who encounter the sentence. Given a population G, an artefact s is a sentence for G if it is serviceable for testimony in G. This does not mean that every instance of the sentence must be produced with the actual intention of testifying: it might have been uttered as a lie, or as a joke, or as fiction. But it must be serviceable for testimony, or it does not count as a sentence at all. So the Faculty Model can propose the following teleological analysis of *use*:

> *Definition of use*: 'G use s to say that κ' $=_{df}$ among G, the design end of s is testimony that κ.

Note that the teleological theory can say that the use of '$0 = 1$' is to testify that $0 = 1$, even if no one would ever in fact use the sentence to say that $0 = 1$; for it is conceivable that someone might believe that $0 = 1$, in which case the sentence '$0 = 1$' would be serviceable for testimony accordingly.

The fact that a sentence is serviceable for testimony allows the Faculty Model to explain how the sentence can also serve other possible purposes of the speaker—not only testimony, but also deceit and pretence. The model can also cope easily with the problem, fatal to the Frequency Model, of sentences that are rarely used. For example, the sentence 'Fido is a cur' might never actually be uttered, for example because it is thought to be bad manners. Still, expressing the content *that Fido is a dog* is the sentence's design end—it can have a design end, even if it is not frequently, or not ever, used for its design end. The Faculty Model also copes with ambiguous sentences—a sentence can have more than one meaning because an artefact can have more than one design end. For example, a claw hammer has two uses: hammering nails in, and clawing nails out. The design end of most words is at least somewhat disjunctive, as is confirmed by their dictionary entries. A practical problem is that because an ambiguous sentence has more than one meaning, one cannot be sure that it will be heard with the intended meaning. Someone who hears the sentence 'N went to the bank' may or may not have an experience of aurally reading that N went to the (river) bank, just as someone who looks at the duck–rabbit drawing may or may not have a visual experience as of seeing a duck. If someone asks 'What was it that N saw at the bank?' and you answer by drawing a duck–rabbit, the conversational exchange may or may not be an illuminating one. In practice people usually succeed in finding disambiguating contextual cues when confronted with ambiguous sentences and drawings, which is why a degree of ambiguity is tolerable and indeed efficient in a natural language.

8

The Constitutive Thesis and the Causal Thesis

A fact may cause knowledge of that very fact. For example, an environmental fact may cause a sense organ to cause a perceptual experience, in virtue of which one has knowledge of the environmental fact. It might also cause a memory, in virtue of which one continues to have knowledge of the fact. But what is this 'in virtue of' relation? Is it the constitutive 'in virtue of', so that one's knowing is nothing over and above one's believing? Or is it the causal 'in virtue of', so that one's believing causes one's knowing, but is not identical with it?

Many philosophers say that the knowing and the believing are not distinct existences; in the right circumstances, they say, knowing just *is* believing. I shall call the Constitutive Thesis this claim that, in the right context, one's knowing is nothing over and above one's believing:

> *Constitutive Thesis*: We know in virtue of believing, because in a suitable context belief is knowledge.

There are two versions of the Constitutive Thesis. The first is the Type Identity version, which says that the property of knowing is the property of believing in a certain way, i.e., that knowledge is a type of belief. The second is the Token Identity version, which makes the weaker claim that every instance of knowing is constituted by an instance of believing. According to both the Type Identity version and the Token Identity version of the Constitutive Thesis, the predicate 'knows' does not stand for a *sui generis* and fundamental relation: the truthmaker for 'S knows that A' is only that the subject S is in a certain belief state, which is related to the context in a certain way.

The Constitutive Thesis contradicts the hypothesis for which I was arguing in previous chapters, that knowledge is a conceptually primitive and metaphysically fundamental relation. That hypothesis is inconsistent with the Constitutive Thesis and would require an alternative account of the relation between knowledge and belief. One such alternative is the Causal Thesis, according to which the predicate 'knows' stands for a distinct relation that is dependent upon belief only causally:

Causal Thesis: We know in virtue of believing, because in a suitable context belief causes knowledge.

The Causal Thesis is not committed to a temporal sequence of events, first the believing, then the knowing; it requires only that the believing and the knowing are different events, and that in the context the believing causally determines the knowing, or at any rate nomically necessitates it.

In previous chapters I offered accounts in terms of knowledge of a number of topics that are of importance in metaphysics; to the extent that these accounts succeed, they give support to the view that knowledge is metaphysically fundamental, and hence they give support to the Causal Thesis. The converse also holds. If the Causal thesis is false, and the Constitutive Thesis is true, then the metaphysical accounts I gave in previous chapters must be mistaken. In this chapter I examine the Constitutive Thesis. I argue that there is no successful positive argument in its favour, and that it does not therefore stand in the way of the metaphysics of knowledge.

In the form in which I stated it above, the Constitutive Thesis is not very illuminating. It needs to be supplemented by an independent account of belief, which must explain belief without appeal to the concept of knowledge. As an illustration of such an account, I discuss functionalism, which seeks without mentioning knowledge to give a definition of belief in terms of the joint roles of belief, desire and experience in the causation of action. Functionalism and the Constitutive Thesis complement each other, since together they purport to identify each instance of knowledge with an instance of being in the right psychological state in the right context. But the Causal Thesis must deny that functionalism on its own can be the whole account of the psychological states. The Causal Thesis says that reference must at some point be made to the concept of knowledge. It therefore prefers the account given by the Faculty Theory, according to which belief and experience are characterised as states that arise in us by the operation of our epistemic faculties. But although the Causal Thesis must take functionalism to be incomplete, it need not entirely reject it; on the contrary, it can define belief and experience as states that (1) conform to the definition given by functionalism and (2) are potential causes of knowledge.

The plan of this chapter is as follows. In section 1 I discuss functionalism, and contrast it with the faculty theory. In section 2 I discuss and reject Type Identity versions of the Constitutive Thesis, which say that knowing is a kind of believing. In section 3 I consider whether the argument from the causal efficacy of the psychological proves the Constitutive Thesis; in section 4 I consider whether the argument from the causal efficacy of the physical proves it. These are both 'completeness arguments' which say that if knowledge is not epiphenomenal, then it must be identical with belief; I argue that both arguments fail. In section 5 I argue that the Constitutive Thesis has difficulty coping with the problem of consciousness. I conclude that the Constitutive Thesis is by no means compulsory. Therefore we should prefer the Causal Thesis, in view of the explanatory power in metaphysics of the concept of knowledge.

8.1 Functionalism and the Faculty Theory

What do the psychological terms mean? It seems likely that 'belief', 'desire', 'experience' and 'action' cannot be separately defined. For example, it would be hard to say what a belief is, without mentioning desire or experience; and similarly for the other psychological terms. If none of them can be defined independently of the others, then they need to be defined by a simultaneous definition if they are to be defined at all.

A simultaneous definition needs a term-introducing theory. Believers in 'Folk Psychology' say there really is a psychological theory, which we all know at least tacitly, which 'implicitly defines' the psychological terms. They suppose it to be a set of tacit beliefs about psychological states; the beliefs are human universals that all of us share, and which may even be innate. They comprise a theory which could have served as a term-introducing theory for the psychological terms, and which can be taken to implicitly define them. So if the psychological terms are to have referents, Folk Psychology needs to be the truth about human psychology.

Functionalists say functionalism, which is a development of behaviourism, is the truth about human psychology. Behaviourism is the formerly popular theory that attempts to define the psychological states of belief, experience and desire as dispositions to behaviour. It says all mental properties are to be understood dispositionally; for example, vanity is the disposition to boast if praised. But what is a disposition? We cannot define dispositions by counterfactuals. It is not correct to say that one is vain if and only if, if one were praised, one would boast; for there are many ordinary circumstances in which even a vain person would not boast if praised. Thus it looks as if vanity cannot be analysed by a simple counterfactual; some mention is needed of the internal state that makes the counterfactual true. At a given moment a person instantiates very many mental states: it is the complex interaction of all of them that causes the person's resultant actual behaviour. Thus behaviourism is an unstable position, and will naturally tend to develop in a direction that lays emphasis less on actual and counterfactual behaviour, and more on the internal states that ground it.

Such a development is functionalism. Functionalism can allow for the causal interactions between internal states; for example, a vain person is in an internal state that disposes them to boast if praised; but perhaps they will not boast if praised, if at the time they are in pain. Thus functionalism explains behaviour by the complex interactions of many mental states: and it defines each mental state by its causal powers and its causal interactions with other mental states. But it retains the fundamental behaviourist assumption that the psychological terms can be introduced from an old language which does not mention knowledge, or anything else mental, and which could in principle be the language of physics. That is exactly how our solipsist of Chapter 6 thought of mental events, when he was still a solipsist, before he hit on the idea that functional states need also to be connected with the conscious states expressed in the private Lichtenbergian language.

The Language of Thought

A sketch of functionalism might go somewhat as follows. For simplicity let us restrict attention to the principal psychological states, i.e., *experience, belief, desire* and *action*. Experiences are caused by states of the sense organs, and these in turn cause beliefs; beliefs and desires cooperate in causing basic actions, which functionalism can take to be body movements. (A more refined version could allow also for certain species of purely mental actions, e.g. voluntary imaginings, considerings.) Suppose we knew the whole truth about these causal patterns, and wrote down what we knew in a theory. What shape could we expect such a theory to take?

We are thinking of experiences, beliefs and desires as psychological states which collectively cause basic actions, i.e., voluntary body movements. Now there are a range of experiential states a person might be in, a range of beliefs and desires they might have, and a range of basic actions they might undertake. The range of experiential states form a determinable, each determinate of which is a particular experiential state. Similarly, the range of belief states form another determinable, and so on. Unlike some other determinables, the determinates of the functional determinables are not contraries, for a mental subject may simultaneously instantiate many different experiential, belief and desire states.

Whenever we have a determinable, there is need for an appropriate notation to label the determinates. If there are infinitely many determinates, as for example in the case of the lengths, we do not name them but *index* them by numbers, e.g., the length 1.51 metres. Experiences, beliefs and desires also are infinite in number, but we do not say that S is 'in belief state 51', or in 'desire state 108'. Instead we say that S 'believes that snow is white', or 'desires that the cup is full'. The reason we use sentences instead of numbers to index the mental states is just convenience of the subsequent theory—the sentential indexing allows a more surveyable formulation of the psychological laws that are to follow. However, at this stage it is only the syntactic properties of sentences that are being exploited in the labelling, for a Gödel numbering could in principle do the job just as well; the semantic meanings, if any, of the sentences are ignored for the time being. Thus we can index the experience, belief and desire determinables by the sentences of any reasonable uninterpreted language L, provided it is sufficiently rich; we can regard the indexing language L as the 'Language of Thought'.

We can use sets of sentences of L to specify a person's total psychological state. To say what a person is currently experiencing, we give a set E of sentences of L, such that for each of these sentences, the person instantiates the determinate of the *experience* determinable indexed by that sentence. Similarly, to specify what the person is believing, we give a set of sentences B, each of which indexes a determinate of the *belief* determinable instantiated by the person; the person's desires are specified by a third set of sentences D, and their actions by a fourth set A.[1] We can thus specify a person's *narrow psychological state* at any time t as the quadruple:

$$\nu_t = \langle E, B, D, A \rangle$$

where E, B, D and A are respectively the sets of sentences of L that specify the person's experience, belief, desire and action states at t.

The job of functionalism is to tell how a person's psychological state will evolve over time. Thus functionalism needs to specify the function Ψ such that if C_t is the person's context at time t, then the following Functional Equation holds:

Functional Equation: $\nu_{(t+\delta t)} = \Psi(\nu_t, C_t)$

The functionalist needs to claim that Ψ is some not too complicated function that can actually be humanly known, at least tacitly and approximately. Perhaps Ψ is given by some reasonably simple general laws; or in a Bayesian version of functionalism, it will perhaps be given to a fair approximation by some version of decision theory.

The Functional Equation is 'narrow', in the sense that it makes little or no reference to what is going on outside the boundaries of the subject's body. We do not need to know very much about the subject's context, in order to know how the subject's state of experience will be changing from one moment to the next, and how the subject's body will be moving. It is not necessary to know the 'distal' causes of the subject's experiences; 'proximal' facts about stimulation of the subject's 'sensory surfaces' are sufficient. Similarly, we do not need to predict what the distal consequences of the subject's actions will be; it is enough to predict how the subject's body will move. Thus the narrow Functional Equation does not say, e.g., that *seeing a tiger* caused the subject *to run away*; it says only that light falling on the subject's eye caused a certain experiential state, indexed by a certain uninterpreted sentence, and that there ensued a certain basic action, namely a body movement, indexed by another uninterpreted sentence. Thus the Functional Equation deals with behaviour only in the narrow sense.

---

[1] In a Bayesian version of functionalism, we might want to assign to each belief a degree of belief, and to each desire a strength or valuation. In that case a Bayesian functionalism would replace the set of sentences B with a credence function C which gives for each sentence of the language of thought a number d which gives the degree to which the person believes the sentence; similarly we replace the set D with a function V which gives for each sentence a number ν which gives the value the person places on that sentence.

Functionalism defines the psychological states by their causal role; such a definition in and of itself leaves it an entirely open question which properties the psychological states are. But it opens the way to an identification of psychological states with physical properties of the agent. Since psychological states are defined functionally by their causal role in moving the body, it follows that a psychological state is realised by whatever underlying physical state actually has the causal role. For example, pain is functionally defined by its characteristic causal role. Suppose it turns out empirically that in humans having one's C-fibres firing has exactly this causal role. Then functionalists conclude that the functional state of pain in humans must be identical with the physical state of having one's C-fibres firing, and they say that C-fibre firing realises pain in humans.

Interpretation

Having a mind normally implies having a certain pattern of narrow behaviour that in the right context allows one to cope effectively with one's environment. Therefore it implies that one's psychological states are keyed to the environment in such a way that a change in the environment produces (by perception) a change in the states, which in turn produces a change in the environment (by action) that makes sense in the light of one's beliefs and desires. That is what justifies us in saying that the agent has a mind, that the agent's experiential states represent the environment, and that the agent's behaviour is rational.

The Functional Equation given earlier is 'narrow', dealing only with the agent and what goes in within the boundaries of the agent's body. Interpretation is the project of making sense of the agent within the broader context. To interpret an agent is to say how they perceive the world to be, how they believe it to be, and how they desire it to be. The narrow Functional Equation allows one to speak of narrow 'experiential states', 'belief states' and 'desire states', using uninterpreted sentences of the LoT to index the psychological states. But interpretation requires one to speak of experiences, beliefs and desires proper, indexed by interpreted sentences that give their semantic content. Thus one must make a sharp distinction between the 'narrow' belief-state indexed by 'snow is white' and the 'broad' belief proper *that snow is white.*

To attribute a belief-state to a subject is to characterise the subject internally, i.e., in a way that does not look outside the boundaries of the subject's body. In contrast, to attribute a belief to a subject is to characterise the subject externally or relationally. For example, the belief concerning snow that it is white entails a relation between the believer and snow. On Twin Earth, where they have only twin snow, no one can believe that snow is white. The Twin Earthers are intrinsic or qualitative duplicates of ourselves, so they like us are in the narrow belief-state indexed by the LoT sentence 'snow is white'; but they are not our relational duplicates, for we stand in a certain relation to snow, whereas they stand in that relation not to snow but to twin snow. Because they are not our relational duplicates, they lack the belief concerning snow that it is white.

What is the relation between the narrow belief-state and the belief proper? If attribution of a narrow belief-state describes the subject only internally, whereas attribution of a belief describes the subject extrinsically or relationally, we might suppose that the narrow belief-state and the belief proper are two different things. But in fact we can take the belief to be just the belief-state under a relational description. Our system of indexing beliefs by sentential 'that'-clauses re-employs the interpreted sentences in a psychological role to generate relational definite descriptions of narrow belief-states.

The functionalist account as we have given it so far therefore requires supplementation to tell us how broad beliefs are attributed in a context. In Chapter 3 I gave a theory of interpretation, i.e., of reference, in terms of knowledge. That account began with the thought that quite often we gain knowledge in virtue of our belief-states and our experiential states. If one apprehends the fact that A in virtue of being in the narrow belief-state indexed by s, that suggests that the correct interpretation of s can only be *that-A*. Similarly, if one learns that A in virtue of being in the narrow experiential state s, that suggests that *that-A* must be the correct interpretation of state s. Of course we have many beliefs which do not give us knowledge of a fact—false beliefs, for example. But we can assign content to these beliefs also by their structural and compositional connections with other beliefs that do give us knowledge.

Is it possible to analyse interpretation in a different way, without appeal to the concept of knowledge? One strategy is to appeal to counterfactual covariation: we assign the content *that-A* to the belief-state s only if s covaries with A, i.e., if the belief-state s exists only if the fact that A exists. In view of the prevalence of erroneous beliefs, a more plausible version of this restricts the extent of the required covariation, for example by saying that s must at least covary with A in 'ideal circumstances'. An alternative strategy is to appeal to information theory. The state of affairs B carries the information that A if $P(A|B) = 1$, so we can say that a necessary condition of the belief-state s indicating that A is that it carries the information that A, i.e., that $P(A|s) = 1$. Again this is only plausible if we say that $P(A|s) = 1$ 'in ideal circumstances'. The difficulty then is to say what constitute 'ideal circumstances'. If the arguments I gave in Chapter 3 are correct, then an interpretation cannot in fact be determined without appeal to the concept of knowledge.

To summarise then, functionalism will claim that a physical state σ of a system is a belief that A provided two conditions are satisfied:

(1) A *narrow psychological* condition: there must be families E, B, D and A of states of the system which, when indexed by the sentences of the LoT, together satisfy the Functional Equation; and for some sentence s of the LoT, the state σ must realise the belief-state indexed by the sentence s in this indexing.

(2) An *interpretational* condition: the family of belief-states of the system must all indicate facts, and in particular the belief-state s must indicate the fact that A.

The Faculty Theory

The Faculty Theory can be very similar to functionalism, except that instead of explaining knowledge as a kind of belief, it explains belief in terms of knowledge. It can retain what functionalism has to say about the functional role of belief; in particular, it retains what it has to say about the way beliefs guide action, and the way in which beliefs are updated in the light of experience. But although the faculty theory says that having the correct functional role is a necessary condition for a state to be a belief, it denies it is a sufficient condition. It says that states with the functional role of belief really are beliefs only if some of them at least cause knowledge.

Functionalism defines the psychological terms *via* the psychological 'platitudes', in an 'old language' that contains only behavioural and causal terms. In contrast, the faculty theory says that the 'old language' must already express our subjective conscious states and have a term for knowledge. Moreover, the faculty theory draws a sharp distinction between psychological terms and mental terms. It says that for all we know there are minds that do not share our psychology. Something has a mind if it has knowledge, but perhaps not every knower is a believer, and perhaps not every knower is a perceiver. For example, we can conceive of an omniscient knower; but such a knower would have no use for beliefs; for a belief is a disposition to judge, but an omniscient knower never needs to make any judgements, since it already knows everything. Similarly an omniscient knower has no use for perception—why look to see how things are, when you already know? Thus having a mind (possessing knowledge) is conceptually distinct from having a psychology, and there can perhaps be mental terms that are not psychological terms.

8.2 Type Identity Versions of the Constitutive Thesis

In this section I discuss the Type Identity version of the Constitutive Thesis, according to which knowing is a kind of believing. I think we may set aside here the view that knowledge is a nominal kind of belief, i.e., that the knowings are a definable subclass of the believings. On this view, the logical relation between the concepts of knowledge and belief would be like the relation between the concepts *bachelor* and *person*. The bachelors do not form a distinct natural kind of persons, for a bachelor is simply an ordinary person who happens to be male and unmarried; similarly, the knowings would not form a distinct natural kind of believing but be simply ordinary believings that happen to be (e.g.) true and justified. But no one has been able to discover the supposed definition of 'knowledge', or at any rate to find a definition that has won general acceptance. If knowledge is a nominal kind of belief, then its definition ought to be known, or at least discoverable. The fact that it has not been found despite a thorough search strongly suggests that knowledge is not a precisely definable kind of belief.

But knowledge could still be a kind of belief, even if not a precisely definable kind, if it were a vague kind. Or if by 'kind' we mean a natural kind, then knowledge can be a kind of believing that is defined by giving examples, which is the disjunctivist position. In this section I consider these two further possibilities.

Is Knowledge a Vague Kind of Belief?

Vague terms do not have exact definitions, but that does not prevent them from naming kinds. For example, 'thin' is a vague term, but that does not prevent it picking out a kind of person, namely the thin kind. So even if 'knowledge' has no exact definition, it might still be a kind of belief.

Is 'knowledge' vague? For example, suppose N is a borderline case of 'thin'. Suppose S knows all the relevant precise facts about N's height and weight: does S know that N is thin? Perhaps we have here a borderline case of knowledge that N is thin. But we need not blame the vagueness of 'S knows N is thin' on any vagueness in 'knows'. We have the alternative of saying the complex sentence is vague because of the vague atomic sentence embedded within it. To show that the term 'knowledge' is vague, we would need to find borderline cases of knowledge of something that is not itself a borderline case. It might be suggested that a borderline case of belief is a borderline case of knowledge. But it seems plainly false that borderline belief yields only borderline knowledge: some higher animals definitely have knowledge, since they are definitely conscious, but their psychological states are at best a borderline case of belief. Thus the vagueness of belief does not entail the vagueness of knowledge.

Do variations in the quantity and quality of evidence give rise to borderline cases of knowledge? Sometimes our evidence is clearly sufficient for knowledge, sometimes it is clearly insufficient, and sometimes we do not know whether the evidence is sufficient or not. An example is the following. Suppose S last saw N some time ago, when N looked in excellent health, and that S has had no subsequent information about N. If N is now alive, does S know N is now alive? We might try to argue that we have a clear case of knowledge if it is 20 seconds since S last saw N, a clear case of ignorance if it is 20 years; and that there are intermediate borderline cases of knowledge at say 20 weeks, or perhaps 20 months. Certainly we can construct here a series from knowledge to ignorance indexed by the time dimension. But it remains to be shown that this is a sorites series. For intermediate times, it is true that we do not know whether to say that S knows. But that does not prove that these are borderline cases: perhaps in the intermediate cases we simply do not have enough information to make an informed judgement. Whether S's inductive belief is knowledge that N is alive depends on whether there are any defeaters. If N has been exposed to serious danger in the meantime, then even if N chances still to be alive, S does not know that N is alive, for the danger is a defeater of S's evidence that N is alive. The longer the elapsed time, the more likely it is that there is such a defeater, and hence the more likely it is that S's belief is not knowledge. Thus this is not a sorites series, but merely a series in which the probability that knowledge is present starts at a high value and sinks to a low value.

For a genuine sorites series, we need to be able to arrange cases in order along some dimension, starting from clear cases, ending with clear non-cases, and with borderline cases in between. We can do this for *heaps* along a dimension of a decreasing number of grains of sand, and for *baldness* along a dimension of an increasing number of hairs. Is there a sorites series from knowledge to ignorance, along a dimension of decreasing probability on one's evidence?

To answer this, we must ask how probable A has to be, before we have a clear case of knowledge that A. As I argued in section 1.6, if we wish to avoid scepticism about knowledge of the future, we must allow that one can know something that is less than 100% certain on one's evidence. We live in a chancy world, so for each of one's beliefs about the contingent future, there is some chance that it is false. Hence on the assumption that one has any knowledge at all about the contingent future, there must be some things that one knows will happen that nevertheless have some present chance of not happening. For example, I am to meet Mark at noon tomorrow. Since Mark is an extremely punctual person, I know he will arrive at noon; which he duly does, as I knew he would. Still, there was some chance that something could have gone wrong. His journey here could have suffered an unexpected chance delay, and then he would have been late. The probability on my evidence that he will arrive at noon ought not to exceed my estimate of the objective chance that he will arrive at noon. My estimate of the objective chance is less than 100%, so the probability on my evidence should be less than 100%. And not just infinitesimally less either; no doubt the objective chance of his being here on time did not exceed 99%, so my confidence should not exceed 99% either. Nevertheless, I knew he would be here; to deny that we have such knowledge is to concede scepticism about the future.

This seems to show that one can know a future contingent, even though there is only a 99% chance that one's belief is true. But the Lottery Paradox shows one can lack knowledge even if there is a more than 99% chance that one's belief is true. It is 99% probable on my evidence that Mark will arrive at noon, whereas it is 99.9% probable on my evidence that your ticket will not win the lottery. Nevertheless, I know Mark will arrive on time, but I do not know your ticket will not win the lottery. Therefore there is no sorites series from knowledge to ignorance along the dimension of probability of truth on one's evidence.

To say that there is a 1% chance today that I don't know that A is to say that I don't know today that A at 1% of the worlds with the same past and laws as the actual world. That is perfectly consistent with my knowing at the actual world. But it may be objected that chancy knowledge conflicts with a central intuition about knowledge, namely that one's knowledgeable belief cannot be true by mere chance. But we must distinguish between a belief that has a chance of not being true, and a belief that is true by chance. For example, I know today that Mark will be here punctually at noon tomorrow; my belief that he will be here at noon, and his being here at noon, have a common cause, namely his habitual punctuality, so the belief is not true by mere chance, even though there is a chance it is not true. Contrast this with the case where I believe that ticket 1234 will not win the lottery, and it does not win. My belief is true, but that is just an (extremely likely) coincidence. There is no common cause of my belief and the outcome of the lottery, so my belief is true by mere chance, and I did not know the ticket would not win.

It might alternatively be objected that if knowledge is a relation to a fact, and there is a chance that the fact won't come into existence, then one cannot know the fact now, as it cannot have come into existence yet. There is the case of tomorrow's sea-fight, where Aristotle and others have argued that at present it is neither true nor false that there will be a sea-fight tomorrow. If they are right, there is not at the present time any fact about tomorrow's sea-fight for anyone to know today. But Aristotle's suggestion is in conflict with the Principle of Bivalence, to which there can be no counterexamples, since one contradicts oneself if one says of any given proposition that it is neither true nor false. For example, suppose one says it is neither true nor false today that there will be a sea-fight tomorrow. Then since it is not true, it follows by the Disquotation Schema that it is not the case that there will be a sea-fight tomorrow. Since it is not false, then again by the Disquotation Schema, it is not the case that it is not the case that there will be a sea-fight tomorrow. But $(\neg A) \wedge \neg(\neg A)$ is a contradiction in any logic. Therefore either it is true today that there will be a sea-fight tomorrow, or it is false. So there is nothing to prevent one knowing a future contingent today, even though today there is still some chance it will not happen. If it will happen, it is true today that it will happen, so the fact exists today and is available today for one to know.

On pain of scepticism, we must allow that we know future contingents that have a finite chance of being false. Therefore there is no sorites series from ignorance to knowledge along a dimension of increasing probability on one's evidence: because for each future contingent one knows, there is a Lottery Paradox proposition which is more likely on one's evidence, but which one does not know.

Contextualism

A different argument for the vagueness of knowledge is contextualism, according to which standards for counting a belief as knowledge vary with the conversational context. (DeRose 1995; Lewis 1996.) I cannot do justice to the very extensive literature on contextualism here, but I shall mention four arguments for contextualism that I find unconvincing.

The first argument is that we are conversationally permitted to say we know when we can exclude all contextually relevant alternatives; there may be other possibilities that our evidence does not exclude, but we still rightly say we know, if we can exclude all the possibilities relevant to the conversation. This is perfectly true, but it does nothing to show that knowledge is vague. For in any conversation there is what Stalnaker (1999) calls the 'context set', i.e., the set of worlds which are consistent with what everyone in the conversation takes everyone in the conversation to be assuming to be the case. Suppose that at a particular stage in a conversation the context set is expressed by a proposition B. Then in this context one is counted as having 'ruled out' every relevant alternative to A, if one knows not that A, but only that $B \rightarrow A$. The contextual variability of the relevant alternatives therefore does nothing to show that knowledge itself is vague. Of course there may be some vagueness about which proposition B accurately gives the context set at any particular stage of the conversation, but that is a separate matter and has nothing to do with vagueness in knowledge.

The second argument for contextualism is that conversational standards of evidence can be made more and more demanding without limit. It is claimed that for any contingent fact, conversational standards can be made so demanding that, by those standards, one does not know that fact. This is supposed to show that there is no absolute standard of knowledge. But to concede this is to concede scepticism. On pain of scepticism, we must insist that we know many things, by any conversational standard, no matter how demanding.

The third argument for contextualism is that whether or not in a context we can be said to know depends on how important the outcome is in the context. If the outcome is vitally important, for example because someone's life depends on it, then you had better not say that A unless you are perfectly certain that A. But if the outcome is vitally important, what matters is not so much whether you know, as whether there is any chance of your not knowing; you should not say you know that A, unless there is a vanishing chance of your being wrong. Thus although I know Mark will arrive at noon tomorrow, I would not bet someone's life on it, for I am less than perfectly certain that he will come. In such conversational circumstances perhaps I ought not to say that I know that he will come. Nevertheless, that does not show I do not know he will come.

A fourth argument for contextualism concerns challenges to one's knowledge. I know where my bicycle is; it is in the cycle rack outside the philosophy department. Suppose a friend asks if I know it hasn't been stolen by a thief who is even now riding it away. I will now admit that I don't know that my bicycle is in the cycle rack. However, this is not because the question causes a new conversational standard to be set where the evidence I previously had is no longer good enough. It is because my friend's question is a defeater of my evidence. If someone asks me outside the philosophy room how I know my bicycle is in the cycle rack, I assume they have some constructive purpose in asking. Perhaps they know of a recent spate of bicycle thefts! The fact that they ask the question therefore acts as a defeater of my previous evidence that the bicycle is in the cycle rack, and destroys my knowledge. It is not that the question creates a context requiring stronger evidence: even by the standards previously in force, I now no longer know; for the question has defeated my evidence. That this is the correct explanation is proved by the fact that things are quite different if it is the sceptic who asks me the same question, rather than my practically-minded friend. The sceptic's question has no power to defeat my evidence, for now that I am familiar with the ways of sceptics I no longer take their questions seriously. A merely sceptical doubt expressed by a known sceptic is not a defeater, and does not undercut my evidence; to the sceptic's question I rightly reply that I know that the bicycle is in the cycle rack, because I remember putting it there.

I conclude that we have no positive reason to assert that knowledge is vague. Do we have positive reason to deny it? It seems to me that the phenomenon of consciousness is such a reason. Consciousness is a kind of knowledge, for a conscious state is a state which its subject is aware of. But consciousness does not seem to admit borderline cases, and it seems implausible that we can find a sorites series from the clearly conscious to the clearly not conscious. It is of course possible to construct a series of conscious sensations ranging from the very intense to the almost imperceptible. But consciousness of a slight sensation is not slight consciousness of a sensation; with consciousness, as Chapter 6 suggests, it is a case of all or nothing; the light of (present) consciousness is either on, or it is off; we cannot make imaginative sense of a borderline case of consciousness. This gives us reason to reject the suggestion that knowledge is a vague kind of belief.

Disjunctivism

Another way for knowledge to be a kind of belief, without being a definable kind, is by being a natural kind of belief. That is the thesis of disjunctivism. Just as the substance jade comes in two natural kinds, namely nephrite and jadeite, so belief comes in two natural kinds, according to disjunctivism, namely knowledge and opinion (McDowell 1982).

Williamson notes that disjunctivism does not define 'opinion'; the best disjunctivism can do is tell us that opinion is belief that is not knowledge (2000: 44–7). However, the disjunctivist view of belief can dispense with the need for a conceptual analysis of opinion—no analysis is needed, when natural kinds are in play. We do not need to be able to give necessary and sufficient conditions for being nephrite or jadeite, for it is sufficient to think of them under a demonstrative mode of presentation—jadeite is *this* kind of jade, nephrite *that* kind. In the same way, the disjunctivist can suggest, knowledge is this kind of belief, opinion that kind.

But the claim that opinion is a natural kind immediately leads to a fresh objection. Although disjunctivism agrees with the tripartite conception and its variants that knowledge is a kind of belief, it radically disagrees with the idea that knowledge is just an ordinary belief with something extra added. According to disjunctivism, there is no 'highest common factor' between opinion that falls short of knowledge, and knowledge itself; there is nothing one can add to mere opinion to turn it into knowledge, no circumstances in which what is in fact opinion could have been knowledge. So it is no more possible that *this* belief, which is in fact opinion, could have been knowledge, than it is possible that this piece of jade, which in fact is nephrite, could have been jadeite. Suppose I believed that Mark will arrive at noon, but that by chance he is delayed, and does not arrive at noon. Then my mental state not only was not knowledge, but could not have been, according to disjunctivism. That is not to say that things could not have turned out otherwise, so that I would have known that Mark would arrive at noon; but in that case my actual mental state of opinion would not have existed; it would have been replaced by the different mental state of knowledge, with which it shares no common factor.

But if knowledge and opinion never co-occur, disjunctivism will have a problem in explaining the office or proper function of opinion. Why do we have opinion at all, if it is so distinct from knowledge? The non-disjunctivist can say that the proper function of opinion is the getting of knowledge—sometimes our opinion is mere opinion, of course, but at other times it is in virtue of opinions we hold that we attain knowledge. But this simple solution is not available to the disjunctivist: if knowledge and opinion are mutually exclusive, then the proper function of opinion cannot be the getting of knowledge, so we are left with no account of the proper function of opinion in the economy of the mind.

It might be suggested that opinion has no proper function, but is merely an unavoidable by-product of the mind's mechanisms for getting knowledge.[2] The idea would be that sub-doxastic states operate in us, whose function is to cause knowledge; without them knowledge would be impossible. But the states do not always succeed in causing knowledge, if circumstances are unfavourable. When they fail to cause knowledge, they

---

[2] I owe this suggestion to Mark Textor.

cause opinion instead, by a kind of misfire; that is why we have opinion, as well as knowledge.

What are these sub-doxastic states that are the cause of both knowledge and opinion? A natural suggestion is that they are the narrow belief-states of the functionalist. The functionalist says that knowledge just is the narrow state under a relational description, but the disjunctivist will say that the narrow state is only the cause of the knowledge; where there is error the narrow state does not cause knowledge but instead causes opinion. But now it is unclear what theoretical work is done by positing the opinion, in addition to the narrow belief-state. The functionalist says the narrow belief-state in context is a belief; in virtue of the belief, the subject may or may not have knowledge, depending on the context. It seems that here we already have everything that theory needs, whether or not an opinion is present as well. Therefore it seems theoretically simpler either to dispense with the opinion altogether, or else to identify it with the belief, i.e., the belief-state. If we take the latter option, the opinion will after all be present even in the case when we do have knowledge; for since we know in virtue of the belief-state, we know in virtue of the opinion with which the belief-state is identical. Thus it seems theoretically simpler to reject the disjunctivist view that knowledge and opinion are mutually exclusive, and hence to reject the view that knowledge is a natural kind of belief. I conclude that there is no very persuasive version of the thesis that knowledge is a type of belief.

8.3 The Argument for the Constitutive Thesis from Functionalism

The Constitutive Thesis is not committed to Type Identity. Token Identity will do; it is enough if each instance of knowing is identical with an instance of believing. A Token Identity version of the Constitutive Thesis would be similar in form to Token Identity theories of the relation between the mental and the physical, which claim that every instance of a mental state is identical with some instance of a physical state, though they do not claim that the property of a mental subject of being in the mental state is identical to any physical property.

In this section I examine a Completeness Argument for the Token Identity version of the Constitutive Thesis. The first premiss of the Completeness

Argument is that our actions are often caused by our knowledge, so that knowledge is causally efficacious and not an epiphenomenon. The second premiss is the explanatory completeness of functionalism, i.e., the claim that the functionally defined mental states constitute a maximally complete psychological explanation of behaviour. To say that the functional explanation is maximally complete is not to say that it fits the behaviour perfectly; no doubt there will be small idiosyncrasies in any individual's behaviour, so that it may fail to conform perfectly to the functionalist laws. What is claimed, however, is that no other theory does any better in this respect: a functional explanation of an episode of behaviour is the most complete psychological explanation possible, for what has a psychological explanation at all has a functional explanation.

The Completeness Argument now proceeds as follows. By the first premiss, knowledge sometimes causes behaviour. By the second premiss, every mental cause of behaviour is some functionally defined state. The conclusion of the argument is that therefore each causally efficacious instance of knowledge must be identical with some instance of a functionally defined state. For example, my knowledge that it will rain causes me to take my umbrella. But the functionalist explanation of my taking it is that I believe it will rain. The Completeness Argument therefore invites us to identify the fact that I know it will rain with the causally efficacious fact of my believing that it will rain. A similar argument applies to experience. For example, it is my perceptual knowledge that it is raining that causes me to open the umbrella. The functionalist explanation of my opening it is that I have a perceptual experience as of its raining. The Completeness Argument invites us to identify the perceptual knowledge with the causally efficacious perceptual experience. The invited conclusion is that every causally efficacious instance of knowledge is either an instance of belief, or an instance of perceptual experience.

Physical and Mental

One way to avoid the conclusion of the Completeness Argument would be to deny its premiss that knowledge is causally efficacious. Following the epiphenomenalists, we could say that knowledge is distinct from belief but causally inert. Epiphenomenalism has had a bad press; indeed, most philosophers treat a proof that a theory entails it as a refutation of the theory. However, it seems far from certain that epiphenomenalism deserves to be regarded in quite so unfavourable a light, for it turns out that many of the common sense things we desire to say about our mental lives can still be said, with some re-parsing, even if epiphenomenalism is true. Still, it is clear that epiphenomenalism is not without its difficulties, and we would prefer to avoid it, if we can.

So it remains to deny the second premiss, that it is beliefs that cause actions in cooperation with desires. A difficulty with seeing knowledge as the cause of action is that it seems one might behave in just the same way if one lacked knowledge and had a true but unjustified belief—or even a false belief. The conclusion would be that it is not knowing that A that causes the action, but merely believing that A.

We can rescue a causal role for knowledge if with the disjunctivist we say that to believe that A is either to know that A, or to have the opinion that A, and that these are mutually exclusive states. For if knowledge causes action, this is not because the knowledge is a belief, which would have caused the action even if the belief had not been knowledge. Admittedly if the belief had not been knowledge then an opinion to the same effect would have been present, and the opinion would have caused the same action that the knowledge caused. But because the knowledge was in fact present, the opinion was absent, and could not actually have caused the action. Thus knowledge is vindicated as the cause of the action, as the only candidate that remains.

Although disjunctivism avoids opinion making knowledge redundant as a cause, it has worse problems of its own. For the disjunctivist has to recognise that knowledge has causes, and that some of these, such as states of the visual system, are very plausibly the narrow states of the functionalist; in a favourable context, a narrow state causes knowledge; in an unfavourable context, it causes only opinion. But now the narrow state threatens to preempt both knowledge and opinion as the cause of the behaviour. And it can be argued that the narrow state is indeed a more plausible candidate than is opinion for this causal role. Whether the person had possessed knowledge or opinion, their 'narrow' behaviour would have been exactly the same. Knowledge and opinion are supposedly very different states, so it seems odd that they should have indiscriminable physical effects. Of course we are used to the claim that they are different yet subjectively indiscriminable, but it stretches credulity to be told that they are also causally indiscriminable so far as narrow behaviour is concerned. It seems more plausible to suppose that if it makes no difference to narrow behaviour whether it is knowledge or opinion that is present, then the cause is not the knowledge, and not the opinion either, but their common cause, viz., the underlying narrow functional states. Thus disjunctivism seems to push us towards regarding the narrow states as the true cause of the body movement. Disjunctivism is in danger of treating both knowledge and opinion as causally inefficacious epiphenomena, so it does not offer an attractive avenue of escape from the Completeness Argument.

The Principle of Acquaintance

According to functionalism, beliefs are defined by their causal role in causing action in cooperation with desires. Thus it can be claimed that beliefs are already fulfilling the role of action-causers, preempting knowledge in that role. But knowledge could still cause action, even if it is not identical with the belief that is the immediate cause of the action. For it may happen that knowledge is the cause of the belief that is the cause of the action, so that, by transitivity of causation, it is a cause of the action, and so is not causally inert.

Here the distinction between narrow functional state and broad psycho-logical state is important. Suppose you intentionally go up to Bismarck and speak with him. What casually explains your action? If by 'your action' is meant the fact that you addressed the man in front of you, then your action is the narrow body-movement, and its causes are narrow functional states. But if the fact to be explained is that it was Bismarck you spoke to, then although the narrow belief state causally explains the body movement, it does not explain why it was specifically Bismarck, and not any other person, that you intentionally addressed. To find the cause of that, we need to go beyond the narrow belief-state to its interpretation, and so to the belief proper that you hold—for example, your belief that this man is Bismarck. Now if some knowledge you have is part of the total cause of your having the belief proper about Bismarck, then that knowledge is not causally inert after all.

Your belief about Bismarck is an example of a singular belief. In a singular belief about an object, the object itself is a constituent of the Russellian proposition believed, so singular beliefs are broad by definition. According to Russell's Principle of Acquaintance, which I argued for in Chapter 3, one cannot have a singular belief about an object unless one is acquainted with the object. To be acquainted with an object is to have some knowledge about it. So if the singular belief causes an action, and the acquaintance is a causally necessary condition of the singular belief, then the knowledge is a causally necessary condition of the action, and hence is a cause of it. Thus someone who subscribes to the Principle of Acquaintance is not forced to accept the Completeness Argument from functionalism.

8.4 A Completeness Argument from Physics

The Completeness Argument from functionalism said that beliefs are the psychological cause of actions, which leaves nothing for knowledge to do, in the way of causing narrow behaviour, unless knowledge is belief. Our reply was that knowledge can still have a causal role, by causing the singular beliefs that cause our 'broad' actions. But there is a further challenge to the causal efficacy of knowledge, that steps outside of psychology altogether. For another version of the Completeness Argument can be given, appealing this time to the completeness of physics.

The laws of physics are complete; this is a statement for which at present we have strong inductive evidence, and which we expect to continue to confirm as we discover more about the laws. Therefore a complete explanation of body movements can be given in the language of physics; it is physical states that explain body movements; so we are invited to conclude that either knowledge is a physical state, or it does not move the body. The Constitutive Thesis can allow knowledge to be causally efficacious by identifying knowledge with belief in a context: assuming functionalism, it can then in turn identify the belief with a physical state, namely the brain state that moves the body. But the Causal Thesis denies that knowledge is a belief, so *a fortiori* it denies that knowledge is a brain state, and thereby it seems to deprive knowledge of its causal role. We are back with the problem that knowledge appears to be epiphenomenal. Its causal role has been preempted this time not by something psychological, the belief, but by something physical, namely the underlying physical state that realises the belief.

We can set out the Completeness Argument from physics as follows:

(1) Some instances of knowledge cause physical events.
(2) Every caused physical event has a complete physical cause.
(3) Therefore, some instances of knowledge are physical events.

This Completeness Argument for the Constitutive Thesis is just a special case of the well-known argument of Hopkins and Peacocke for the Identity Theory (Hopkins 1978: 223–4; Peacocke 1979: 134–5). This argument says that since mental events have physical effects, and since every caused physical event has a complete physical cause, it must follow that some mental events are physical events. The above Completeness Argument is the special case of this for the mental event of knowledge.

Distinguishing Causes and Laws

If the Causal Thesis is to be upheld despite the Completeness Argument, then it is necessary to deny one of the premisses. Since we shall not wish to deny premiss (1), that knowledge is non-redundantly causally efficacious, it will be necessary to deny premiss (2), which I shall call the premiss of Mechanism:

> *Mechanism*: Every caused physical event has a complete physical cause.

Have we any reason to believe the Mechanism premiss? The grounds usually given for believing it are the success of current physics, which it is said will soon give a complete description of the physical events of our world; or at any rate, as complete a description as it is possible to give. How complete the description is depends on whether the laws of physics are deterministic. If they are then we have the Deterministic Nomological Completeness of physics:

> *Deterministic Nomological Completeness*. If worlds w and w' have the same physical past and the same physical laws, then they have the same physical future.

Is our world a world of Deterministic Nomological Completeness? We do not know, but it may well not be, for if quantum mechanics is correct then ours is an objectively chancy world. In that case the past and the laws do not completely determine the future, and there exist alternative futures each with some chance of happening. But even if ours is a chancy world, there is an alternative completeness claim that can still be made, for it may be that the physical past and laws completely determine the chances of any future physical event. In that case we can endorse:

Indeterministic Nomological Completeness. If worlds w and w' have the same physical past and the same physical laws, then for any physical future F the chances of F at w and w' are the same.

The Indeterministic Nomological Completeness of physics supposes that the laws of physics include laws of chance; these laws together with the past determine the present chance of any physical event.

The nomological completeness of physics in either deterministic or indeterministic form seems to be quite plausible in light of present knowledge. But does the completeness of physics entail the Mechanism premiss, that every caused physical event has a complete physical cause? I shall argue that it does not, either in the deterministic case or in the indeterministic case. To show this I shall discuss interactionism, the version of dualism that holds that the mental and the physical are distinct, and that there is two-way causal interaction between them. Interactionism is inconsistent with Mechanism, because according to interactionism some physical events such as body movements are partially or completely caused by mental events, yet these mental events are not identical with any physical event. I shall argue that interactionism is consistent with both the deterministic and the indeterministic nomological completeness of physics; so since interactionism is inconsistent with Mechanism, it follows that completeness does not entail Mechanism. Thus whether or not interactionism is true, completeness is at least consistent with causation by mental facts that are not physical facts; in particular it leaves room for causation by knowledge, even if the fact of knowledge is not identical with any physical fact; so the Completeness Argument from physics for the Constitutive Thesis fails.

The Deterministic Case

Interactionism is the view that mental events are not identical with physical events, but that there is two-way causal interaction between the mental and the physical: physical events, for example brain states such as C-fibre firings, sometimes cause mental events, for example a headache; and mental events, for example a headache, sometimes cause physical events, for example swallowing an aspirin. Now it is often suggested that interactionism is inconsistent with the deterministic completeness of the laws of physics, for the following reason. Suppose that we live in a world of physical determinism, so that the physical past of the universe and the laws of physics completely determine the physical future. If I swallow an aspirin, that is a physical event, which by physical determinism was already predetermined by the laws of physics and the past. The mental event of my headache therefore seems in danger of being redundant as a cause of my swallowing the aspirin; to avoid this danger we must conclude that the headache is identical with some physical event, contrary to interactionism.

Let M be the event of my having a headache, let P_1 be the state of my brain that is, according to the interactionist, the immediate neural cause of my headache M, and let P_2 be my swallowing the aspirin. So the causal and nomological dependencies, according to the interactionist, can be diagrammed in Figure 8.1.

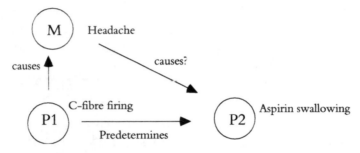

Figure 8.1. Psychophysical causation

The argument against interactionism can now be set out as follows.

(1) The occurrence of P_1 physically predetermined the occurrence of P_2.

(2) Therefore once P_1 had occurred, P_2 was going to occur anyway, whether or not M had occurred.

(3) Therefore if M had not occurred, P_2 would have happened anyway.

(4) Therefore M did not cause P_2.

Here the step from (3) to (4) might be questioned. It is quite often the case that A causes B, even though had A not happened, B would have happened anyway. For example, A might preempt some other potential cause C of B; had A not happened, C would have happened, and C would have caused B, so that B would have happened anyway. But the interactionist is not claiming that we have that sort of case here: the headache is not preempting some other potential cause of the aspirin-taking. We may therefore agree that the truth of the counterfactual (3) does indeed entail (4): if the aspirin-taking would have occurred anyway even if the headache had not occurred, then the headache did not cause the aspirin-taking.

Does (3) follow from (2)? It is conceded that the occurrence of P_1, together with the laws, entails the occurrence of P_2. Therefore if P_1 had occurred, and M had not occurred, P_2 would have occurred anyway. But this complex counterfactual does not entail the simple counterfactual (3) in which we are interested, namely that if M had not occurred, P_2 would have occurred anyway. For in the logic of counterfactuals, $(P_1 \wedge \neg M) \,\square\!\!\rightarrow P_2$ does not entail $\neg M \,\square\!\!\rightarrow P_2$. The interactionist can therefore claim that even if (2) is true, still (3) is not true: if M had not occurred, P_2 would not have occurred either. Thus the interactionist denies that (3) follows from (2). Instead the interactionist asserts the following counterfactual:

> *The Interactionist Counterfactual*: If I had not had a headache, I would not have taken the aspirin.

Can the Interactionist Counterfactual be true, even given (2)? As a first step in investigating this, we may note that the interactionist needs to assume that psychophysical causation is deterministic. This may not seem immediately obvious, since the Deterministic Nomological Completeness of physics is a premiss only about physical determinism. Since the interactionist denies that mental events are physical events, it might appear open to the interactionist either to assert or to deny psychophysical determinism. But in fact this appearance is illusory; under the supposition of physical determinism, interactionism is inconsistent with psychophysical indeterminism. For psychophysical indeterminism entails that although P_1 actually causes M, there was a chance that P_1 could occur without M. Therefore there is a world $w^\star$ with exactly the same laws as the actual world, where P_1 occurs but M chances not to occur. But since at the actual world the physical past and the laws of physics determine the physical future, then since the laws at $w^\star$ are the same, it follows that P_2 occurs at $w^\star$. Thus $w^\star$ is a closest world to the actual world where M does not occur, and P_2 happens anyway at $w^\star$. So the Interactionist Counterfactual 'If I had not had a headache, I would still have taken the aspirin' is false; therefore the headache is not the cause of the aspirin-taking, contrary to interactionism. So if the actual world is a world of physical determinism, then the interactionist must say it is also a world of psychophysical determinism. In that case if P_1 occurs and M occurs, there was no chance of M not occurring; thus there is no world $w^\star$ with the same past as the actual world up to the time of P_1, and with the same laws, at which M does not occur; so we are not yet obliged to reject the Interactionist Counterfactual as untrue.

Whether the Interactionist Counterfactual is true or not is determined by whether the aspirin-taking P_2 occurs at the closest world to actuality at which the headache M does not occur. Which world is that? Consider the following worlds, from all of which M is missing:

w_1: Shortly before the time t_1 when P_1 actually occurs, a physical 'divergence miracle' occurs, which prevents P_1 at w_1. In the absence of P_1, M does not occur, and P_2 does not occur either.

w_2 : P_1 occurs at t_1 but a psychophysical divergence miracle occurs, and P_1 fails to have its expected effect M. P_2 occurs anyway.

w_3 : P_1 occurs at t_1, but as at w_2, M does not occur. P_2 does not occur either.

To evaluate the Interactionist Counterfactual, we have to decide which of w_1, w_2 and w_3 is closest to the actual world. The methodology I shall adopt in evaluating their comparative closeness is that of Lewis (1986b: 73–7).

According to Lewis, in determining closeness for the purposes of evaluating counterfactuals, we do not insist that the closest world should have an absolutely perfect match with the actual past before t_1. We are willing to trade a small amount of 'backtracking', in order to ensure that events unfold in a continuous way. We count as the closest world one that has perfect match with almost all of the past, up to the commencement of a 'transition period', in which there is a tiny divergence from the actual laws and the actual past, after which things develop in a continuously lawful way to make the antecedent of the counterfactual true. For example, consider the counterfactual:

If the match had been struck at noon, it would have lit.

If the match was actually a foot from the matchbox all morning, we do not take the closest world where the antecedent is true to be one where you pick up the match exactly at noon and move it at warp speed to the striking surface of the matchbox. Rather, we judge the closest world to be one where a tiny difference in the neural firings in your brain causes you to pick up the match a few moments before noon, and then to strike it at normal human speed. A match moving at warp speed is a large violation of law; a tiny difference in neural firings is a small violation of law; we willingly trade off a small amount of backtracking to avoid the need for a big 'miracle'.

By considering such cases, Lewis concludes that in evaluating the relative closeness of two possible worlds, we must apply the following criteria, in descending order of priority:

(1) Do the worlds have the same laws, or at least very similar laws that differ at most by one 'small' miracle?
(2) Do the worlds perfectly match with respect to the past?
(3) Do the worlds have at least fairly similar laws, differing at most by some 'big' miracle?
(4) Do the worlds have exactly the same future?[3]

In our case of the headache and the aspirin-taking, we can apply Lewis's criteria to determine which of the three worlds w_1, w_2 and w_3 is closest to the actual world. At w_1 a tiny divergence miracle suppresses P_1, the normal neural precursor of the headache M and the aspirin-taking P_2; at w_2, P_1 and P_2 occur, but M does not occur; at w_3, P_1 occurs, but neither M nor P_2 occurs.

We find first that w_1 is closer to actuality than w_3, because w_3 involves two miracles: a psychophysical law is violated, since P_1 does not have its expected effect M; and a physical law is also violated, since P_1 does not have its expected effect P_2. So even though w_3 has a better match with the actual past than has w_1, still w_1 is closer to actuality than w_3, because the laws at w_1 differ less from the actual laws; by Lewis's criteria, similarity of law counts for more than exact similarity of the past.

w_1 is also closer to actuality than w_2. Because P_1 does occur at w_2, we do get a longer period of perfect match with the actual past than we do at w_1, where P_1 does not occur. But this is more than offset by the much larger miracle required at w_2. Both w_1 and w_2 diverge from the laws of the actual world. At w_1 some tiny physical miracle occurs: perhaps a solitary neurone fails to fire, so a cascade of neural effects follow that end in P_1 not occurring. That is a small violation of law. At w_2 the physical event P_1 fails to have its

---

[3] Thus in Lewis (1986b). The better known criteria in Lewis (1979) are a generalisation to allow for esoteric possibilities in the philosophy of time that are irrelevant here. In a world like ours, the (1979) criteria coincide with those given here.

expected mental effect, so M does not occur. But that is a large violation of law. The event P_1 is the total state of my brain, not just the firing of one particular neurone; the event M is the exact particular headache I had. At w_2 we are to suppose that the total state of my brain is exactly the same, yet I have not a minutely different headache, but no headache at all. That is a big miracle; it is worth trading off a little backtracking to avoid it. So w_1, where the headache is absent in virtue of a tiny physical miracle, is closer to actuality than w_2, where there is perfect match with slightly more of the past, but at the price of a major psychophysical divergence miracle.

Here I am assuming that psychophysical causation is 'inter-level' causation, which is simultaneous causation, not the 'same-level' causation of events that occur in succession. Same-level causation occurs when a physical event causes another physical event: the speed at which such a physical effect can propagate is limited by the velocity of light, as Relativity tells us. In contrast, inter-level causation occurs when an event at one level, say an event of physics, causes an event at another level, say a biological event. For example, at the level of physics there is the event of all the components of a virus particle being assembled in the correct way. At the level of biology, there is the coming into existence of that virus. The cause of there being a virus there is the assembling of the physical components; but there is no delay between the event of the arranging of the components and the event of the coming into being of the virus. The arranging of the physical components simultaneously causes the existence of the virus, by inter-level causation.

Inter-level causation is often called nomological supervenience. For example, at the actual world, the biological supervenes upon the physical; thus identically arranged sets of particles either both compose a virus, or neither do. But this is only nomological supervenience. It does not on its own entail that the biological properties of the virus are nothing over and above physical properties of the arrangement of its constituent particles; for if the laws of physics were slightly different, the viral mechanisms might not work properly, so the same physical arrangement of particles might not compose a living virus. Vitalists might be tempted to conclude that the biological does not metaphysically supervene on the physical, but that does not follow. For anti-vitalists will reply that the biological supervenes on physical properties and physical laws. They will assert:

Metaphysical Supervenience At any world with the same physical laws as the actual world, any duplicate of an actual virus is a virus.

If we assume Metaphysical Supervenience, then the existence of a virus at a world presupposes facts about what the physical laws are at that world. Now suppose we are evaluating a counterfactual about the life of a particular virus. For example, consider the counterfactual:

If the temperature had been lower, the virus would not have replicated.

Under determinism, if the laws and the past at a world are the same as at the actual world, the temperature will be the same too. So at the closest world *w* where most of the past is the same, yet where the temperature is lower, the laws must be different. Therefore the question arises whether this arrangement of physical particles would still compose a virus at world *w*. By Metaphysical Supervenience, the existence of the virus at a world is partly a fact about the laws at that world; since the laws at *w* are different from the actual laws, it may seem an open question whether we are to assume that the particles would still compose a virus. However, it is evident that in evaluating this counterfactual we would work on the assumption that there would still be a virus there at *w*, even if some small physical divergence miracle occurs and the laws are slightly different at *w*. So we appear to impose the requirement that the closest world is one where the laws of physics are not changed in such a way as to upset the biophysical laws connecting the physical and biological state of the virus. We may conclude that any breach of biophysical law counts as a 'big' miracle for the purpose of evaluating counterfactuals.

So suppose the interactionist holds that psychophysical causation is inter-level causation, and that the mental nomologically supervenes upon the physical. This is perfectly consistent with interactionism, for it does not say that the mental reduces to the physical, or even that it is ontologically dependent on the physical, since the supervenience in question is not metaphysical but only nomological supervenience, according to interactionism. If psychophysical causation is indeed by simultaneous inter-level causation, then any breach of the inter-level laws would be a breach of psychophysical law. Just as in the case of biophysical law, a breach of psychophysical law would count as a 'big' miracle, for purposes of evaluating counterfactuals. The interactionist can therefore very plausibly claim that it is a 'big' departure from actuality for my brain to be in the very physical state P_1 it is in when I actually have a headache, without my having a headache. It seems we are closer to actuality if we avoid the violation of psychophysical law, and instead get rid of M by a tiny physical divergence miracle, so that my brain fails to enter state P_1 in the first place, and so I do not get the headache.

Here are some further intuitive reasons to count the violation of psychophysical law as a 'big' miracle. One is that the headache lasts for a long time, which is why it eventually causes me to take the aspirin. To suppress the entire headache despite the continuing presence of its normal physical causes requires a miracle that goes on for a long time; but long-lasting miracles are bigger miracles than momentary miracles. Another reason is that a violation of psychophysical law may induce subsequent failures of rationality. At w_2, the brain-state P_1 occurs but the headache M does not occur; nevertheless the whole physical history of the world is just as it is in actuality. Therefore at the later time t_2 my brain is in just the same physical state at w_2 as it is in actually at t_2. The state of my brain causes me at the actual world to remember being in pain at t_1. If the violation of psychophysical law is small and localised in time to t_1, then at w_2 this same brain state will cause me at t_2 to seem to remember having a headache at t_1. Thus at w_2 I will believe I had a headache even though I did not in fact have a headache. At w_2 my beliefs fail to track the truth in a way that is inexplicable at the level of psychology. Moreover if w_2 really were the closest world where M does not occur, then the following counterfactual would be true:

If I had not had a headache, I would still have believed I had a headache

But in fact we know this counterfactual is false. It follows that we regard w_2 as not the closest world to actuality. w_2 is a world where I acquire false memories in a way that is psychologically miraculous, and therefore it is to be counted as remote from actuality.

I conclude that interactionism is perfectly consistent with physical predetermination, provided the interactionist holds that psychophysical causation is by deterministic nomological supervenience. Mental events can consistently be held to cause physical events in a world of physical determinism, even if the mental events are not identical with physical events. It follows that Deterministic Nomological Completeness of physics does not entail the Mechanism premiss, that every caused physical event has a complete physical cause, which is needed by the Completeness Argument for the Constitutive Thesis. Therefore it can consistently be claimed both that knowledge causes physically predetermined events, and that knowledge is not constituted by physical events.

The Indeterministic Case

The thesis of Deterministic Nomological Completeness does not appear to be actually empirically supported by contemporary physics. For according to quantum mechanics, the world evolves deterministically by the unfolding of the Schrödinger equation only until a measurement is made. Thereupon there is a random collapse of the wave-function, which then proceeds to evolve Schrödinger-style again until there is a further measurement, whereupon the wave-function collapses randomly once again, and so on.

What is a 'measurement', in the sense of quantum mechanics? No one seems to know exactly, but in a puzzling way it seems to be an event that is somehow connected with an observer coming to know the value of the quantity measured. If that is correct, and we take the empirical evidence from contemporary physics at face value, it seems we should all perhaps be interactionists. But many philosophers of mind prefer to say that the 'measurement problem' shows only that there must be some non-epistemic interpretation of 'measurement'. Some conclude more radically that current quantum mechanics cannot be the finally correct physical theory. Thus Lewis writes:

The idea that a unique microphysical process takes place when a person makes a measurement seems about as credible as the idea that a unique kind of vibration takes place when two people fall truly in love. (1986c: 59)

Lewis presumes that quantum mechanics will eventually give way to some improved theory, free of the measurement problem. However, he says that probably quantum mechanics will at least be vindicated in its hypothesis that ours is an indeterministic world of objectively random events.

It is of interest to enquire whether interactionism is compatible with a physically chancy world, under the assumption of the Indeterministic Nomological Completeness of physics:

Indeterministic Nomological Completeness. If worlds w and w' have the same physical past and the same physical laws, then for any physical future F the chances of F at w and w' are the same.

Is this inconsistent with interactionism? An argument that it is might go as follows. The physical event P_1 of my brain's being in a certain state completely determines the chances of the later physical event P_2 of my taking an aspirin. If the mental event M of my headache is not identical with P_1, then M can make no difference to the chance of occurrence of P_2, and so M is causally irrelevant to P_2. Again we are invited to conclude that M must be either an epiphenomenon or identical with P_2, contrary to interactionism.

To evaluate this argument, we must again consider which is the closest world to actuality where I do not have the headache. If with the interactionist we assume that the headache M is not identical with the corresponding brain-state P_1, then the following worlds w_4 and w_5 seem to be the only relevant candidates:

w_4: shortly before t_1 there is a tiny chance divergence from the actual world—a neurone fails to fire. In consequence my brain at t_1 is not in the state P_1, and I fail to have the headache M. The chance of P_2 given that not-P_1 is very low.

w_5: The past is exactly as the actual past until t_1. At t_1, P_1 occurs but fails to have its expected effect M. The chance of P_2 given that P_1 occurs is very high.

The comparison here is similar to the deterministic case. At w_4 no law is broken, but a chance occurrence shortly before t_1 leads smoothly into a scenario where both P_1 and M are missing. At w_5 there is a better match with the actual past, for there is perfect match at every time before t_1. But the price paid for the perfect match is a violation of psychophysical law. By our previous discussion, that is a 'big' miracle, in a chancy world just as much as in a deterministic world; so since similarity of law counts for more than exact match with the past, we conclude that w_4 is closer to actuality than w_5. So w_4 is the relevantly closest world for evaluation of the counterfactual. In straightforward cases at least, the test under indeterminism of whether C (immediately) causes E is whether C 'raises the chance' of E; i.e., whether the chance of E is higher at the closest C-world than it is at the closest not-C world. We see that at the actual world I have a headache and the chance of my taking the aspirin is high: whereas at w_4, the closest world where I do not have a headache, the chance is low. Thus the headache is indeed the cause of my taking the aspirin, just as interactionism requires. The interactionist can again consistently claim that the mental event caused the physical event, without the mental event being identical with any physical event.

Thus whether or not interactionism is in itself a plausible doctrine, it is at any rate not logically inconsistent with either the Deterministic or the Indeterministic Nomological Completeness of physics. It follows that the completeness of physics does not entail the Mechanism premiss; therefore the completeness of physics does not entail that knowledge must be identical with some physical state if it is to be causally efficacious. Appeal to the nomological completeness of physics gives no support to the Constitutive Thesis.

8.5 An Inductive Argument Against the Constitutive Thesis

The Constitutive Thesis says that we know by believing, because in a suitable context, knowing *is* believing—*S*'s knowledge that *A* is merely *S*'s belief that *A* under a relational description. The Token Identity version of the Constitutive Thesis asserts only a token identity: every instance of knowing is identical with some instance of believing. It does not claim that knowing is a particular kind of believing, and it is under no obligation to define knowledge in terms of belief.

In this section I present an argument against the Token Identity version of the Constitutive Thesis, if it takes believing to be a functional state. The argument is that one can imagine the knowing without the functional state, and that one can also imagine the functional state without the knowing. I take this to be an inductively strong argument against the alleged identity. It is not a so-called 'conceivability' argument for non-identity, however, but only an ordinary inductive argument.

Conceivability arguments have been advanced in connection with the mind-brain identity theory. It has been argued that it is certainly conceivable that the mind is not the brain, and hence that it is possible that the mind is not the brain; however, if the mind were the brain, it would not be possible that the mind is not the brain; from which it is concluded that the mind is not the brain. But this sort of argument founders, because conceivability under a single mode of presentation does not imply possibility; according to the point of view argued for in Chapter 4, only what is conceivable under every mode of presentation is possible. For example, 'Hesperus ≠ Phosphorus' is perfectly conceivable under that mode of presentation, since 'Hesperus = Phosphorus' is not *a priori*; nevertheless 'Hesperus ≠ Phosphorus' is impossible, because it is not conceivable under the mode of presentation 'Hesperus ≠ Hesperus'.

It follows that if a conceivability argument is to prove that mind and brain are non-identical, it will have to show that their non-identity is conceivable under every mode of presentation. But if 'mind = brain' is true, there will certainly exist a mode of presentation of the mind and of the brain under which their non-identity is not conceivable, viz., 'mind ≠ mind'. Therefore we can know that the non-identity of mind and brain is conceivable under every mode of presentation only if we already know that mind and brain are non-identical; which is just what was to be proved in the first place.

Conceivability arguments can therefore throw little light on whether the mind is the brain, or whether knowledge is belief. To settle such questions of identity, we must proceed more directly. Non-trivial identities are *a posteriori* necessities, which we discover by induction: for example, that is how we discovered that Hesperus is Phosphorus. It is also by induction that we discover difference; for example, that is how we know the non-identity of Venus and Mercury. What follows is an argument against the Constitutive Thesis that appeals to what one can imagine. The imagining is not being used to prove conceivability, however, but is simply used in the service of induction.

Argument Against the Realiser States Version of the Constitutive Thesis

What does the Constitutive Thesis mean by the expression 'belief that *A*?' From a functionalist perspective, the belief that *A* is a belief-state of the agent which in the context is interpretable as having the propositional content that *A*. But 'belief-state' is ambiguous between the 'realiser state' (i.e., the physical state that plays the functional role) and the 'role state' (i.e., the functional state itself). Depending on how we resolve the ambiguity, we get two different versions of the Constitutive Thesis:

(*Realiser States version*) In a suitable context, being in physical state σ constitutes *S*'s knowledge that *A*.

(*Role States version*) In a suitable context, being in functional state s constitutes S's knowledge that A.

I will now give arguments against each version of the Constitutive Thesis. The argument against the Realiser States version is that it is probable that human minds are not the only minds there are; it is likely that other beings also are knowers, though they are not in the human realiser states. The argument against the Role States version is that it is likely that systems that lack minds could be in the relevant role states; these other systems fail to be knowers, despite being in the human role states. Therefore knowledge is not constituted by being in either the realiser states or the role states that are associated with belief in human beings.

The argument against the Realiser States version is that it is likely that beings other than human beings could have knowledge, despite not being in the human physical states. This claim is supported by the consideration that the higher animals at least are knowers; but they do not have exactly the same physical states as human knowers, for their brains are different from ours. Perhaps it will be replied that in the relevant respects their brains are just like ours. But we can point to the probably quite alien physiology of the intelligent inhabitants of other planets. It is inductively probable, considering the size of the universe, that other intelligent beings exist, and there seems no more reason to think that the Earth is the centre of the universe with respect to the biochemistry of intelligent life than to think it is central in any other respect. So it seems inductively probable that there are intelligent beings in other parts of the universe whose brains if any take quite a different form from ours.

Can the Realiser States version of the Constitutive Thesis be adapted to allow for the existence of non-human knowers? One strategy would be for it to broaden its definition of knowledge. Instead of allowing only the human realiser states to constitute knowledge, it might lay down a disjunctive list of physical states, any one of which can constitute knowledge that A. For example, we can imagine that in a given suitable environment, human beings would know that A by having their X-fibres firing, while Martians would know that A by having their Y-fibres firing. Then it might be suggested that knowledge can be constituted by any of an exhaustive list of cases, as follows:

'S knows that A' $=_{df}$ In a suitable environment, S is human and has X-fibres firing, or S is a Martian and has Y-fibres firing, or ...

But of course no such list is known to us, and none is built into the meaning of the term 'knowledge'. Nor is it open to us to draw up such a list now 'by convention'. When we meet advanced civilisations around other stars, it would be absurd to suppose that it will be a matter of human verbal convention whether the inhabitants 'know' anything or 'are conscious'. They may be physically unlike human beings, but the fact that they are living beings who show every sign of sentience and intelligence is strong inductive evidence that they are conscious, regardless of any convention of ours. So it seems inductively likely that knowledge is not identical with any realiser states.

The Role States Version of the Constitutive Thesis

We are not in a position to stipulate, for each candidate physical state, whether or not that state constitutes knowledge. But although we cannot specify the knowledge-constituting physical states individually, perhaps we can specify them by a general characterisation: perhaps *any* physical state that realises the appropriate belief constitutes knowledge that *A* in the right context. We thus arrive at the Role States version of the Constitutive Thesis:

> (*Role States version*) In a suitable context, being in the belief-state indexed by LoT sentence *s* constitutes knowledge that *A*.

On this view, in a suitable environment knowing that *A* is nothing over and above having the sentence *s* written in one's belief box. The view is un–chauvinist, because it allows the Martians, as well as ourselves, to be thinking intelligent beings. But it is open to the objection that it seems inductively probable that a system could have exactly the human functional organisation, yet not be conscious.

Current computers can simulate complex processes, such as a weather system, or a nuclear explosion; human behaviour is more complex than even these processes, but still it is conceivable that a future computer might perfectly simulate a human being. If it did, then by definition it would have the human functional organisation. But that is no reason to think the computer would be conscious: no one supposes that a computer simulation of an explosion is a real explosion, so why suppose that a computer simulation of consciousness is real consciousness?

Turing believed that a good enough simulation would indeed be conscious. He thought it would soon be possible to make a computer whose linguistic behaviour would be indiscriminable from the linguistic behaviour of a human being. In that case it would not be possible to tell from the linguistic behaviour alone that one was not speaking with a human being. Turing concluded that any machine that could pass this 'Turing Test' of conversational indiscriminability from a human being would have just as much right as a human being, or just as little, to be treated as 'conscious'. But his argument appears to rely on verificationism as a premiss. Certainly one would not be able to tell in this situation whether one was speaking to a conscious being or a computer simulation. But only a verificationist would immediately conclude that there is not a real difference between a conscious being and a simulation of a conscious being.

The question whether the computer would be conscious is a substantive question of fact, even if we are not in a position to determine the answer with certainty. By directing our attention on our own conscious states, we can give ourselves an inner demonstration of consciousness as *this*, in a sort of private ostensive definition. Now we can ask the following substantive question: 'I have *this* consciousness: does everything that is functionally similar to me have consciousness like this too?' And to this question the honest answer is that we simply do not know. There are a range of cases of systems with some functional similarity to ourselves: for some of these we know or are fairly sure that they do have this consciousness; for some we are fairly sure that they do not; and for some we are simply in doubt.

The sceptical problem of 'Other Minds' arises when one asks oneself if other people also have consciousness like *this*. The Constitutive Thesis would offer a quick way with the problem of Other Minds, since if one knew that the Constitutive Thesis was true one could immediately deduce that others are conscious from their functional similarity to oneself. But this seems too facile a 'solution' to the sceptical problem, for the functional resemblance alone does not seem to settle as a matter of definition that other people have consciousness like this. Of course if we are not sceptics, we do in fact know that other people are conscious, for they are functionally like us, and moreover their bodies are physically like ours. But this is a matter not of definitions, but of evidential support: the functional resemblance together with the physical resemblance is strong inductive evidence for one's natural belief that other people are conscious too.

Do other animals have consciousness like this? Here we perhaps feel more uncertain, but it does seems evidentially probable that the higher animals at least do have consciousness, for they are functionally and physically somewhat similar to ourselves. But when it comes to simple animals, for example the insects, it seems very doubtful whether they have consciousness or not. Perhaps our uncertainty would not be resolved even if we knew all there is to know about the functional organisation of an insect; the question whether an insect has consciousness like *this* seems to be one to which we genuinely do not know the answer.

Thus it is a substantive question of fact whether a given thing has consciousness. Suppose we knew all there is to know about a computer's program. It would not be possible to assert as a matter of definition that any computer running that program is thereby conscious; we would need inductive evidence. I myself think it implausible that we will ever have inductive evidence that a computer of the type of present day machines was conscious, even if it ran a program that perfectly simulated a human being. Such a computer is not a living thing; indeed it is not a genuinely unitary being at all; it is only some circuit boards connected together. The Constitutive Thesis notwithstanding, the fact that the computer's states are functional duplicates of the states of a conscious being does not seem to be any sort of inductively strong evidence that the computer is conscious.

The conclusion to which we are led is that it is inductively likely that some but not all knowers have the human realiser (physical) states, and some but not all systems with the human role (functional) states have knowledge. Therefore the Realiser States version of the Constitutive Thesis is wrong; knowledge is not constituted by being in the right physical states in the right context, because probably there are knowers that do not have the human realiser states. And the Role States version is also wrong: knowledge is not constituted by being in the human role states in the right context, because probably there will be non-living systems with the human role states, which are not knowers.

The Causal Thesis does not face these difficulties, for it takes human knowledge not to be constituted by functional states, but to be caused by them. It says that the human role states, when realised by the human physical states, can cause knowledge, but do not constitute it. When sufficiently similar role states are realised somewhat differently, it is inductively probable that they too can cause knowledge, as no doubt they do in the intelligent inhabitants of other planets. When sufficiently similar physical states realise a somewhat different role state, again they cause knowledge, as no doubt they do in the higher animals. But the Causal Thesis declines to assert that every realisation of the role states causes knowledge. It can deny that a computer simulation of a human being would be conscious, even though it has exactly the right role states; for a computer has the wrong realiser states, since it is not alive.

Bibliography

Aczel, P. (1988). *Non-Well-Founded Sets*. Stanford, Calif.: Center for the Study of Language and Information.

Almog J., Perry J., and Wettstein, H. (1989). *Themes from Kaplan*. Oxford: Oxford University Press.

Aristotle (1941). *The Basic Works of Aristotle*, ed. R. McKeon. New York: Random House.

Austin, J. L. (1962). *How to do Things with Words*. Oxford: Oxford University Press.

Boolos, G. (1993). *The Logic of Provability*. Cambridge: Cambridge University Press.

Brentano, F. (1995). *Psychology from an Empirical Standpoint*, ed. O. Kraus, trans. A. Rancurello, D. Terrell, and L. McAlister. London: Routledge.

Campbell, J. (1994). *Past, Space and Self*. Cambridge, Mass.: The MIT Press.

Carruthers, P. (1996). *Language, Thought and Consciousness*. Cambridge: Cambridge University Press.

Cassam, Q. (1997). *Self and World*. Oxford: Oxford University Press.

Chomsky, N. (1986). *Knowledge of Language*. New York: Praeger.

Cresswell, M. J. (1990). *Entities and Indices*. Dordrecht: Kluwer Academic Publishers.

Davidson, D. (1967). 'Truth and Meaning'. *Synthese*, 17: 304–23. Page references to reprinting in Davidson (1984).

——— (1980). 'The Logical Form of Action Sentences'. In his *Essays on Actions and Events*. Oxford: Oxford University Press, 105–48.

——— (1984). *Inquiries into Truth and Interpretation*. Oxford: Oxford University Press.

Davies, M. (1981). *Meaning, Quantification, Necessity*. London: Routledge & Kegan Paul.

Dennett, D. (1991). *Consciousness Explained*. London: The Penguin Press.

DeRose, K. (1995). 'Solving the Skeptical Problem'. *Philosophical Review*, 104: 1–52.

Dummett, M. (1978). 'The Justification of Deduction'. *Proceedings of the British Academy*, 59: 201–32. Page references to reprinting in his *Truth and Other Enigmas*, London: Duckworth.

——— (1981). *Frege—Philosophy of Language*, 2nd edn. London: Duckworth.

Evans, G. (1979). 'Reference and Contingency'. *The Monist*, 62: 161–89.

——— (1982). *The Varieties of Reference*. Oxford: Oxford University Press.

Fodor, J. (1975). *The Language of Thought*. New York: Crowell.

——— (1998). *Concepts*. Oxford: Oxford University Press.

Frege, G. (1891). 'Function and Concept'. In Frege (1966: 21–41).

———— (1892a). 'On Concept and Object'. In Frege (1966: 42–55).

———— (1892b). 'On Sense and Reference'. Page references to Frege (1966: 68–78).

———— (1918). 'Logical Investigations'. Page references to Frege (1984: 351–406).

———— (1966). *Translations from the Philosophical Writings of Gottlob Frege*, ed. P. Geach and M. Black. Oxford: Blackwell.

———— (1967). *The Basic Laws of Arithmetic*, trans. M. Furth. Berkeley, Calif.: University of California Press.

———— (1968). *The Foundations of Arithmetic*, trans. J. L. Austin. Oxford: Blackwell.

———— (1979). *Posthumous Writings*, ed. H. Kermes, F. Kambartel and F. Kaulbach, trans. P. Long and R. White. Oxford: Basil Blackwell.

———— (1984). *Collected Papers in Mathematics, Logic and Philosophy*, ed. B. McGuiness. Oxford: Blackwell.

Geach, P. T. (1971). *Mental Acts: their Contents and their Objects*. London: Routledge & Kegan-Paul.

Gettier, E. L. (1963). 'Is Justified True Belief Knowledge?' *Analysis*, 23: 121–3.

Grice, P. (1957). 'Meaning'. *Philosophical Review*, 66: 377–88. Page references to reprinting in Grice (1989).

———— (1969). 'Utterer's Meaning and Intentions'. *Philosophical Review*, 78: 147–77. Page references to reprinting in Grice (1989).

———— (1989). *Studies in the Ways of Words*. Cambridge, Mass.: Harvard University Press.

Gupta, A. (1982). 'Truth and Paradox'. *Journal of Philosophical Logic*, 11: 1–60.

Hopkins, J. (1978). 'Mental States, Natural Kinds and Psychophysical Laws'. *Proceedings of the Aristotelian Society, Supplementary Volume* 52: 221–36.

Hossack, K. (2000). 'Plurals and Complexes'. *British Journal for Philosophy of Science*, 51: 411–43.

Jackson, F. (1982). 'Epiphenomenal Qualia'. *Philosophical Quarterly*, 32: 127–36.

Kant, I. (1929). *Critique of Pure Reason*, trans. N. Kemp-Smith. London: MacMillan.

Kaplan, D. (1977). 'Demonstratives'. In Almog, Perry and Wettstein (1989: 481–563).

Kitcher, P. (1980). 'Apriority and Necessity'. *Australasian Journal of Philosophy*, 58: 89–101. Page references to reprinting in Moser (1987).

Kripke, S. A. (1975). 'Outline of a Theory of Truth'. *Journal of Philosophy*, 72: 690–716.

———— (1980). *Naming and Necessity*. Oxford: Blackwell.

Leibniz, G. (1982). *New Essays on Human Understanding*, abridged edn., trans. P. Remnant and J. Bennett. Cambridge: Cambridge University Press.

Lewis, D. (1969). *Convention*. Oxford: Blackwell.

Lewis, D. (1970a). 'How to Define Theoretical Terms.' *Journal of Philosophy*, 67: 427–46.

____ (1970b). 'General Semantics'. *Synthese*, 22: 18–67. Page references to reprinting in Lewis (1983).

____ (1972a). 'Psychophysical and Theoretical Identifications.' *Australasian Journal of Philosophy*, 50: 249–58. Page references to reprinting in Lewis (1999a).

____ (1972b). 'Language and Languages'. In Lewis (1983:163–88).

____ (1978). 'Truth in Fiction'. *American Philosophical Quarterly*, 15: 37–46. Page references to reprinting in Lewis (1983).

____ (1979). 'Counterfactual Dependence and Time's Arrow'. *Noûs*, 13: 455–76.

____ (1983). *Philosophical Papers, Volume 1*. Oxford: Oxford University Press.

____ (1986a). *On the Plurality of Worlds*. Oxford: Blackwell.

____ (1986b). *Counterfactuals*. Oxford: Blackwell.

____ (1986c). 'Postscripts to "Counterfactual Dependence and Time's Arrow"'. In his *Philosophical Papers, Volume II*, Oxford: Oxford University Press, 52–66.

____ (1987). 'New Work for a Theory of Universals'. *Australasian Journal of Philosophy*, 61: 343–77. Page references to reprinting in Lewis (1999a).

____ (1996). 'Elusive Knowledge'. *Australasian Journal of Philosophy*, 74: 549–67. Page references to reprinting in Lewis (1999a).

____ (1999a). *Papers in Metaphysics and Epistemology*. Cambridge: Cambridge University Press.

____ (1999b). 'Why Conditionalise?' In Lewis (1999a: 403–7).

Lichtenberg, G. C. (1990). *Aphorisms*, trans. R. J. Hollingdale. London: Penguin.

Locke, J. (1979). *An Essay Concerning Human Understanding*, ed. with an Introduction by P. H. Nidditch. Oxford: Oxford University Press.

MacBride, F. (1999). 'Could Armstrong Have Been A Universal?' *Mind*, 108: 471–501.

____ (2004). 'Whence the Particular-Universal Distinction?' *Grazer Philosophische Studien*, 67: 181–94.

____ (2005). 'The Particular-Universal Distinction: A Dogma of Metaphysics?' *Mind*, 114: 565–614.

McDowell, J. (1982). 'Criteria, Defeasibility, and Knowledge'. *Proceedings of the British Academy*, 68: 455–79.

McGee, V. (1991). *Truth, Vagueness and Paradox*. Indianapolis, Indiana: Hackett Publishing Company.

McGinn, C. (1982). *The Character of Mind*. Oxford: Oxford University Press.

Madell, G. (1989). 'Personal Identity and the Mind/Body Problem.' In *The Case for Dualism*, ed. J. R. Smithies and J. Beloff. Charlottesville, Va.: University of Virginia Press, 25–41.

Mates, B. (1952). 'Synonymity'. In *Semantics and the Philosophy of Language*, ed. L. Linsky. Urbana, Ill.: University of Illinois Press, 101–36.

Mellor, D. H. (1995). *The Facts of Causation*. London: Routledge.

Mendelson, E. (1987). *Introduction to Mathematical Logic*, 3rd edn. Monterey, Calif.: Wadsworth and Brooks/Cole Advanced Books and Software.

Moser, P. (ed.) (1987). *A Priori Knowledge*. Oxford: Oxford University Press.

Neale, S. (1990). *Descriptions*. Cambridge, Mass.: The MIT Press.

Nozick, R. (1981). *Philosophical Explanations*. Oxford: Oxford University Press.

Papineau, D. (2002). *Thinking About Consciousness*. Oxford: Oxford University Press.

Parfit, D. (1971). 'Personal Identity'. *The Philosophical Review*, 80: 3–27.

Peacocke, C. (1979). *Holistic Explanation: Action, Space, Interpretation*. Oxford: Oxford University Press.

—— (1992). *A Study of Concepts*. Cambridge, Mass: The MIT Press.

—— (1999). *Being Known*. Oxford: Oxford University Press.

Perry, J. (1979). 'The Problem of the Essential Indexical.' *Noûs*, 13: 3–21.

Plantinga, A. (1993). *Warrant and Proper Function*. Oxford: Oxford University Press.

Plato (1963). *The Collected Dialogues*, ed. E. Hamilton and H. Cairns. Princeton, N. J.: Princeton University Press.

Priest, G. (1995). *Beyond the Limits of Thought*. Cambridge: Cambridge University Press.

Quine, W. V. (1956). 'Quantifiers and Attitudes'. Page references to reprinting in Quine (1976: 185–96).

—— (1976). *The Ways of Paradox*. Cambridge, Mass.: Harvard University Press.

—— (1986). *Philosophy of Logic*, 2nd edn. Cambridge, Mass.: Harvard University Press.

—— (1990). *Pursuit of Truth*. Cambridge, Mass.: Harvard University Press.

—— (1995) 'Variables Explained Away'. In his *Selected Logic Papers*, enlarged edn. Cambridge, Mass.: Harvard University Press, 227–35.

Ramsey, F. P. (1925). 'Universals'. *Mind*, 34: 401–17.

—— (1927). 'Facts and Propositions'. In Ramsey (1990: 34–51).

—— (1990). *Philosophical Papers*, ed. D. H. Mellor. Cambridge: Cambridge University Press.

Reid, T. (1846). 'Essays on the Intellectual Powers of Man'. In *The Works of Thomas Reid*, ed. W. Hamilton, 215–508. Edinburgh: McLachlan, Stewart & Co.

Rescher, N. (1991). *G. W. Leibniz's Monadology*. London: Routledge.

Rosenthal, D. (1993). 'Thinking That One Thinks'. In *Consciousness*, ed. M. Davies and G. Humphreys, 197–223. Oxford: Blackwell.

Russell, B. (1908). 'Mathematical Logic as Based on the Theory of Types'. *American Journal of Mathematics*, 30: 222–62. Reprinted in Russell (1956).

—— (1918) 'The Philosophy of Logical Atomism'. Page references to reprinting in Russell (1956: 177–281).

—— (1956). *Logic and Knowledge*, ed. R. C. Marsh. London: George Allen & Unwin.

—— (1959). *The Problems of Philosophy*. London: Oxford University Press.

—— (1994). *Philosophical Essays*. London: Routledge.

—— and Whitehead, A. N. (1970). *Principia Mathematica*. Cambridge: Cambridge University Press.

Sainsbury, R. M. (1997). 'Easy Possibilities'. *Philosophy and Phenomenological Research*, 57: 907–19.

Schiffer, S. (1987). *Remnants of Meaning*. Cambridge, Mass.: The MIT Press.

Shoemaker, S. (1996). *The First Person Perspective*. Cambridge: Cambridge University Press.

Stalnaker, R. (1968). 'A Theory of Conditionals'. *Studies in Logical Theory, American Philosophical Quarterly*, Monograph 2. Oxford: Blackwell, 98–112.

—— (1978). 'Assertion'. *Syntax and Semantics*, 9: 315–32.

—— (1987). *Inquiry*. Cambridge, Mass.: The MIT Press.

—— (1999). 'Belief Attribution and Context'. In his *Context and Content*, Oxford: Oxford University Press, 150–66.

Stebbing, L. S. (1930). *A Modern Introduction to Logic*. London: Methuen.

Strawson, P. F. (1950). 'Truth'. *Proceedings of the Aristotelian Society, Supplementary Volume 24*. Page references to Strawson (1971: 191–213).

—— (1964). 'Intention and Convention in Speech Acts'. *Philosophical Review*, 73: 439–60. Page references to reprinting in Strawson (1971).

—— (1966). *The Bounds of Sense*. London: Methuen.

—— (1971). *Logico-Linguistic Papers*. London: Methuen.

Swinburne, R. G. (1974). 'Personal Identity'. *Proceedings of the Aristotelian Society*, 74: 231–47.

Tarski, A. (1944). 'The Semantic Conception of Truth and the Foundation of Semantics'. *Philosophy and Phenomenological Research*, 4: 341–76.

—— (1983). 'The Concept of Truth in Formalised Languages'. In his *Logic, Semantics, Meta-Mathematics*, 2nd edn., trans. J. H. Woodger. Indianapolis, Ind.: Hackett Publishing Company, 227–35.

Taylor, B. and Hazen, A. P. (1992). 'Flexibly Structured Predication'. *Logique et Analyse*, 139–140: 375–93.

Unger, P. (1975). *Ignorance: A Case for Scepticism*. Oxford: Oxford University Press.

Williams, B. (1970). 'The Self and the Future'. *The Philosophical Review*, 79: 161–80. Page references to reprinting in ed. J. Perry (1975) *Personal Identity*, Berkeley Calif.: University of California Press.

Williamson, T. (1992). 'Inexact Knowledge'. *Mind*, 101: 217–42.

—— (1994). *Vagueness*. London: Routledge.

—— (1996). 'The Necessity and Determinacy of Distinctness'. In *Essays for David Wiggins: Identity Truth and Value*, ed. S. Lovibond and S. Williams. Oxford: Blackwell, 1–17.

—— (1998). 'Bare possibilia'. *Erkenntnis*, 48: 257–73.

—— (2000). *Knowledge and its Limits*. Oxford: Oxford University Press.

Wittgenstein, L. (1958). *The Blue and Brown Books*. Oxford: Blackwell.

—— (1961a). *Notebooks 1914–1916*, ed. G. H. von Wright and G. E. M. Anscombe, trans. G. E. M. Anscombe. Oxford: Blackwell.

—— (1961b). *Tractatus Logico-Philosophicus*, trans. D. F. Pears and B. F. McGuiness. Oxford: Blackwell.

—— (1967a) *Remarks on the Foundations of Mathematics*, trans. G. E. M. Anscombe. Oxford: Blackwell.

—— (1967b). *Philosophical Investigations*. Oxford: Blackwell.

—— (1975). *Philosophical Remarks*, ed. R. Rhees, trans. R. Hargreaves and R. White. Oxford: Blackwell.

Wright, C. (1989). 'Wittgenstein and the Central Project in Theoretical Linguistics'. In *Reflections on Chomsky*, ed. A. George. Oxford: Blackwell, 233–64.

Index